PATTERNS OF EXPOSITION 7

RANDALL E. DECKER

PATTERNS OF EXPOSITION 7

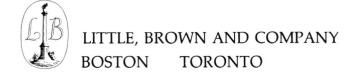

LITTLE, BROWN AND COMPANY
BOSTON TORONTO

LIBRARY OF CONGRESS CATALOG CARD NO. 79-90129

FIRST PRINTING

Published simultaneously in Canada
by Little, Brown & Company (Canada) Limited

PRINTED IN THE UNITED STATES OF AMERICA

To the Instructor

Patterns of Exposition 7 retains the basic principles and the general format of the former editions. Use of the book continues to remain high (the publisher tells me that *Patterns 6* is still the most widely adopted composition anthology in the country) and we continue to poll instructor-users for evaluations of the selections and about the need for basic changes in the framework. In preparing this edition we mailed out and received more user questionnaires than ever before. We also reviewed the responses of students who returned questionnaires like the one at the back of this book. Although obviously we are unable to comply with all requests, we have incorporated many suggestions into this new edition, and we have seriously considered and fully appreciated all of them.

We continue the policy, started in the last edition, of using the "Further Readings" section for a few classical or near-classical selections, all of which can be shown to have *some elements* of argument or persuasion. Instructors apparently found the section useful in varying ways and liked the fact that essays there are presented without suggestions or questions. In the instructor's manual, however, we still include a brief discussion of the special techniques and hazards of argument, as well as a few suggestions for using the various selections.

But throughout *Patterns of Exposition 7* we have tried, as always, to make possible the convenient use of all materials in whatever ways instructors think best for their own classes. Only complete essays or free-standing units of larger works have been included. With their inevitable overlap of patterns, they are more complicated than excerpts illustrating single principles, but they are also more realistic examples of exposition and more useful for other classroom purposes. Versatility is one important standard in choosing materials.

The total number of selections has been increased. Twenty-three of those best liked in the previous edition have been retained; five favorites from still earlier editions have been returned in response to numerous requests. Sixteen are entirely new, and several of these are anthologized here for the first time anywhere.

Their arrangement is but one of many workable orders; the instructor can easily develop another if he so desires. To make such variations convenient, we have nearly always placed interessay questions at the end of sequences, where they can be quickly detected and, if not suitable, easily eliminated or modified.

We have tried to vary the study questions—and undoubtedly have included far more than any one teacher will want—from the purely objective to those calling for some serious self-examination by the students. (The booklet, *Instructor's Manual to Accompany Patterns of Exposition 7*, is available, placing further materials at the instructor's disposal.)

Suggestions for writing assignments to be developed from ideas in the essays are located immediately after each selection. But for classes in which the instructor prefers writing to be done according to the expository pattern under study at the time, regardless of subject matter, topic suggestions are located at the end of each section.

"A Guide to Terms," where matters from *Abstract* to *Unity* are briefly discussed, refers whenever possible to the essays themselves for illustrations. To permit unity and easy access, it is located at the back of the book, but there are continuing cross-references to it in the study questions.

In all respects—in size, content, arrangement, format—we have tried to keep *Patterns of Exposition 7* uncluttered and easy to use.

The editor wishes to express appreciation for the helpful criticism and suggestions provided by his friends and colleagues, especially Richard Albert, Mary Allen, Carol Anderson, Beverly Beem, Raymond Beirne, Marian Berliner, Susan Bessel, Barbara Bixby, Charles Bordogna, George Boyd, Jean Bridges, Daniel Brislane, Jane Brown, W. K. Buckley, Cheryl Burghdorf, Terre Burton, William Byers, Janet Carnesi, Rick Christman, Gary Collison, Dorothy Condry, Betty Mae Conkin, India Cooper, Stephen Curry, Lois Craig, Robert Dees, Barbara DuBois, Barbara Eckstein, Elinor Evans, Margaret Falls, Marilyn Fisher, Francine Foltz, Valerie Foulkes, George Geckle, James Gifford, G. Dale Gleason, H. W. Gleason, Jr., Dorothy Gott, Thomas Grace, Janice Gratz, Gordon Green, Nancy Gundersen,

Tori Haring-Smith, Margaret Hennessey, R. Herzog, Stephen Hind, Dan Hise, Julian Hogan, Mary Hogue, Phillip Holcomb, Sandra Hytken, Martin Jacobi, Phyllis Katz, John T. Kelly, Duane Kessler, Muriel Klafehn, Janice LeFevre, T. N. Lane, Bette Lansdowne, Charles LaPierre, Russell Larson, Paul Lehmburg, Mary F. Lewis, Richard Lewis, D. A. Light, Marie Lively, James Lucas, Michael Lund, Jo W. Lyday, C. Mablikos, Margaret Mack, Crystal MacLean-Field, John Mann, Thomas Martin, Caroline Matalene, Jay Maurer, Nellie McCrory, L. F. McKeown, Kathleen McKnight, Brian Milim, Dean Minihan, Monroe Morgret, William Mullinex, R. T. Mundhenk, Dan Myers, Lois Nachman, Thomas Neal, James R. Neale, Jr., Harold Nelson, Sherry Anne Nelson, Harvey Netterville, Ronald Newman, Frederic Orensky, Huey Owings, Elaine Palm, Jeannette Perrin, Maureen Potts, R. C. Raymond, Rosemary Reagan, Morgan Romans, Kathryn Rosengren, Ruth Ross, Timothy Scheurer, Suzanne Sidhu, H. M. Simon, Jr., Peggy Skagg, Sara Skolnik, Hassel Sledd, Donald Smith, Carol Snyder, Stephen Sossaman, Jacqueline Stark, Frank Steel, Rebecca Stevenson, Hazel Stewart, Donald Stuart, Charlotte Tannheimer, Janet Tassel, Carol Thomas, Eloise Thompson, Charles Wagner, K. M. Ward, Emily Ware, Samuel Whyte, Peter Williams, Jack Wills, and Jean Wilson. He would also like to thank Douglas Cope, and certainly the many cooperative members of the Little, Brown staff, especially Charles H. Christensen, Timothy J. Kenslea, and Elizabeth Philipps.

PUBLISHER'S NOTE

We maintain an unusual revision policy on *Patterns of Exposition.* It is revised every two years to ensure that its popular framework is always well stocked with fresh selections. However, for those who do not like to change texts so frequently, the previous edition does *not* go out of print. Thus, two editions of *Patterns of Exposition* are available at all times.

An Instructor's Manual for *Patterns of Exposition 7* is available from the publisher. Instructors wishing to obtain a complementary copy of the manual may address their requests (on school letterhead) to College Marketing, Little, Brown and Company, 34 Beacon Street, Boston, Massachusetts 02106.

Table of Contents

Introduction

Exposition is one of the four basic forms of communication, more important to most people than any of the others—narration, description, or argumentation (including persuasion). The novelist and to some extent the sports reporter use narration and description; the lawyer, the salesman, the preacher become skilled in logical argument and persuasion. But these persons are in specialized fields, prepared by specialized training. People in such professions, like the rest of us, are also frequent users of exposition in one way or another.

Exposition means explanation, simply an *exposing* of information or ideas. Its primary function is not to tell a story or relate a happening, although exposition often *uses* narration as one of many techniques. Its primary function is not to create vivid pictures for the reader, although description, too, may at times be a valuable technique of exposition. The primary function of exposition is not to convince or persuade, although, conversely, logical argument and persuasion frequently use exposition as one of their techniques. But the primary function of exposition itself is merely *to explain.*

Even beyond our increasing need for informally written and spoken explanations, we use the processes of written exposition throughout college—in reports, term papers, essay examinations. Most of us use exposition throughout our working lives—in letters, in memoranda, in business and professional reports. Hence there are practical reasons why most college composition courses are devoted primarily to study and practice in exposition. And these, of course, are the reasons this book concentrates on patterns of expository writing and other techniques commonly used. (An exception is the last part, "Further Readings," which offers a wider variety of composition forms and subject matter.)

There is nothing new about the ten basic patterns of exposition;

we have been using most of them since we first tried to explain why some types of birds fly south in the winter. But mature writing depends partly on the author's being able to use *deliberately* whichever techniques will do the job best, with the least chance of misunderstanding. We study them to get a clearer view of their functions and possibilities, with the aim of being able to use them more effectively in our own writing.

We examine and practice these techniques separately, realizing they are seldom used separately in practical writing. After all, when we observe and practice for hours a skill involved in tennis or golf, we are not assuming that an entire game will be made up of serving or putting. In writing, we know there is no reason why a process analysis should not be used to assist comparison in some explanations, why illustration might not be valuably aided in certain developments by narration. In good writing, if the patterns do not overlap, it is simply because one alone is sufficient for the purpose.

But besides the study of writing techniques in a college anthology, we have a right to expect real benefit from the reading itself. Reading and thinking about new ideas or experiences is an excellent way to widen horizons, to broaden our interests—and that is an important phase of becoming educated. In general, each set of essays in this book progresses in complexity and depth. Challenges help our understanding to reach an ever higher level.

The manner of approaching each reading, or the study of it, may be suggested by the instructor. If not, a worthwhile system for the student to give at least a fair trial is this:

1. For the first reading relax. Read the selection casually, as you would some magazine article, for whatever enjoyment or new ideas you can get without straining. Do not stop to look up new words unless the sentences in which they are used are meaningless until you do. But have a pencil in hand and mark all words you are doubtful about, then go on.
2. When finished with the first reading, put the book down; for a few minutes think over what you have read.
3. Then use the dictionary to help you understand the words you have marked. Do not make the mistake of finding the first or the shortest definition, and trying to memorize it. Instead, look at the various meanings, and for the word's uses as noun, verb, and modifier. *Think* about them. Pronounce the word. Use it in a few sen-

tences. Identify it with similar words you already know. Then see how the author has used it.

4. After you understand all the words, read and think briefly about the assigned questions and remarks following the selection. (The paragraphs in each selection are numbered for easy reference.)

5. Then reread the essay, pausing sometimes to think and to *question,* underlining important ideas, marking sentences or phrases that seem to you especially interesting, misleading, amusing, or well expressed.

6. Then return to the questions at the end. You will probably find that you have already provided most of the answers. If not, give them further thought, referring again to the essay and to "A Guide to Terms" or earlier explanations wherever necessary for thorough understanding.

7. Next, try to *evaluate* the selection. What was the author trying to explain? Did he succeed in explaining? Was his endeavor worthwhile?

Useful as these selections can be, however, they are not intended as models for imitation by students. Each was written, as all expository projects should be, to give a particular audience a particular explanation. The style of some is much too informal for most college writing. Other styles, perhaps from a slower and more sedate age than ours, would be too stately for today. Pure imitation is not the purpose of our study.

But each of the selections does demonstrate one or more of the *patterns* of exposition, which are as useful now as ever. Each can provide, too, some profitable study of other sound principles of writing—principles of effective sentences and paragraphs, mature diction, forceful introductions and closings. The consideration of all these principles, instead of being handled in separate sections, is a continuing study within the basic framework of the expository patterns. The book is designed so that instructors and students can use it in several ways.

PATTERNS OF EXPOSITION 7

1

Illustrating Ideas by Use of *Example*

The use of examples to illustrate an idea under discussion is the most common, and frequently most efficient, pattern of exposition. It is a method we use almost instinctively; for instance, instead of talking in generalities about the qualities of a good city manager, we cite Harry Hibbons as an example. We may go further and illustrate Harry's virtues by a specific account of his handling of a crucial situation during the last power shortage or hurricane disaster. In this way we put our abstract ideas into concrete form — a process that is always an aid to clarity. (As a matter of fact, with the "for instance" in this very paragraph, examples are employed to illustrate even the *use* of example.)

Lack of clear illustrations may leave the reader with only a hazy conception of the points the writer has tried to make. Even worse, the reader may try to supply examples from his own knowledge or experience, and these might do the job poorly or even lead him to an impression different from that intended by the author. Since the writer is the one trying to communicate, clarity is primarily his responsibility.

Not only do good examples put into clear form what otherwise might remain vague and abstract, but the writing also becomes more interesting, with a better chance of holding the reader's attention. With something specific to be visualized, a statement also becomes more convincing — but convincing within certain limitations. If we use the Volvo as an example of Swedish workmanship, the reader is probably aware that this car may not be entirely typical. Although isolated examples will not hold up well in logical argument, for ordinary purposes of explanation the Volvo example could make its point convincingly enough.

As in the selection and use of all materials for composition, of course, the successful writer selects and uses examples cautiously, always keeping in mind the nature of his reader-audience and his own specific purpose for communicating. To be effective, each example must be pertinent, respecting the chief qualities of the generality it illustrates. Its function as an example must be either instantly obvious to the reader or fully enough developed so that he learns exactly what it illustrates, and how. Sometimes, however, illustration may be provided best by something other than a real-life example — a fictional anecdote, an analogy, or perhaps a parable that demonstrates the general idea. Here even greater care is needed to be sure these examples are both precise and clear.

Illustration is sometimes used alone as the basic means of development; but it also frequently assists other basic techniques, such as comparison and contrast. In either of its functions, the author may find his purpose best served by one well-developed example, possibly with full background information and descriptive details. But sometimes citing several shorter examples is best, particularly if the author is attempting to show a trend or a prevalence. In more difficult explanations, of course, a careful combination of the two techniques — using both one well-developed example and several shorter examples — may be worth the extra time and effort required.

Whichever method is used, the writer is following at least one sound principle of writing: he is trying to make the general more specific, the abstract more concrete.

RUSSELL BAKER

RUSSELL BAKER was born in 1925, in Virginia, and now lives in New York. He has a B.A. degree from Johns Hopkins University. For several years he was a reporter and London bureau chief for the Baltimore *Sun,* and later served in the Washington Bureau of *The New York Times.* He now writes a widely syndicated column, the "Observer," and is a contributor to many magazines, such as *Saturday Evening Post, The New York Times Magazine, Sports Illustrated, Ladies Home Journal,* and *McCall's.* In 1979 he won the Pulitzer Prize — journalism's highest award — for commentary. *Poor Russell's Almanac,* a collection of his newspaper articles and columns, was published in 1972.

The Trouble with Baseball

"The Trouble with Baseball" (editor's title) is a selection from *Poor Russell's Almanac.* Like most of Baker's writing, it is a thoughtful blend of humor and wisdom — a wistful sort that never makes the mistake of taking itself too seriously. In this piece Baker uses short examples liberally (in conjunction with other patterns, primarily comparison and contrast) to show the trend, or prevalence, that establishes his central theme.

The trouble with baseball is that it grew up and became engineering. 1
When the country loved it with a passion, baseball was boyhood eternal, all bluster, innocence and bravado flashing across green meadows in the sunlight. The whole game was suffused with a mythic sense so gross that only boyhood could entertain it.

The names of today's teams reflect its original innocence. The 2
Giants, the Dodgers, the Sox, the Tigers, the Orioles, the Cardinals, the Indians. The names are so upright and innocent of modern public-relations flummery that they could only have been created by small boys gathered under an apple tree on a spring morning.

The uniform, too, is out of boyhood past. Knickers and beanie 3 caps for two-hundred-pound men are ridiculous except as a device for preserving the illusion that the wearers are not men at all, but merely boys grown to mythic size.

Like the gods, a boy who played baseball was capable of trans- 4
formation. If he was short, simply by walking onto the field he became "Pee-Wee," and if he was skinny he could become "Slim" or "Bones." At the professional level, this power of transformation became absolutely Jovian as sports writers competed to drape the players in names of heroic proportion. George could become "The Sultan of Swat" simply by knocking baseballs over a fence.

Until quite recently, in fact, hardly anybody in baseball was 5
allowed to appear in public as Charlie or Pete or Nick. Baseball had the boy's love of overstatement, melodrama and comedy. Charlie, Pete and Nick might be all right for the guys who dropped in on the old man on Saturday night, but not for baseball.

Baseball, like boyhood, was life with all the dullness distilled 6
out. The kind of people who capered in that golden sunshine had to be unforgettable. And so we had "the Big Train," "the Big Chief," "the Fordham Flash," "the Iron Horse," and "the Rajah." And they lived in the same world with "Joltin' Joe," and "Poosh-em-up Tony," with "Twinkletoes" Selkirk and "King Kong" Keller, with "Bananas" Bonura and "the Georgia Peach." "Sal the Barber" contended with "Stan the Man" and "Leo the Lip," and the correct question among the inside crowd was whether "Double X" could ever beat "the Bambino's" record.

One sign of baseball's outgrowing boyhood is the decline in 7
nickname voltage. The Mets, who won the World Series a few years ago, despite much publicity suggesting boyish gaudiness, were a dull bunch to pronounce; an eminently forgettable collection of Als, Rons, Jerrys, Eds, Georges and Tommys. There is some suspicion that "Marvelous Marv" Throneberry was carried on the Mets roster for several years mostly because he was the only fellow on the team with a reasonably memorable nickname.

The same dull condition prevails throughout both major leagues. 8
Without going to the record books, it is hard to remember more than one or two players ("Blue Moon" Odom and "No-Neck" Williams come to mind) whose names celebrate the fact that baseball is, after all, just a game that boys can play.

In growing up, baseball has become too self-conscious to tolerate 9
the boyish absurdity of ridiculous nicknames. The game has been

infected by the American passion for perfection, and one of the prices commonly paid for perfection is the sacrifice of sheer fun.

10 And so we have baseball now lost in the pursuit of engineering, in consonance with the contemporary American faith that technology leads to the end of the rainbow. The possibility of error is being engineered out of the game with gloves so error-proof that any player who now bobbles the ball should have his pay docked.

11 Fields are engineered to amplify the strengths and diminish the weaknesses of the host team. Pitcher-development now begins in highly engineered leagues for preadolescents in which baseball is no longer an exuberant afternoon of capering in the orchard, but a systematically organized pressure cooker to condition boys to the strain of professional play.

12 As a result of all this, baseball today is probably executed more skillfully than at any time since it began. It is also rather dull. If he wants to see perfection of execution, the spectator might just as well be at the ballet.

13 Football, another human-engineering business that also specializes in perfect execution, altered its rules to keep the audience entertained by a constant rat-tat-tat of touchdowns. Baseball cannot bring itself to do this. It is sentimentally attached to its memory of boyhood and fears that changing the rules it played by long ago in the sun-swept meadows will destroy the charm.

14 And so, torn between its sentimental yearning for what was, and doubts about where it is going, it becomes less exuberant and increasingly neurotic. Typically, when "the Bambino's" record was finally broken a few years ago, it went into a sulk because the man who broke it was named, new style, "Roger."

Meanings and Values

1a. What is Baker's attitude toward his subject?
 b. To what extent, if at all, is this attitude reflected in his tone? (See Guide to Terms: *Style/Tone.*)
 c. Do you find any evidence of sentimentality? (Guide: *Sentimentality.*)
 d. If so, can it be justified? How?

2. Is the selection a better illustration of concrete or abstract writing? Why? (Guide: *Concrete/Abstract.*)

3. At how much disadvantage is the reader who is not well versed in the history of baseball? Why?

4a. What irony do you find in paragraph 11? (Guide: *Irony.*)

b. Why is it ironical?
c. What kind of irony is it?

Expository Techniques

1a. The first six paragraphs contain examples of varying degrees of specificity. (Guide: *Specific/General.*) If the second sentence of paragraph 1 is seen as a broad generality, what four somewhat more specific statements help to illustrate it?
b. Which of these are in turn illustrated by still more specific examples?

2a. For each set of examples used in the rest of the selection, choose one and tell what generality it illustrates.
b. What are the benefits of such narrowing down to specific examples?

3a. How well does paragraph 1 perform the three essential functions of a good introduction? (Guide: *Introductions.*)
b. Which of the standard techniques does the introduction employ?

4a. Which closing techniques does the author use? (Guide: *Closings.*)
b. Do you consider it an effective closing? Why, or why not?

Diction and Vocabulary

1a. How can you best describe Baker's style, as demonstrated by this selection? (Guide: *Style/Tone.*)
b. What are the chief ingredients of his style? (It will be best to generalize in this answer, then to illustrate by examples from the writing itself.)

2a. Throughout this composition Baker uses one subtle personification. What is it? (Guide: *Figures of Speech.*)
b. Why do you classify it as personification?

3a. Explain the reference and meaning of the allusion in paragraph 4. (Guide: *Figures of Speech.*)
b. Paragraphs 10 and 11 also contain figures of speech. What are they?
c. What kinds are they? Why?

4. Distinguish between Baker's use of "entertain" (par. 1) and that with which you are more familiar.

Suggestions for Writing and Discussion

1. Discuss the broader implications of the "American faith that technology leads to the end of the rainbow" (par. 10).

2. What is your estimation of the "organized pressure cooker" by which preadolescents are trained for baseball — e.g., the harm versus the good that it does (par. 11)?

3. Just how were the rules of football altered to keep the audience better entertained (par. 13)?
4. Discuss some other activity that started out as fun but was (or sometimes is) diverted from its original purpose.

(NOTE: Suggestions for topics requiring development by use of EXAMPLE are on page 43, at the end of this section.)

ELAINE MORGAN

ELAINE MORGAN, born in 1920 in Wales, is married to a teacher and has three children; she still lives in Wales. She has a B.A. degree from Oxford University and has been employed as a supply teacher and lecturer in adult education courses. Morgan has written numerous plays and TV scripts, many of them performed for BBC and in various London theatres. Her most recent book, *Falling Apart: The Rise and Fall of Urban Civilization,* was published in 1977. Although *The Descent of Woman* (1972) was greeted with both derision and praise upon its release, it became a best-seller and was a selection of Book-of-the-Month Club and the *Psychology Today* Book Club. Anthony Storr, an author Morgan sharply disagrees with in the selection below, describes the book as "brimful of ideas" and refers to Morgan herself as "formidably intelligent, extremely well informed, provocative, and original."

The Murderous Species

"The Murderous Species" (editor's title) is an excerpt from *The Descent of Woman.* The piece is a good illustration of the use of examples — sometimes in an unconventional manner — in order to make generalities more specific. The author attempts to convert each of her abstract ideas into easier-to-visualize, concrete images.

Scores of books and articles have been written recently on [the problem of human aggression], and the question usually posed is something like: Why has the species Homo sapiens been cursed from its earliest beginnings with a propensity for murder and violence unparalleled in the whole of the animal kingdom? 1

Anthony Storr states clearly: "The somber fact is that we are the cruellest and most ruthless species that has ever walked the earth." And when his book *On Human Aggression* went into paperback his publishers picked out this sentence to print in large letters on the front cover, in the belief (justified, I don't doubt) that this is the kind of stuff people like to read about themselves. 2

If you read these books and articles with close attention you will 3
find they don't seem to be talking about the species as a whole. They are talking only about the subsection Homo sapiens ♂. They are saying that human males are more aggressive than the males of any other species.

Suppose we try to define this allegation a little more closely. Is 4
a man more bloodthirsty than a shark? Or a piranha? Obviously not: so the claim probably refers only to mammals. Is he fiercer than a wolverine? Is he more murderous than a rat? No, he's not. Perhaps the comparison had better be confined to primates. Speaking frankly, then, which would you be more chary of annoying, a man or a gorilla? Or, if we withdraw the gorilla because he's bigger, compare the aggressiveness of a man with that of some of the smaller primates — for instance, the charming and cuddly-looking wooly monkey of South America, who, if he takes offense, will hurtle from a treetop onto your shoulders, get a stranglehold on your throat with his prehensile tail, and claw at your face and eyes while hammering his sharp canine teeth repeatedly into the top of your skull. How exactly has man become more maniacally aggressive than all of these?

Or has he? 5

Try a bit of fieldwork. Go out of your front door and try to spot 6
some live specimens of Homo sapiens in his natural habitat. It shouldn't be difficult because the species is protected by law and in no immediate danger of extinction. Observe closely the behavior and interactions of *the first twenty you encounter at random.* Then, next time you read a sonorous statement about man, try mentally replacing the collective noun by the image of one of those twenty faces.

"That window cleaner is one of the most sophisticated predators 7
the world has ever seen."

"The weapon is my grocer's principal means of expression, and 8
his only means of resolving differences."

"The postman's aggressive drive has acquired a paranoid poten- 9
tial because his young remain dependent for a prolonged period."

You will instantly suspect that the writers are not thinking about 10
people like that at all, and that you have foolishly been watching the wrong species. But if you're going to be any good as an ethologist, you must learn to trust the evidence of your own senses above that of the printed word and the television image. Remember, you have been living among thousands of these large carnivores all your life, on more intimate terms than those on which Jane Goodall lived among the chimpanzees or Phyllis Jay among the langurs.

Some observers, watching small bands of primates over periods of up to one thousand hours, have carefully recorded the number of "agonistic encounters involving physical contact" that took place per baboon-hour or per chimpanzee-hour. You are well placed to compile a similar logbook dealing with the naked ape. If it is more than six months since you saw one of them fling himself on another and inflict grievous bodily harm, then you are qualified to bring the good news from Ghent to Aix[1] that as far as uncontrollable aggressiveness is concerned, this species is nowhere in the top ten. 11

You may say: "What about Vietnam?" This, of course, is why the statements about man's aggressiveness are so frequently swallowed whole. The writers are thinking about war. War is a special case and . . . I only want to make four points about it. 12

1. It is by no means an activity common to the whole species, or even to the male half of it. Most men have always lived and died without ever being involved in war. The wars that dominate the history books were waged by a small mobile minority, while the rest of the population carried on with plowing and milking and making wheels and feeding the pigs. Even in the terrible years of the two "world" wars, the overwhelming majority of extant males never at any time destroyed another human life. This is not to minimize the horrors of war; but lately men have been so obsessed by the experience of the last two holocausts that they tend to write of war as an ineradicable species-specific behavior pattern, or a biological imperative like breathing and eating, and this is absurd. 13

2. Neither is it a "primitive heritage" we are trying vainly to outgrow. In most of the remaining Stone Age cultures warfare is unknown. For instance, the African Bushmen, as Marshall Sahlins has pointed out, "find the idea of war incomprehensible." 14

3. We are sometimes told that man is the only animal which has ever been observed to behave in this way, slaughtering its own kind. This isn't true, either. Rats will fight and kill not only rats of another species, but those from a different group of the same species. And there was one terrible day in London Zoo when fighting broke out among hamadryad baboons on Monkey Hill with such ferocity that no keeper dared to intervene, and when it was over the bat- 15

[1]From the Robert Browning poem, "How They Brought the Good News from Ghent to Aix." (Editor's note)

tlefield was littered with the maimed and dismembered bodies of the dying and the dead.

Ethologists will quickly point out that animals behave in this way only under unnatural and "pathological" conditions, and that the Monkey Hill debacle is now known to have been due to human ignorance and mismanagement. I accept this unreservedly. Only I would say the same about the Somme.[2] 16

4. If you had visited the Somme, and walked behind the lines among the British and German soldiers, and picked out twenty at random, and stuck electrodes on their temples and measured their blood pressure and skin temperature and adrenalin level, you wouldn't have found them all seething with ungovernable hate and rage, as those baboons undoubtedly were. You'd have found the window cleaner and the grocer and the postman, cold and wet and fed up to the teeth and sick for home. Something had gone badly wrong for those creatures or they wouldn't have been there; but it wasn't a paranoid level of violence and aggression. 17

Meanings and Values

1. Where would you place this piece on an objective–subjective continuum? Why? (See Guide to Terms: *Objective/Subjective.*)
2. Use the selection to demonstrate the relationship between tone and the attitude of the author. (Guide: *Style/Tone.*)
3. Do you find any evidence of sentimentality in Morgan's writings? (Guide: *Sentimentality.*) If so, explain.

Expository Techniques

1a. Cite the first use of example in this selection.
 b. What generality does it make more specific?
 c. Why is this a particularly valuable function?

2a. Paragraph 4 is a rather novel arrangement — a chain, so to speak, of implied generalities and illustrating examples in the form of questions. What is the effect of this particular arrangement and technique in general? (Remember, the author *chooses* such things: they seldom just "happen.")
 b. Experiment with other, more conventional ways of presenting the same material. Are they more, or less, effective? Why?

[2]River in northern France and the scene of violent battles in both world wars. (Editor's note)

3a. Still another manner of presenting examples is illustrated in paragraphs 7–9. What is the effect?
b. Would they have been more, or less, effective if handled in some other way? Why?
c. Why do you think the author selected these particular examples — the grocer, the window cleaner, the postman?
d. What was gained later when we encountered these same three at the Somme?
4. Cite three other uses of examples.
5. What are the structural and rhetorical benefits of using a single sentence for paragraph 5?
6a. You can find at least two examples of parallel structure in paragraph 17. What are they? (Guide: *Parallel Structure.*)
b. Consider the last one carefully and state what subtle effect is achieved by its use.

Diction and Vocabulary

1. Cite the allusion in paragraph 11. (Guide: *Figures of Speech.*) Why does it qualify as an allusion?
2. Use the dictionary as needed to understand the meanings of the following words: propensity (par. 1); Homo sapiens (3, 6); allegation, piranha, prehensile (4); sonorous (6); ethologist (10, 16); carnivore (10); agonistic (11); extant, holocaust, ineradicable (13).

Suggestions for Writing and Discussion

1. Do you think this is really the "kind of stuff" (par. 2) we like to read about ourselves? Explain.
2. Which do you believe is more normal to the human race — Morgan's grocer, window washer, and postman, or Anthony Storr's "cruellest and most ruthless species"? Why?
3. If you have some fresh insight or observations to bring to the task, use "war as an ineradicable species-specific behavior pattern, . . . a biological imperative," as a basis for discussion. Organize your ideas, whether pro or con, in a coherent pattern.

(NOTE: Suggestions for topics requiring development by use of EXAMPLE are on page 43, at the end of this section.)

JAMES THURBER

JAMES THURBER (1894–1961) was a writer and cartoonist whose essays, short stories, and line drawings have helped enliven and illuminate American life for half a century. He joined the staff of *The New Yorker* in 1925, and most of his writings were first published in that magazine. Some of his collections are *Is Sex Necessary?* (1929, with E. B. White), *The Owl in the Attic* (1931), *Let Your Mind Alone!* (1937), *The Thurber Carnival* (1945), *The Thurber Album* (1952), and *Thurber Country* (1953). His more recent books are *Alarms and Diversions* (1957), *The Years with Ross* (1959), and *Lanterns and Lances* (1961).

Courtship Through the Ages

"Courtship Through the Ages" was first published in 1939 by *The New Yorker*, and was included the same year in Thurber's book *My World — and Welcome to It.* Although it would be misleading to call any one selection "typical" of writing as varied as Thurber's, this one is at least representative of the kind of humor that made him famous. It also serves, for us, to illustrate example usage to show a "prevalence."

Surely nothing in the astonishing scheme of life can have nonplussed Nature so much as the fact that none of the females of any of the species she created really cared very much for the male, as such. For the past ten million years Nature has been busily inventing ways to make the male attractive to the female, but the whole business of courtship, from the marine annelids up to man, still lumbers heavily along, like a complicated musical comedy. I have been reading the sad and absorbing story in Volume 6 (Cole to Dama) of the *Encyclopaedia Britannica.* In this volume you can learn all about cricket, cotton, costume designing, crocodiles, crown jewels, and Coleridge, but none of these subjects is so interesting as the Courtship of Animals, which recounts the sorrowful lengths to which all males must go to arouse the interest of a lady.

We all know, I think, that Nature gave man whiskers and a mustache with the quaint idea in mind that these would prove attractive to the female. We all know that, far from attracting her, whiskers and mustaches only made her nervous and gloomy, so that man had to go in for somersaults, tilting with lances, and performing feats of parlor magic to win her attention; he also had to bring her candy, flowers, and the furs of animals. It is common knowledge that in spite of all these "love displays" the male is constantly being turned down, insulted, or thrown out of the house. It is rather comforting, then, to discover that the peacock, for all his gorgeous plumage, does not have a particularly easy time in courtship; none of the males in the world do. The first peahen, it turned out, was only faintly stirred by her suitor's beautiful train. She would often go quietly to sleep while he was whisking it around. The *Britannica* tells us that the peacock actually had to learn a certain little trick to wake her up and revive her interest: he had to learn to vibrate his quills so as to make a rustling sound. In ancient times man himself, observing the ways of the peacock, probably tried vibrating his whiskers to make a rustling sound; if so, it didn't get him anywhere. He had to go in for something else; so, among other things, he went in for gifts. It is not unlikely that he got this idea from certain flies and birds who were making no headway at all with rustling sounds. 2

One of the flies of the family Empidae, who had tried everything, finally hit on something pretty special. He contrived to make a glistening transparent balloon which was even larger than himself. Into this he would put sweetmeats and tidbits and he would carry the whole elaborate envelope through the air to the lady of his choice. This amused her for a time, but she finally got bored with it. She demanded silly little colorful presents, something that you couldn't eat but that would look nice around the house. So the male Empis had to go around gathering flower petals and pieces of bright paper to put into his balloon. On a courtship flight a male Empis cuts quite a figure now, but he can hardly be said to be happy. He never knows how soon the female will demand heavier presents, such as Roman coins and gold collar buttons. It seems probable that one day the courtship of the Empidae will fall down, as man's occasionally does, of its own weight. 3

The bowerbird is another creature that spends so much time courting the female that he never gets any work done. If all the male 4 bowerbirds became nervous wrecks within the next ten or fifteen years, it would not surprise me. The female bowerbird insists that a playground be built for her with a specially constructed bower at the entrance. This bower is much more elaborate than an ordinary nest and is harder to build; it costs a lot more, too. The female will not come to the playground until the male has filled it up with a great many gifts: silvery leaves, red leaves, rose petals, shells, beads, berries, bones, dice, buttons, cigar bands, Christmas seals, and the Lord knows what else. When the female finally condescends to visit the playground, she is in a coy and silly mood and has to be chased in and out of the bower and up and down the playground before she will quit giggling and stand still long enough even to shake hands. The male bird is, of course, pretty well done in before the chase starts, because he has worn himself out hunting for eyeglass lenses and begonia blossoms. I imagine that many a bowerbird, after chasing a female for two or three hours, says the hell with it and goes home to bed. Next day, of course, he telephones someone else and the same trying ritual is gone through with again. A male bowerbird is as exhausted as a night-club habitué before he is out of his twenties.

The male fiddler crab has a somewhat easier time, but it can 5
hardly be said that he is sitting pretty. He has one enormously large and powerful claw, usually brilliantly colored, and you might suppose that all he had to do was reach out and grab some passing cutie. The very earliest fiddler crabs may have tried this, but, if so, they got slapped for their pains. A female fiddler crab will not tolerate any caveman stuff; she never has and she doesn't intend to start now. To attract a female, a fiddler crab has to stand on tiptoe and brandish his claw in the air. If any female in the neighborhood is interested — and you'd be surprised how many are not — she comes over and engages him in light badinage, for which he is not in the mood. As many as a hundred females may pass the time of day with him and go on about their business. By nightfall of an average courting day, a fiddler crab who has been standing on tiptoe for eight or ten hours waving a heavy claw in the air is in pretty sad shape. As in the case of the males of all species, however, he gets out of bed next morning, dashes some water on his face, and tries again.

The next time you encounter a male web-spinning spider, stop 6
and reflect that he is too busy worrying about his love life to have any desire to bite you. Male web-spinning spiders have a tougher life than any other males in the animal kingdom. This is because the female web-spinning spiders have very poor eyesight. If a male lands

on a female's web, she kills him before he has time to lay down his cane and gloves, mistaking him for a fly or a bumblebee who has tumbled into her trap. Before the species figured out what to do about this, millions of males were murdered by ladies they called on. It is the nature of spiders to perform a little dance in front of the female, but before a male spinner could get near enough for the female to see who he was and what he was up to, she would lash out at him with a flat-iron or a pair of garden shears. One night, nobody knows when, a very bright male spinner lay awake worrying about calling on a lady who had been killing suitors right and left. It came to him that this business of dancing as a love display wasn't getting anybody anywhere except the grave. He decided to go in for web-twitching, or strand-vibrating. The next day he tried it on one of the nearsighted girls. Instead of dropping in on her suddenly, he stayed outside the web and began monkeying with one of its strands. He twitched it up and down and in and out with such a lilting rhythm that the female was charmed. The serenade worked beautifully; the female let him live. The *Britannica*'s spider-watchers, however, report that this system is not always successful. Once in a while, even now, a female will fire three bullets into a suitor or run him through with a kitchen knife. She keeps threatening him from the moment he strikes the first low notes on the outside strings, but usually by the time he has got up to the high notes played around the center of the web, he is going to town and she spares his life.

Even the butterfly, as handsome a fellow as he is, can't always 7
win a mate merely by fluttering around and showing off. Many butterflies have to have scent scales on their wings. Hepialus carries a powder puff in a perfumed pouch. He throws perfume at the ladies when they pass. The male tree cricket, Oecanthus, goes Hepialus one better by carrying a tiny bottle of wine with him and giving drinks to such doxies as he has designs on. One of the male snails throws darts to entertain the girls. So it goes, through the long list of animals, from the bristle worm and his rudimentary dance steps to man and his gift of diamonds and sapphires. The golden-eye drake raises a jet of water with his feet as he flies over a lake; Hepialus has his powder puff, Oecanthus his wine bottle, man his etchings. It is a bright and melancholy story, the age-old desire of the male for the female, the age-old desire of the feamle to be amused and entertained. Of all the creatures on earth, the only males who could be figured as putting any irony into their courtship are the grebes and certain other diving

birds. Every now and then a courting grebe slips quietly down to the bottom of a lake and then, with a mighty "Whoosh!," pops out suddenly a few feet from his girl friend, splashing water all over her. She seems to be persuaded that this is a purely loving display, but I like to think that the grebe always has a faint hope of drowning her or scaring her to death.

I will close this investigation into the mournful burdens of the male with *Britannica*'s story about a certain Argus pheasant. It appears that the Argus displays himself in front of a female who stands perfectly still without moving a feather. . . . The male Argus the *Britannica* tells about was confined in a cage with a female of another species, a female who kept moving around, emptying ashtrays and fussing with lampshades all the time the male was showing off his talents. Finally, in disgust, he stalked away and began displaying in front of his water trough. He reminds me of a certain male (Homo sapiens) of my acquaintance who one night after dinner asked his wife to put down her detective magazine so that he could read a poem of which he was very fond. She sat quietly enough until he was well into the middle of the thing, intoning with great ardor and intensity. Then suddenly there came a sharp, disconcerting *slap!* It turned out that all during the male's display, the female had been intent on a circling mosquito and had finally trapped it between the palms of her hands. The male in this case did not stalk away and display in front of a water trough; he went over to Tim's and had a flock of drinks and recited the poem to the fellas. I am sure they all told bitter stories of their own about how their displays had been interrupted by females. I am also sure that they all ended up singing "Honey, Honey, Bless Your Heart." 8

Meanings and Values

1a. Clarify the meaning of "irony of situation" by using at least one example from this essay. (See Guide to Terms: *Irony.*)

b. Use at least three examples to illustrate the meaning of "verbal irony."

2. Thurber's writing is sometimes said to have nearly universal appeal — not only because of the humor, but also because of his subjects and his attitude toward them. What appeals would this subject have to various types of people you know?

3a. The author's themes are ordinarily deeper than they may appear to be on the surface, and they are sometimes quite serious. How seriously is he concerned about the mating foolishness of human males? How can you tell?

b. Explain the relation of this matter of attitude to that of tone in writing. (Guide: *Style/Tone.*)

c. Describe Thurber's tone in this essay, using no more than two or three descriptive words.

4. How much literal truth, if any, is in the allegation that "none of the females . . . really cared very much for the male, as such" (par. 1)?

5. Do you think we are really laughing at the animals themselves when we go to the zoo? If not, what do we laugh at? Explain carefully.

Expository Techniques

1. How does the author remind us with each new example, without making an issue of it, that he is describing people as well as (perhaps even more than) wildlife?

2. List the general ways in which humor is achieved in this selection and illustrate each with a specific example.

3. Briefly explain why some people would classify these examples as personification, whereas others would not. (Guide: *Figures of Speech.*)

4a. Which of the common transitional devices is (or are) used to bridge between paragraphs 2 and 3? (Guide: *Transition.*)

b. Between 3 and 4?

c. Between 4 and 5?

d. How do such matters relate to coherence? (Guide: *Coherence.*)

Diction and Vocabulary

1. Which, if any, of the ways listed in answering question 2 of "Expository Techniques" are matters of diction? Why? (Guide: *Diction.*)

2. If you are not already familiar with the following words as used in this essay, study their meanings as given in the dictionary; non-plussed, lumbers (par. 1); condescends, habitué (4); brandish, badinage (5); doxies (7); intoning, disconcerting (8).

Suggestions for Writing and Discussion

1. Explain fully, using specific examples, the real reasons for amusement at a zoo (or, for some people, a barnyard).

2. How do young men today try to impress the young women they are interested in?

3. Examine the possibility that women are interested in male "displays"

because such reactions have been "programmed" into them from their earliest childhood.

4. If you are familiar with the aims and methods of the women's liberation movement, how do you think its more radical members would react to Thurber's impressions of courtship?

(NOTE: Suggestions for topics requiring development by use of EXAMPLE are on page 43, at the end of this section.)

LAURENCE J. PETER and RAYMOND HULL

LAURENCE J. PETER was born in Canada in 1919 and received his Ed.D. from Washington State University. Based on his wide experience as a teacher, counselor, school psychologist, prison instructor, consultant, and university professor, he has written numerous articles for professional journals. His books include *Prescriptive Teaching* (1965), *Teaching System: Vol. 1, Individual Instruction* (1972), *The Peter Prescription* (1972), *Competencies for Teaching*, 4 vols. (1975), and *The Peter Plan* (1977). Peter is now associate professor of education, director of the Evelyn Frieden Center for Prescriptive Teaching, and coordinator of programs for emotionally disturbed children at the University of Southern California.

RAYMOND HULL, also born in 1919, the son of an English Methodist minister, has lived in British Columbia since 1947. He has been a prolific writer of television and stage plays, and his published works cover a wide range, including such subjects as surveying, meat curing, weaving, wine and beer making, and public speaking. Hull's articles have been featured in *Punch, Maclean's, Esquire,* and other magazines.

The Peter Principle

"The Peter Principle," as it follows, combines the first two chapters of the book by that name, which was published in 1969. It is a clear and orderly illustration of the use of developed examples to give concrete form to an abstract central theme.

When I was a boy I was taught that the men upstairs knew what they 1
were doing. I was told, "Peter, the more you know, the further you go." So I stayed in school until I graduated from college and then went forth into the world clutching firmly these ideas and my new teaching certificate. During the first year of teaching I was upset to find that a number of teachers, school principals, supervisors and

superintendents appeared to be unaware of their professional responsibilities and incompetent in executing their duties. For example my principal's main concerns were that all window shades be at the same level, that classrooms should be quiet and that no one step on or near the rose beds. The superintendent's main concerns were that no minority group, no matter how fanatical, should ever be offended and that all official forms be submitted on time. The children's education appeared farthest from the administrator mind.

At first I thought this was a special weakness of the school system in which I taught so I applied for certification in another province. I filled out the special forms, enclosed the required documents and complied willingly with all the red tape. Several weeks later, back came my application and all the documents! 2

No, there was nothing wrong with my credentials; the forms were correctly filled out; an official departmental stamp showed that they had been received in good order. But an accompanying letter said, "The new regulations require that such forms cannot be accepted by the Department of Education unless they have been registered at the Post Office to ensure safe delivery. Will you please remail the forms to the Department, making sure to register them this time?" 3

I began to suspect that the local school system did not have a monopoly on incompetence. 4

As I looked further afield, I saw that every organization contained a number of persons who could not do their jobs. 5

A UNIVERSAL PHENOMENON

Occupational incompetence is everywhere. Have you noticed it? Probably we all have noticed it. 6

We see indecisive politicians posing as resolute statesmen and the "authoritative source" who blames his misinformation on "situational imponderables." Limitless are the public servants who are indolent and insolent; military commanders whose behavioral timidity belies their dreadnaught rhetoric, and governors whose innate servility prevents their actually governing. In our sophistication, we virtually shrug aside the immoral cleric, corrupt judge, incoherent attorney, author who cannot write and English teacher who cannot spell. At universities we see proclamations authored by administra- 7 tors whose own office communications are hopelessly muddled; and droning lectures from inaudible or incomprehensible instructors.

Seeing incompetence at all levels of every hierachy — political, 8
legal, educational and industrial — I hypothesized that the cause was some inherent feature of the rules governing the placement of employees. Thus began my serious study of the ways in which employees move upward through a hierarchy, and of what happens to them after promotion.

For my scientific data hundreds of case histories were collected. 9
Here are three typical examples.

Municipal Government File, Case No. 17. J. S. Minion[1] was a maintenance 10
foreman in the public works department of Excelsior City. He was a favorite of the senior officials at City Hall. They all praised his unfailing affability.

"I like Minion," said the superintendent of works. "He has good 11
judgment and is always pleasant and agreeable."

This behavior was appropriate for Minion's position: he was not 12
supposed to make policy, so he had no need to disagree with his superiors.

The superintendent of works retired and Minion succeeded him. 13
Minion continued to agree with everyone. He passed to his foreman every suggestion that came from above. The resulting conflicts in policy, and the continual changing of plans, soon demoralized the department. Complaints poured in from the Mayor and other officials, from taxpayers and from the maintenance-workers' union.

Minion still says "Yes" to everyone, and carries messages briskly 14
back and forth between his superiors and his subordinates. Nominally a superintendent, he actually does the work of a messenger. The maintenance department regularly exceeds its budget, yet fails to fulfill its program of work. In short, Minion, a competent foreman, became an incompetent superintendent.

Service Industries File, Case No. 3. E. Tinker was exceptionally zealous 15
and intelligent as apprentice at G. Reece Auto Repair Inc., and soon rose to journeyman mechanic. In this job he showed outstanding ability in diagnosing obscure faults, and endless patience in correcting them. He was promoted to foreman of the repair shop.

[1]Some names have been changed, in order to protect the guilty.

But here his love of things mechanical and his perfectionism 16
became liabilities. He will undertake any job that he thinks looks interesting, no matter how busy the shop may be. "We'll work it in somehow," he says.

He will not let a job go until he is fully satisfied with it. 17

He meddles constantly. He is seldom to be found at his desk. He 18
is usually up to his elbows in a dismantled motor and while the man who should be doing the work stands watching, other workmen sit around waiting to be assigned new tasks. As a result the shop is always overcrowded with work, always in a muddle, and delivery times are often missed.

Tinker cannot understand that the average customer cares little 19
about perfection — he wants his car back on time! He cannot understand that most of his men are less interested in motors than their pay checks. So Tinker cannot get on with his customers or with his subordinates. He was a competent mechanic, but is now an incompetent foreman.

Military File, Case No. 8. Consider the case of the late renowned 20
General A. Goodwin. His hearty, informal manner, his racy style of speech, his scorn for petty regulations and his undoubted personal bravery made him the idol of his men. He led them to many well-deserved victories.

When Goodwin was promoted to field marshall he had to deal, 21
not with ordinary soldiers, but with politicians and allied generalissimos.

He would not conform to the necessary protocol. He could not 22
turn his tongue to the conventional courtesies and flatteries. He quarreled with all the dignitaries and took to lying for days at a time, drunk and sulking, in his trailer. The conduct of the war slipped out of his hands into those of his subordinates. He had been promoted to a position that he was incompetent to fill.

AN IMPORTANT CLUE!

In time I saw that all such cases had a common feature. The employee 23
had been promoted from a position of competence to a position of incompetence. I saw that, sooner or later, this could happen to every employee in every hierarchy.

Hypothetical Case File, Case No. 1 Suppose you own a pill-rolling fac- 24
tory, Perfect Pill Incorporated. Your foreman pill roller dies of a
perforated ulcer. You need a replacement. You naturally look among
your rank-and-file pill rollers.

Miss Oval, Mrs. Cylinder, Mr. Ellipse and Mr. Cube all show 25
various degrees of incompetence. They will naturally be ineligible for
promotion. You will choose—other things being equal — your most
competent pill roller, Mr. Sphere, and promote him to foreman.

Now suppose Mr. Sphere proves competent as foreman. Later, 26
when your general foreman, Legree, moves up to Works Manager,
Sphere will be eligible to take his place.

If, on the other hand, Sphere is an incompetent foreman, he will 27
get no more promotion. He has reached what I call his "level of
incompetence." He will stay there till the end of his career.

Some employees, like Ellipse and Cube, reach a level of incom- 28
petence in the lowest grade and are never promoted. Some, like
Sphere (assuming he is not a satisfactory foreman), reach it after one
promotion.

E. Tinker, the automobile repair-shop foreman, reached his level 29
of incompetence on the third stage of the hierarchy. General Goodwin reached his level of incompetence at the very top of the hierarchy.

So my analysis of hundreds of cases of occupational incompe- 30
tence led me on to formulate *The Peter Principle:*

In a Hierarchy Every Employee Tends
to Rise to His Level of Incompetence

A NEW SCIENCE!

Having formulated the Principle, I discovered that I had inadver- 31
tently founded a new science, hierarchiology, the study of hierarchies.

The term "hierarchy" was originally used to describe the system 32
of church government by priests graded into ranks. The contemporary meaning includes any organization whose members or employees are arraged in order of rank, grade or class.

Hierarchiology, although a relatively recent discipline, appears 33
to have great applicability to the fields of public and private administration.

THIS MEANS YOU!

My Principle is the key to an understanding of all hierarchal systems, 34
and therefore to an understanding of the whole structure of civilization. A few eccentrics try to avoid getting involved with hierarchies, but everyone in business, industry, trade-unionism, politics, government, the armed forces, religion and education is so involved. All of them are controlled by the Peter Principle.

Many of them, to be sure, may win a promotion or two, moving 35
from one level of competence to a higher level of competence. But competence in that new position qualifies them for still another promotion. For each individual, for *you,* for *me,* the final promotion is from a level of competence to a level of incompetence.[2]

So, given enough time — and assuming the existence of enough 36
ranks in the hierarchy — each employee rises to, and remains at, his level of incompetence. Peter's Corollary states:

In time, every post tends to be occupied by an employee who is incompe- 37
tent to carry out its duties.

WHO TURNS THE WHEELS?

You will rarely find, of course, a system in which *every* employee has 38
reached his level of incompetence. In most instances, something is being done to further the ostensible purposes for which the hierarchy exists.

Work is accomplished by those employees who have not yet reached their 39
level of incompetence.

* * *

A study of a typical hierarchy, the Excelsior City school system, 40
will show how the Peter Principle works within the teaching profession. Study this example and understand how hierarchiology operates within every establishment.

Let us begin with the rank-and-file classroom teachers. I group 41
them, for this analysis, into three classes: competent, moderately competent and incompetent.

[2]The phenomena of "percussive sublimation" (commonly referred to as "being kicked upstairs") and of "the lateral arabesque" are not, as the casual observer might think, exceptions to the Principle. They are only pseudo-promotions. . . .

Distribution theory predicts, and experience confirms, that 42
teachers will be distributed unevenly in these classes: the majority in the moderately competent class, minorities in the competent and incompetent classes. This graph illustrates the distribution:

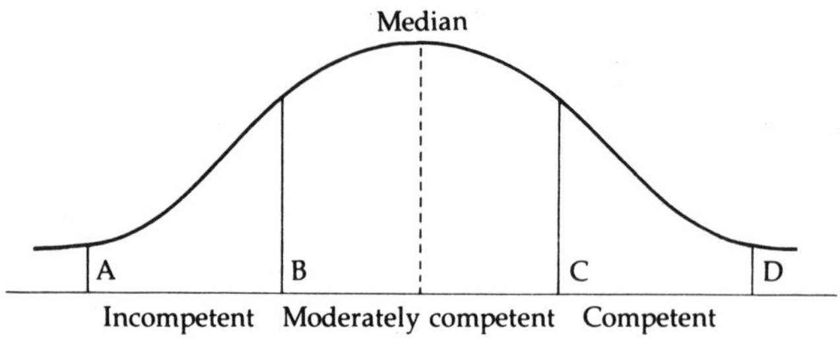

THE CASE OF THE CONFORMIST

An incompetent teacher is ineligible for promotion. Dorothea D. 43
Ditto, for example, had been an extremely conforming student in college. Her assignments were either plagiarisms from textbooks and journals, or transcriptions of the professors' lectures. She always did exactly as she was told, no more, no less. *She was considered to be a competent student.* She graduated with honors from the Excelsior Teachers' College.

When she became a teacher, she taught exactly as she herself 44
had been taught. She followed precisely the textbook, the curriculum guide and the bell schedule.

Her work goes fairly well, except when no rule or precedent is 45
available. For example, when a water pipe burst and flooded the classroom floor, Miss Ditto kept on teaching until the principal rushed in and rescued the class.

"Miss Ditto!" he cried. "In the Name of the Superintendent! 46
There are three inches of water on this floor. Why is your class still here?"

She replied. "I don't hear the emergency bell signal. I pay atten- 47
tion to those things. You know I do. I'm certain you didn't sound the bell." Flummoxed before the power of her awesome *non sequitur,* the principal invoked a provision of the school code giving him emergency powers in an extraordinary circumstance and led her sopping class from the building.

So, although she never breaks a rule or disobeys an order, she 48
is often in trouble, and will never gain promotion. Competent as a student, *she has reached her level of incompetence as a classroom teacher, and willl therefore remain in that position throughout her teaching career.*

THE ELIGIBLE MAJORITY

Most beginning teachers are moderately competent or competent — 49
see the area from B to D on the — graph and *they will all be eligible for promotion.* Here is one such case.

A Latent Weakness. Mr. N. Beeker had been a competent student, and 50
became a popular science teacher. His lessons and lab periods were inspiring. His students were co-operative and kept the laboratory in order. Mr. Beeker was not good at paper work, but this weakness was offset, in the judgment of his superiors, by his success as a teacher.

Beeker was promoted to head of the science department where 51
he now had to order all science supplies and keep extensive records. *His incompetence is evident!* For three years running he has ordered new Bunsen burners, but no tubing for connecting them. As the old tubing deteriorates, fewer and fewer burners are operable, although new ones accumulate on the shelves.

Beeker is not being considered for further promotion. *His ulti-* 52
mate position is one for which he is incompetent.

Higher up the Hierarchy. B. Lunt had been a competent student, teacher 53
and department head, and was promoted to assistant principal. In this post he got on well with teachers, students and parents, and was intellectually competent. He gained a further promotion to the rank of principal.

Till now, he had never dealt directly with school-board mem- 54
bers, or with the district superintendent of education. It soon appeared that he lacked the required finesse to work with these high officials. *He kept the superintendent waiting* while he settled a dispute between two children. Taking a class for a teacher who was ill, *he missed a curriculum revision committee meeting* called by the assistant superintendent.

He worked so hard at running his school that *he had no energy* 55
for running community organizations. He declined offers to become program chairman of the Parent-Teacher Association, president of

the Community Betterment League and consultant to the Committee for Decency in Literature.

His school lost community support and he fell out of favor with 56
the superintendent. Lunt came to be regarded, by the public and by his superiors, as an incompetent principal. When the assistant superintendent's post became vacant, the school board declined to give it to Lunt. He remains, and will remain till he retires, unhappy and incompetent as a principal.

The Autocrat. R. Driver, having proved his competence as student, 57
teacher, department head, assistant principal and principal, was promoted to assistant superintendent. Previously he had only to interpret the school board's policy and have it efficiently carried out in his school. Now, as assistant superintendent, he must participate in the policy discussions of the board, using democratic procedures.

But Driver dislikes democratic procedures. He insists on his 58
status as an expert. He lectures the board members much as he used to lecture his students when he was a classroom teacher. He tries to dominate the board as he dominated his staff when he was a principal.

The board now considers Driver an incompetent assistant super- 59
intendent. He will receive no further promotion.

Soon Parted. G. Spender was a competent student, English teacher, 60
department head, assistant principal and principal. He then worked competently for six years as an assistant superintendent — patriotic, diplomatic, suave and well liked. He was promoted to superintendent. Here he was obliged to enter the field of school finance, in which he soon found himself at a loss.

From the start of his teaching career, Spender had never both- 61
ered his head about money. His wife handled his pay check, paid all household accounts and gave him pocket money each week.

Now Spender's incompetence in the area of finance is revealed. 62
He purchased a large number of teaching machines from a fly-by-night company which went bankrupt without producing any programs to fit the machines. He had every classroom in the city equipped with television, although the only programs available in the area were for secondary schools. Spender has found his level of incompetence.

ANOTHER PROMOTION MECHANISM

The foregoing examples are typical of what are called "line promotions." There is another mode of upward movement: the "staff promotion." The case of Miss T. Totland is typical. 63

Miss Totland, who had been a competent student and an outstanding primary teacher, was promoted to primary supervisor. She now has to teach, not children, but teachers. Yet *she still uses the techniques which worked so well with small children.* 64

Addressing teachers, singly or in groups, she speaks slowly and distinctly. She uses mostly words of one or two syllables. She explains each point several times in different ways, to be sure it is understood. She always wears a bright smile. 65

Teachers dislike what they call her false cheerfulness and her patronizing attitude. Their resentment is so sharp that, instead of trying to carry out her suggestions, they spend much time devising excuses for *not* doing what she recommends. 66

Miss Totland has proved herself incompetent in communicating with primary teachers. She is therefore ineligible for further promotion, *and will remain as primary supervisor, at her level of incompetence.* 67

YOU BE THE JUDGE

You can find similar examples in any hierarchy. Look around you where you work, and pick out the people who have reached their level of incompetence. You will see that in every hierarchy *the cream rises until it sours.* Look in the mirror and ask whether . . . 68

Meanings and Values

1a. Has it been your experience that incompetence is really widespread enough to make this selection worthwhile?

b. Support your answer, either way, by examples from your own or your family's experience. (You will not be *proving* anything — merely supporting an observation.)

2. Does it seem feasible to you that our highly successful, complex industrial and educational systems were devised and are run either by incompetent top executives and engineers or by underlings in the hierarchy? Why, or why not?

3. To what extent are people in elective public office subject to the Peter Principle?

4. Clarify the distinction between "line" and "staff" promotions, as referred to in paragraph 63.

5. Specify at least two ways in which an understanding of the Peter Principle might be of value.

6. Why do people permit themselves to be promoted to levels of incompetence?

Expository Techniques

1. Show how at least two of the standard methods of introduction are used for this exposition. (See Guide to Terms: *Introductions.*)

2a. Where do the authors first give a simple statement of their central theme? (Guide: *Unity.*)
b. How, if at all, is the statement qualified? (Guide: *Qualification.*)
c. Do all portions of the essay serve as "tributaries" into the central theme, thus giving unity to the writing? If not, what are the exceptions?

3a. Several short, undeveloped examples are used in paragraph 1 to show a "prevalence." What is the generality they support?
b. What generality does the list of short examples in paragraph 7 support?

4a. A brief comparison between the examples of paragraph 1 and those of paragraph 7 can be used to show that examples, like words, can achieve differing degrees of specificity. (Guide: *Specific/General.*) Which of the two sets is more general?
b. Is one set then necessarily more, or less, effective than the other? Explain.

5. Paragraphs 2 and 3 comprise a more fully developed example. Which paragraph contains the generalization it supports?

6. All the authors' case file reports, themselves fully developed examples, also *use* example. Analyze any one of these reports for its basic structure, its use of this kind of interior example, and the effectiveness of presentation.

7a. Of the "hundreds of case histories" (par. 9) at the authors' disposal, why do you think cases 17, 3, and 8 were chosen to use as examples?
b. Were these good choices?

8a. How is the series of developed examples beginning in paragraph 43 organized?
b. How is organization superior, or inferior, to a less structured, more casual arrangement?
c. Can you think of some other order that would have been as effective? Explain.
d. What advantage is derived from the similar formats and endings of these examples?

Diction and Vocabulary

1. If you are not familiar with the meanings of any of the following words, consult your dictionary: phenomenon (subheading before par. 6); indolent, dreadnaught, innate, servility, incoherent, inaudible (7); hypothesized, inherent (8); succeeded, demoralized (13); protocol (22); inadvertently (31); eccentrics (34); corollary (36); ostensible (38); plagiarisms (43); flummoxed, *non sequitur* (47); latent (50).

Suggestions for Writing and Discussion

1. How is it possible, if at all in this complex society, to avoid getting involved with hierarchies (par. 34), other than in occasional dealings with them in the necessary conduct of personal affairs? Consider such pertinent matters as methods, penalties, rewards.
2. If one's work is necessarily involved in a hierarchy, what practical methods would you suggest for reaching and remaining on the highest level of *competence,* thereby defying the Peter Principle?
3. From your own knowledge, select an example of incompetence dissimilar to any of those discussed in this essay. Show as well as you can the way in which a person passed his highest level of competence and, if possible, the results of the mistake for himself and others.
4. If you have reason to doubt the Peter Principle's rather broad claims, show the nature of and justification for your doubts. You should not try to "prove" the principle wrong unless you have at least as much ammunition as the authors do. Remember that they do qualify most of their major generalizations.

(NOTE: Suggestions for topics requiring development by use of EXAMPLE are on page 43, at the end of this section.)

DICK GREGORY

DICK GREGORY was born in St. Louis in 1932. He won the Missouri mile-run championship in 1951 and while attending Southern Illinois University (1951–1953 and 1955–1956) was named the school's outstanding athlete. He served in the United States Army from 1953 to 1955. Gregory is one of America's sharpest social satirists. Once a popular night club comedian and recording artist, Gregory retired from his career as an entertainer in the mid-seventies to concentrate on his second career, as a lecturer and political activist. He fasted for several years to protest the war in Southeast Asia, and is now fasting to protest nuclear power. In 1968 he ran unsuccessfully for President as the U. S. Peace and Freedom Party candidate. Gregory's books include the autobiographical *Nigger* (1964), *No More Lies: The Myths of American History* (1971), *Dick Gregory's Political Primer* (1972), and *Up from Nigger* (1976). He has also recorded several albums, among them *Dick Gregory in Living Black and White.* Gregory lives in Chicago with his wife and ten children.

The Ghetto Cop

"The Ghetto Cop" (editor's title) is an excerpt from Gregory's book *The Shadow That Scares Me,* published in 1968. Although in this selection Gregory is less dependent on example as a means of primary development than the previous authors have been, his liberal and informal use of varied examples is consistent with his essay's familiar style.

The power structure cannot expect to solve the social problems of the ghetto by the mere physical presence of cops. The violence and strife in the ghetto cannot be contained or suppressed because they do not represent a riot. Five disciplined cops can stop a riot, but the best trained armies in the world cannot contain a legitimate protest. 1

The attitude of the cop is much more important than his physical 2 presence. If you live in a city whose baseball team has just won the World Series, or which has been chosen by the Shriners as the site for their national convention, you will see people take over the town. They get drunk in the streets, damage property, and bother passersby. The cop will look the other way because a big convention is bringing the city millions of dollars. If a cop can be taught to change his attitude because a convention is bringing a city a lot of money, he had also better be taught not to mistreat people who are demanding human dignity, which is more than all the money in the world can buy.

People insist that it is unfair to generalize about the police. The good cop is held up for public inspection and he is supposed to be the example of law-enforcement officers everywhere. Just as the one rabbi, priest or minister who goes to Alabama to demonstrate is supposed to represent the whole church. The one beautiful cop in a neighborhood *will* stand out. He has pride in his job. He is sensitive to human problems and knows how to talk to the person on the street corner. He has not chosen his job because he couldn't get hired any place else. He is a cop because he wants to be; perhaps his father and grandfather before him had devoted their lives to law enforcement. 3

The problem cops, and there are many, are those who resented their job when they took it. They are the cops who act like the judge and the jury when they make an arrest. Their resentment shows twenty-four hours a day. This situation will never change until society gives law enforcement a status which is comparable to the job it is expected to do. 4

Policemen labor under two basic injustices: inadequate salary and lack of proper training. The cop is the most underpaid man in American society today. Cops in the large cities should begin with a minimum salary of ten thousand dollars per year. You must pay a proper dollar for the job required. More and more potential teachers are lost to the vocation of education because industry is able to pay more money. The cop is so important to solving the social problems which beset the ghetto that America should take the chance of overpaying him, not underpaying him. 5

Being an entertainer, I am constantly reminded of the financial injustice which the cop suffers. I have done benefit performances all over the country for Policemen's Wives, Policemen's Widows, Policemen's Benevolence Associations, and so on. But I never did a show for the politician's wife or the nightclub owner's wife. They are 6 able to provide for their family in case of emergency, because their earnings are at a higher level than the cop's. If America treated the cop with the respect his job deserves, the family of a cop killed in the line of duty would automatically become the responsibility of government. Some local governments have accepted this responsibility, but such legislation should be enacted across the country in a uniform way.

Imagine yourself a cop in a major urban area. When you put on that uniform in the morning and leave the house, you never know if you will make it back home in the evening. The policeman must live daily with a basic human fright which few other professions share. Yet the cop pays the same price for his haircut that Rockefeller pays. He pays the same amount for the education of his children that the rich executive pays. If a policeman is killed in the line of duty, it is an ethical and moral imperative that society accept the responsibility of scholarships for his children, a home for his family, and other necessary benefits. 7

Somehow we seem to be able to give foreign aid to countries all over the world, even those countries who openly tell us to "go to hell." We should be able to find the money to give some aid to the cop — proper salary and proper training. Domestic aid to the cop at home is more important than foreign aid to countries abroad. We have a crisis in this country which can destroy us from within. . . . The number one place to begin to solve this problem which calls attention to itself with the haunting chant, "Burn, baby, burn," is through enlightened law enforcement. 8

There is a psychological factor operating in the injustice to the cop. A man knows when he is being mistreated and it is bound to affect his attitude. This applies to both Negroes and cops. When we finally create an atmosphere in this country where law-enforcement officers are trained and paid in direct proportion to the importance of their job, a new attitude of vocational pride will be evident. If society does not have enough pride in its law-enforcement officers to pay them what they are worth, the cop is more likely to be susceptible to the bribe. If the pay scale is high enough, the cop does not want to risk getting caught taking a bribe for fear of losing his job. He knows he cannot get another job at the same high salary. Honesty and devotion are basic ingredients in vocational pride. 9

There is also the consideration of security, which is especially important in a dangerous profession. The soldier has security, although often he is not even aware of it. Count up his benefits and 10 you will find that he has much more security than the cop. And the soldier's job is easier than the cop's, because the soldier knows where his enemy is. The enemy even wears a uniform to identify himself. But the cop doesn't know what his enemy looks like. It might be that nut the Army rejected! The same man who is too crazy to go to Vietnam and kill Vietcong is back home in your neighborhood waiting to assault you. The cop has to deal with him.

Each new technological advance and the prospect of life in a cybernetic society will place more demands upon the cop. We will see unions demanding shorter and shorter work weeks. There will be an increase of leisure time. People will have more time on their hands, perhaps to be out in the streets. When a man works a forty-hour week, the cop can count on the foreman watching him at least eight hours a day! 11

The prophet Micah insisted that the Lord requires simply that man "do justice." He seems to imply that other problems of human relationship will be solved when a climate of justice is established. Justice in America today requires the investment of funds for the proper training and schooling of law-enforcement officers. The cop's job is too important for him to be allowed to put on the uniform without proper training. When I travel to England, it is frightening to see that the cabdriver in London receives a longer period of training than the average cop in America. Surely we must see our cops as more crucial to the total health of society than England does its cabdrivers. Only through basic research and proper training can just and enlightened law enforcement become a reality. And this enlightenment and sensitivity must come *before* the cop gets out into the street. Society simply cannot send the cop out into the street with his nightstick to get on-the-job training on my head or with my problems, which he has not been trained to understand. He must become thoroughly aware of my social problems while he is still in school. All the force in the world will never totally suppress a legitimate problem. Those who would deal with social problems must have a basic human understanding. 12

The cop must be taught the unique problems of ghetto living *before* he ever goes out on his beat. He must know, for example, why the man in the ghetto rarely shops at the supermarket. The supermarket requires him to pay cash. So the man in the ghetto goes to the white local merchant across the street. The prices in that little store are too high already, and the local merchant will try to cheat even more. The ghetto brother knows he is being cheated and it worries 13 him. So when the white merchant turns his back to get the stale day-old loaf of bread, his customer wipes out the cookie rack. It is the customer's way of making up for the cheat. While the merchant is busy putting his thumb on the scale, his pickles disappear.

The cop must understand this injustice. He will see that there is more to the issue than a customer stealing. But if the customer gets caught stealing, the merchant calls a cop. When the ghetto kid gets caught stealing, the merchant grabs him by the ears and holds him until the cops arrive. But what happens when that same kid gets short-changed by the merchant? The kid can't call a cop and get a fair hearing. Cops must be taught to have a responsive and sympathetic ear and listen when that ghetto mother complains that her kids are being shortchanged. Once a cop becomes aware of such practices from the beginning, he can go immediately to the local merchant and say, "We have tremendously explosive social problems in this neighborhood which you could tip off at any moment. Don't shortchange the kids." And if complaints continue to come in, the cop should investigate the basis of the complaint immediately. Such activity would go a long way toward establishing a new image of respect for the cop in the ghetto. And the resentment and frustration which lead to breaking the local merchant's window and looting his store would begin to be alleviated. 14

Understanding ghetto kids presents a special problem for the cop. When a riot breaks out in a high school, the damage is already done and there is little the cop can do besides try to contain the violence. But if the cop had been sensitive to the history of the problem, the riot might have been avoided. For example, two kids have a gun duel in the schoolyard. The incident will very probably be hushed up by the school principal to keep his own record clean downtown. He doesn't want the superintendent of schools questioning his ability to control his pupils. But the seed for further trouble has been sown. A full-scale school riot may erupt which is certainly a more destructive mark on the principal's record. 15

Cops need to learn to work hand in hand with the school. They need to learn to meet ghetto kids on their own level — the " 'cause why" level. It is that basic, raw, instinctive level of life which seeks honest and open answers to very basic questions. High school kids know that the cops will be on hand when they throw their dance. 'Cause why is that the only time the cops are around? The cop has the image of only coming around to break up a party. 16

When cops learn to meet kids on their own level, they will learn the answer to many adolescent mysteries. Like why so many kids choose the street corner or the local hangout instead of the brand-new recreational facilities in the neighborhood. It is a simple fact of Nature. Recreational facilities are geared to a program for boys. But the boys are going to choose to be where the girls are. The girls are at the local hangout. There are certain biological factors which take precedence even over basketball! 17

When cops learn the conditions of the home environment in the ghetto, they will find out why kids act as they do. How many cops on the beat have actually seen their mother have an affair with their own daddy, let alone another man? Or how many cops have seen their mother take a needle and stick it in her arm and get high? The ghetto kid has seen this. He has looked at his own mother have an affair with a stranger. Of course, she told him it was one of Daddy's friends who came by to talk to her. So they went into the bedroom to talk, closing the door behind them. But Mother never thought that her little seven-year-old kid would peek through the keyhole. After he peeked through the keyhole and saw what he saw, he came back out into the street. He has just seen his mother have an affair with a stranger and the cop is going to tell him to be good? Naturally he will start swinging on the cop because he has to react against something. He can't swing on Momma. 18

The cop has to go back home with the ghetto kid and find out where he learned that language he uses. Mother and Father would never curse in front of the kid, until they get angry. Then the curse words fly. When you hear these words at age seven, you assume that a dirty word is something to be used as a defensive weapon. So when you walk down the street and a little girl says to you, "You stink," quite naturally you are angry and threatened. It is only natural to turn and say, "Kiss my butt." It is natural because the little seven-year-old has heard Mother and Father use dirty language under the same threatening conditions. The little kid doesn't take a bite out of a good piece of chicken and curse. He smacks his lips and makes funny little grunting noises, just like Momma and Daddy. But when he is threatened, angry, and misused, the little kid curses. His home environment has taught him that response. 19

Cops must be trained to understand, on the human level, the conditions of life and the home environment. It is amazing to see the results of juvenile police who have received private grants to work 20 with kids. They accept the gang leader and work with him. They do not start out resenting him and trying to force him to behave. A loyalty is established between cop and gang, so that the cops often know when and where the big rumble is going to be. By really becoming involved in the life of the gang, and accepting kids on their own level, juvenile cops have been able to contain potentially troublesome situations.

Just and proper training of cops must take into account the tremendous responsibility placed upon law-enforcement officers and the great pressures under which they live. Can you imagine a cop running through the streets of New York City, chasing a burglar, and he shoots, missing the culprit and hitting the Russian diplomat coming out of the United Nations Building? That is World War Three! Such is the awesome responsibility placed upon the man with the gun. 21

Imagine the mental pressure a cop must live under daily in the ordinary line of duty. He sees daily the horror we only read about in the newspapers. We read about a three-year-old girl being sexually molested, mutilated, and murdered. The cop sees it for himself. He walks into an apartment minutes after a man has gone berserk and chopped up his wife and mutilated his kids. Perhaps the cop has little kids of his own waiting for him to come home. What does such a gruesome sight do to a man's mind? How does it affect a man mentally to daily smell and touch dead human beings? It is the cop's job to live in an atmosphere of death — to see dead kids, to hear people moaning, groaning, and crying for help. Society expects the cop to experience such sickening horror and to take it in his stride. He is expected to forget what he has seen and walk back out on the street without holding a grudge. Have we done enough basic research to find out what such an occupational atmosphere does to a cop, as a man? Without such basic research, he cannot be adequately trained to deal with the conditions which his job imposes upon him. The cop's daily work is certain to affect him mentally. One cannot witness daily the horrible reminders of the worst that man can do without developing a low evaluation of humanity. Just and proper training for the cop must take this inevitable reaction into account. 22

Respect for law and order can never be expected until a climate of justice is created which encompasses both the cop and the man in the ghetto. The cop has to be an authority before he gets into the neighborhood. He must be trained to be an expert in understanding 23 human behavior. He must be skilled in the art of human relationships. He must be a general practitioner trained to doctor social ills. If the cop is not adequately trained, he may be doing the very best he can given the conditions of his job; but his best is still wrong. A man does not become a brain surgeon by receiving on-the-job training in the emergency room of a hospital. The surgeon receives basic knowledge and training in medical school. Then he is ready to operate on a cracked skull and see the raw horror of an exposed brain. He will become a better surgeon with each new operation. But he is trained for his task before he is allowed to perform his very first operation. Basic knowledge and training precede actual practice. And the same thing must happen with law enforcement.

If the man on the street is to respect law and order, the cop must 24
behave like a trained, enlightened authority. A man does not want his authority getting angry, swinging a nightstick, and cursing. Such behavior is like the brain surgeon panicking at the sight of a skull fracture after an automobile accident. If that happens, you might just as well close down the hospital. The patient will die when he sees the look of horror on the surgeon's face. The surgeon is expected to take the crisis in his stride and do his job.

It is the same with the cop. It is easy for the cop to walk down 25
the street when nothing is going on, beating his stick on the lamppost and waving with a friendly word for everyone sitting on the tenement stoop. But can the cop keep this same air of cool, calm, and authority in the midst of crisis?

Almost every day a cop performs duties as a matter of routine 26
which would scare me to death. A woman giving birth to a baby in the back seat of my car, for example. It doesn't scare the average cop because he has been trained to know what to do when that water bag bursts before the woman gets to the hospital. He recognizes that it is an act of Nature and he knows how to deal with it.

The social revolution in the sore spots of this nation is another 27
act of Nature, a natural response to oppressive conditions. It bears the same marks of pain, violence, and struggle which accompany any birth. From this violent, painful struggle a new America will be born. For the first time, the nation will be christened in the name of freedom, dignity, and justice. During this transitory period of pregnancy, justice demands that the cop be trained to display the same authority and sophistication in the midst of social crisis as he does when a woman gives birth to a baby in the back of his patrol wagon.

It has been said, "Justice belongs to all men, or it belongs to none." Aristotle wrote, "The way to gain good will is to show good will." And the prophet Micah reminds us what the Lord requires for men to live together in peace, love, and harmony, "do justice, love kindness and walk humbly with your God." What better description could there be for a climate in which respect for law and order is guaranteed? To *do* justice means to treat all men with respect and human dignity — Negroes, whites, cops, and all of creation. To love kindness is to consciously seek an atmosphere of human dwelling in which the rights and needs of all men are respected. To walk humbly means to maintain an air of sensitivity which seeks first to understand human expression rather than to thwart or suppress it. Such is the climate of justice. And when that climate is created, respect for law and order — even an increase of genuine love — will follow. 28

Meanings and Values

1a. What apparently is the author's attitude toward his subject matter? (See Guide to Terms: *Point of View*.)
 b. How did you determine the preceding answer?
 c. How, if at all, is tone involved in the matter? (Guide: *Style/Tone*.)

2a. Is there any evidence of sentimentality in this essay? (Guide: *Sentimentality*.) If so, is it sufficient to damage the writing's effectiveness?
 b. Explain how this is, or would be, a matter of tone.

3a. What criticism, if any, would an ultra-liberal be apt to make of this essay?
 b. An ultra-conservative?
 c. Judging by "The Ghetto Cop," where would you place Gregory on the liberal-conservative spectrum?

4. How valid and appropriate is the comparison with foreign aid in paragraph 8? Explain.

5. If you see any irony in the comparison of cops and cabdrivers in paragraph 12, what kind is it? Why? (Guide: *Irony*.)

6. Give this essay our three-step critical evaluation. (Guide: *Evaluation*.)

7. If you have read the "The Peter Principle," do you think the principle applies to police departments as much as to schools and commercial enterprises? Explain.

Expository Techniques

1a. Cite the paragraphs that use example to achieve concreteness.
 b. Which of these examples, if any, would have benefited by further development?

c. Which examples, if any, seem poorly chosen for their purposes? How could the choice have been improved?

2. By what methods does the author gain emphasis? (Guide: *Emphasis.*) Provide one example of each method.

3. Consider the following sentences in relation to each other and to the essay's general subject matter: the last sentence in paragraph 4, the first in paragraph 5, and the last in paragraph 8.
 a. Which of these three, if any, seems to you a good statement of the overall central theme? (Guide: *Unity*.)
 b. Do *all* parts of the essay pertain to this statement?
 c. If not, does the writing therefore lack unity — or was your answer to 3a incorrect? Explain.

4a. Which of the author's statements, if they are to be taken literally, should have been more carefully qualified? (Guide: *Qualification*.)
 b. Give your reasons for each.
 c. Indicate how qualification for each could have been achieved with least difficulty.
 d. Which of these generalizations, as used in their own context, do you consider permissible as mere obvious exaggerations (a technique sometimes useful for shock value alone)?
 e. Briefly explain how a writer may jeopardize the effectiveness of his writing (even aside from possible damage to other people) by careless generalizing. Illustrate by using quotations from this essay, if any apply.

5a. What standard techniques are used here for closing. (Guide: *Closings*.)
 b. How effectively?

6a. How does its style help qualify this selection as a familiar essay? (Guide: *Essay; Style/Tone*.)
 b. How, if at all, are its organization and development also involved in the matter?

7a. If you have read "The Peter Principle," point out at least three basic ways in which the writing techniques differ decidedly between it and Gregory's essay.
 b. Is either more effectively written, considering the subject matter with which the authors were working? Explain.

Diction and Vocabulary

1a. Which of the elements of style dicussed in your answer to question 6a in "Expository Techniques" are primarily matters of diction? (Guide: *Diction*.) Cite examples.
 b. Which are primarily matters of syntax? (Guide: *Syntax*.) Cite examples.

2a. Gregory consistently uses colloquial and slang terms (Guide: *Colloquial*.) List or mark these. (Dictionaries will differ as to which are colloquial and which slang, but for our purposes we need not be concerned with the distinction.)

b. Comment briefly on the appropriateness for this essay of such liberal usage?

3a. What do you think is the usual connotation of the word "cop"? (Guide: *Connotation/Denotation*.)

b. Do you think Gregory intends this connotation here? Why, or why not?

c. List the possible alternatives to "cop" and indicate for each whether its choice would have been better or worse.

d. Be prepared to justify your answers.

4. Consult the dictionary as needed for an understanding of the following words: Shriners (par. 2); potential, beset (5); imperative (7); cybernetic (11); alleviated (14); encompasses (23).

Suggestions for Writing and Discussion

1. Consider the statement that "five disciplined cops can stop a riot" (par 1.). If you have had sufficient training or experience to speak with some authority, explain how a relatively small police squad (perhaps five is too small) *can* stop a riot.

2. Compare, with facts if you can, the security of the soldier with that of the policeman (par. 10).

3. What problems other than those of police (par. 11) do you think would multiply or worsen with shorter work weeks? Explain.

4. If you have carefully observed a policeman with special training and the time to work with ghetto children (par. 2), explain how he went about this project and, if possible, how successful and long-lasting were the results.

5. Most British city police (officially designated as *peace* officers) do not carry guns. Weigh objectively and explain the feasibility of such a policy in American cities.

6. Consider the statement that "one cannot witness daily the horrible reminders of the worst that man can do without developing a low evaluation of humanity" (par. 22). If you believe this is even generally true, what kind of advance training could possibly offset that devastating effect? Be objective and as thorough as possible.

Writing Suggestions for Section 1

Illustration by Example

Use one of the following statements or another suggested by them as your central theme. Develop it into a unified composition, using examples from history, current events, or personal experience to illustrate your ideas. Be sure to have your reader-audience clearly in mind, as well as your specific purpose for the communication.

1. Successful businesses keep employees at their highest level of *competence.*
2. Not all women want to be "liberated."
3. Women's liberation achievements present dilemmas for both males and females.
4. Laws holding parents responsible for their children's crimes would (or would not) result in serious injustices.
5. You can't always tell a nonconformist by the way he looks.
6. One thing is certain about styles: they cannot stay the same.
7. Good sportsmanship is far more than shaking hands with the winner.
8. Religion in the United States is not dying.
9. Democracy is not always the best form of government.
10. Colonialism was not entirely bad.
11. Nearly anyone can have a creative hobby.
12. The general quality of television commercials may be improving (or deteriorating).
13. "Some books are to be tasted; others swallowed; and some few to be chewed and digested." (*Francis Bacon,* English scientist-author, 1561–1626.)

2

Analyzing a Subject by *Classification*

People naturally like to sort and classify things. The untidiest urchin, moving into a new dresser of his own, will put his handkerchiefs together, socks and underwear in separate stacks, and perhaps his toads and snails (temporarily) into a drawer of their own. He may classify animals as those with legs, those with wings, and those with neither. As he gets older, he finds that schoolteachers have ways of classifying *him,* not only into a reading group but, periodically, into an "A" or "F" category, or somewhere in between. On errands to the grocery store, he discovers the macaroni in the same department as noodles, the pork chops somewhere near the ham. In reading the local newspaper, he observes that its staff has done some classifying for him, putting most of the comics together and seldom mixing sports stories with the news of bridal showers. Eventually he finds courses neatly classified in the college catalogue, and he knows enough not to look for biology courses under "Social Science." (Examples again — used to illustrate a "prevalence.")

However, our main interest in classification here is its use as a structural pattern for explanatory writing. Many subjects about which either student or graduate may need to write will remain a hodgepodge of facts and opinions unless he can find some system of analyzing the material, dividing the subject into categories, and classifying individual elements into those categories. Here we have the distinction usually made between the rhetorical terms *division* and *classification* — for example, dividing "meat" into pork, beef, mutton, and fowl, then classifying ham and pork chops into the category of "pork." But this distinction is one we need scarcely pause for here; once the need for analysis is recognized, the dividing and classifying become inevitable companions and result in the single scheme of "classification" itself, as we have been discussing it. The original division into parts merely sets up the system that, if well chosen, best serves our purpose.

Obviously, no single system of classification is best for all purposes. Our untidy urchin may at some point classify girls according to athletic prowess, then later by size or shape or hair color. Other people may need entirely different systems of classification: the music instructor classifies girls as sopranos, altos, contraltos; the psychologist, according to their behavioral patterns; the sociologist, according to their ethnic origins.

Whatever the purpose, for the more formal uses of classification ("formal," that is, to the extent of most academic and on-the-job writing), we should be careful to use a logical system that is complete and that follows a consistent principle throughout. It would not be logical to divide Protestantism into the categories of Methodist, Baptist, and Lutheran, because the system would be incomplete and misleading. But in classifying Protestants attending some special conference — a different matter entirely — such a limited system might be both complete and logical. In any case, the writer must be careful that classes do not overlap: to classify the persons at the conference as Methodists, Baptists, Lutherans, and clergy would be illogical, because some are undoubtedly both Lutheran, for instance, and "clergy."

In dividing and classifying we are really using the basic process of outlining. Moreover, if we are dealing with classifiable *ideas,* the resulting pattern *is* our outline, which has been our aim all along — a basic organizational plan.

This process of classification frequently does, in fact, organize much less tangible things than the examples mentioned. We might wish to find some orderly basis for discussing the South's post–Civil War problems. Division might give us three primary categories of information: economic, political, and social. But for a full-scale consideration of these, the major divisions themselves may be subdivided for still more orderly explanation: the economic information may be further divided into agriculture and industry. Now it is possible to isolate and clarify such strictly industrial matters as shortage of investment capital, disrupted transportation systems, and lack of power development.

Any plan like this seems almost absurdly obvious, of course — *after* the planning is done. It appears less obvious, however, to the inexperienced writer who is dealing with a jumble of information he must explain to someone else. This is when he should be aware of the patterns at his disposal, and one of the most useful of these, alone or combined with others, is classification.

ERIC BERNE (1910–1970) was a graduate of McGill University's School of Medicine. A psychiatrist, he wrote extensively in that field, lectured at various universities, and served on the psychiatric staff of Mount Sinai Hospital in New York City. He later engaged in private practice and research in California. His books include *Games People Play* (1964), *The Happy Valley* (1968), *Sex in Human Loving* (1970), and *What Do You Say After You Say Hello?* (1972).

Can People Be Judged by Their Appearance?

"Can People Be Judged by Their Appearance?" was originally published in Berne's *Mind in Action* (1947) and was later included in a revised edition of his book, *A Layman's Guide to Psychiatry and Psychoanalysis.* This explanation of one theory of basic human types is an example of a scientific subject made readable for non-scientists. Using division and classification as his primary pattern of development, Berne also relies to varying extents on most of the other expository patterns: illustration, comparison and contrast, process analysis, cause and effect, definition, and description.

Everyone knows that a human being, like a chicken, comes from an egg. At a very early stage, the human embryo forms a three-layered tube, the inside layer of which grows into the stomach and lungs, the middle layer into bones, muscles, joints, and blood vessels, and the outside layer into the skin and nervous system. 1

Usually these three grow about equally, so that the average human being is a fair mixture of brains, muscles, and inward organs. In some eggs, however, one layer grows more than the others, and when the angels have finished putting the child together, he may have more gut than brain, or more brain than muscle. When this happens, the individual's activities will often be mostly with the overgrown layer. 2

We can thus say that while the average human being is a mixture, some people are mainly "digestion-minded," some "muscle-minded," and some "brain-minded," and correspondingly digestion-bodied, muscle-bodied, or brain-bodied. The digestion-bodied people look thick; the muscle-bodied people look wide; and the brain-bodied people look long. This does not mean the taller a man is the brainier he will be. It means that if a man, even a short man, looks long rather than wide or thick, he will often be more concerned about what goes on in his mind than about what he does or what he eats; but the key factor is slenderness and not height. On the other hand, a man who gives the impression of being thick rather than long or wide will usually be more interested in a good steak than in a good idea or a good long walk. 3

Medical men use Greek words to describe these types of body-build. For the man whose body shape mostly depends on the inside layer of the egg, they use the word *endomorph.* If it depends mostly upon the middle layer, they call him a *mesomorph.* If it depends mostly upon the outside layer, they call him an *ectomorph.* We can see the same roots in our English words "enter," "medium," and "exit," which might just as easily have been spelled "ender," "mesium," and "ectit." 4

Since the inside skin of the human egg, or endoderm, forms the inner organs of the belly, the viscera, the endomorph is usually belly-minded; since the middle skin forms the body tissues, or soma, the mesomorph is usually muscle-minded; and since the outside skin forms the brain, or cerebrum, the ectomorph is usually brain-minded. Translating this into Greek, we have the viscerotonic endomorph, the somatotonic mesomorph, and the cerebrotonic ectomorph. 5

Words are beautiful things to a cerebrotonic, but a viscerotonic knows you cannot eat a menu no matter what language it is printed in, and a somatotonic knows you cannot increase your chest expansion by reading a dictionary. So it is advisable to leave these words and see what kinds of people they actually apply to, remembering again that most individuals are fairly equal mixtures and that what we have to say concerns only the extremes. Up to the present, these types have been thoroughly studied only in the male sex. 6

Viscerotonic Endomorph. If a man is definitely a thick type rather than a broad or long type, he is likely to be round and soft, with a big chest but a bigger belly. He would rather eat than breathe comfortably. He 7 is likely to have a wide face, short, thick neck, big thighs and upper arms, and small hands and feet. He has overdeveloped breasts and looks as though he were blown up a little like a balloon. His skin is soft and smooth, and when he gets bald, as he does usually quite early, he loses the hair in the middle of his head first.

The short, jolly, thickset, red-faced politician with a cigar in his mouth, who always looks as though he were about to have a stroke, is the best example of this type. The reason he often makes a good politician is that he likes people, banquets, baths, and sleep; he is easygoing, soothing, and his feelings are easy to understand. 8

His abdomen is big because he has lots of intestines. He likes to take in things. He likes to take in food, and affection and approval as well. Going to a banquet with people who like him is his idea of a fine time. It is important for a psychiatrist to understand the natures of such men when they come to him for advice. 9

Somatotonic Mesomorph. If a man is definitely a broad type rather than a thick or long type, he is likely to be rugged and have lots of muscle. He is apt to have big forearms and legs, and his chest and belly are well formed and firm, with the chest bigger than the belly. He would rather breathe than eat. He has a bony head, big shoulders, and a square jaw. His skin is thick, coarse, and elastic, and tans easily. If he gets bald, it usually starts on the front of the head. 10

Dick Tracy, Li'l Abner, and other men of action belong to this type. Such people make good lifeguards and construction workers. They like to put out energy. They have lots of muscles and they like to use them. They go in for adventure, exercise, fighting, and getting the upper hand. They are bold and unrestrained, and love to master the people and things around them. If the psychiatrist knows the things which give such people satisfaction, he is able to understand why they may be unhappy in certain situations. 11

Cerebrotonic Ectomorph. The man who is definitely a long type is likely to have thin bones and muscles. His shoulders are apt to sag and he has a flat belly with a dropped stomach, and long, weak legs. His neck and fingers are long, and his face is shaped like a long egg. His skin is thin, dry, and pale, and he rarely gets bald. He looks like an absent-minded professor and often is one. 12

Though such people are jumpy, they like to keep their energy and don't fancy moving around much. They would rather sit quietly 13 by themselves and keep out of difficulties. Trouble upsets them, and they run away from it. Their friends don't understand them very well. They move jerkily and feel jerkily. The psychiatrist who understands how easily they become anxious is often able to help them get along better in the sociable and aggressive world of endomorphs and mesomorphs.

In the special cases where people definitely belong to one type or another, then, one can tell a good deal about their personalities from their appearance. When the human mind is engaged in one of its struggles with itself or with the world outside, the individual's way of handling the struggle will be partly determined by his type. If he is a viscerotonic he will often want to go to a party where he can eat and drink and be in good company at a time when he might be better off attending to business; the somatotonic will want to go out and do something about it, master the situation, even if what he does is foolish and not properly figured out, while the cerebrotonic will go off by himself and think it over, when perhaps he would be better off doing something about it or seeking good company to try to forget it. 14

Since these personality characteristics depend on the growth of the layers of the little egg from which the person developed, they are very difficult to change. Nevertheless, it is important for the individual to know about these types, so that he can have at least an inkling of what to expect from those around him, and can make allowances for the different kinds of human nature, and so that he can become aware of and learn to control his own natural tendencies, which may sometimes guide him into making the same mistakes over and over again in handling his difficulties. 15

Meanings and Values

1. Consider men you have known who fit, or nearly fit, into one or another of the three categories of build.
   a. Do they also have the traits described by Berne in paragraphs 8, 9, 11, and 13? Or do you know, perhaps, a "thick" man who hates banquets, a "wide" man who writes poetry, or a "long" man who bullies people?
   b. If so, should we assume that these are learned characteristics? Explain.
2. Illustrate clearly how an understanding of basic types of people can be important to the layman.

3. In view of the fact that so many of a person's characteristics are determined before he is born, what room does the author leave for the possibility of altering or controlling these natural tendencies?
4. If you have read "The Peter Principle" in Section 1, show by use of a clear example how an understanding of Berne's theory might benefit an individual in his personal application of the Peter Principle.

Expository Techniques

1a. Most people, according to the author, are not classifiable in the categories he discusses. Is the classification system then faulty, since it does not include everyone?
b. Explain the difference, if any, between this system and the faulty classification of Protestants mentioned in the introduction to this section.

2. Study the general organization of this essay.
a. Which paragraphs give an overall preview of Berne's classification system?
b. Which paragraphs are devoted to explanations of individual categories?
c. Where does the author bring the categories together again to show the importance of the whole analysis?
d. Can you work out another plan that would have presented his material as meaningfully?

3. The author ends each detailed account of type characteristics with a statement of why the psychiatrist needs to know these things (pars. 9, 11, 13). Why is this a valuable technique, even though the essay was not written for psychiatrists?

4. Show the value of the parallel structures in paragraphs 4 and 5. (See Guide to Terms: *Parallel Structure.)*

5. In your opinion, do Berne's occasional attempts at humor — e.g., "the angels" and "cannot eat a menu" — benefit or detract from his explanation? Why?

Diction and Vocabulary

1a. Are the numerous Greek words as bothersome as you expected them to be when you first glanced at the essay? Why, or why not?
b. Do you think the author expects us really to master them? If not, why did he use them?

2. Aside from the Greek words, you probably found no words with which you were not already familiar. Is this a result of the type of subject matter, the author's concern for his audience, or something else? Explain.

Suggestions for Writing and Discussion

1. At the time this essay was written, the types had been "thoroughly studied only in the male sex." Even if the same general traits were characteristic of women, might tradition and social pressures tend to modify the natural tendencies more in women than in men (e.g., women are "not supposed" to go around flexing their muscles or getting into fist fights)? Explain any differences that you would expect.
2. Using examples for illustration, show that basic nature can be changed — or, if you prefer, that such change is very difficult or impossible.
3. Show the practical importance — especially for success in your future carrer — of understanding people and why they act as they do.
4. Develop the thesis that people of opposite types can sometimes get along more congenially than those of the same type.

(NOTE: Suggestions for topics requiring development by use of CLASSIFICATION are on page 85, at the end of this section.)

GILBERT HIGHET

GILBERT HIGHET (1906–1978) was born in Scotland but spent most of his life in this country. He was a classical scholar, poet, critic, author, and for many years professor of Latin language and literature at Columbia University. At one time he was chief literary critic for *Harper's.* Highet's fourteen books include *The Powers of Poetry* (1960); *Explorations* (1971); and *The Immortal Profession: The Joys of Teaching and Learning* (1976).

The Pleasures of Learning

"The Pleasures of Learning," a condensation from *The Immortal Profession,* was first published in *Reader's Digest.* It provides a reasonably clear-cut illustration of how division (and then, classification) can be used informally to bring order to a profusion of ideas.

As most schools are set up today, learning is compulsory. It is an Ought: even worse, a Must, enforced by regular hours and rigid discipline. And the young sneer at the Oughts and resist the Musts with all their energy. The feeling often lasts through a lifetime. For too many of us, learning appears to be a surrender of our own will to external direction, a sort of enslavement. 1

This is a mistake. Learning is a natural pleasure, inborn and instinctive, one of the essential pleasures of the human race. Watch a small child, at an age too young to have had any mental habits implanted by training. Some delightful films made by the late Dr. Arnold Gesell of Yale University show little creatures who can barely talk investigating problems with all the zeal and excitement of explorers, making discoveries with the passion and absorption of dedicated scientists. At the end of each successful investigation, there comes over each tiny face an expression of pure heart-felt pleasure. 2

When Archimedes discovered the principle of specific gravity by observing his own displacement of water in a bathtub, he leaped out 3 with delight, shouting, *"Heurēka, heurēka!"* ("I have found it, I have found it!") The instinct which prompted his outburst, and the rapture of its gratification, are possessed by all children.

But if the pleasure of learning is universal, why are there so many dull, incurious people in the world? It is because they were *made* dull, by bad teaching, by isolation, by surrender to routine; sometimes, too, by the pressure of hard work and poverty; or by the toxin of riches, with all their ephemeral and trivial delights. With luck, resolution and guidance, however, the human mind can survive not only poverty but even wealth. 4

This pleasure is not confined to learning from textbooks, which are too often tedious. But it does include learning from books. Sometimes, when I stand in a big library like the Library of Congress, or Butler Library at Columbia, and gaze round me at the millions of books, I feel a sober, earnest delight hard to convey except by a metaphor. These are not lumps of lifeless paper, but *minds* alive on the shelves. From each of them goes out its own voice, as inaudible as the streams of sound conveyed by electric waves beyond the range of our hearing; and just as the touch of a button on our stereo will fill the room with music, so by opening one of these volumes, one can call into range a voice far distant in time and space, and hear it speaking, mind to mind, heart to heart. 5

But, far beyond books, learning means keeping the mind open and active to receive all kinds of experience. One of the best-informed men I ever knew was a cowboy who rarely read a newspaper and never a book, but who had ridden many thousands of miles through one of the western states. He knew his state as thoroughly as a surgeon knows the human body. He loved it, and understood it. Not a mountain, not a canyon which had not much to tell him; not a change in the weather that he could not interpret. And so, among the pleasures of learning, we should include travel: travel with an open mind, an alert eye and a wish to understand other peoples, other places, rather than looking in them for a mirror image of oneself. If I were a young man today, I should resolve to see — no, to learn — all the 50 states before I was 35. 6

Learning also means learning to practice, or at least to appreciate, an art. Every new art you learn appears like a new window on the universe; it is like acquiring a new sense. Because I was born and brought up in Glasgow, Scotland, a hideous 19th-century industrial city, I did not understand the slightest thing about architecture until I was in my 20s. Since then, I have learned a little about the art, and 7 it has been a constant delight. In my mind I have a permanent album containing bright pictures of the Blue Mosque in Istanbul, the little church of St. John Nepomuk in Munich, the exquisite acropolis of Lindos standing high above the shining Rhodian sea.

Crafts, too, are well worth exploring. A friend of mine took up 8 book-binding because his doctor ordered him to do something that would give him relaxation and activity without tension. It was a difficult challenge at first, but he gradually learned to square off the paper and the boards, sew the pages, fasten on the backstrip, and maintain precision and neatness throughout.

Within a few years, this initially rather dull hobby had led him 9 into fresh fields of enjoyment. He began to collect fine books from the past five centuries; he developed an interest in printing; eventually, he started a private press and had the joy of producing his own elegant books. Many other crafts there are, and most of them contain one essential pleasure: the pleasure of making something that will last.

As for *reading* books, this contains two different delights. One 10 is the pleasure of apprehending the unexpected, such as when one meets a new author who has a new vision of the world. The other pleasure is of deepening one's knowledge of a special field. One might enjoy reading about the Civil War, and then be drawn to a particularly moving part of it — the underground railway, say, which carried escaping slaves northword to freedom. One would then be impelled to visit the chief way stations along the route, reconstructing the lives of those resolute organizers and thankful fugitives.

Tradition says that Ptolemy, the great astronomer of the Greek 11 and Roman world, worked peacefully in his observatory under the clear skies of northern Egypt for 40 years. Many and great were his explorations of the starry universe. For instance, he described astronomical refraction in a way that was not improved for over 1000 years. Ptolemy wrote just one poem, but it expressed his whole life:

> Mortal I know I am, short-lived; and yet, whenever
>   I watch the multitude of swirling stars,
> then I no longer tread this earth, but rise to feast
>   with God, and enjoy the food of the immortals.

Learning extends our lives (as Ptolemy said) into new dimen- 12 sions. It is cumulative. Instead of diminishing in time, like health and strength, its returns go on increasing, provided . . .

Provided that you aim, throughout your life, as you continue 13
learning, to integrate your thought, to make it harmonious. If you happen to be an engineer and also enjoy singing in a glee club, connect these two activities. They unite in you; they are not in conflict. Both choral singing and engineering are examples of the architectonic ability of man: of his power to make a large plan and to convey it clearly to others. Both are esthetic and depend much on symmetry. Think about them not as though they were dissociated, but as though each were one aspect of a single unity. You will do them better, and be happier.

This is hard advice to give to young students. They are explo- 14
sive, exploratory and insurrectionary. Instead of integrating their lives, they would rather seek outward, and even try to move in opposite directions simultaneously.

Much unhappiness has been suffered by those people who have 15
never recognized that it is as necessary to make themselves into whole and harmonious personalities as to keep themselves clean, healthy and financially solvent. Wholeness of the mind and spirit is not a quality conferred by nature, or by God. It is like health, virtue and knowledge. Man has the capacity to attain it; but to achieve it depends on his own efforts. It needs a long, deliberate effort of the mind and the emotions, and even the body.

During our earthly life, the body gradually dies; even the emo- 16
tions become duller. But the mind in most of us continues to live, and even grows more lively and active, enjoys itself more, works and plays with more expansion and delight.

Many people have played themselves to death, or eaten and 17
drunk themselves to death. Nobody has ever thought himself to death. The chief danger confronting us is not age. It is laziness, sloth, routine, stupidity — forcing their way in like wind through the shutters, seeping into the cellar like swamp water. Many who avoid learning, or abandon it, find that life is drained dry. They spend 30 years in a club chair looking glumly out at the sand and the ocean; on a porch swing waiting for somebody to drive down the road. But that is not how to live.

No learner has ever run short of subjects to explore. The plea- 18
sures of learning are indeed pleasures. In fact, the word should be changed. The true name is happiness. You can live longest and best and most rewardingly by attaining and preserving the happiness of learning.

Meanings and Values

1. Do you consider this essay primarily objective or subjective? Why? (See Guide to Terms: *Objective/Subjective.*)

2a. How would you describe the tone of Highet's writing? (Guide: *Style/Tone.*)
 b. Is the tone consistent throughout?

3a. What kind of essay is it — formal, informal, or familiar? (Guide: *Essay.*
 b. Why does it not fit well into either of the other categories?

4a. Cite any passages where you think the author tends to overgeneralize.
 b. Would the writing be significantly improved by the use of qualification? (Guide: *Qualification.*)
 c. If so, how might this have been accomplished?

5a. Consider Highet's implication that it is even harder for the mind to survive wealth than poverty (par. 4). Does this seem to be a valid observation?
 b. If so, what are the greater impediments of wealth? If not, why do you think poverty is the greater?

Expository Techniques

1a. What are the four major diversions of learning pleasure, as discussed by the author?
 b. Did he intend the first paragraph on books (par. 5) to be a part of his classification system? Why, or why not?
 c. Demonstrate how each of the divisions, or categories, may be used to *classify* any number of more specific examples.

2a. List by paragraph the use of examples in this selection, and for each cite the generality that it demonstrates.
 b. Are the examples well chosen for their individual purposes?
 c. Cite any exceptions, and state why you consider them as such.

3a. What seems to be the main purpose of the passage on Ptolemy, including the poem?
 b. What application does it have beyond the mere study of astronomy?

Diction and Vocabulary

1a. Who was Archimedes (par. 3)?
 b. Why is the word *Heurēka* in italics?

2a. Where in this essay do you find an extended metaphor? (Guide: *Figures of Speech.*)
 b. Why may it be classified as such?

c. Cite as many other figures of speech as you can find, and identify each as to kind.

3. Use the dictionary as necessary to understand how the author uses the following words: toxin, ephermeral (par. 4); esthetic, symmetry (13); insurrectionary (14).

Suggestions for Writing and Discussion

1. To what extent did you and other young people of your acquaintance "sneer at the Oughts and resist the Musts" or consider learning "a sort of enslavement"? What were the causes, and how might they have been avoided?
2. Select one of the crafts (preferably one with which you have had some personal experience) and show how it can involve a real learning process. Does it contain the "one essential pleasure," mentioned by Highet in paragraph 9?
3. If you can think of still another category of pleasure that learning can give, explain what it is and how it can also "extend our lives into new dimensions."

(NOTE: Suggestions for topics requiring development by CLASSIFICATION are on page 85, at the end of this section.)

DONALD HALL

DONALD HALL, educator and writer, was born in Connecticut in 1928. He earned a B.A. degree from Harvard University and a B.Litt. degree at Oxford, later doing postgraduate work at Stanford University. This versatile author has written about universities for *The Atlantic Monthly,* about baseball for *Playboy,* about the sculptor Henry Moore for *The New Yorker.* Besides his seven books of poems, he has written two children's books, a collection of limericks, a biography, literary criticism, short stories in *Esquire* and *The New Yorker,* a best-selling freshman composition text, two plays, one of which ran off Broadway, and *Remembering Poets,* a book about Dylan Thomas, Robert Frost, T. S. Eliot, and Ezra Pound. Until recently Hall taught creative writing, literature, and freshman English at the University of Michigan. He now lives on the old family farm in Danbury, New Hampshire, where he continues to write, and sometimes emerges to give a poetry reading or to teach a class at Dartmouth or Colby-Sawyer College.

Four Kinds of Reading

"Four Kinds of Reading" is a piece of purely subjective writing, and as such is nearly as likely to provoke disagreement as favor. Hall's problem was simple: having asserted that some reading is simply narcotic and of no value in itself, he was faced with the task of telling us *which* reading, as well as what other kinds he believes do have value. The project, of course, demands some clear system of division/classification.

Everywhere one meets the idea that reading is an activity desirable in itself. It is understandable that publishers and librarians — and even writers — should promote this assumption, but it is strange that the idea should have general currency. People surround the idea of reading with piety, and do not take into account the purpose of reading or the value of what is being read. Teachers and parents praise the child who reads, and praise themselves, whether the text 1

Reprinted by permission of the publisher from *The New York Times* (January 26, 1969).

be *The Reader's Digest* or *Moby Dick.* The advent of TV has increased the false values ascribed to reading, since TV provides a vulgar alternative. But this piety is silly; and most reading is no more cultural nor intellectual nor imaginative than shooting pool or watching *What's My Line.*

It is worth asking how the act of reading became something to value in itself, as opposed for instance to the act of conversation or the act of taking a walk. Mass literacy is a recent phenomenon, and I suggest that the aura which decorates reading is a relic of the importance of reading to our great-great-grandparents. Literacy used to be a mark of social distinction, separating a small portion of humanity from the rest. The farm laborer who was ambitious for his children did not daydream that they would become schoolteachers or doctors; he daydreamed that they would learn to read, and that a world would therefore open up to them in which they did not have to labor in the fields fourteen hours a day for six days a week in order to buy salt and cotton. On the next rank of society, ample time for reading meant that the reader was free from the necessity to spend most of his waking hours making a living of any kind. This sort of attitude shades into the contemporary man's boast of his wife's cultural activities. When he says that his wife is interested in books and music and pictures, he is not only enclosing the arts in a delicate female world; he is saying that he is rich enough to provide her with the leisure to do nothing. Reading is an inactivity, and therefore a badge of social class. Of course, these reasons for the piety attached to reading are never acknowledged. They show themselves in the shape of our attitudes toward books; reading gives off an air of gentility. 2

It seems to me possible to name four kinds of reading, each with a characteristic manner and purpose. The first is reading for information — reading to learn about a trade, or politics, or how to accomplish something. We read a newspaper this way, or most textbooks, or directions on how to assemble a bicycle. With most of this sort of material, the reader can learn to scan the page quickly, coming up with what he needs and ignoring what is irrelevant to him, like the rhythm of the sentence, or the play of metaphor. Courses in speed reading can help us read for this purpose, training the eye to jump quickly across the page. If we read *The New York Times* with the attention we should give a novel or a poem, we will have time for nothing else, and our mind will be cluttered with clichés and dead 3 metaphor. Quick eye-reading is a necessity to anyone who wants to keep up with what's happening, or learn much of what has happened in the past. The amount of reflection, which interrupts and slows down the reading, depends on the material.

But it is not the same activity as reading literature. There ought 4
to be another word. If we read a work of literature properly, we read slowly, and we hear all the words. If our lips do not actually move, it's only laziness. The muscles in our throats move, and come together when we see the word "squeeze." We hear the sounds so accurately that if a syllable is missing in a line of poetry we hear the lack, though we may not know what we are lacking. In prose we accept the rhythms, and hear the adjacent sounds. We also register a track of feeling through the metaphors and associations of words. Careless writing prevents this sort of attention, and becomes offensive. But the great writers reward this attention. Only by the full exercise of our powers to receive language can we absorb their intelligence and their imagination. This kind of reading goes through the ear — though the eye takes in the print, and decodes it into sound — to the throat and the understanding, and it can never be quick. It is slow and sensual, a deep pleasure that begins with touch and ends with the sort of comprehension that we associate with dream.

Too many intellectuals read in order to reduce images to abstrac- 5
tions. With a philosopher one reads slowly, as if it were literature, but much time must be spent with the eyes turned away from the pages, reflecting on the text. To read literature this way is to turn it into something it is not — to concepts clothed in character, or philosophy sugar-coated. I think that most literary intellectuals read this way, including the brighter Professors of English, with the result that they miss literature completely, and concern themselves with a minor discipline called the history of ideas. I remember a course in Chaucer at my University in which the final exam largely required the identification of a hundred or more fragments of Chaucer, none as long as a line. If you liked poetry, and read Chaucer through a couple of times slowly, you found yourself knowing them all. If you were a literary intellectual, well-informed about the great chain of being, chances are you had a difficult time. To read literature is to be intimately involved with the words on the page, and never to think of them as the embodiments of ideas which can be expressed in other terms. On the other hand, intellectual writing — closer to mathematics on a continuum that has at its opposite pole lyric poetry — re-

quires intellectual reading, which is slow because it is reflective and because the reader must pause to evaluate concepts.

But most of the reading which is praised for itself is neither literary nor intellectual. It is narcotic. Novels, stories and biographies — historical sagas, monthly regurgitations of book clubs, four- and five-thousand word daydreams of the magazines — these are the opium of the suburbs. The drug is not harmful except to the addict himself, and is no more injurious to him than Johnny Carson or a bridge club, but it is nothing to be proud of. This reading is the automated daydream, the mild trip of the housewife and the tired businessman, interested not in experience and feeling but in turning off the possibilities of experience and feeling. Great literature, if we read it well, opens us up to the world, and makes us more sensitive to it, as if we acquired eyes that could see through things and ears that could hear smaller sounds. But by narcotic reading, one can reduce great literature to the level of *The Valley of the Dolls.* One can read *Anna Karenina* passively and inattentively, and float down the river of lethargy as if one were reading a confession magazine: "I Spurned My Husband for a Count." 6

I think that everyone reads for narcosis occasionally, and perhaps most consistently in late adolescence, when great readers are born. I remember reading to shut the world out, away at a school where I did not want to be; I invented a word to name my disease: "bibliolepsy," on the analogy of narcolepsy. But after a while the books became a window on the world, and not a screen against it. This change doesn't always happen. I think that late adolescent narcotic reading accounts for some of the badness of English departments. As a college student, the boy loves reading and majors in English because he would be reading anyway. Deciding on a career, he takes up English teaching for the same reason. Then in graduate school he is trained to be a scholar, which is painful and irrelevant, and finds he must write papers and publish them to be a Professor — and at about this time he no longer requires reading for narcosis, and he is left with nothing but a Ph.D. and the prospect of fifty years of teaching literature; and he does not even like literature. 7

Narcotic reading survives the impact of television, because this type of reading has even less reality than melodrama; that is, the reader is in control: once the characters reach into the reader's feelings, he is able to stop reading, or glance away, or superimpose his own daydream. The trouble with television is that it writes its own 8 script. Literature is often valued precisely because of its distance from the tangible. Some readers prefer looking into the text of a play to seeing it performed. Reading a play, it is possible to stage it oneself by an imaginative act; but it is also possible to remove it from real people. Here is Virginia Woolf, who was lavish in her praise of the act of reading, talking about reading a play rather than seeing it: "Certainly there is a good deal to be said for reading *Twelfth Night* in the book if the book can be read in a garden, with no sound but the thud of an apple falling to the earth, or of the wind ruffling the branches of the trees." She sets her own stage; the play is called *Virginia Woolf Reads Twelfth Night in a Garden.* Piety moves into narcissism, and the high metaphors of Shakespeare's lines dwindle into the flowers of an English garden; actors in ruffles wither, while the wind ruffles branches.

Meanings and Values

1. Why is this essay classifiable as subjective writing? (See headnotes and Guide to Terms: *Objective/Subjective.*)

2a. What kind of people would be apt to read something like this piece on their own?

b. As which of the four kinds of reading does the author apparently intend his own essay to be viewed?

3. Does it seem to you that the remarks about Virginia Woolf (par. 8) are entirely merited? Explain.

4. Do you agree that reading is not justifiable in itself? Why, or why not?

5a. What inconsistency do you see, if any, between the author's criticisms in paragraph 1 and the account of his own early reading in paragraph 7?

b. If you find any such inconsistency, does it seriously damage credibility?

6. In the first paragraph Hall insinuates that teachers and parents have no reason to praise the child who reads *Reader's Digest.* Do you agree, or disagree, with this low estimation of the magazine — which the author seems to place, by implication, on the intellectual level of shooting pool or watching *What's My Line* (par. 1)?

Expository Techniques

1a. How well does Hall's system of division/classification meet the requirements of logic and completeness?

b. Does the fact that reading matter of any category may be treated differently by different people make the system itself less valid? Explain.

2. Cite three paragraphs in which Hall uses examples to make the general more specific. (Guide: *Specific/General.*)

3a. In paragraph 6 the author calls stories and novels "the opium of the suburbs." What reason have we to doubt that he intends to include *all* stories and novels?

b. Demonstrate how a simple use of qualification could have prevented this misrepresentation (Guide: *Qualification.*)

c. If you find other statements that could have benefited by qualification, show how this could have been achieved.

4. This author frequently employs sarcasm as a means of emphasis. (Guide: *Emphasis.*) Cite at least three examples of this technique and comment on their effectiveness.

5. What closing techniques does Hall use? (Guide: *Closings.*)

Diction and Vocabulary

1. In what sense does TV provide a "vulgar alternative" to reading (par. 1)?

2a. Select three of the author's best metaphors by which to demonstrate how style may be affected by figurative language. (Guide: *Figures of Speech.*)

b. Cite three examples in which his nonfigurative diction clearly becomes an important element of his style. (Guide: *Style/Tone.*)

3. Consult the dictionary as needed for an understanding of the following words, as used in this essay: currency (par. 1); concepts, embodiments (5); sagas, regurgitations, lethargy (6); narcolepsy (7); narcissism (8).

Suggestions for Writing and Discussion

1. Discuss the tendency of some people to "enclose the arts in a delicate female world" (par. 2) — e.g., the reasons for that attitude, or your own experiences in the face of it.

2. Explain how it is that our minds can become "cluttered with clichés and dead metaphor" (par. 3), using examples from current newspapers to illustrate their prevalence.

3. If you believe that any reading is better than no reading at all (in general, or for any particular type of person), explain why your views differ from Hall's.

(NOTE: Suggestions for topics requiring development by use of CLASSIFICATION are on page 85, at the end of this section.)

JAMES DAVID BARBER

JAMES DAVID BARBER was born in Charleston, West Virginia, in 1930. He received his B.A. and M.A. degrees from the University of Chicago and holds a Ph.D. degree in political science from Yale University. Barber has served in various capacities on the faculties of Stetson, Yale, and Columbia universities, and he is a frequent guest lecturer at other universities throughout the country. At present he is a professor of the political science at Duke University. Barber has contributed steadily to both scholarly and popular periodicals and has written and edited several important books in this field, including *Race for the Presidency* (1978) and *The Pulse of Politics* (1980).

Four Types of President

"Four Types of President" (editor's title) is selected from Barber's most widely known book, *Presidential Character: Predicting Performance in the White House.* In this piece he attempts to explain, by division and classification, a much more complex subject than those of the other authors of this section; the resulting system, however, is admirably simple. Also worth a beginning writer's study are the distinctive elements of Barber's style.

Who the President is at a given time can make a profound difference 1
in the whole thrust and direction of national politics. Since we have only one President at a time, we can never prove this by comparison, but even the most superficial speculation confirms the commonsense view that the man himself weighs heavily among other historical factors. A Wilson re-elected in 1920, a Hoover in 1932, a John F. Kennedy in 1964 would, it seems very likely, have guided the body politic along rather different paths from those their actual successors chose. Or try to imagine a Theodore Roosevelt ensconced behind today's "bully pulpit" of a Presidency, or Lyndon Johnson as Presi-

dent in the age of McKinley. Only someone mesmerized by the lures of historical inevitability can suppose that it would have made little or no difference to government policy had Alf Landon replaced FDR in 1936, and Dewey beaten Truman in 1948, or Adlai Stevenson reigned through the 1950s. Not only would these alternative Presidents have advocated different policies — they would have approached the office from very different psychological angles. It stretches credibility to think that Eugene McCarthy would have run the institution the way Lyndon Johnson did.

The first baseline in defining Presidential types is *activity-pas-* 2
sivity. How much energy does the man invest in his Presidency? Lyndon Johnson went at his day like a human cyclone, coming to rest long after the sun went down. Calvin Coolidge often slept eleven hours a night and still needed a nap in the middle of the day. In between the Presidents array themselves on the high or low side of the activity line.

The second baseline is *positive-negative affect* toward one's activ- 3
ity — that is, how he feels about what he does. Relatively speaking, does he seem to experience his political life as happy or sad, enjoyable or discouraging, positive or negative in its main effect. The feeling I am after here is not grim satisfaction in a job well done, not some philosophical conclusion. The idea is this: is he someone who, on the surfaces we can see, gives forth the feeling that he has *fun* in political life? Franklin Roosevelt's Secretary of War, Henry L. Stimson wrote that the Roosevelts "not only understood the *use* of power, they knew the *enjoyment* of power, too. . . . Whether a man is burdened by power or enjoys power; whether he is trapped by repsonsibility or made free by it; whether he is moved by other people and outer forces or moves them — that is the essence of leadership."

The positive-negative baseline, then, is a general symptom of 4
the fit between the man and his experience, a kind of register of *felt* satisfaction.

Why might we expect these two simple dimensions to outline 5
the main character types? Because they stand for two central features of anyone's orientation toward life. In nearly every study of personality, some form of the active-passive contrast is critical; the general tendency to act or be acted upon is evident in such concepts as dominance-submission, extraversion-introversion, aggression-timidity, attack-defense, fight-flight, engagement-withdrawal, approach-avoidance. In everyday life we sense quickly the general energy

output of the people we deal with. Similarly we catch on fairly quickly to the affect dimension — whether the person seems to be optimistic or pessimistic, hopeful or skeptical, happy or sad. The two baselines are clear and they are also independent of one another: all of us know people who are very active but seem discouraged, others who are quite passive but seem happy, and so forth. The activity baseline refers to what one does, the affect baseline to how one feels about what he does.

Both are crude clues to character. They are leads into four basic 6
character patterns long familiar in psychological research. In summary form, these are the main configurations:

Active-positive: There is a congruence, a consistency, between much 7
activity and the enjoyment of it, indicating relatively high self-esteem and relative success in relating to the environment. The man shows an orientation toward productiveness as a value and an ability to use his styles flexibly, adaptively, suiting the dance to the music. He sees himself as developing over time toward relatively well-defined personal goals — growing toward his image of himself as he might yet be. There is an emphasis on rational mastery, on using the brain to move the feet. This may get him into trouble; he may fail to take account of the irrational in politics. Not everyone he deals with sees things his way and he may find it hard to understand why.

Active-negative: The contradiction here is between relatively intense 8
effort and relatively low emotional reward for that effort. The activity has a compulsive quality, as if the man were trying to make up for something or to escape from anxiety into hard work. He seems ambitious, striving upward, power-seeking. His stance toward the environment is aggressive and he has a persistent problem in managing his aggressive feelings. His self-image is vague and discontinuous. Life is a hard struggle to achieve and hold power, hampered by the condemnations of a perfectionistic conscience. Active-negative types pour energy into the political system, but it is an energy distorted from within.

Passive-positive: This is the receptive, compliant, other-directed char- 9
acter whose life is a search for affection as a reward for being agreeable and cooperative rather than personally assertive. The contradiction is between low self-esteem (on grounds of being un-

lovable, unattractive) and a superficial optimism. A hopeful attitude helps dispel doubt and elicits encouragement from others. Passive-positive types help soften the harsh edges of politics. But their dependence and the fragility of their hopes and enjoyments make disappointment in politics likely.

Passive-negative: The factors are consistent — but how are we to ac- 10
count for the man's *political* role-taking? Why is someone who does little in politics and enjoys it less there at all? The answer lies in the passive-negative's character-rooted orientation toward doing dutiful service; this compensates for low self-esteem based on a sense of uselessness. Passive-negative types are in politics because they think they ought to be. They may be well adapted to certain nonpolitical roles, but they lack the experience and flexibility to perform effectively as political leaders. Their tendency is to withdraw, to escape from the conflict and uncertainty of politics by emphasizing vague principles (especially prohibitions) and procedural arrangements. They become guardians of the right and proper way, above the sordid politicking of lesser men.

Active-positive Presidents want most to achieve results. Active- 11
negatives aim to get and keep power. Passive-positives are after love. Passive-negatives emphasize their civic virtue. The relation of activity to enjoyment in a President thus tends to outline a cluster of characteristics, to set apart the adapted from the compulsive, compliant, and withdrawn types.

The first four Presidents of the United States, conveniently, ran 12
through this gamut of character types. (Remember, we are talking about tendencies, broad directions; no individual man exactly fits a category.) George Washington — clearly the most important President in the pantheon — established the fundamental legitimacy of an American government at a time when this was a matter in considerable question. Washington's dignity, judiciousness, his aloof air of reserve and dedication to duty fit the passive-negative or withdrawing type best. Washington did not seek innovation, he sought stability. He longed to retire to Mount Vernon, but fortunately was persuaded to stay on through a second term, in which, by rising above the political conflict between Hamilton and Jefferson and inspiring confidence in his own integrity, he gave the nation time to develop the organized means for peaceful change.

John Adams followed, a dour New England Puritan, much given 13
to work and worry, an impatient and irascible man — an active-negative President, a compulsive type. Adams was far more partisan than Washington; the survival of the system through his Presidency demonstrated that the nation could tolerate, for a time, domination by one of its nascent political parties. As President, an angry Adams brought the United States to the brink of war with France, and presided over the new nation's first experiment in political repression: the Alien and Sedition Acts, forbidding, among other things, unlawful combinations "with intent to oppose any measure or measures of the government of the United States," or "any false, scandalous, and malicious writing or writings against the United States, or the President of the United States, with intent to defame . . . or to bring them or either of them, into contempt or disrepute."

Then came Jefferson. He too had his troubles and failures — in 14
the design of national defense, for example. As for his Presidential character (only one element in success or failure), Jefferson was clearly active-positive. A child of the Enlightenment, he applied his reason to organizing connections with Congress aimed at strengthening the more popular forces. A man of catholic interests and delightful humor, Jefferson combined a clear and open vision of what the country could be with a profound political sense, expressed in his famous phrase, "Every difference of opinion is not a difference of principle."

The fourth President was James Madison, "Little Jemmy," the 15
constitutional philosopher thrown into the White House at a time of great international turmoil. Madison comes closest to the passive-positive, or compliant, type; he suffered from irresolution, tried to compromise his way out, and gave in too readily to the "warhawks" urging combat with Britain. The nation drifted into war, and Madison wound up ineptly commanding his collection of amateur generals in the streets of Washington. General Jackson's victory at New Orleans saved the Madison administration's historical reputation; but he left the Presidency with the United States close to bankruptcy and secession.

These four Presidents — like all Presidents — were persons try- 16
ing to cope with the roles they had won by using the equipment they had built over a lifetime. The President is not some shapeless organism in a flood of novelties, but a man with a memory in a system with a history. Like all of us, he draws on his past to shape his future. The

pathetic hope that the White House will turn a Caligula into a Marcus Aurelius is as naive as the fear that ultimate power inevitably corrupts. The problem is to understand — and to state understandably — what in the personal past foreshadows the Presidential future.

Meanings and Values

1. Is this selection more nearly objective or subjective writing? Why? (See Guide to Terms: *Objective/Subjective.*)
2. What seems to be the author's opinion of "historical inevitability" (par.1)? Justify your answer.
3. What have been some of the most important "historical factors" (par. 1) which have combined with the character of recent presidents to shape their conduct in office?

4a. How, if at all, could a person be "made free" by responsibility (par. 3)?

b. Does Stimson's statement constitute a paradox? Why, or why not? (Guide: *Paradox.*)

5. Why was the "fundamental legitimacy of an American government" in question (par. 12), even after the Revolutionary War was won?

6a. In paragraph 5, Barber makes clear that his classification system applies to ordinary people, not just to presidents. If you have also read Berne's system of classifying types of people, do you find any parallels between the two?

b. If you do, show the parallels. If not, are they then contradictory to each other? Why, or why not?

Expository Techniques

1a. If this seems to be a more complicated classification system than the others in this section, try to determine why.

b. Devise, if you can, a simpler way to present the material. Is yours more, or less, effective? Why?

2. In paragraph 12, Barber says that no individual man exactly fits a category. Must we therefore conclude that it is not a complete and logical system? Why, or why not?

3a. Cite the paragraphs in which the author uses examples as an expository technique.

b. Do the examples improve the effectiveness of the writing, or merely slow down the reading? Why?

4a. Cite examples of parallel structure in at least two paragraphs. (Guide: *Parallel Structure.*)

b. How is their use a matter of syntax and of style? (Guide: *Syntax, Style/Tone.*)

5. What other qualities of Barber's writing are relevant to style? Use examples to illustrate.

6a. What is the apparent purpose of paragraph 11 and the last sentence of paragraph 5?

b. Would you use this technique if you were doing similar writing? Why, or why not?

Diction and Vocabulary

1a. Which, if any, of your answers to question 5 of "Expository Techniques" are also matters of diction? (Guide: *Diction.*)

b. If none of them are, why did you not consider diction a distinctive element of Barber's style? (Guide: *Style/Tone.*)

2a. Why are the baselines "crude" clues to character (par. 6)?

b. Are they therefore not valid? Why, or why not?

3a. The author uses two qualifications in the final sentence of paragraph 7. What are they? (Guide: *Qualification.*)

b. What is gained by their use?

4a. How might the careless reader misunderstand the meaning of "His stance toward the environment is aggressive . . ." (par. 8)?

b. In view of the author's apparent purpose and reader-audience, is there any reason to believe he would be concerned about this possible ambiguity? Explain.

c. How, if at all, is this a matter of connotation? (Guide: *Connotation/Denotation.*)

5a. What are the meanings, both literal and figurative, of the allusions in paragraph 16? (Guide: *Figure of Speech.*)

b. Cite at least one example each of simile and metaphor in paragraph 2 or 7.

6. Consult the dictionary as needed for full understanding of the following words: ensconced, mesmerized (par. 1); array (2); essence (3); configurations (6); congruence (7); discontinuous (8); dispel, elicits (9); compliant (9, 15); gamut, pantheon, judiciousness (12); dour, irascible, nascent, defame (13); catholic (14); irresolution, ineptly (15).

Suggestions for Writing and Discussion

1. Analyze your own character patterns and determine which category they best fit. For what practical purposes might such analysis be used?

2. How can we reliably analyze and categorize a candidate's character during the fakery of a presidential campaign?

3. To what extent should we consider the national situation or "other historical factors" at the time of election, in relation to the candidates' character types?
4. If Barber's meaning of "character" differs from your own — e.g., if it is more or less concerned with integrity — explain the differences.
5. Where do the three most recent presidents best fit into Barber's classification system? Justify your answer.

(NOTE: Suggestions for topics requiring development by use of CLASSIFICATION are on page 85, at the end of this section.)

DESMOND MORRIS

DESMOND MORRIS was born in 1928, in England, and educated at Birmingham University (B.S. degree) and Oxford (Ph.D. degree). He was later researcher in animal behavior at the Department of Zoology, Oxford, and for several years served as curator of mammals at the Zoological Society of London. Morris has increasingly specialized in human behavior and now holds a Research Fellowship at Oxford, where he spends much of his time writing. He is the author of some fifty scientific papers and a dozen books. In 1967 he published *The Naked Ape,* which has sold over 8 million copies and been translated into twenty-three languages. Other recent books have been *The Human Zoo* (1970), *Intimate Behaviour* (1972), and *Manwatching* (1977).

Territorial Behaviour

"Territorial Behaviour" is a chapter from *Manwatching.* The selection is straightforward in purpose and execution: Morris's divisions of territorial behavior, though simple and obvious, provide a firm and valid structure for the writing.

A territory is a defended space. In the broadest sense, there are three kinds of human territory: tribal, family and personal. 1

It is rare for people to be driven to physical fighting in defence of these "owned" spaces, but fight they will, if pushed to the limit. The invading army encroaching on national territory, the gang moving into a rival district, the trespasser climbing into an orchard, the burglar breaking into a house, the bully pushing to the front of a queue, the driver trying to steal a parking space, all of these intruders are liable to be met with resistance varying from the vigorous to the savagely violent. Even if the law is on the side of the intruder, the urge to protect a territory may be so strong that otherwise peaceful citizens abandon all their usual controls and inhibitions. Attempts to evict families from their homes, no matter how socially valid the 2 reasons, can lead to siege conditions reminiscent of the defence of a medieval fortress.

3 The fact that these upheavals are so rare is a measure of the success of Territorial Signals as a system of dispute prevention. It is sometimes cynically stated that "all property is theft," but in reality it is the opposite. Property, as owned space which is *displayed* as owned space, is a special kind of sharing system which reduces fighting much more than it causes it. Man is a co-operative species, but he is also competitive, and his struggle for dominance has to be structured in some way if chaos is to be avoided. The establishment of territorial rights is one such structure. It limits dominance geographically. I am dominant in my territory and you are dominant in yours. In other words, dominance is shared out spatially, and we all have some. Even if I am weak and unintelligent and you can dominate me when we meet on neutral ground, I can still enjoy a thoroughly dominant role as soon as I retreat to my private base. Be it ever so humble, there is no place like a home territory.

4 Of course, I can still be intimidated by a particularly dominant individual who enters my home base, but his encroachment will be dangerous for him and he will think twice about it, because he will know that here my urge to resist will be dramatically magnified and my usual subservience banished. Insulted at the heart of my own territory, I may easily explode into battle — either symbolic or real — with a result that may be damaging to both of us.

5 In order for this to work, each territory has to be plainly advertised as such. Just as a dog cocks its leg to deposit its personal scent on the trees in its locality, so the human animal cocks its leg symbolically all over his home base. But because we are predominantly visual animals we employ mostly visual signals, and it is worth asking how we do this at the three levels: tribal, family and personal.

6 First: the Tribal Territory. We evolved as tribal animals, living in comparatively small groups, probably of less than a hundred, and we existed like that for millions of years. It is our basic social unit, a group in which everyone knows everyone else. Essentially, the tribal territory consisted of a home base surrounded by extended hunting grounds. Any neighbouring tribe intruding on our social space would be repelled and driven away. As these early tribes swelled into agricultural super-tribes, and eventually into industrial nations, their territorial defence systems became increasingly elaborate. The tiny, ancient home base of the hunting tribe became the

great capital city, the primitive war-paint became the flags, emblems, uniforms and regalia of the specialized military, and the war-chants became national anthems, marching songs and bugle calls. Territorial boundary-lines hardened into fixed borders, often conspicuously patrolled and punctuated with defensive structures — forts and look-out posts, checkpoints and great walls, and, today, customs barriers.

Today each nation flies its own flag, a symbolic embodiment of 7
its territorial status. But patriotism is not enough. The ancient tribal hunter lurking inside each citizen finds himself unsatisfied by membership in such a vast conglomeration of individuals, most of whom are totally unknown to him personally. He does his best to feel that he shares a common territorial defence with them all, but the scale of the operation has become inhuman. It is hard to feel a sense of belonging with a tribe of fifty million or more. His answer is to form sub-groups, nearer to his ancient pattern, smaller and more personally known to him — the local club, the teenage gang, the union, the specialist society, the sports association, the political party, the college fraternity, the social clique, the protest group, and the rest. Rare indeed is the individual who does not belong to at least one of these splinter groups, and take from it a sense of tribal allegiance and brotherhood. Typical of all these groups is the development of Territorial Signals — badges, costumes, headquarters, banners, slogans, and all the other displays of group identity. This is where the action is, in terms of tribal territorialism, and only when a major war breaks out does the emphasis shift upwards to the higher group level of the nation.

Each of these modern pseudo-tribes sets up its own special kind 8
of home base. In extreme cases non-members are totally excluded, in others they are allowed in as visitors with limited rights and under a control system of special rules. In many ways they are like miniature nations, with their own flags and emblems and their own border guards. The exclusive club has its own "customs barrier": the doorman who checks your "passport" (your membership card) and prevents strangers from passing in unchallenged. There is a government: the club committee; and often special displays of the tribal elders: the photographs or portraits of previous officials on the walls. At the heart of the specialized territories there is a powerful feeling of security and importance, a sense of shared defence against the outside world. Much of the club chatter, both serious and joking, directs itself against the rottenness of everything outside the club boundaries — in that "other world" beyond the protected portals.

In social organizations which embody a strong class system, such 9
as military units and large business concerns, there are many territorial rules, often unspoken, which interfere with the official hierarchy. High-status individuals, such as officers or managers, could in theory enter any of the regions occupied by the lower levels in the peck order, but they limit this power in a striking way. An officer seldom enters a sergeant's mess or a barrack room unless it is for a formal inspection. He respects those regions as alien territories even though he has the power to go there by virtue of his dominant role. And in businesses, part of the appeal of unions, over and above their obvious functions, is that with their officials, headquarters and meetings they add a sense of territorial power for the staff workers. It is almost as if each military organization and business concern consists of two warring tribes: the officers versus the other ranks, and the management versus the workers. Each has its special home base within the system, and the territorial defence pattern thrusts itself into what, on the surface, is a pure social hierarchy. Negotiations between managements and unions are tribal battles fought out over the neutral ground of a boardroom table, and are as much concerned with territorial display as they are with resolving problems of wages and conditions. Indeed, if one side gives in too quickly and accepts the other's demands, the victors feel strangely cheated and deeply suspicious that it may be a trick. What they are missing is the protracted sequence of ritual and counter-ritual that keeps alive their group territorial identity.

Likewise, many of the hostile displays of sports fans and teenage 10
gangs are primarily concerned with displaying their group image to rival fan-clubs and gangs. Except in rare cases, they do not attack one another's headquarters, drive out the occupants, and reduce them to a submissive, subordinate condition. It is enough to have scuffles on the borderlands between the two rival territories. This is particularly clear at football matches, where the fan-club headquarters becomes temporarily shifted from the club-house to a section of the stands, and where minor fighting breaks out at the unofficial boundary line between the massed groups of rival supporters. Newspaper reports play up the few accidents and injuries which do occur on such occasions, but when these are studied in relation to the total numbers of displaying fans involved it is clear that the serious incidents represent only a tiny fraction of the overall group behaviour. For every actual punch or kick there are a thousand war-cries, war-dances, chants and gestures.

Second: the Family Territory. Essentially, the family is a breeding unit and the family territory is a breeding ground. At the centre of this space, there is the nest — the bedroom — where, tucked up in bed, we feel at our most territorially secure. In a typical house the bedroom is upstairs, where a safe nest should be. This puts it farther away from the entrance hall, the area where contact is made, intermittently, with the outside world. The less private reception rooms, where intruders are allowed access, are the next line of defence. Beyond them, outside the walls of the building, there is often a symbolic remnant of the ancient feeding grounds — a garden. Its symbolism often extends to the plants and animals it contains, which cease to be nutritional and become merely decorative — flowers and pets. But like a true territorial space it has a conspicuously displayed boundary-line, the garden fence, wall, or railings. Often no more than a token barrier, this is the outer territorial demarcation, separating the private world of the family from the public world beyond. To cross it puts any visitor or intruder at an immediate disadvantage. As he crosses the threshold, his dominance wanes, slightly but unmistakably. He is entering an area where he senses that he must ask permission to do simple things that he would consider a right elsewhere. Without lifting a finger, the territorial owners exert their dominance. This is done by all the hundreds of small ownership "markers" they have deposited on their family territory: the ornaments, the "possessed" objects positioned in the rooms and on the walls; the furnishings, the furniture, the colours, the patterns, all owner-chosen and all making this particular home base unique to them. 11

It is one of the tragedies of modern architecture that there has been a standardization of these vital territorial living units. One of the most important aspects of a home is that it should be similar to other homes only in a general way, and that in detail it should have many differences, making it a *particular* home. Unfortunately, it is cheaper to build a row of houses, or a block of flats, so that all the family living-units are identical, but the territorial urge rebels against this trend and house-owners struggle as best they can to make their mark on their mass-produced properties. They do this with garden-design, with front-door colours, with curtain patterns, with wallpaper and all the other decorative elements that together create a unique and different family environment. Only when they have completed this nest-building do they feel truly "at home" and secure. 12

When they venture forth as a family unit they repeat the process in a minor way. On a day-trip to the seaside, they load the car with personal belongings and it becomes their temporary, portable territory. Arriving at the beach they stake out a small territorial claim, marking it with rugs, towels, baskets and other belongings to which they can return from their seaboard wanderings. Even if they all leave it at once to bathe, it retains a characteristic territorial quality and other family groups arriving will recognize this by setting up their own "home" bases at a respectful distance. Only when the whole beach has filled up with these marked spaces will newcomers start to position themselves in such a way that the inter-base distance becomes reduced. Forced to pitch between several existing beach territories they will feel a momentary sensation of intrusion, and the established "owners" will feel a similar sensation of invasion, even though they are not being directly inconvenienced. 13

The same territorial scene is being played out in parks and fields and on riverbanks, wherever family groups gather in their clustered units. But if rivalry for spaces creates mild feelings of hostility, it is true to say that, without the territorial system of sharing and space-limited dominance, there would be chaotic disorder. 14

Third: the Personal Space. If a man enters a waiting-room and sits at one end of a long row of empty chairs, it is possible to predict where the next man to enter will seat himself. He will not sit next to the first man, nor will he sit at the far end, right away from him. He will choose a position about halfway between these two points. The next man to enter will take the largest gap left, and sit roughly in the middle of that, and so on, until eventually the latest newcomer will be forced to select a seat that places him right next to one of the already seated men. Similar patterns can be observed in cinemas, public urinals, airplanes, trains and buses. This is a reflection of the fact that we all carry with us, everywhere we go, a portable territory called a Personal Space. If people move inside this space, we feel threatened. If they keep too far outside it, we feel rejected. The result is a subtle series of spatial adjustments, usually operating quite unconsciously and producing ideal compromises as far as this is possible. If a situation becomes too crowded, then we adjust our reactions accordingly and allow our personal space to shrink. Jammed into an elevator, a rush-hour compartment, or a packed room, we give up altogether and allow body-to-body contact, but when we relinquish our Personal Space in this way, we adopt certain special techniques. 15

In essence, what we do is to convert these other bodies into "nonpersons." We studiously ignore them, and they us. We try not to face them if we can possibly avoid it. We wipe all expressiveness from our faces, letting them go blank. We may look up at the ceiling or down at the floor, and we reduce body movements to a minimum. Packed together like sardines in a tin, we stand dumbly still, sending out as few social signals as possible.

Even if the crowding is less severe, we still tend to cut down our 16
social interactions in the presence of large numbers. Careful observations of children in play groups revealed that if they are high density groupings there is less social interaction between the individual children, even though there is theoretically more opportunity for such contacts. At the same time, the high-density groups show a higher frequency of aggressive and destructive behaviour patterns in their play. Personal Space — "elbow room" — is a vital commodity for the human animal, and one that cannot be ignored without risking serious trouble.

Of course, we all enjoy the excitement of being in a crowd, and 17
this reaction cannot be ignored. But there are crowds and crowds. It is pleasant enough to be in a "spectator crowd," but not so appealing to find youself in the middle of a rush-hour crush. The difference between the two is that the spectator crowd is all facing in the same direction and concentrating on a distant point of interest. Attending a theatre, there are twinges of rising hostility towards the stranger who sits down immediately in front of you or the one who squeezes into the seat next to you. The shared armrest can become a polite, but distinct, territorial boundary-dispute region. However, as soon as the show begins, these invasions of Personal Space are forgotten and the attention is focused beyond the small space where the crowding is taking place. Now, each member of the audience feels himself spatially related, not to his cramped neighbours, but to the actor on the stage, and this distance is, if anything, too great. In the rush-hour crowd, by contrast, each member of the pushing throng is competing with his neighbours all the time. There is no escape to a spatial relation with a distant actor, only the pushing, shoving bodies all around.

Those of us who have to spend a great deal of time in crowded 18
conditions become gradually better able to adjust, but no one can ever become completely immune to invasions of Personal Space. This is because they remain forever associated with either powerful hos-

tile or equally powerful loving feelings. All through our childhood we will have been held to be loved and held to be hurt, and anyone who invades our Personal Space when we are adults is, in effect, threatening to extend his behavior into one of these two highly charged areas of human interaction. Even if his motives are clearly neither hostile nor sexual, we still find it hard to suppress our reactions to his close approach. Unfortunately, different countries have different ideas about exactly how close is close. It is easy enough to test your own "space reaction": when you are talking to someone in the street or in any open space, reach out with your arm and see where the nearest point on his body comes. If you hail from western Europe, you will find that he is at roughly fingertip distance from you. In other words, as you reach out, your fingertips will just about make contact with his shoulder. If you come from eastern Europe you will find you are standing at "wrist distance." If you come from the Mediterranean region you will find that you are much closer to your companion, at little more than "elbow distance."

Trouble begins when a member of one of these cultures meets 19
and talks to one from another. Say a British diplomat meets an Italian or an Arab diplomat at an embassy function. They start talking in a friendly way, but soon the fingertips man begins to feel uneasy. Without knowing quite why, he starts to back away gently from his companion. The companion edges forward again. Each tries in this way to set up a Personal Space relationship that suits his own background. But it is impossible to do. Every time the Mediterranean diplomat advances to a distance that feels comfortable for him, the British diplomat feels threatened. Every time the Briton moves back, the other feels rejected. Attempts to adjust this situation often lead to a talking pair shifting slowly across a room, and many an embassy reception is dotted with western-European fingertip-distance men pinned against the walls by eager elbow-distance men. Until such differences are fully understood and allowances made, these minor differences in "body territories" will continue to act as an alienation factor which may interfere in a subtle way with diplomatic harmony and other forms of international transaction.

If there are distance problems when engaged in conversation, 20
then there are clearly going to be even bigger difficulties where people must work privately in a shared space. Close proximity of others, pressing against the invisible boundaries of our personal body-territory, makes it difficult to concentrate on non-social matters. Flat-

mates, students sharing a study, sailors in the cramped quarters of a ship, and office staff in crowded work-places, all have to face this problem. They solve it by "cocooning." They use a variety of devices to shut themselves off from the others present. The best possible cocoon, of course, is a small private room — a den, a private office, a study or a studio — which physically obscures the presence of other nearby territory-owners. This is the ideal situation for non-social work, but the space-sharers cannot enjoy this luxury. Their cocooning must be symbolic. They may, in certain cases, be able to erect small physical barriers, such as screens and partitions, which give substance to their invisible Personal Space boundaries, but when this cannot be done, other means must be sought. One of these is the "favoured object." Each space-sharer develops a preference, repeatedly expressed until it becomes a fixed pattern, for a particular chair, or table, or alcove. Others come to respect this, and friction is reduced. This system is often formally arranged (this is my desk, that is yours), but even where it is not, favoured places soon develop. Professor Smith has a favourite chair in the library. It is not formally his, but he always uses it and others avoid it. Seats around a mess-room table, or a boardroom table, become almost personal property for specific individuals. Even in the home, father has his favourite chair for reading the newspaper or watching television. Another device is the blinkers-posture. Just as a horse that over-reacts to other horses and the distractions of the noisy race-course is given a pair of blinkers to shield its eyes, so people studying privately in a public place put on pseudo-blinkers in the form of shielding hands. Resting their elbows on the table, they sit with their hands screening their eyes from the scene on either side.

21 A third method of reinforcing the body-territory is to use personal markers. Books, papers and other personal belongings are scattered around the favoured site to render it more privately owned in the eyes of companions. Spreading out one's belongings is a well-known trick in public-transport situations, where a traveller tries to give the impression that seats next to him are taken. In many contexts carefully arranged personal markers can act as an effective territorial display, even in the absence of the territory owner. Experiments in a library revealed that placing a pile of magazines on the table in one seating position successfully reserved that place for an average of 77 minutes. If a sports-jacket was added, draped over the chair, then the "reservation effect" lasted for over two hours.

In these ways, we strengthen the defences of our Personal Spaces, keeping out intruders with the minimum of open hostility. As with all territorial behaviour, the object is to defend space with signals rather than with fists and at all three levels — the tribal, the family and the personal — it is a remarkably efficient system of space-sharing. It does not always seem so, because newspapers and newscasts inevitably magnify the exceptions and dwell on those cases where the signals have failed and wars have broken out, gangs have fought, neighbouring families have feuded, or colleagues have clashed, but for every territoral signal that has failed, there are millions of others that have not. They do not rate a mention in the news, but they nevertheless constitute a dominant feature of human society — the society of a remarkably territorial animal. 22

Meanings and Values

1. What are the characteristics that enable you to classify this selection as formal, informal, or familiar? (See Guide to Terms: *Essay.*)

2a. What are some of the "socially valid" reasons that justify evicting a family from its home (par. 3)?

b. If you think there are no such valid reasons, justify your stand.

3a. List other subgroups that give members a "powerful feeling of security and importance" (par. 8).

b. What are the territorial signals of each group?

4a. In one sentence, state the central theme of this selection. (Guide: *Unity.*)

b. Does the writing have good unity? Why, or why not?

5a. What was the author's apparent purpose?

b. How successfully does he perform this function?

c. How worthwhile was it? Why?

Expository Techniques

1a. Is this classification system logical, complete, and consistent in all respects? Cite any exceptions and state what is wrong.

b. What other basis can you suggest for organizing the discussion of man's territorial behavior? Which do you prefer? Why?

2a. Into how many categories does the author divide the solutions of people sharing cramped living or working quarters?

b. Cite two of the solutions in each division.

3a. Demonstrate the value of using examples by eliminating them entirely from any one portion of this selection, leaving only the generalities.

b. What would be the effect on the reader?

4a. It is possible (but not very rewarding) to argue about whether this writing has a one-paragraph or a five-paragraph introduction. Assuming the latter to be the author's intention, which of the standard introductory techniques does he use? (Guide: *Introductions.*)

b. How successfully does he perform the four potential functions of an introduction? Be specific.

Diction and Vocabulary

1. How can you account for the unusual spelling of some of the words, such as behaviour (title), defence (par. 2), and colours (par. 11)?

2. Why do you think the author considered the word "displayed" important enough to be italicized (par. 3)?

3a. Of what might a "symbolic" exploding into battle consist (par. 4)?

b. What makes some of the barriers listed in paragraph 20 "symbolic"?

c. Explain how the uses of "symbolic" and "symbolically" in these paragraphs and in paragraphs 5, 7, and 11 are, or are not, consistent with the discussion of "symbol" in this book. (Guide: *Symbol.*)

4a. What, if anything, is noteworthy about the diction or syntax of this selection? (Guide: *Diction, Syntax.*)

a. To what extent, if at all, is Morris's writing characterized by his style? (Guide: *Style/Tone.*) You may want to compare his style, or lack of it, with that of an author previously read.

Suggestions for Writing and Discussion

1. You may select one of the subgroups listed in answering Question 3 of Meanings and Values to discuss more fully — explaining, perhaps, just what the members get out of belonging.

2. The owners of a home also assert their dominance in subtle and unconscious actions as well as objects. Discuss these actions and explain why such asserted dominance is not resented by the average visitor.

3. Most of Morris's discussion of family territory seems to refer to family-owned homes. What are the limitations on renters, especially of apartments, in displaying their territorial signals? To what extent do you suppose a desire for greater territorial display contribute to most people's dream of one day owning their own homes?

Writing Suggestions for Section 2

Classification

Use division and classification (into at least three categories) as your basic method of analyzing one of the following subjects from one interesting point of view. (Your instructor may have good reason to place limitations on your choice of subject.) Narrow the topic as necessary to enable you to do a thorough job.

1. College students.
2. College teachers.
3. Athletes.
4. Coaches.
5. Salespeople.
6. Hunters (or fishermen).
7. Parents.
8. Marijuana users.
9. Policemen.
10. Summer (or part-time) jobs.
11. Sailing vessels.
12. Horses (or other animals).
13. Television programs.
14. Motivations for study.
15. Methods of studying for exams.
16. Lies.
17. Selling techniques.
18. Tastes in clothes.
19. Contemporary music.
20. Love.
21. Immorality.
22. Attitudes toward life.

3

Explaining by Means of *Comparison* and *Contrast*

One of the first expository methods we used as children was *comparison,* noticing similarities of objects, qualities, and actions, or *contrast,* noticing their differences. We compared the color of the new puppies with that of their mother, contrasted our father's height with our own. Then the process became more complicated. Now we employ it frequently in college essay examinations or term papers when we compare or contrast forms of government, reproductive systems of animals, or ethical philosophies of man. Later, in the business or professional world, we may prepare important reports based on comparison and contrast — between kinds of equipment for purchase, the personnel policies of different departments, or precedents in legal matters. Nearly everyone uses the process, though he may not be aware of this, many times a day — in choosing a head of lettuce, in deciding what to wear to school, in selecting a house or a friend or a religion.

In the more formal scholastic and professional uses of comparison and contrast, however, an ordered plan is needed to avoid having a mere list of characteristics or a frustrating jumble of similarities and differences. If the author wants to avoid communication blocks that will prevent his "getting through" to his reader, he will observe a few basic principles of selection and development. These principles apply mostly to comparisons between two subjects only; if three or more are to be considered, the usual method is to compare or contrast them in pairs.

A *logical* comparison or contrast can be made only between subjects of the same general type. (Analogy, a special form of comparison used for another purpose, is discussed in the next section.) For example, contrasting a pine and a maple could be useful or meaningful, but little would be gained, except exercise in sentence construction, by contrasting the pine and the pansy.

Of course, logical but informal comparisons that are merely incidental to the basic structure, and hence follow no special pattern, may be made in any writing. Several of the preceding selections make limited use of comparison and contrast; Baker relies heavily on contrast between the old and the new baseball, and Hall, in his fifth paragraph, to distinguish between two of his types of reading. But once committed to a formal, full-scale analysis by comparison and contrast, the careful writer ordinarily gives the subjects similar treatment. Points used for one should also be used for the other, and usually in the same order. All pertinent points should be explored — pertinent, that is, to the purpose of the comparison.

The purpose and the complexity of materials will usually indicate their arrangement and use. Sometimes the purpose is merely to point out *what* the likenesses and differences are, sometimes it is to show the *superiority* of one thing over another — or possibly to convince the reader of the superiority, as this is also a technique of argumentation. The purpose may be to explain the *unfamiliar* (wedding customs in Ethiopia) by comparing to the *familiar* (wedding customs in Kansas). Or it may be to explain or emphasize some other type of *central idea,* as in most of the essays in this section.

One of the two basic methods of comparison is to present all the information on the two subjects, one at a time, and to summarize by combining their most important similarities and differences. This method may be desirable if there are few points to compare, or if the individual points are less important than the overall picture they present. Therefore, this procedure might be a satisfactory means of showing the relative difficulty of two college courses, or comparing two viewpoints concerning an automobile accident. (Of course, as in all other matters of expository arrangement, the last subject discussed is in the most emphatic position.)

However, if there are several points of comparison to be considered, or if the points are of individual importance, alternation of the material would be a better arrangement. Hence, in a detailed comparison of Oak Valley and Elm Hill hospitals, we might compare their sizes, locations, surgical facilities, staffs, and so on, always in the same order. To tell all about Oak Valley and then all about Elm Hill would create a serious communication block, requiring the reader constantly to call on his memory of what was cited earlier, or to turn back to the first group of facts again and again in order to make the meaningful comparisons that the author should have made for him.

Often the subject matter or the purpose itself will suggest a more casual treatment, or some combination or variation of the two basic methods. We might present the complete information on the first subject, then summarize it point by point within the complete information on the second. In other circumstances (as in "The Spider and the Wasp" in Section 5), it may be desirable simply to set up the thesis of likeness or difference, and then to explain a *process* that demonstrates this thesis. And, although expository comparisons and contrasts are frequently handled together, it is sometimes best to present all similarities first, then all differences — or vice versa, depending on the emphasis desired.

In any basic use of "comparison" (conveniently, the term is most often used in a general sense to cover both comparison and contrast), the important thing is to have a plan that suits the purpose and material thoughtfully worked out in advance.

MARK TWAIN

MARK TWAIN was the pen name of Samuel Clemens (1835–1910). He was born in Missouri and became the first author of importance to emerge from "beyond the Mississippi." Although best known for bringing humor, realism, and western local color to American fiction, Mark Twain wanted to be remembered as a philosopher and social critic. Still widely read, in most languages and in all parts of the world, are his numerous short stories (his "tall tales," in particular), autobiographical accounts, and novels, especially *Adventures of Huckleberry Finn* (1884). Ernest Hemingway called the latter "the best book we've had," an appraisal with which many critics agree.

Two Ways of Seeing a River

"Two Ways of Seeing a River" (editor's title) is from Mark Twain's "Old Times on the Mississippi," which was later expanded and published in book form as *Life on the Mississippi* (1883). It is autobiographical. The prose of this selection is vivid, as in all of Mark Twain's writing, but considerably more reflective in tone than most.

Now when I had mastered the language of this water and had come 1
to know every trifling feature that bordered the great river as familiarly as I knew the letters of the alphabet, I had made a valuable acquisition. But I had lost something, too. I had lost something which could never be restored to me while I lived. All the grace, the beauty, the poetry, had gone out of the majestic river! I still kept in mind a certain wonderful sunset which I witnessed when steamboating was new to me. A broad expanse of the river was turned to blood; in the middle distance the red hue brightened into gold, through which a solitary log came floating, black and conspicuous; in one place a long, slanting mark lay sparkling upon the water; in another the surface was broken by boiling, tumbling rings, that were as many-tinted as an opal; where the ruddy flush was faintest, was a smooth spot that was covered with graceful circles and radiating lines, ever so deli-

cately traced; the shore on our left was densely wooded and the somber shadow that fell from this forest was broken in one place by a long, ruffled trail that shone like silver; and high above the forest wall a clean-stemmed dead tree waved a single leafy bough that glowed like a flame in the unobstructed splendor that was flowing from the sun. There were graceful curves, reflected images, woody heights, soft distances, and over the whole scene, far and near, the dissolving lights drifted steadily, enriching it every passing moment with new marvels of coloring.

I stood like one bewitched. I drank it in, in a speechless rapture. 2
The world was new to me and I had never seen anything like this at home. But as I have said, a day came when I began to cease from noting the glories and the charms which the moon and the sun and the twilight wrought upon the river's face; another day came when I ceased altogether to note them. Then, if that sunset scene had been repeated, I should have looked upon it without rapture, and should have commented upon it inwardly after this fashion: "This sun means that we are going to have wind to-morrow; that floating log means that the river is rising, small thanks to it; that slanting mark on the water refers to a bluff reef which is going to kill somebody's steamboat one of these nights, if it keeps on stretching out like that; those tumbling 'boils' show a dissolving bar and a changing channel there; the lines and circles in the slick water over yonder are a warning that that troublesome place is shoaling up dangerously; that silver streak in the shadow of the forest is the 'break' from a new snag and he has located himself in the very best place he could have found to fish for steamboats; that tall dead tree, with a single living branch, is not going to last long, and then how is a body ever going to get through this blind place at night without the friendly old landmark?"

No, the romance and beauty were all gone from the river. All the 3
value any feature of it had for me now was the amount of usefulness it could furnish toward compassing the safe piloting of a steamboat. Since those days, I have pitied doctors from my heart. What does the lovely flush in a beauty's cheek mean to a doctor but a "break" that ripples above some deadly disease? Are not all her visible charms sown thick with what are to him the signs and symbols of hidden decay? Does he ever see her beauty at all, or doesn't he simply view her professionally and comment upon her unwholesome condition all to himself? And doesn't he sometimes wonder whether he has gained most or lost most by learning his trade?

Meanings and Values

1. No selection could better illustrate the intimate relationship of several skills with which students of writing should be familiar, especially the potentials in "point of view" (and attitude), "style," "tone."
   a. What is the point of view in paragraph 1? (See Guide to Terms: *Point of View.*)
   b. Where, and how, does it change in paragraph 2?
   c. Why is the shift important to the author's contrast?
   d. Show how the noticeable change of tone is related to this change in point of view. (Guide: *Style/Tone.*)
   e. Specifically, what changes in style accompany the shift in tone and attitude?
   f. How effectively do they all relate to the central theme itself? (Remember that such effects seldom just "happen"; the writer *makes* them happen.)

2a. Is the first paragraph primarily objective or subjective? (Guide: *Objective/Subjective.*)
 b. How about the latter part of paragraph 2?
 c. Are your answers to "a" and "b" related to point of view? If so, how?

3a. Does the author permit himself to engage in sentimentality? (Guide: *Sentimentality.*) If so, how could it have been avoided without damage to his theme's development?
 b. If not, what restraints does the author use?

4. Do you think the last sentence refers only to doctors? Why, or why not?

5. List other vocations in which you assume (or perhaps have occasion to know) that the beauty and romance eventually give way to practical realities; state briefly, for each, why this hardening should be expected.

Expository Techniques

1a. Where do you find a second comparison or contrast? Which is it?
 b. Is the comparison/contrast made within itself, with something external, or both? Explain.
 c. Is this part of the writing closely enough related to the major contrast to justify its use? Why or why not?

2a. In developing the numerous points of the major contrast, would an alternating, point-to-point system have been better? Why, or why not?
 b. Show how the author uses organization within the groups to assist in the overall contrast.

3a. What is the most noteworthy feature of syntax in paragraphs 1 and 2? (Guide: *Syntax.*)

b. How effectively does it perform the function intended?

4. What is gained by the apparently deliberate decision to use rhetorical questions only toward the end? (Guide: *Rhetorical Questions.*)

Diction and Vocabulary

1. Why would the colloquialism in the last sentence of paragraph 2 have been inappropriate in the first paragraph? (Guide: *Colloquial Expressions.*)

2a. Compare the quality of metaphors in the quotation of paragraph 2 with the quality of those preceding it. (Guide: *Figures of Speech.*)

b. Is the difference justified? Why, or why not?

Suggestions for Writing and Discussion

1. Select for further development one of the vocations in your answer to question 5 of "Meanings and Values." How would one's attitude be apt to change from the beginning romantic appeal?
2. Show how, if at all, Mark Twain's contrast might be used to show parallels to life itself — e.g., differences in the idealism and attitudes of youth and maturity.
3. Explore the possibility, citing examples if possible, of being able to retain *both* the "rapture" and the "usefulness."

(NOTE: Suggestions for topics requiring development by use of COMPARISON and CONTRAST are on page 124, at the end of this section.)

BRUCE CATTON

BRUCE CATTON (1899–1978) was a Civil War specialist whose early career included reporting for various newspapers. In 1954 he received both the Pulitzer Prize for historical work and the National Book Award. He served as director of information for the United States Department of Commerce and wrote many books, including *Mr. Lincoln's Army* (1951), *Glory Road* (1952), *A Stillness at Appomattox* (1953), *The Hallowed Ground* (1956), *America Goes to War* (1958), *The Coming Fury* (1961), *Terrible Swift Sword* (1963), *Never Call Retreat* (1966), *Waiting for the Morning Train: An American Boyhood* (1972), and *Gettysburg: The Final Fury* (1974). For five years, Catton edited *American Heritage.*

Grant and Lee: A Study in Contrasts

"Grant and Lee: A Study in Contrasts" was written as a chapter of *The American Story,* a collection of essays by noted historians. In this study, as in most of his other writing, Catton does more than recount the facts of history: he shows the significance within them. It is a carefully constructed essay, using contrast and comparison as the entire framework for his explanation.

When Ulysses S. Grant and Robert E. Lee met in the parlor of a modest house at Appomattox Court House, Virginia, on April 9, 1865, to work out the terms for the surrender of Lee's Army of Northern Virginia, a great chapter in American life came to a close, and a great new chapter began. 1

These men were bringing the Civil War to its virtual finish. To be sure, other armies had yet to surrender, and for a few days the fugitive Confederate government would struggle desperately and vainly, trying to find some way to go on living now that its chief support was gone. But in effect it was all over when Grant and Lee signed the papers. And the little room where they wrote out the terms 2

From *The American Story,* ed. by Earl Schenk Miers.

was the scene of one of the poignant, dramatic contrasts in American History.

They were two strong men, these oddly different generals, and they represented the strengths of two conflicting currents that, through them, had come into final collision. 3

Back of Robert E. Lee was the notion that the old aristocratic concept might somehow survive and be dominant in American life. 4

Lee was tidewater Virginia, and in his background were family, culture, and tradition . . . the age of chivalry transplanted to a New World which was making its own legends and its own myths. He embodied a way of life that had come down through the age of knighthood and the English country squire. America was a land that was beginning all over again, dedicated to nothing much more complicated than the rather hazy belief that all men had equal rights and should have an equal chance in the world. In such a land Lee stood for the feeling that it was somehow of advantage to human society to have a pronounced inequality in the social structure. There should be a leisure class, backed by ownership of land; in turn, society itself should be keyed to the land as the chief source of wealth and influence. It would bring forth (according to this ideal) a class of men with a strong sense of obligation to the community; men who lived not to gain advantage for themselves, but to meet the solemn obligations which had been laid on them by the very fact that they were privileged. From them the country would get its leadership; to them it could look for the higher values — of thought, of conduct, of personal deportment — to give it strength and virtue. 5

Lee embodied the noblest elements of this aristocratic ideal. Through him, the landed nobility justified itself. For four years, the Southern states had fought a desperate war to uphold the ideals for which Lee stood. In the end, it almost seemed as if the Confederacy fought for Lee; as if he himself was the Confederacy . . . the best thing that the way of life for which the Confederacy stood could ever have to offer. He had passed into legend before Appomattox. Thousands of tired, underfed, poorly clothed Confederate soldiers, long since past the simple enthusiasm of the early days of the struggle, somehow considered Lee the symbol of everything for which they had been willing to die. But they could not quite put this feeling into words. If the Lost Cause, sanctified by so much heroism and so many 6 deaths, had a living justification, its justification was General Lee.

Grant, the son of a tanner on the Western frontier, was everything Lee was not. He had come up the hard way and embodied nothing in particular except the eternal toughness and sinewy fiber of the men who grew up beyond the mountains. He was one of a body of men who owed reverence and obeisance to no one, who were self-reliant to a fault, who cared hardly anything for the past but who had a sharp eye for the future. 7

These frontier men were the precise opposites of the tidewater aristocrats. Back of them, in the great surge that had taken people over the Alleghenies and into the opening Western country, there was a deep, implicit dissatisfaction with a past that had settled into grooves. They stood for democracy, not from any reasoned conclusion about the proper ordering of human society, but simply because they had grown up in the middle of democracry and knew how it worked. Their society might have privileges, but they would be privileges each man had won for himself. Forms and patterns meant nothing. No man was born to anything, except perhaps to a chance to show how far he could rise. Life was competition. 8

Yet along with this feeling had come a deep sense of belonging to a national community. The Westerner who developed a farm, opened a shop, or set up in business as a trader, could hope to prosper only as his own community prospered — and his community ran from the Atlantic to the Pacific and from Canada down to Mexico. If the land was settled, with towns and highways and accessible markets, he could better himself. He saw his fate in terms of the nation's own destiny. As its horizons expanded, so did his. He had, in other words, an acute dollars-and-cents stake in the continued growth and development of his country. 9

And that, perhaps, is where the contrast between Grant and Lee becomes most striking. The Virginia aristocrat, inevitably, saw himself in relation to his own region. He lived in a static society which could endure almost anything except change. Instinctively, his first loyalty would go to the locality in which that society existed. He would fight to the limit of endurance to defend it, because in defending it he was defending everything that gave his own life its deepest meaning. 10

The Westerner, on the other hand, would fight with an equal tenacity for the broader concept of society. He fought so because 11 everything he lived by was tied to growth, expansion, and a constantly widening horizon. What he lived by would survive or fall with the nation itself. He could not possibly stand by unmoved in the face of an attempt to destroy the Union. He would combat it with everything he had, because he could only see it as an effort to cut the ground out from under his feet.

So Grant and Lee were in complete contrast, representing two 12
diametrically opposed elements in American life. Grant was the modern man emerging; beyond him, ready to come on the stage, was the great age of steel and machinery, of crowded cities and a restless burgeoning vitality. Lee might have ridden down from the old age of chivalry, lance in hand, silken banner fluttering over his head. Each man was the perfect champion of his cause, drawing both his strengths and his weaknesses from the people he led.

Yet it was not all contrast, after all. Different as they were — in 13
background, in personality, in underlying aspiration — these two great soldiers had much in common. Under everything else, they were marvelous fighters. Furthermore, their fighting qualities were really very much alike.

Each man had, to begin with, the great virtue of utter tenacity 14
and fidelity. Grant fought his way down the Mississippi Valley in spite of acute personal discouragement and profound military handicaps. Lee hung on in the trenches at Petersburg after hope itself had died. In each man there was an indomitable quality . . . the born fighter's refusal to give up as long as he can still remain on his feet and lift his two fists.

Daring and resourcefulness they had, too; the ability to think 15
faster and move faster than the enemy. These were the qualities which gave Lee the dazzling campaigns of Second Manassas and Chancellorsville and won Vicksburg for Grant.

Lastly, and perhaps greatest of all, there was the ability, at the 16
end, to turn quickly from war to peace once the fighting was over. Out of the way these two men behaved at Appomattox came the possibility of a peace of reconciliation. It was a possibility not wholly realized, in the years to come, but which did, in the end, help the two sections to become one nation again . . . after a war whose bitterness might have seemed to make such a reunion wholly impossible. No part of either man's life became him more than the part he played in their brief meeting in the McLean house at Appomattox. Their behavior there put all succeeding generations of Americans in their

debt. Two great Americans, Grant and Lee — very different, yet under everything very much alike. Their encounter at Appomattox was one of the great moments of American history.

Meanings and Values

1a. Clarify the assertions that through Lee "the landed nobility justified itself" and that "if the Lost Cause . . . had a living justification," it was General Lee (par. 6).
b. Why are these assertions pertinent to the central theme?

2a. Does it seem reasonable that "thousands of tired, underfed, poorly clothed Confederate soldiers" (par. 6) had been willing to fight for the aristocratic system in which they would never have had even a chance to be aristocrats? Why, or why not?
b. Can you think of more likely reasons why there were willing to fight?

3. Under any circumstances today might such a social structure as the South's be best for a country? Explain.

4a. What countries of the world have recently been so torn by internal war and bitterness that reunion has seemed, or still seems, impossible?
b. Do you see any basic differences between the trouble in those countries and that in America at the time of the Civil War?

5a. The author calls Lee a symbol (par. 6). Was Grant also a symbol? If so, of what? (See guide to Terms: *Symbol.*)
b. How would you classify this kind of symbolism?

Expository Techniques

1. Make an informal list of paragraph numbers from 3 to 16, and note by each whether the paragraph is devoted primarily to Lee, to Grant, or to direct comparison or contrast of the two. This chart will show you Catton's basic pattern of development. (Notice, for instance, how the broad information of paragraphs 4–6 and 7–9 seems almost to "funnel" down through the narrower summaries in 10 and 11 and into paragraph 12, where the converging elements meet and the contrast is made specific.)

2. What new technique of development is started in paragraph 13?

3a. What is gained, or lost, by using one sentence for paragraph 3?
b. For paragraph 4?

4a. How many paragraphs does the introduction comprise?
b. How successfully does it fulfill the three basic requirements of a good introduction? (Guide: *Introductions.*)

5. Show how Catton has constructed the beginning of each paragraph so that there is a smooth transition from the one preceding it. (Guide: *Transition.*)

6. The author's conclusion is really only the expanation of one of his integral points — and this method, if not carefully planned, runs the risk of ending too abruptly and leaving the reader unsatisfied. How has Catton avoided this hazard? (Guide: *Closings.*)

7a. What seems to be the author's attitude toward Grant and Lee?
 b. Show how his tone reflects this attitude. (Guide: *Style/Tone.*)

Diction and Vocabulary

1. Why would a use of colloquialisms have been inconsistent with the tone of this writing?

2a. List or mark all metaphors in paragraphs 1, 3, 5, 7–11, 16. (Guide: *Figures of Speech.*)
 b. Comment on their general effectiveness.

3. If you are not already familiar with the following words, study their meanings as given in the dictionary and as used in this essay: virtual, poignant (par. 2); concept (4); sinewy, obeisance (7); implicit (8); tenacity (11); diametrically, burgeoning (12); aspiration (13); fidelity, profound, indomitable (14); succeeding (16).

4. Explain how the word "poignant" aptly describes this contrast of two men (par. 2).

Suggestions for Writing and Discussion

1. Find, by minor research, an incident in the life of Grant or Lee that will, in suitable essay form, illustrate one of Catton's points.

2. Select some other dramatic moment in history and show its long-range significance.

3. Select some important moment in your life and show its long-range significance.

4. Explain how someone you know symbolizes a philosophy or way of life.

(NOTE: Suggestions for topics requiring development by use of COMPARISON and CONTRAST are on page 124, at the end of this section.)

ARTHUR L. CAMPA

ARTHUR L. CAMPA (1905–1978), born of missionary parents in Guaymas, Mexico, received degrees at the University of New Mexico and Columbia University. Before becoming chairman of the Department of Modern Languages at the University of Denver in 1946, Campa served in the United States Air Force, had moved from instructor to professor at the University of New Mexico, and had already become a versatile and prolific writer. Campa served the Department of State as cultural affairs officer in foreign embassies and as director of training projects for the Peace Corps. From 1946 until his death Campa was director of the Center of Latin American Studies in Denver. His books include *Spanish Folk Poetry in New Mexico* (1946); *Treasure of the Sangres des Christos* (1963); and *Hispanic Culture in the Southwest* (1978).

Anglo vs. Chicano: Why?

"Anglo vs. Chicano: Why?" was written for *Western Review* and condensed somewhat for *Intellectual Digest;* we use the briefer version here. Campa goes further than most writers on this subject to develop a careful, point-by-point analysis of not only differences, but their origins and implications as well.

1 The cultural differences between Hispanic and Anglo-American people have been dwelt upon by so many writers that we should all be well informed about the values of both. But audiences are usually of the same persuasion as the speakers, and those who consult published works are for the most part specialists looking for affirmation of what they believe. So, let us consider the same subject, exploring briefly some of the basic cultural differences that cause conflict in the Southwest, where Hispanic and Anglo-American cultures meet.

2 Cultural differences are implicit in the conceptual content of the languages of these two civilizations, and their value systems stem from a long series of historical circumstances. Therefore, it may be

Reprinted by permission of Lucille Campa from *Intellectual Digest* (January 1973). First published in *Western Review,* vol. IX (Spring 1972).

well to consider some of the English and Spanish cultural configurations before these Europeans set foot on American soil. English culture was basically insular, geographically and ideologically; was more integrated on the whole, except for some strong theological differences; and was particularly zealous of its racial purity. Spanish culture was peninsular, a geographical circumstance that made it a catchall of Mediterranean, central European and north African peoples. The composite nature of the population produced a market regionalism that prevented close integration, except for religion, and led to a strong sense of individualism. These differences were reflected in the colonizing enterprise of the two cultures. The English isolated themselves from the Indians physically and culturally; the Spanish, who had strong notions about *pureza de sangre* [purity of blood] among the nobility, were not collectively averse to adding one more strain to their racial cocktail. Cortés led the way by siring the first *mestizo* in North America, and the rest of the conquistadores followed suit. The ultimate products of these two orientations meet today in the Southwest.

Anglo-American culture was absolutist at the onset; that is, all the dominant values were considered identical for all, regardless of time and place. Such values as justice, charity, honesty were considered the superior social order for all men and were later embodied in the American Constitution. The Spaniard brought with him a relativistic viewpoint and saw fewer moral implications in man's actions. Values were looked upon as the result of social and economic conditions. 3

The motives that brought Spaniards and Englishmen to America also differed. The former came on an enterprise of discovery, searching for a new route to India initially, and later for new lands to conquer, the fountain of youth, minerals, the Seven Cities of Cíbola and, in the case of the missionaries, new souls to win for the Kingdom of Heaven. The English came to escape religious persecution, and once having found a haven, they settled down to cultivate the soil and establish their homes. Since the Spaniards were not seeking a refuge or running away from anything, they continued their explorations and circled the globe 25 years after the discovery of the New World. 4

This peripatetic tendency of the Spaniard may be accounted for in part by the fact that he was the product of an equestrian culture. Men on foot do not venture far into the unknown. It was almost a 5 century after the landing on Plymouth Rock that Governor Alexander Spotswood of Virginia crossed the Blue Ridge Mountains, and it was not until the nineteenth century that the Anglo-Americans began to move west of the Mississippi.

The Spaniard's equestrian role meant that he was not close to the soil, as was the Anglo-American pioneer, who tilled the land and built the greatest agricultural industry in history. The Spaniard cultivated the land only when he had Indians available to do it for him. The uses to which the horse was put also varied. The Spanish horse was essentially a mount, while the more robust English horse was used in cultivating the soil. It is therefore not surprising that the viewpoints of these two cultures should differ when we consider that the pioneer is looking at the world at the level of his eyes while the *caballero* [horseman] is looking beyond and down at the rest of the world. 6

One of the most commonly quoted, and often misinterpreted, characteristics of Hispanic peoples is the deeply ingrained individualism in all walks of life. Hispanic individualism is a revolt against the incursion of collectivity, strongly asserted when it is felt that the ego is being fenced in. This attitude leads to a deficiency in those social qualities based on collective standards, an attitude that Hispanos do not consider negative because it manifests a measure of resistance to standardization in order to achieve a measure of individual freedom. Naturally, such an attitude has no *reglas fijas* [fixed rules]. 7

Anglo-Americans who achieve a measure of success and security through institutional guidance not only do not mind a few fixed rules but demand them. The lack of a concerted plan of action, whether in business or in politics, appears unreasonable to Anglo-Americans. They have a sense of individualism, but they achieve it through action and self-determination. Spanish individualism is based on feeling, on something that is the result not of rules and collective standards but of a person's momentary, emotional reaction. And it is subject to change when the mood changes. In contrast to Spanish emotional individualism, the Anglo-American strives for objectivity when choosing a course of action or making a decision. 8

The Southwestern Hispanos voiced strong objections to the lack of courtesy of the Anglo-Americans when they first met them in the early days of the Santa Fe trade. The same accusation is leveled at the *Americanos* today in many quarters of the Hispanic world. Some of 9 this results from their different conceptions of polite behavior. Here too one can say that the Spanish have no *reglas fijas* because for them courtesy is simply an expression of the way one person feels toward another. To some they extend the hand, to some they bow and for the more *íntimos* there is the well-known *abrazo.* The concepts of "good or bad" or "right and wrong" in polite behavior are moral considerations of an absolutist culture.

Another cultural contrast appears in the way both cultures share part of their material substance with others. The pragmatic Anglo-American contributes regularly to such institutions as the Red Cross, the United Fund and a myriad of associations. He also establishes foundations and quite often leaves millions to such institutions. The Hispano prefers to give his contribution directly to the recipient so he can see the person he is helping. 10

A century of association has inevitably acculturated both Hispanos and Anglo-Americans to some extent, but there still persist a number of culture traits that neither group has relinquished altogether. Nothing is more disquieting to an Anglo-American who believes that time is money than the time perspective of Hispanos. They usually refer to this attitude as the "*mañana* psychology." Actually, it is more of a "today psychology," because Hispanos cultivate the present to the exclusion of the future; because the latter has not arrived yet, it is not a reality. They are reluctant to relinquish the present, so they hold on to it until it becomes the past. To an Hispano, nine is nine until it is ten, so when he arrives at nine-thirty, he jubilantly exclaims: "¡Justo!" [right on time]. This may be why the clock is slowed down to a walk in Spanish while in English it runs. In the United States, our future-oriented civilization plans our lives so far in advance that the present loses its meaning. January magazine issues [including ID's] are out in December; 1973 cars have been out since October; cemetery plots and even funeral arrangements are bought on the installment plan. To a person engrossed in living today the very idea of planning his funeral sounds like the tolling of the bells. 11

It is a natural corollary that a person who is present oriented should be compensated by being good at improvising. An Anglo-American is told in advance to prepare for an "impromptu speech," but an Hispano usually can improvise a speech because *"Nosotros lo improvisamos todo"* [we improvise everything]. 12

Another source of cultural conflict arises from the difference 13 between *being* and *doing.* Even when trying to be individualistic, the Anglo-American achieves it by what he does. Today's young generation decided to be themselves, to get away from standardization, so they let their hair grow, wore ragged clothes and even went barefoot in order to be different from the Establishment. As a result they all ended up doing the same things and created another stereotype. The freedom enjoyed by the individuality of *being* makes it unnecessary for Hispanos to strive to be different.

In 1963 a team of psychologists from the University of Guadalajara in Mexico and the University of Michigan compared 74 upper-middle-class students from each university. Individualism and personalism were found to be central values for the Mexican students. This was explained by saying that a Mexican's value as a person lies in his *being* rather than, as is the case of the Anglo-Americans, in concrete accomplishments. Efficiency and accomplishments are derived characteristics that do not affect worthiness in the Mexican, whereas in the American it is equated with success, a value of highest priority in the American culture. Hispanic people disassociate themselves from material things or from actions that may impugn a person's sense of being, but the Anglo-American shows great concern for material things and assumes responsibility for his actions. This is expressed in the language of each culture. In Spanish one says, *"Se me cayó la taza"* [the cup fell away from me] instead of "I dropped the cup." 14

In English, one speaks of money, cash and all related transactions with frankness because material things of this high order do not trouble Anglo-Americans. In Spanish such materialistic concepts are circumvented by referring to cash as *efectivo* [effective] and when buying or selling as something *al contado* [counted out], and when without it by saying *No tengo fondos* [I have no funds]. This disassociation from material things is what produces *sobriedad* [sobriety] in the Spaniard according to Miguel de Unamuno, but in the Southwest the disassociation from materialism leads to *dejadez* [lassitude] and *desprendimiento* [disinterestedness]. A man may lose his life defending his honor but is unconcerned about the lack of material things. *Desprendimiento* causes a man to spend his last cent on a friend, which when added to lack of concern for the future may mean that tomorrow he will eat beans as a result of today's binge. 15

The implicit differences in words that appear to be identical in meaning are astonishing. Versatile is a compliment in English and an 16 insult in Spanish. An Hispano student who is told to apologize cannot do it, because the word doesn't exist in Spanish. *Apologia* means words in praise of a person. The Anglo-American either apologizes, which is a form of retraction abhorrent in Spanish, or compromises, another concept foreign to Hispanic culture. *Compromiso* means a date, not a compromise. In colonial Mexico City, two hidalgos once entered a narrow street from opposite sides, and when they could not go around, they sat in their coaches for three days until the viceroy ordered them to back out. All this because they could not work out a compromise.

It was that way then and to some extent now. Many of today's conflicts in the Southwest have their roots in polarized cultural differences, which need not be irreconcilable when approached with mutual respect and understanding. 17

Meanings and Values

1a. What is this author's point of view? (See Guide to Terms: *Point of View.*)
 b. Does he maintain this viewpoint consistently? If not where does he lose it?
2. Where, if at all, does he engage in sentimentality? (Guide: *Sentimentality.*)
3. Differentiate the meanings of "objective" and/or "subjective" by citing portions of this essay. (Guide: *Objective/Subjective.*)
4. Why do you suppose the author ignored Indian influence in explaining present-day Chicano culture?
5. What type of essay is "Anglo vs. Chicano: Why?" (Guide: *Essay.*)
6. Give this selection our three-step critical evaluation. (Guide: *Evaluation.*)

Expository Techniques

1a. Is Campa's development primarily by comparison or by contrast?
 b. Are there any exceptions? If so, where?
 c. Given his particular subject, does this seem to indicate a one-sided analysis? Explain.
2a. Which of the basic means of organizing comparison/contrast does the author use?
 b. Would the other method have been better? Why, or why not?
3a. How many individual items of comparison/contrast has he developed?

b. Cite the paragraphs devoted to each.

4. Would the essay have benefited by greater use of qualification? (Guide: *Qualification.*) If so, how?

5. Demonstrate by specific passages how generalizations can be made more specific through the use of examples. (Guide: *Specific/General.*)

6. Does the last sentence seem fully justified, prepared for by the preceding analysis? Why, or why not?

Diction and Vocabulary

1a. For the average American reader, does this author overuse foreign words and expressions? Explain the reasons for your answer.

b. Most of these words are defined, but not all of them — e.g., *mestizo* (par. 2) and *abrazo* (9). Why do you think he made exceptions of these?

c. The Spanish word "conquistadores" is not printed in italics (par. 2). Why?

2. Familiarize yourself with the following words and their meanings, consulting a dictionary as necessary: implicit, conceptual, configurations, insular, ideological, peninsular (par. 2); relativistic (3); peripatetic (5); equestrian (5, 6); incursion (7); recipient (10); acculturated (11); corollary (12); impugn (14); retraction (16).

3. Can the relatively large number of "dictionary-type" words be explained in terms of Campa's expected reader-audience? If so, how?

Suggestions for Writing and Discussion

1. Use one of Campa's major points for still further development or for analytic refutation.

2. If you can do so with any reliable knowledge of the subject, show what effects Indian culture had on that of today's Chicano.

3. In areas where Anglo and Chicano cultures have long been in contact, what effects have they already had on each other?

4. Select some other American ethnic group and show how cultural background differences have also caused conflict when confronted with Anglo culture. If possible, show how this conflict was, or is being, resolved.

5. Agree or disagree with Campa's assertion that the young generation of Anglo-Americans merely created another stereotype (par. 13). Support your stand.

(NOTE: Suggestions for topics requiring development by use of COMPARISON and CONTRAST are on page 124, at the end of this section.)

ANNE ROIPHE

ANNE RICHARDSON ROIPHE (born 1935) is a native New Yorker. After graduating from Sarah Lawrence she pursued further studies in Munich, Germany. Upon her return to the United States Roiphe worked for a public relations firm and did research for Forbes. Her first novel, *Digging Out,* published in 1968, was met with great enthusiasm. She has since published *Up The Sandbox* (1971), which was made into a movie, *Long Division* (1973), and *Torch Song* (1977). Her articles appear frequently in *Vogue* and *The New York Times Magazine.* Roiphe and her husband live in New York City with their family.

Confessions of a Female Chauvinist Sow

"Confessions of a Female Chauvinist Sow" first appeared in the magazine *New York.* This is an informal essay (which some would classify as "familiar"), and the author uses personal examples liberally to illustrate her central theme. It is a theme, however, that depends directly on comparison and contrast for its primary development.

I once married a man I thought was totally unlike my father and I imagined a whole new world of freedom emerging. Five years later it was clear even to me — floating face down in a wash of despair — that I had simply chosen a replica of my handsome daddy-true. The updated version spoke English like an angel but — good God! — underneath he was my father exactly: wonderful, but not the right man for me. 1

Most people I know have at one time or another been fouled up by their childhood experiences. Patterns tend to sink into the unconscious only to reappear, disguised, unseen, like marionette strings, pulling us this way or that. Whatever ails people — keeps them up at night, tossing and turning — also ails movements no matter how historically huge or politically important. The women's movement 2 cannot remake consciousness, or reshape the future, without acknowledging and shedding all the unnecessary and ugly baggage of the past. It's easy enough now to see where men have kept us out of clubs, baseball games, graduate schools; its easy enough to recognize the hidden directions that limit Sis to cake-baking and Junior to bridge-building; it's now possible for even Miss America herself to identify what *they* have done to us, and, of course, *they* have and *they* did and *they* are. . . . But along the way we also developed our own hidden prejudices, class assumptions and an anti-male humor and collection of expectations that gave us, like all oppressed groups, a secret sense of superiority (co-existing with a poor self-image — it's not news that people can believe two contradictory things at once).

Listen to any group that suffers materially and socially. They 3
have a lexicon with which they tease the enemy: ofay, goy, honky gringo. "Poor pale devils," said Malcolm X loud enough for us to hear, although blacks had joked about that to each other for years. Behind some of the women's liberation thinking lurk the rumors, the the prejudices, the defense systems of generations of oppressed women whispering in the kitchen together, presenting one face to their menfolk and another to their card clubs, their mothers and sisters. All this is natural enough but potentially dangerous in a revolutionary situation in which you hope to create a future that does not mirror the past. The hidden anti-male feelings, a result of the old system, will foul us up if they are allowed to persist.

During my teen years I never left the house on my Saturday 4
night dates without my mother slipping me a few extra dollars — mad money, it was called. I'll explain what it was for the benefit of the new generation in which people just sleep with each other: the fellow was supposed to bring me home, lead me safely through the asphalt jungle, protect me from slithering snakes, rapists and the like. But my mother and I knew young men were apt to drink too much, to slosh down so many rye-and-gingers that some hero might well lead me in front of an oncoming bus, smash his daddy's car into Tiffany's window or, less gallantly, throw up on my new dress. Mad money was for getting home on your own, no matter what form of insanity your date happened to evidence. Mad money was also a wallflower's rope ladder; if the guy you came with suddenly fancied someone else, well, you didn't have to stay there and suffer, you could go home. Boys were fickle and likely to be unkind; my mother and I knew that, as surely as we knew they tried to make you do things in the dark

they wouldn't respect you for afterwards, and in fact would spread the word and spoil your rep. Boys liked to be flattered; if you made them feel important they would eat out of your hand. So talk to them about their interests, don't alarm them with displays of intelligence — we all knew that, we groups of girls talking into the wee hours of the night in a kind of easy companionship we thought impossible with boys. Boys were prone to have a good time, get you pregnant, and then pretend they didn't know your name when you came knocking on their door for finances or comfort. In short, we believed boys were less moral than we were. They appeared to be hypocritical, self-seeking, exploitative, untrustworthy and very likely to be showing off their precious masculinity. I never had a girl friend I thought would be unkind or embarrass me in public. I never expected a girl to lie to me about her marks or sports skill or how good she was in bed. Altogether — without anyone's directly coming out and saying so — I gathered that men were sexy, powerful, very interesting, but not very nice, not very moral, humane and tender, like us. Girls played fairly while men, unfortunately, reserved their honor for the battlefield.

Why are there laws insisting on alimony and child support? 5
Well, everyone knows that men don't have an instinct to protect their young and, given half a chance, with the moon in the right phase, they will run off and disappear. Everyone assumes a mother will not let her child starve, yet it is necessary to legislate that a father must not do so. We are taught to accept the idea that men are less than decent; their charms may be manifold but their characters are riddled with faults. To this day I never blink if I hear that a man has gone to find his fortune in South America, having left his pregnant wife, his blind mother and taken the family car. I still gasp in horror when I hear of a woman leaving her asthmatic infant for a rock group in Taos because I can't seem to avoid the assumption that men are naturally heels and women the ordained carriers of what little is moral in our dubious civilization.

My mother never gave me mad money thinking I would ditch 6
a fellow for some other guy or that I would pass out drunk on the floor. She knew I would be considerate of my companion because, after all, I was more mature than the boys that gathered about. Why was I more mature? Women just are people-oriented; they learn to be empathetic at an early age. Most English students (students interested in humanity, not artifacts) are women. Men and boys — so the

myth goes—conceal their feelings and lose interest in anybody else's. Everyone knows that even little boys can tell the difference between one kind of a car and another — proof that their souls are mechanical, their attention directed to the non-human.

I remember shivering in the cold vestibule of a famous men's athletic club. Women and girls are not permitted inside the club's door. What are they doing in there, I asked? They're naked, said my mother, they're sweating, jumping up and down a lot, telling each other dirty jokes and bragging about their stock market exploits. Why can't we go in? I asked. Well, my mother told me, they're afraid we'd laugh at them. 7

The prejudices of childhood are hard to outgrow. I confess that every time my business takes me past that club, I shudder. Images of large bellies resting on massage tables and flaccid penises rising and falling with the Dow Jones average flash through my head. There it is, chauvinism waving its cancerous tentacles from the depths of my psyche. 8

Minorities automatically feel superior to the oppressor because, after all, they are not hurting anybody. In fact, they feel morally better. The old canard that women need love, men need sex — believed for too long by both sexes — attributes moral and spiritual superiority to women and makes of men beasts whose urges send them prowling into the night. This false division of good and bad, placing deforming pressures on everyone, doesn't have to contaminate the future. We know that the assumptions we make about each other become a part of the cultural air we breathe and, in fact, become social truths. Women who want equality must be prepared to give it and to believe in it, and in order to do that it is not enough to state that you are as good as any man, but also it must be stated that he is as good as you and both will be humans together. If we want men to share in the care of the family in a new way, we must assume them as capable of consistent loving tenderness as we. 9

I rummage about and find in my thinking all kinds of antimale prejudices. Some are just jokes and others I will have a hard time abandoning. First, I share an emotional conviction with many sisters that women given power would not create wars. Intellectually I know that's ridiculous; great queens have waged war before; the likes of Lurleen Wallace, Pat Nixon and Mrs. General Lavelle can be depended upon in the future to guiltlessly condemn to death other people's children in the name of some ideal of their own. Little girls, 10 of course, don't take toy guns out of their hip pockets and say "Pow, pow" to all their neighbors and friends like the average well-adjusted little boy. However, if we gave little girls the six-shooters, we would soon have double the pretend body count.

Aggression is not, as I secretly think, a male-sex-linked characteristic: brutality is masculine only by virtue of opportunity. True, there are 1,000 Jack the Rippers for every Lizzie Borden, but that surely is the result of social forms. Women as a group are indeed more masochistic than men. The practical result of this division is that women seem nicer and kinder, but when the world changes, women will have a fuller opportunity to be just as rotten as men and there will be fewer claims of female moral superiority. 11

Now that I am entering early middle age, I hear many women complaining of husbands and ex-husbands who are attracted to younger females. This strikes the older woman as unfair, of course. But I remember a time when I thought all boys around my age and grade were creeps and bores. I wanted to go out with an older man: a senior or, miraculously, a college man. I had a certain contempt for my coevals, not realizing that the freshman in college I thought so desirable, was some older girl's creep. Some women never lose that contempt for men of their own age. That isn't fair either and may be one reason why some sensible men of middle years find solace in young women. 12

I remember coming home from school one day to find my mother's card game dissolved in hysterical laughter. The cards were floating in black rivers of running mascara. What was so funny? A woman named Helen was lying on a couch pretending to be her husband with a cold. She was issuing demands for orange juice, aspirin, suggesting a call to a specialist, complaining of neglect, of fate's cruel finger, of heat, of cold, of sharp pains on the bridge of the nose that might indicate brain involvement. What was so funny? The ladies explained to me that all men behave just like that with colds, they are reduced to temper tantrums by simple nasal congestion, men cannot stand any little physical discomfort—on and on the laughter went. 13

The point of this vignette is the nature of the laughter — us laughing at them, us feeling superior to them, us ridiculing them behind their backs. If they were doing it to us we'd call it male chauvinist pigness; if we do it to them, it is inescapably female chauvinist sowness and, whatever its roots, it leads to the same 14 isolation. Boys are messy, boys are mean, boys are rough, boys are stupid and have sloppy handwriting. A cacophony of childhood memories rushes through my head, balanced, of course, by all the well-documented feelings of inferiority and envy. But the important thing, the hard thing, is to wipe the slate clean, to start again without the meanness of the past. That's why it's so important that the women's movement not become anti-male and allow its most prejudiced spokesmen total leadership. The much-chewed-over abortion issue illustrates this. The women's-liberation position, insisting on a woman's right to determine her own body's destiny, leads in fanatical extreme to a kind of emotional immaculate conception in which the father is not judged even half-responsible — he has no rights, and no consideration is to be given to his concern for either the woman or the fetus.

Woman, who once was abandoned and disgraced by an un- 15
wanted pregnancy, has recently arrived at a new pride of ownership or disposal. She has traveled in a straight line that still excludes her sexual partner from an equal share in the wanted or unwanted pregnancy. A better style of life may develop from an assumption that men are as human as we. Why not ask the child's father if he would like to bring up the child? Why not share decisions, when possible, with the male? If we cut them out, assuming an old-style indifference on their part, we perpetrate the ugly divisiveness that has characterized relations between the sexes so far.

Hard as it is for many of us to believe, women are not really 16
superior to men in intelligence or humanity — they are only equal.

Meanings and Values

1a. How would you describe the author's point of view in this selection? (See Guide to Terms: *Point of View.*)
 b. How did the tone help determine your answer? (Guide: *Style/Tone.*)

2. In the last sentence of paragraph 2 is an example of irony. (Guide: *Irony.*)
 a. What kind is it?
 b. Could it also be used to illustrate the meaning of "paradox"? (Guide: *Paradox.*) Why, or why not?

3a. Exactly what is the "myth" with which Roiphe is primarily concerned?
 b. Is it explained more by comparison or by contrast?

c. Which aspects of it, if any, do young women of your acquaintance still seem to believe? Explain.

4. Show the special significance, in relation to the theme, of the author's mother's last answer in paragraph 7.

5. How is it possible, if at all, to "guiltlessly" condemn to death other people's children (par. 10)?

Expository Techniques

1. The central theme of this essay becomes clear more slowly than in most expository writings. (Guide: *Unity.*)
   a. At what point did you first become aware of it?
   b. Where is it first clearly stated?
   c. Is this statement specific or general? (Guide: *Specific/General.*)
   d. What is the primary function of the rest of the essay?

2a. Is the further development accomplished more by comparison or contrast? Explain.
   b. Cite paragraphs by which your answer to 2a can best be illustrated.
   c. Which pattern of exposition previously studied does the author use more freely in her comparison/contrast? How effectively?

3. Which of the standard means of introducing an exposition are used in this essay? (Guide: *Introductions.*)

4a. In paragraphs 6 and 7 can be found examples of both rhetorical and non-rhetorical questions. (Guide: *Rhetorical Question.*) Identify one of each and show the difference.
   b. Cite one further question used as a rhetorical device.

5a. Cite two examples of parallel structure in paragraph 14. (Guide: *Parallel Structure.*)
   b. What advantage, if any, is gained by use of this technique?

6. How effective is the brief closing paragraph? (Guide: *Closings.*) Why?

Diction and Vocabulary

1a. What is the significance of the word "sow," as used in the title?
   b. How, if at all, is this significance a matter of connotation? (Guide: *Connotation/Denotation.*)

2a. Cite five figures of speech that you consider particularly effective. (Guide: *Figures of Speech.*)
   b. Indicate the kind of each.

3a. Which, if any, of the author's figures of speech could also be classed as a cliché. (Guide: *Clichés.*)
   b. If any, is its use justified here? Why, or why not?

4. Would you consider any of the author's expressions colloquial? (Guide: *Colloquial Expressions.*) If so, which?
5. Explain briefly how your answers to questions 2–4 are related to matters of style. (Guide: *Style/Tone.*)
6. Use the dictionary as necessary to understand the meanings of the following words: lexicon (par. 3); empathetic, artifacts (6); flaccid (8); chauvinism (8, 14); canard (9); masochistic (11); coevals, solace (12); vignette, cacophony (14).

Suggestions for Writing and Discussion

1. Show by use of examples that it is also possible in other matters to "believe two contradictory things at once" (par.2).
2. Has it been your observation that girls are less likely than boys to embarrass one in public or lie about such things as grades or sexual prowess (par. 4)? Explain the difference, if any.
3. What justification is there for laws forcing men to pay alimony and/or child support (par. 5)?
4. Is there any *natural* reason that mothers are less apt to desert their children than fathers? In your estimation, is one desertion more reprehensible than the other? Explain.
5. Explore the author's assertion (par. 11) that women are more masochistic than men.
6. If applicable, select any one aspect of Roiphe's "myth" about men-women differences and show why you still consider the difference more fact than myth.

(NOTE: Suggestions for topics requiring development by use of COMPARISON and CONTRAST are on page 124, at the end of this section.)

ALVIN TOFFLER

ALVIN TOFFLER (born 1928), a native of New York City and graduate of New York University, has been a Washington correspondent for various newspapers and magazines. His freelance articles still appear regularly in professional journals and in numerous magazines, most often in *Seventeen* and *Saturday Evening Post.* At one time he was an associate editor of *Fortune.* Toffler has served on the faculty of the New School for Social Research and has lectured at Cornell and other universities. In addition to *Future Shock* (1970), his most famous book, he has written *The Culture Consumers* (1964), and has edited *Schoolhouse in the City* (1968), *The Futurists* (1972), *Learning for Tomorrow* (1974), and *The Eco-Spasm Report: Why Our Economy is Running Out of Control* (1975).

The 800th Lifetime

"The 800th Lifetime," as it appears here, is an excerpt from the introductory section by that title in *Future Shock.* The author builds a sharp contrast between ours and all previous lifetimes, and in so doing shows that results can be devastating to the human psyche.

Western society for the past 300 years has been caught up in a fire storm of change. This storm, far from abating, now appears to be gathering force. Change sweeps through the highly industrialized countries with waves of ever accelerating speed and unprecedented impact. It spawns in its wake all sorts of curious social flora — from psychedelic churches and "free universities" to science cities in the Arctic and wife-swap clubs in California. 1

It breeds odd personalities, too: children who at twelve are no longer childlike; adults who at fifty are children of twelve. There are rich men who playact poverty, computer programmers who turn on with LSD. There are anarchists who, beneath their dirty denim shirts, are outrageous conformists, and conformists who, beneath their button-down collars, are outrageous anarchists. There are married 2 priests and atheist ministers and Jewish Zen Buddhists. We have pop ... and op ... and *art cinétique* ... There are Playboy Clubs and homosexual movie theaters ... amphetamines and tranquilizers ... anger, affluence, and oblivion. Much oblivion.

Is there some way to explain so strange a scene without recourse to the jargon of psychoanalysis or the murky clichés of existentialism? A strange new society is apparently erupting in our midst. Is there a way to understand it, to shape its development? How can we come to terms with it? 3

Much that now strikes us as incomprehensible would be far less so if we took a fresh look at the racing rate of change that makes reality seem, sometimes, like a kaleidoscope run wild. For the acceleration of change does not merely buffet industries or nations. It is a concrete force that reaches deep into our personal lives, compels us to act out new roles, and confronts us with the danger of a new and powerfully upsetting psychological disease. This new disease can be called "future shock," and a knowledge of its sources and symptoms helps explain many things that otherwise defy rational analysis. 4

The parallel term "culture shock" has already begun to creep into the popular vocabulary. Culture shock is the effect that immersion in a strange culture has on the unprepared visitor. Peace Corps volunteers suffer from it in Borneo or Brazil. Marco Polo probably suffered from it in Cathay. Culture shock is what happens when a traveler suddenly finds himself in a place where yes may mean no, where a "fixed price" is negotiable, where to be kept waiting in an outer office is no cause for insult, where laughter may signify anger. It is what happens when the familiar psychological cues that help an individual to function in society are suddenly withdrawn and replaced by new ones that are strange or incomprehensible. 5

The culture shock phenomenon accounts for much of the bewilderment, frustration, and disorientation that plagues Americans in their dealings with other societies. It causes a breakdown in communication, a misreading of reality, an inability to cope. Yet culture shock is relatively mild in comparison with the much more serious malady, future shock. Future shock is the dizzying disorientation brought on by the premature arrival of the future. It may well be the most important disease of tomorrow. 6

Future shock will not be found in *Index Medicus* or in any listing of psychological abnormalities. Yet, unless intelligent steps are taken 7 to combat it, millions of human beings will find themselves increasingly disoriented, progressively incompetent to deal rationally with their environments. The malaise, mass neurosis, irrationality, and free-floating violence already apparent in contemporary life are merely a foretaste of what may lie ahead unless we come to understand and treat this disease.

Future shock is a time phenomenon, a product of the greatly accelerated rate of change in society. It arises from the superimposition of a new culture on an old one. It is culture shock in one's own society. But its impact is far worse. For most Peace Corps men, in fact most travelers, have the conforting knowledge that the culture they left behind will be there to return to. The victim of future shock does not. 8

Take an individual out of his own culture and set him down suddenly in an environment sharply different from his own, with a different set of cues to react to — different conceptions of time, space, work, love, religion, sex, and everything else — then cut him off from any hope of retreat to a more familiar social landscape, and the dislocation he suffers is doubly severe. Moreover, if this new culture is itself in constant turmoil, and if — worse yet — its values are incessantly changing, the sense of disorientation will be still further intensified. Given few clues as to what kind of behavior is rational under the radically new circumstances, the victim may well become a hazard to himself and others. 9

Now imagine not merely an individual but an entire society, an entire generation — including its weakest, least intelligent, and most irrational members — suddenly transported into this new world. The result is mass disorientation, future shock on a grand scale. 10

This is the prospect that man now faces. Change is avalanching upon our heads and most people are grotesquely unprepared to cope with it. 11

Is all this exaggerated? I think not. It has become a cliché to say that what we are now living through is a "second industrial revolution." This phrase is supposed to impress us with the speed and profundity of the change around us. But in addition to being platitudinous, it is misleading. For what is occurring now is, in all likelihood, bigger, deeper, and more important than the industrial revolution. Indeed, a growing body of reputable opinion asserts that the present moment represents nothing less than the second great 12 divide in human history, comparable in magnitude only with that first great break in historic continuity, the shift from barbarism to civilization. . . .

13 One of the most striking statements of this theme has come from Kenneth Boulding, an eminent economist and imaginative social thinker. In justifying this view that the present moment represents a crucial turning point in human history, Boulding observes that "as far as many statistical series related to activities of mankind are concerned, the data that divides human history into two equal parts is well within living memory." In effect, our century represents The Great Median Strip running down the center of human history. Thus he asserts, "The world of today . . . is as different from the world in which I was born as that world was from Julius Caesar's. I was born in the middle of human history, to date, roughly. Almost as much has happened since I was born as happened before."

14 This startling statement can be illustrated in a number of ways. It has been observed, for example, that if the last 50,000 years of man's existence were divided into lifetimes of approximately sixty-two years each, there have been about 800 such lifetimes. Of these 800, fully 650 were spent in caves.

15 Only during the last seventy lifetimes has it been possible to communicate effectively from one lifetime to another — as writing made it possible to do. Only during the last six lifetimes did masses of men ever see a printed word. Only during the last four has it been possible to measure time with any precision. Only in the last two has anyone anywhere used an electric motor. And the overwhelming majority of all the material goods we use in daily life today have been developed within the present, the 800th, lifetime.

16 This 800th lifetime marks a sharp break with all past human experience because during this lifetime man's relationship to resources has reversed itself. This is most evident in the field of economic development. Within a single lifetime, agriculture, the original basis of civilization, has lost its dominance in nation after nation. Today in a dozen major countries agriculture employs fewer than 15 percent of the economically active population. In the United States, whose farms feed 200,000,000 Americans plus the equivalent of another 160,000,000 people around the world, this figure is already below 6 percent and it is still shrinking rapidly.

17 Moreover, if agriculture is the first stage of economic development and industrialism the second, we can now see that still another

stage — the third — has suddenly been reached. In about 1956 the United States became the first major power in which more than 50 percent of the non-farm labor force ceased to wear the blue collar of factory or manual labor. Blue-collar workers were outnumbered by those in the so-called white-collar occupations — in retail trade, administration, communications, research, education, and other service categories. Within the same lifetime a society for the first time in human history not only threw off the yoke of agriculture, but managed within a few brief decades to throw off the yoke of manual labor as well. The world's first service economy had been born.

Since then, one after another of the technologically advanced 18
countries have moved in the same direction. Today, in those nations in which agriculture is down to the 15 percent level or below, white collars already outnumber blue in Sweden, Britain, Belgium, Canada, and the Netherlands. Ten thousand years for agriculture. A century or two for industrialism. And now, opening before us — super-industrialism.

Jean Fourastié, the French planner and social philosopher, has 19
declared that "Nothing will be less industrial than the civilization born of the industrial revolution." The significance of this staggering fact has yet to be digested. Perhaps U Thant, Secretary General of the United Nations, came closest to summarizing the meaning of the shift to super-industrialism when he declared that "The central stupendous truth about developed economies today is that they can have — in anything but the shortest run — the kind and scale of resources they decide to have. . . . It is no longer resources that limit decisions. It is the decision that makes the resources. This is the fundamental revolutionary change — perhaps the most revolutionary man has ever known." This monumental reversal has taken place in the 800th lifetime.

This lifetime is also different from all others because of the 20
astonishing expansion of the scale and scope of change. Clearly, there have been other lifetimes in which epochal upheavals occurred. Wars, plagues, earthquakes, and famine rocked many an earlier social order. But these shocks and upheavals were contained within the borders of one or a group of adjacent societies. It took generations, even centuries, for their impact to spread beyond these borders.

In our lifetime the boundaries have burst. Today the network of 21
social ties is so tightly woven that the consequences of contemporary events radiate instantaneously around the world. A war in Vietnam

alters basic political alignments in Peking, Moscow, and Washington, touches off protests in Stockholm, affects financial transactions in Zurich, triggers secret diplomatic moves in Algiers.

Indeed, not only do *contemporary* events radiate instantaneously 22
— now we can be said to be feeling the impact of all *past* events in a new way. For the past is doubling back on us. We are caught in what might be called a "time skip."

An event that affected only a handful of people at the time of 23
its occurrence in the past can have large-scale consequences today. The Peloponnesian War, for example, was little more than a skirmish by modern standards. While Athens, Sparta and several nearby city-states battled, the population of the rest of the globe remained largely unaware of and undisturbed by the war. The Zapotec Indians living in Mexico at the time were wholly untouched by it. The ancient Japanese felt none of its impact.

Yet the Peloponnesian War deeply altered the future course of 24
Greek history. By changing the movement of men, the geographical distribution of genes, values, and ideas, it affected later events in Rome, and, through Rome, all Europe. Today's Europeans are to some small degree different people because that conflict occurred.

In turn, in the tightly wired world of today, these Europeans 25
influence Mexicans and Japanese alike. Whatever trace of impact the Peloponnesian War left on the genetic structure, the ideas, and the values of today's Europeans is now exported by them to all parts of the world. Thus today's Mexicans and Japanese feel the distant, twice-removed impact of that war even though their ancestors, alive during its occurrence, did not. In this way, the events of the past, skipping as it were over generations and centuries, rise up to haunt and change us today.

When we think not merely of the Peloponnesian War but of the 26
building of the Great Wall of China, the Black Plague, the battle of the Bantu against the Hamites — indeed, of all the events of the past — the cumulative implications of the time-skip principle take on weight. Whatever happened to some men in the past affects virtually all men today. This was not always true. In short, all history is catching up with us, and this very difference, paradoxically, underscores our break with the past. Thus the scope of change is fundamentally altered. Across space and through time, change has a power and reach in this, the 800th lifetime, that it never did before.

But the final, qualitative difference between this and all previous 27 lifetimes is the most easily overlooked. For we have not merely extended the scope and scale of change, we have radically altered its pace. We have in our time released a totally new social force — a stream of change so accelerated that it influences our sense of time, revolutionizes the tempo of daily life, and affects the very way we "feel" the world around us. We no longer "feel" life as men did in the past. And this is the ultimate difference, the distinction that separates the truly contemporary man from all others. For this acceleration lies behind the impermanence — the transience — that penetrates and tinctures our consciousness, radically affecting the way we relate to other people, to things, to the entire universe of ideas, art and values.

To understand what is happening to us as we move into the age of super-industrialism, we must analyze the processes of acceleration and confront the concept of transience. If acceleration is a new social force, transience is its psychological counterpart and without an understanding of the role it plays in contemporary human behavior, all our theories of personality, all our psychology, must remain premodern. Psychology without the concept of transience cannot take account of precisely those phenomena that are peculiarly contemporary. 28

By changing our relationship to the resources that surround us, by violently expanding the scope of change, and, most crucially, by accelerating its pace, we have broken irretrievably with the past. We have cut ourselves off from the old ways of thinking, of feeling, of adapting. We have set the stage for a completely new society and we are now racing toward it. This is the crux of the 800th lifetime. . . . 29

Meanings and Values

1a. Summarize briefly the differences between culture shock and future shock.
  b. Does it seem likely that the potential effects of the latter on society are as severe as the author believes? Why, or why not?
2. Cite examples of "new roles" we may be compelled to act out (par. 4).
3. Why may the phrase "second industrial revolution" be both "platitudinous" and "misleading" (par. 12)?
4a. How is it possible for advanced economies to have the "kind and scale of resources they decide to have" (par. 19)?
  b. Is this statement a paradox? (See Guide to Terms: *Paradox*.) Why?

5. Is Toffler justified in referring to the fourth sentence of paragraph 26 as paradoxical?
6. Explain why it may be true, or may not be, that we no longer "feel" life as people did in the past (par. 27).
7. Explain in your own way the "concept of transience" (par. 28). How is it the "psychological counterpart" of acceleration?

Expository Techniques

1a. In the first major comparative analysis of this piece, why do you suppose Toffler devoted nearly two paragraphs to culture shock before taking up future shock, his primary concern?
b. Is the analysis devoted more to comparison or to contrast? Explain.

2a. What is contrasted in paragraph 12?
b. Why is it important to dispose of this contrast before continuing the discussion?

3a. Beginning with paragraph 16, list the various ways in which the "800th lifetime" differs from all that have gone before.
b. Cite the paragraphs in which each contrast is made.
c. Is this a convincing comparative analysis? Why, or why not?

4a. What do you think governed the selection of details in paragraphs 1 and 2?
b. Are these examples? If so, what do they illustrate?
c. What is the effect of the two-word sentence ending paragraph 2?

5a. What is the purpose of the series of statements in paragraph 14 and 15?
b. What is the advantage of the particular order in which they are presented?
c. What is gained by presenting them in parallel structure? (Guide: *Parallel Structure.*)

6a. Why do you think Toffler chose to use the quotation from Kenneth Boulding (par. 13)?
b. Does it matter greatly whether or not you ever heard of him? Why, or why not?

Diction and Vocabulary

1a. Cite three good figures of speech in paragraphs 1 and 4, and identify as to kind. (Guide: *Figures of Speech.*)
b. Does the use of figurative language seem to be an important characteristic of Toffler's style? (Guide: *Style/Tone.*)

2. Use one or more of the details in paragraph 2 to demonstrate the meaning of "paradox." (Guide: *Paradox.*)

3. If not already familiar with the following words as they are used in this selection, consult your dictionary for their meanings: affluence (par. 2); jargon, murky, existentialism (3); kaleidoscope, buffet (4); malaise, neurosis (7); profundity, platitudinous (12); epochal (20); tinctures (27); crux (29).

Suggestions for Writing and Discussion

1. Have you ever been a victim of culture shock? Is so, relate your experience.
2. Do you sometimes have the feeling that you may be afflicted with future shock? If not, do you then conclude that Toffler exaggerates the threat — or do you think the real effects are yet to come, as the acceleration of events grows more and more pronounced?
3. Do you also see the peculiar examples of paragraphs 1 and 2 as evidence that a "strange new society" is erupting in our midst (par. 3) — or does it seem more likely they are merely indicative of a normal wave of change?
4. Discuss the possibility that the perpetrators of today's "free-floating violence" (par. 7) may themselves be early victims of future shock.
5. What do you think is the most noticeable result of having fewer people engaged in agriculture? Show how this result itself contributes to future shock for large numbers of people.
6. What, if anything, can the individual or individual family do to minimize the effects of future shock?

Writing Suggestions for Section 3

Comparison and Contrast

Base your central theme on one of the following, and develop your composition primarily by use of comparison and/or contrast. Use examples liberally for clarity and concreteness, chosen always with your purpose and reader-audience in mind.

1. Two kinds of home life.
2. The sea at two different times.
3. The innate qualifications needed for success in two careers.
4. The natural temperaments of two acquaintances.
5. Two poets.
6. The teaching techniques of two instructors or former teachers.
7. Two methods of parental handling of teenage problems.
8. Two family attitudes toward the practice of religion.
9. Two "moods" of the same town at different times.
10. The personalities (or atmospheres) of two cities or towns of similar size.
11. Two acquaintances who exemplify different ways of serving humanity.
12. Two acquaintances who seem to symbolize different philosophies of life.
13. Two different attitudes toward the same thing or activity: one "practical," the other romantic or aesthetic.
14. The beliefs and practices of two religions or denominations concerning *one* aspect of religion.
15. Two courses on the same subject: one in high school and one in college.
16. The differing styles of two players of some sport or game.
17. The hazards of frontier life and those of today.
18. The views of two recent presidents concerning the trappings of high office.

4

Using *Analogy* as an Expository Device

Analogy is a special form of comparison that is used for a specific purpose: to explain something abstract or difficult to understand by showing its similarity to something concrete or easy to understand. A much less commonly used technique than logical comparison (and contrast), analogy is, nonetheless, a highly efficient means of explaining some difficult concepts or of giving added force to the explanations.

Logical comparison is made between two members of the same general class, usually assuming the same kind of interest in the subject matter of both. But in analogy we are really concerned only with the subject matter of one, using a second just to help explain the first. The two subjects, quite incomparable in most respects, are never of the same general class; if they are, we then have logical comparison, not analogy.

If the analogy is to be effective, the writer should be able to assume that his reader is familiar enough with the easier subject, or can quickly be made so, that it really helps explain the more difficult one. A common example is the explanation of the human circulatory system, which we may have trouble comprehending, by comparing the heart and arteries with a pump forcing water through the pipes of a plumbing system. This analogy has been carried further to liken the effect of cholesterol deposits on the inner walls of the arteries to mineral deposits that accumulate inside water pipes and eventually close them entirely. Although there is little logical similarity between a steel pipe and a human artery, the *analogical* similarity would be apparent to most readers — but the analogy might cause even greater confusion for any who did not know about pumps.

Distinguishing between analogy and metaphor is sometimes difficult. The difference is basically in their purpose: the function of a metaphor is merely *to describe,* to create a brief, vivid image for the reader; the function of analogy is primarily one of exposition, *to explain,* rather than to describe. In this sense, however, the function of a metaphor is actually *to suggest* an analogy: instead of showing the similarities of the heart and the pump, a metaphor might simply refer to "that faithful pump inside my chest," implying enough of a comparison to serve its purpose as description. (We can see here why some people refer to analogy as "extended" metaphor.) The analogist, when trying to explain the wide selection of college subjects and the need for balance in a course of study, could use the easily understood principle of a cafeteria, which serves Jell-o and lemon meringue pie, as well as meat and potatoes. If his purpose had been only to create an image, to describe, he might have referred simply to the bewildering variety in "the cafeteria of college courses" — and that would have been a metaphor.

Sometimes related metaphors, however, through continued use to explain an abstract concept, can in effect work together to *build* a kind of analogy. You may already have seen this process at work in Donald Hall's "*Four Kinds of Reading*" (Sec. 2), in his explanation of the fourth type of reading. (For still another example of the more conventional type of analogy, see the explanation of *Unity,* in Guide to Terms.)

But as useful as analogy can be in exposition, it is a risky technique to use in logical argument. It should never be offered anywhere as *proof.* The two subjects of any analogy, although similar in one or more ways useful for illustration, are basically too unlike for any reliable conclusions to be drawn from their similarity.

MARTIN LUTHER KING, JR.

MARTIN LUTHER KING JR. (1929–1968) was a Baptist clergyman, the president of the Southern Christian Leadership Conference, and a respected leader in the nationwide movement toward equal rights for Negroes. He was born in Atlanta, Georgia, and earned degrees from Morehouse College (A. B., 1948), Crozer Theological Seminary (B. D., 1951), Boston University (Ph.D., 1955), and Chicago Theological Seminary (D. D., 1957). He held honorary degrees from numerous other colleges and universities and was awarded the Nobel Peace Prize in 1964. Some of his books are *Why We Can't Wait* (1964), *Stride Toward Freedom* (1958), and *Strength to Love* (1963). King was assassinated April 4, 1968, in Memphis, Tennessee.

The World House

"The World House" is from King's book *Where Do We Go from Here: Chaos or Community?,* published in 1967. His theme, the absolute necessity for international understanding and cooperation throughout the world, is recognized by most people today but ignored by them as much as possible, perhaps because it seems to present such insoluble problems. We can assume, therefore, that King uses analogy more for emphasis than for primary explanation. It serves his purpose well.

Some years ago a famous novelist died. Among his papers was found 1
a list of suggested plots for future stories, the most prominently underscored being this one: "A widely separated family inherits a house in which they have to live together." This is the great new problem of mankind. We have inherited a large house, a great "world house" in which we have to live together — black and white, Easterner and Westerner, Gentile and Jew, Catholic and Protestant, Moslem and Hindu — a family unduly separated in ideas, culture and

interest, who, because we can never again live apart, must learn somehow to live with each other in peace.

However deeply American Negroes are caught in the struggle to 2
be at last at home in our homeland of the United States, we cannot ignore the larger world house in which we are also dwellers. Equality with whites will not solve the problems of either whites or Negroes if it means equality in a world society stricken by poverty and in a universe doomed to extinction by war.

All inhabitants of the globe are now neighbors. This world-wide 3
neighborhood has been brought into being largely as a result of the modern scientific and technological revolutions. The world of today is vastly different from the world of just one hundred years ago. A century ago Thomas Edison had not yet invented the incandescent lamp to bring light to many dark places of the earth. The Wright brothers had not yet invented that fascinating mechanical bird that would spread its gigantic wings across the skies and soon dwarf distance and place time in the service of man. Einstein had not yet challenged an axiom and the theory of relatively had not yet been posited.

Human beings, searching a century ago as now for better under- 4
standing, had no television, no radios, no telephones and no motion pictures through which to communicate. Medical science had not yet discovered the wonder drugs to end many dread plagues and diseases. One hundred years ago military men had not yet developed the terrifying weapons of warfare that we know today — not the bomber, an airborne fortress raining down death; nor napalm, that burner of all things and flesh in its path. A century ago there were no skyscraping buildings to kiss the stars and no gargantuan bridges to span the waters. Science had not yet peered into the unfathomable ranges of interstellar space, nor had it penetrated oceanic depths. All these new inventions, these new ideas, these sometimes fascinating and sometimes frightening developments came later. Most of them have come within the past sixty years, sometimes with agonizing slowness, more characteristically with bewildering speed, but always with enormous significance for our future.

The years ahead will see a continuation of the same dramatic 5
developments. Physical science will carve new highways through the stratosphere. In a few years astronauts and cosmonauts will probably walk comfortably across the uncertain pathways of the moon. In two or three years it will be possible, because of the new supersonic jets,

to fly from New York to London in two and one-half hours. In the years ahead medical science will greatly prolong the lives of men by finding a cure for cancer and deadly heart ailments. Automation and cybernation will make it possible for working people to have undreamed-of amounts of leisure time. All this is a dazzling picture of the furniture, the workshop, the spacious rooms, the new decorations and the architectural pattern of the large world house in which we are living.

Along with the scientific and technological revolution, we have also witnessed a world-wide freedom revolution over the last few decades. The present upsurge of the Negro people of the United States grows out of a deep and passionate determination to make freedom and equality a reality "here" and "now." In one sense the civil rights movement in the United States is a special American phenomenon which must be understood in the light of American history and dealt with in terms of the American situation. But on another and more important level, what is happening in the United States today is a significant part of a world development. 6

We live in a day, said the philosopher Alfred North Whitehead, "when civilization is shifting its basic outlook; a major turning point in history where the pre-suppositions on which society is structured are being analyzed, sharply challenged, and profoundly changed." What we are seeing now is a freedom explosion, the realization of "an idea whose time has come," to use Victor Hugo's phrase. The deep rumbling of discontent that we hear today is the thunder of disinherited masses, rising from dungeons of oppression to the bright hills of freedom. In one majestic chorus the rising masses are singing, in the words of our freedom song, "Ain't gonna let nobody turn us around." All over the world like a fever, freedom is spreading in the widest liberation movement in history. The great masses of people are determined to end the exploitation of their races and lands. They are awake and moving toward their goal like a tidal wave. You can hear them rumbling in every village street, on the docks, in the houses, among the students, in the churches and at political meetings. For several centuries the direction of history flowed from the nations and societies of Western Europe out into the rest of the world in "conquests" of various sorts. That period, the era of colonialism, is at an end. East is moving West. The earth is being redistributed. Yes, we are "shifting our basic outlooks." 7

These developments should not surprise any student of history. 8

Oppressed people cannot remain oppressed forever. The yearning for freedom eventually manifests itself. The Bible tells the thrilling story of how Moses stood in Pharaoh's court centuries ago and cried, "Let my people go." This was an opening chapter in a continuing story. The present struggle in the United States is a later chapter in the same story. Something within has reminded the Negro of his birthright of freedom, and something without has reminded him that it can be gained. Consciously or unconsciously, he has been caught up by the spirit of the times, and with his black brothers of Africa and his brown and yellow brothers in Asia, South America and the Caribbean, the United States Negro is moving with a sense of great urgency toward the promised land of racial justice.

Nothing could be more tragic than for men to live in these 9
revolutionary times and fail to achieve the new attitudes and the new mental outlooks that the new situation demands. In Washington Irving's familiar story of Rip Van Winkle, the one thing that we usually remember is that Rip slept twenty years. There is another important point, however, that is almost always overlooked. It was the sign on the inn in the little town on the Hudson from which Rip departed and scaled the mountain for his long sleep. When he went up, the sign had a picture of King George III of England. When he came down, twenty years later, the sign had a picture of George Washington. As he looked at the picture of the first President of the United States, Rip was confused, flustered and lost. He knew not who Washington was. The most striking thing about this story is not that Rip slept twenty years, but that he slept through a revolution that would alter the course of human history.

One of the great liabilities of history is that all too many people 10
fail to remain awake through great periods of social change. Every society has its protectors of the status quo and its fraternities of the indifferent who are notorious for sleeping through revolutions. But today our very survival depends on our ability to stay awake, to adjust to new ideas, to remain vigilant and to face the challenge of change. The large house in which we live demands that we transform this world-wide neighborhood into a world-wide brotherhood. Together we must learn to live as brothers or together we will be forced to perish as fools.

We must work passionately and indefatigably to bridge the gulf 11
between our scientific progress and our moral progress. One of the great problems of mankind is that we suffer from a poverty of the

spirit which stands in glaring contrast to our scientific and technological abundance. The richer we have become materially, the poorer we have become morally and spiritually.

Every man lives in two realms, the internal and the external. The 12
internal is that realm of spiritual ends expressed in art, literature, morals and religion. The external is that complex of devices, techniques, mechanisms and instrumentalities by means of which we live. Our problem today is that we have allowed the internal to become lost in the external. We have allowed the means by which we live to outdistance the ends for which we live. So much of modern life can be summarized in that suggestive phrase of Thoreau: "Improved means to an unimproved end." This is the serious predicament, the deep and haunting problem, confronting modern man. Enlarged material powers spell enlarged peril if there is not proportionate growth of the soul. When the external of man's nature subjugates the internal, dark storm clouds begin to form.

Western civilization is particularly vulnerable at this moment, 13
for our material abundance has brought us neither peace of mind nor serenity of spirit. An Asian writer has portrayed our dilemma in candid terms:

> You call your thousand material devices "labor-saving machinery," yet you are forever "busy." With the multiplying of your machinery you grow increasingly fatigued, anxious, nervous, dissatisfied. Whatever you have, you want more; and wherever you are you want to go somewhere else . . . your devices are neither time-saving nor soul-saving machinery. They are so many sharp spurs which urge you on to invent more machinery and to do more business.[1]

This tells us something about our civilization that cannot be cast 14
aside as a prejudiced charge by an Eastern thinker who is jealous of Western prosperity. We cannot escape the indictment.

This does not mean that we must turn back the clock of scientific 15
progress. No one can overlook the wonders that science has wrought for our lives. The automobile will not abdicate in favor of the horse and buggy, or the train in favor of the stagecoach, or the tractor in favor of the hand plow, or the scientific method in favor of ignorance and superstition. But our moral and spirtual "lag" must be redeemed. When scientific power outruns moral power, we end up with guided

[1]Abraham Mitrie Rihbany, *Wise Men from the East and from the West,* Houghton Mifflin, 1922.

missiles and misguided men. When we foolishly minimize the internal of our lives and maximize the external, we sign the warrant for our own day of doom.

Our hope for creative living in this world house that we have inherited lies in our ability to re-establish the moral ends of our lives in personal character and social justice. Without this spiritual and moral reawakening we shall destroy ourselves in the misuse of our own instruments. 16

Meanings and Values

1a. What are the "pre-suppositions" on which society has been structured (par. 7)?
b. What were the "various sorts" of "conquests" which came out of Western Europe (par. 7)?
2. Does it seem to you that the author overgeneralizes in his apparent assumption (pars. 7, 8) that all the world's "rumbling of discontent" is directed toward Western "oppression" of those who are not white? Explain.
3. List at least five of the intervening "chapters" (between the first and the present chapters) of the "continuing story" discussed in paragraph 8.
4. How do you explain the author's reference to "an unimproved end" (par. 12), in view of the many billions of dollars Americans have deliberately taxed themselves during recent years, in order to aid underdeveloped countries all over the world?
5a. Judging from what you see and read, do you agree with Rihbany (par. 13) that Americans are "increasingly fatigued, anxious, nervous, dissatisfied"?
b. Illustrate the meaning of "irony" by using this quotation. (See Guide to Terms: *Irony.*)
6. Use the three-point system of evaluation to measure the success of "The World House." (Guide: *Evaluation.*)

Expository Techniques

1a. Is King's primary analogy well chosen for the job it has to do? Explain.
b. In what sense does the analogy also serve as a "frame" for the essay?
c. Could it have been used effectively to greater extent in explaining the world situation? Justify your answer.
d. Does the author's use of the metaphor "neighborhood" (pars 3, 10), seem consistent with his analogy of a "house"? Explain.

2. Show precisely how the story of Rip Van Winkle also qualifies as an analogy.
3. Cite the paragraphs where illustration by example is an important means of clarification.
4. Of what value, if any, is King's frequent use of direct quotations?
5. What is gained by the author's consistent use of "we" instead of "you" in his various charges, when obviously some of them do not apply to himself?
6. King wrote (as he spoke) to communicate with all kinds of people, including the semiliterate. The fact no doubt accounts for his use of the uncomplicated analogy to give added force, if not added clarity, to his remarks. List the other ways that the nature of his reader-audience apparently influenced this writing. Illustrate with examples from the essay.

7a. Which of the standard techniques for introducing exposition does the author use in the first paragraph? (Guide: *Introductions.*)
 b. How effective is this introduction?

8a. Which of the standard techniques for closing exposition does the author use in the last paragraph? (Guide: *Closing.*)
 b. How effective is this closing?

Diction and Vocabulary

1. King makes liberal use of figures of speech in this essay. (Guide: *Figures of Speech.*)
 a. Within a small part of paragraph 4, you can find three different kinds. What are they?
 b. List or mark the most effective figure of speech in each of the following paragraphs, and identify the type of each: 5, 7, 8, 11–13.

2a. Although King was a well-educated and articulate man, there are few words in any of his public writings (or addresses) that necessitate use of a dictionary. How do you account for this fact?
 b. However, if you are not sure of the following, consult your dictionary: cybernation (par. 5); manifests (8); subjugates (12); vulnerable, indictment (13).

Suggestions for Writing and Discussion

1. Explain how "spiritual ends" (par. 12) may be expressed in art, using examples to clarify your explanation.
2. Select any one of Rihbany's sentences (par. 13) to be your central theme, and change the "you" to "we" and the "your" to "our".

Develop by use of examples and/or by use of comparison and contrast.

3. Projecting King's primary analogy, show the diversity of the "family" by developing a classification system to encompass all the "relatives" trying to live together in the world house. Give examples of countries or peoples that fit into each of the "relative" categories.
4. Projecting King's primary analogy, explain a practical idea for handling the domineering "relative" who is peaceful only as long as he can impose his preferences on others.
5. Explore the possible ways in which an ordinary citizen, having little talent or time, could still help "family" relationships in the new world house. From your findings compose a specific statement of theme and base your writing or discussion on it.

(NOTE: Suggestions for topics requiring development by use of ANALOGY are on page 152, at the end of this section.)

JAMES RETTIE

JAMES RETTIE was an employee of the National Forest Service's experimental station at Upper Darby, Pennsylvania in 1948 when he adapted this fable from a United States Department of Agriculture pamphlet entitled "To Hold This Soil." At the time, he was a member of The Society of the Friends of the Land and an ardent conservationist.

But a Watch in the Night

"But a Watch in the Night"[1] is a highly innovative analogy and serves to illustrate, among other things, the extreme versatility of this pattern of exposition. The analogy itself (a "scientific fable," as the author has called it) is composed almost entirely of narration (a pattern to be studied further in Section 9). While Rettie has taken numerous creative liberties not often available to the student in ordinary college writing, he apparently was very much aware of the same goal we all need to keep in mind when writing: the desired effect, for *his* purposes, on *his* reader-audience.

Out beyond our solar system there is a planet called Copernicus. It 1
came into existence some four or five billion years before the birth of our Earth. In due course of time it became inhabited by a race of intelligent men.

[1]From the Bible, Psalm 90, apparently either slightly altered or using a translation other than the King James version, which reads:

Lord, thou hast been our dwelling place
In all generations.
Before the mountains were brought forth,
Or ever thou hadst formed the earth and the world,
Even from everlasting to everlasting, thou art God.
Thou turnest man to destruction;
And sayest, "Return, ye children of men."
For a thousand years in thy sight
Are but as yesterday when it is past,
And as a watch in the night. . . .

About 750 million years ago the Copernicans had developed the motion picture machine to a point well in advance of the stage that we have reached. Most of the cameras that we now use in motion picture work are geared to take twenty-four pictures per second on a continuous strip of film. When such film is run through a projector, it throws a series of images on the screen and these change with a rapidity that gives the visual impression of normal movement. If a motion is too swift for the human eye to see it in detail, it can be captured and artificially slowed down by means of the slow-motion camera. This one is geared to take many more shots per second — ninety-six or even more than that. When the slow-motion film is projected at the normal speed of twenty-four pictures per second, we can see just how the jumping horse goes over a hurdle. 2

What about motion that is too slow to be seen by the human eye? That problem has been solved by the use of the time-lapse camera. In this one, the shutter is geared to take only one shot per second, or one per minute, or even one per hour — depending upon the kind of movement that is being photographed. When the time-lapse film is projected at the normal speed of twenty-four pic-tures per second, it is possible to see a bean sprout growing up out of the ground. Time-lapse films are useful in the study of many types of motion too slow to be observed by the unaided, human eye. 3

The Copernicans, it seems, had time-lapse cameras some 757 million years ago and they also had superpowered telescopes that gave them a clear view of what was happening upon this Earth. They decided to make a film record of the life history of Earth and to make it on the scale of one picture per year. The photography has been in progress during the last 757 years. 4

In the near future, a Copernican interstellar expedition will arrive upon our Earth and bring with it a copy of the time-lapse film. Arrangements will be made for showing the entire film in one continuous run. This will begin at midnight of New Year's eve and continue day and night without a single stop until midnight of December 31. The rate of projection will be twenty-four pictures per second. Time on the screen will thus seem to move at the rate of twenty-four years per second; 1,440 years per minute; 86,400 years per hour; approximately two million years per day; and 62 million years per month. The normal life-span of individual man will occupy about three seconds. The full period of Earth history that will be unfolded on the screen (some 757 million years) will extend from what the geologists 5 call Pre-Cambrian times up to the present. This will, by no means, cover the full time-span of the Earth's geological history but it will embrace the period since the advent of living organisms.

During the months of January, February and March the picture 6
will be desolate and dreary. The shape of the land masses and the oceans will bear little or no resemblance to those that we know. The violence of geological erosion will be much in evidence. Rains will pour down on the land and promptly go booming down to the seas. There will be no clear streams anywhere except where the rains fall upon hard rock. Everywhere on the steeper ground the stream channels will be filled with boulders hurled down by rushing waters. Raging torrents and dry stream beds will keep alternating in quick succession. High mountains will seem to melt like so much butter in the sun. The shifting of land into the seas, later to be thrust up as new mountains, will be going on at a grand scale.

Early in April there will be some indication of the presence of 7
single-celled living organisms in some of the warmer and sheltered coastal waters. By the end of the month it will be noticed that some of these organisms have become multicellular. A few of them, including the Trilobites, will be encased in hard shells.

Toward the end of May, the first vertebrates will appear, but 8
they will still be aquatic creatures. In June about 60 percent of the land area that we know as North America will be under water. One broad channel will occupy the space where the Rocky Mountains now stand. Great deposits of limestone will be forming under some of the shallower seas. Oil and gas deposits will be in process of formation — also under shallow seas. On land there will still be no sign of vegetation. Erosion will be rampant, tearing loose particles and chunks of rock and grinding them into sand and silt to be spewed out by the streams into bays and estuaries.

About the middle of July the first land plants will appear and 9
take up the tremendous job of soil building. Slowly, very slowly, the mat of vegetation will spread, always battling for its life against the power of erosion. Almost foot by foot, the plant life will advance, lacing down with its root structures whatever pulverized rock material it can find. Leaves and stems will be giving added protection against the loss of the soil foothold. The increasing vegetation will pave the way for the land animals that will live upon it.

Early in August the seas will be teeming with fish. This will be 10
what geologists call the Devonian period. Some of the races of these

fish will be breathing by means of lung tissue instead of through gill tissues. Before the month is over, some of the lung fish will go ashore and take on a crude lizard-like appearance. Here are the first amphibians.

In early September the insects will put in their appearance. Some will look like huge dragon flies and will have a wingspread of 24 inches. Large portions of the land masses will now be covered with heavy vegetation that will include the primitive spore-propagating trees. Layer upon layer of this plant growth will build up, later to appear as the coal deposits. About the middle of this month, there will be evidence of the first seed-bearing plants and the first reptiles. Heretofore, the land animals will have been amphibians that could reproduce their kind only by depositing a soft egg mass in quiet waters. The reptiles will be shown to be freed from the aquatic bond because they can reproduce by means of a shelled egg in which the embryo and its nurturing liquids are sealed in and thus protected from destructive evaporation. Before September is over, the first dinosaurs will be seen — creatures destined to dominate the animal realm for about 140 million years and then to disappear. 11

In October there will be series of mountain uplifts along what is now the eastern coast of the United States. A creature with feathered limbs — half bird and half reptile in appearance — will take itself into the air. Some small and rather unpretentious animals will be seen to bring forth their young in a form that is a miniature replica of the parents and to feed these young on milk secreted by mammary glands in the female parent. The emergence of this mammalian form of animal life will be recognized as one of the great events in geologic time. October will also witness the high water mark of the dinosaurs — creatures ranging in size from that of the modern goat to monsters like Brontosaurus that weighed some 40 tons. Most of them will be placid vegetarians, but a few will be hideous-looking carnivores, like Allosaurus and Tyrannosaurus. Some of the herbivorous dinosaurs will be clad in bony armor for protection against their flesh-eating comrades. 12

November will bring pictures of a sea extending from the Gulf of Mexico to the Arctic in space now occupied by the Rocky Mountains. A few of the reptiles will take to the air on bat-like wings. One of these, called Pteranodon, will have a wingspread of 15 feet. There will be a rapid development of the modern flowering plants, modern trees, and modern insects. The dinosaurs will disappear. Toward the 13 end of the month there will be a tremendous land disturbance in which the Rocky Mountains will rise out of the sea to assume a dominating place in the North American landscape.

As the picture runs on into December it will show the mammals 14
in command of the animal life. Seed-bearing trees and grasses will have covered most of the land with a heavy mantle of vegetation. Only the areas newly thrust up from the sea will be barren. Most of the streams will be crystal clear. The turmoil of geologic erosion will be confined to localized areas. About December 25 will begin the cutting of the Grand Canyon of the Colorado River. Grinding down through layer after layer of sedimentary strata, this stream will finally expose deposits laid down in Pre-Cambrian times. Thus in the walls of that canyon will appear geological formations dating from recent times to the period when the earth had no living organisms upon it.

The picture will run on through the latter days of December and 15
even up to its final day with still no sign of mankind. The spectators will become alarmed in the fear that man has somehow been left out. But not so; sometime about noon on December 31 (one million years ago) will appear a stooped, massive creature of man-like proportions. This will be Pithecanthropus, the Java ape man. For tools and weapons he will have nothing but crude stone and wooden clubs. His children will live a precarious existence threatened on the one side by hostile animals and on the other by tremendous climatic changes. Ice sheets — in places 4000 feet deep — will form in the northern parts of North America and Eurasia. Four times this glacial ice will push southward to cover half the continents. With each advance the plant and animal life will be swept under or pushed southward. With each recession of the ice, life will struggle to reestablish itself in the wake of the retreating glaciers. The wooly mammoth, the musk ox, and the caribou all will fight to maintain themselves near the ice line. Sometimes they will be caught and put into cold storage — skin, flesh, blood, bones and all.

The picture will run on through supper time with still very little 16
evidence of man's presence on the Earth. It will be about 11 o'clock when Neanderthal man appears. Another half hour will go by before the appearance of Cro-Magnon man living in caves and painting crude animal pictures on the walls of his dwelling. Fifteen minutes more will bring Neolithic man, knowing how to chip stone and thus produce sharp cutting edges for spears and tools. In a few minutes

more it will appear that man has domesticated the dog, the sheep and, possibly, other animals. He will then begin the use of milk. He will also learn the arts of basket weaving and the making of pottery and dugout canoes.

The dawn of civilization will not come until about five or six minutes before the end of the picture. The story of the Egyptians, the Babylonians, the Greeks, and the Romans will unroll during the fourth, the third and the second minute before the end. At 58 minutes and 43 seconds past 11:00 P.M. (just 1 minute and 17 seconds before the end) will come the beginning of the Christian era. Columbus will discover the new world 20 seconds before the end. The Declaration of Independence will be signed just 7 seconds before the final curtain comes down. 17

In those few moments of geologic time will be the story of all that has happened since we became a nation. And what a story it will be! A human swarm will sweep across the face of the continent and take it away from the . . . red men. They will change it far more radically than it has ever been changed before in a comparable time. The great virgin forests will be seen going down before ax and fire. The soil, covered for aeons by its protective mantle of trees and grasses, will be laid bare to the ravages of water and wind erosion. Streams that had been flowing clear will, once again, take up a load of silt and push it toward the seas. Humus and mineral salts, both vital elements of productive soil, will be seen to vanish at a terrifying rate. The railroads and highways and cities that will spring up may divert attention, but they cannot cover up the blight of man's recent activities. In great sections of Asia, it will be seen that man must utilize cow dung and every scrap of available straw or grass for fuel to cook his food. The forests that once provided wood for this purpose will be gone without a trace. The use of these agricultural wastes for fuel, in place of returning them to the land, will be leading to increasing soil impoverishment. Here and there will be seen a dust storm darkening the landscape over an area a thousand miles across. Man-creatures will be shown counting their wealth in terms of bits of printed paper representing other bits of a scarce but comparatively useless yellow metal that is kept buried in strong vaults. Meanwhile, the soil, the only real wealth that can keep mankind alive on the face of this Earth is savagely being cut loose from its ancient moorings and washed into the seven seas. 18

We have just arrived upon this Earth. How long will we stay? 19

Meanings and Values

1a. What is the significance of the quotation, as it is used in the title of this essay?
b. Is the title itself an allusion? Why, or why not? (See Guide to Terms: *Figures of Speech.*)
c. Explain why you personally do, or do not, like the title.

2a. What do you find ironical in the latter part of paragraph 18? (Guide: *Irony.*)
b. What kind of irony is it?

3a. Compare the effectiveness of Rettie's unique handling of the soil-loss problem with the methods commonly used for environmental propaganda.
b. Could he have enlarged it effectively to include other environmental problems? Why, or why not?

Expository Techniques

1a. In what respects does "But a Watch in the Night" qualify as analogy?
b. Why could the author not have achieved his purpose as well by showing us more simply, in actual year-spans, the brevity of human existence on earth, rather than by this condensed movie version?

2a. The author devotes five paragraphs just to setting up his analogy. In what way, or ways, might this slow beginning be justified?
b. Does the analogy benefit by such a detailed explanation of the camera's capabilities? How, or why not?
c. Why do you suppose Rettie created a fictional planet?
d. Should he have told us at some point that the whole thing is make-believe? Why, or why not?

3a. Why do you think the author took the trouble to work out the rate of projection to fit exactly into one year?
b. What is gained, or lost, by learning as early as paragraph 5 that the normal life span of individual man would occupy only about three seconds?

4a. What did you believe at first to be the central theme? (Guide: *Unity.*)
b. How did your impression of the theme become modified in paragraph 5?
c. In view of the overall essay, state what you now believe to have been the author's theme.
d. Does the composition have unity — i.e., do all parts serve as tributaries, however indirect, into the central theme?

5a. Explain fully, in terms of "emphasis," why this slow unfolding of real theme helps, or hinders, in achieving the author's apparent purpose. (Guide: *Emphasis.*)

b. This is a more "creative" piece than most expositions. Why would such a slow unfolding be inappropriate to most college and workaday writing?

6. What advantage is gained, if any, by the parallel beginnings of most paragraphs? (Guide: *Parallel Structures.*)

7a. What criteria did Rettie apparently use in selecting, from among thousands, the details to be included in the various time periods?

b. Would it have been better to use some other criteria? Why, or why not?

8a. A rhetorical question is used here in a highly strategic position. Where is it? (Guide: *Rhetorical Questions.*)

b. How effective is its use?

Diction and Vocabulary

1a. The naming of the planet makes use, rather indirectly, of an allusion. To what does it refer? (Guide: *Figures of Speech.*)

b. Why is it appropriate, or inappropriate, for this piece?

2a. What kind of figure of speech do you find in paragraph 6?

b. In paragraph 17 is a figure of speech that is also a cliché. What is it? (Guide: *Figures of Speech, Cliché.*)

c. What kind of figure of speech is it?

d. Why is it also classifiable as a cliché?

Suggestions for Writing and Discussion

1. What practical steps could be taken now to prevent the rest of our "only real wealth" from being washed into the sea? What are the chances of such steps being taken seriously enough, soon enough?

2. Assuming that our food-production technology continues to advance rapidly, is it conceivable that mankind might manage to survive without much soil? Discuss this possibility.

3. If you are particularly interested in the Bible, for either literary or religious reasons, discuss more fully the meanings of the part of Psalm 90 quoted in the introduction. If you like, you may enlarge your discussion to include the entire psalm.

(NOTE: Suggestions for topics requiring development by use of ANALOGY are on page 152, at the end of this section.)

TOM WOLFE

TOM WOLFE was born in 1931 and grew up in Richmond, Virginia, was graduated from Washington and Lee University, and took his doctorate at Yale. After working for several years as a reporter for *The Washington Post,* he joined the staff of the New York *Herald Tribune* in 1962. He has won two Washington Newspaper Guild Awards, one for humor and the other for foreign news. Wolfe has been a regular contributor to *New York, Esquire,* and other magazines. His books include *The Kandy-Kolored Tangerine-Flake Streamline Baby* (1965), *The Electric Kool-Aid Acid Test* (1968), *Radical Chic and Mau-mauing the Flak Catchers* (1970), *The New Journalism* (1973), *The Painted Word* (1975), and *The Right Stuff* (1977).

O Rotten Gotham — Sliding Down into the Behavioral Sink

"O Rotten Gotham — Sliding Down into the Behavioral Sink," as used here, is excerpted from a longer selection by that title in Wolfe's book *The Pump House Gang* (1968). Here, as he frequently does, the author investigates an important aspect of modern life — seriously, but in his characteristic and seemingly freewheeling style. It is a style that is sometimes ridiculed by scholars but is far more often admired. (Wolfe, as the serious student can discover for himself, is always in complete control of his materials and methods, using them to create certain effects, to reinforce his ideas.) In this piece his analogy is particularly noteworthy for the extensive usage he is able to get from it.

I just spent two days with Edward T. Hall, an anthropologist, watching thousands of my fellow New Yorkers short-circuiting themselves into hot little twitching death balls with jolts of their own adrenalin. Dr. Hall says it is overcrowding that does it. Overcrowding gets the adrenalin going, and the adrenalin gets them queer, autistic, sadistic, 1 barren, batty, sloppy, hot-in-the-pants, chancred-on-the-flankers, leering, puling, numb — the usual in New York, in other words, and God knows what else. Dr. Hall has the theory that overcrowding has already thrown New York into a state of behavioral sink. Behavioral sink is a term from ethology, which is the study of how animals relate to their environment. Among animals, the sink winds up with a "population collapse" or "massive die-off." O rotten Gotham.

2 It got to be easy to look at New Yorkers as animals, especially looking down from some place like a balcony at Grand Central at the rush hour Friday afternoon. The floor was filled with the poor white humans, running around, dodging, blinking their eyes, making a sound like a pen full of starlings or rats or something.

3 "Listen to them skid," says Dr. Hall.

4 He was right. The poor old etiolate animals were out there skidding on their rubber soles. You could hear it once he pointed it out. They stop short to keep from hitting somebody or because they are disoriented and they suddenly stop and look around, and they skid on their rubber-soled shoes, and a screech goes up. They pour out onto the floor down the escalators from the Pan-Am Building, from 42nd Street, from Lexington Avenue, up out of subways, down into subways, railroad trains, up into helicopters —

5 "You can also hear the helicopters all the way down here," says Dr. Hall. The sound of the helicopters using the roof of the Pan-Am Building nearly fifty stories up beats right through. "If it weren't for this ceiling" — he is referring to the very high ceiling in Grand Central— " this place would be unbearable with this kind of crowding. And yet they'll probably never 'waste' space like this again."

6 They screech! And the adrenal glands in all those poor white animals enlarge, micrometer by micrometer, to the size of cantaloupes. Dr. Hall pulls a Minox camera out of a holster he has on his belt and starts shooting away at the human scurry. The Sink!

7 Dr. Hall has the Minox up to his eye — he is a slender man, calm, 52 years old, young-looking, an anthropologist who has worked with Navajos, Hopis, Spanish-Americans, Negroes, Trukese. He was the most important anthropologist in the government during the crucial years of the foreign aid program, the 1950's. He directed both the Point Four training program and the Human Relations Area Files. He wrote *The Silent Language* and *The Hidden Dimension,* two books that are picking up the kind of "underground" following his friend Marshall McLuhan started picking up about five years ago. He teaches

at the Illinois Institute of Technology, lives with his wife, Mildred, in a high-ceilinged town house on one of the last great residential streets in downtown Chicago, Astor Street; he has a grown son and daughter, loves good food, good wine, the relaxed, civilized life — but comes to New York with a Minox at his eye to record! — perfect — The Sink.

We really got down in there by walking down into the Lexington Avenue line subway stop under Grand Central. We inhaled those nice big fluffy fumes of human sweat, urine, effluvia, and sebaceous secretions. One old female human was already stroked out on the upper level, on a stretcher, with two policemen standing by. The other humans barely looked at her. They rushed into line. They bellied each other, haunch to paunch, down the stairs. Human heads shone through the gratings. The species North European tried to create bubbles of space around themselves, about a foot and a half in diameter — 8

"See, he's reacting against the line," says Dr. Hall. 9

— but the species Mediterranean presses on in. The hell with bubbles of space. The species North European resents that, this male human behind him presses forward toward the booth . . . *breathing* on him, he's disgusted, he pulls out of the line entirely, the species Mediterranean resents him for resenting it, and neither of them realizes what the hell they are getting irritable about exactly. And in all of them the old adrenals grow another micrometer. 10

Dr. Hall whips out the Minox. Too perfect! The bottom of The Sink. 11

It is the sheer overcrowding, such as occurs in the business sections of Manhattan five days a week and in Harlem, Bedford-Stuyvesant, southeast Bronx every day — sheer overcrowding is converting New Yorkers into animals in a sink pen. Dr. Hall's argument runs as follows: all animals, including birds, seem to have a built-in inherited requirement to have a certain amount of territory, space, to lead their lives in. Even if they have all the food they need, and there are no predatory animals threatening them, they cannot tolerate crowding beyond a certain point. No more than two hundred wild Norway rats can survive on a quarter acre of ground, for example, even when they are given all the food they can eat. They just die off. 12

But why? To find out, ethologists have run experiments on all sorts of animals, from stickleback crabs to Sika deer. In one major 13 experiment, an ethologist named John Calhoun put some domesticated white Norway rats in a pen with four sections to it, connected by ramps. Calhoun knew from previous experiments that the rats tend to split up into groups of ten to twelve and that the pen, therefore, would hold forty to forty-eight rats comfortably, assuming they formed four equal groups. He allowed them to reproduce until there were eighty rats, balanced between male and female, but did not let it get any more crowded. He kept them supplied with plenty of food, water, and nesting materials. In other words, all their more obvious needs were taken care of. A less obvious need — space — was not. To the human eye, the pen did not even look especially crowded. But to the rats, it was crowded beyond endurance.

The entire colony was soon plunged into a profound behavioral 14
sink. "The sink," said Calhoun, "is the outcome of any behavioral process that collects animals together in unusually great numbers. The unhealthy connotations of the term are not accidental: a behavioral sink does act to aggravate all forms of pathology that can be found within a group."

For a start, long before the rat population reached eighty, a status 15
hierarchy had developed in the pen. Two dominant male rats took over the two end sections, acquired harems of eight to ten females each, and forced the rest of the rats into the two middle pens. All the overcrowding took place in the middle pens. That was where the "sink" hit. The aristocrat rats at the end grew bigger, sleeker, healthier, and more secure the whole time.

In The Sink, meanwhile, nest building, courting, sex behavior, 16
reproduction, social organization, health — all of it went to pieces. Normally, Norway rats have a mating ritual in which the male chases the female, the female ducks down into a burrow and sticks her head up to watch the male. He performs a little dance outside the burrow, then she comes out, and he mounts her, usually for a few seconds. When The Sink set in, however, no more than three males — the dominant males in the middle sections — kept up the old customs. The rest tried everything from satyrism to homosexuality or else gave up on sex altogether. Some of the subordinate males spent all their time chasing females. Three or four might chase one female at the same time, and instead of stopping at the borrow entrance for the ritual, they would charge right in. Once mounted, they would hold on for minutes instead of the usual seconds.

Homosexuality rose sharply. So did bisexuality. Some males would mount anything — males, females, babies, senescent rats, anything. Still other males dropped sexual activity altogether, wouldn't fight and, in fact, would hardly move except when the other rats slept. Occasionally a female from the aristocrat rats' harems would come over the ramps and into the middle sections to sample life in The Sink. When she had had enough, she would run back up the ramp. Sink males would give chase up to the top of the ramp, which is to say, to the very edge of the aristocratic preserve. But one glance from one of the king rats would stop them cold and they would return to The Sink. 17

The slumming females from the harems had their adventures and then returned to a placid, healthy life. Females in The Sink, however, were ravaged, physically and psychologically. Pregnant rats had trouble continuing pregnancy. The rate of miscarriages increased significantly, and females started dying from tumors and other disorders of the mammary glands, sex organs, uterus, ovaries, and Fallopian tubes. Typically, their kidneys, livers, and adrenals were also enlarged or diseased or showed other signs associated with stress. 18

Child-rearing became totally disorganized. The females lost the interest or the stamina to build nests and did not keep them up if they did build them. In the general filth and confusion, they would not put themselves out to save offspring they were momentarily separated from. Frantic, even sadistic competition among the males was going on all around them and rendering their lives chaotic. The males began unprovoked and senseless assaults upon one another, often in the form of tail-biting. Ordinarily, rats will supress this kind of behavior when it crops up. In The Sink, male rats gave up all policing and just looked out for themselves. The "pecking order" among males in The Sink was never stable. Normally, male rats set up a three-class structure. Under the pressure of overcrowding, however, they broke up into all sorts of unstable subclasses, cliques, packs — and constantly pushed, probed, explored, tested one another's power. Anyone was fair game, except for the aristocrats in the end pens. 19

Calhoun kept the population down to eighty, so that the next stage, "population collapse" or "massive die-off," did not occur. But the autopsies showed that the pattern — as in the diseases among the female rats — was already there. 20

The classic study of die-off was John J. Christian's study of Sika 21 deer on James Island in the Chesapeake Bay, west of Cambridge, Maryland. Four or five of the deer had been released on the island, which was 280 acres and uninhibited, in 1916. By 1955 they had bred freely into a herd of 280 to 300. The population density was only about one deer per acre at this point, but Christian knew that this was already too high for the Sikas' inborn space requirements, and something would give before long. For two years the number of deer remained 280 to 300. But suddenly, in 1958, over half the deer died; 161 carcasses were recovered. In 1959 more deer died and the population steadied at about 80.

In two years, two-thirds of the herd had died. Why? It was not starvation. In fact, all the deer collected were in excellent condition, with well-developed muscles, shining coats, and fat deposits between the muscles. In practically all the deer, however, the adrenal glands had enlarged by 50 percent. Christian concluded that the die-off was due to "shock following severe metabolic disturbance, probably as a result of prolonged adrenocortical hyperactivity. . . . There was no evidence of infection, starvation, or other obvious cause to explain the mass mortality." In other words, the constant stress of overpopulation, plus the normal stress of the cold of the winter, had kept the adrenalin flowing so constantly in the deer that their systems were depleted of blood sugar and they died of shock. 22

Well, the white humans are still skidding and darting across the floor of Grand Central. Dr. Hall listens a moment longer to the skidding and the darting noises, and then says, "You know, I've been on commuter trains here after everyone has been through one of these rushes, and I'll tell you, there is enough acid flowing in the stomachs in every car to dissolve the rails underneath." 23

Just a little invisible acid bath for the linings to round off the day. The ulcers the acids cause, of course, are the one disease people have already been taught to associate with the stress of city life. But overcrowding, as Dr. Hall sees it, raises a lot more hell with the body than just ulcers. In everyday life in New York — just the usual, getting to work, working in massively congested areas like 42nd Street between Fifth Avenue and Lexington, especially now that the Pan-Am Building is set in there, working in cubicles such as those in the editorial offices at Time-Life, Inc., which Dr. Hall cites as typical of New York's poor handling of space, working in cubicles with low ceilings and, often, no access to a window, while construction crews all over Manhattan drive everybody up the Masonite wall with air- 24 pressure generators with noises up to the boil-a-brain decibel level, then rushing to get home, piling into subways and trains, fighting for time and for space, the usual day in New York — the whole now-normal thing keeps shooting jolts of adrenalin into the body, breaking down the body's defenses and winding up with the work-a-daddy human animal stroked out at the breakfast table with his head apoplexed like a cauliflower out of his $6.95 semi-spread Pima-cotton shirt, and nosed over into a plate of No-Kloresto egg substitute, signing off with the black thrombosis, cancer, kidney, liver, or stomach failure, and the adrenals ooze to a halt, the size of eggplants in July.

25 One of the people whose work Dr. Hall is interested in on this score is Rene Dubos at the Rockefeller Institute. Dubos's work indicates that specific organisms, such as the tuberculosis bacillus or a pneumonia virus, can seldom be considered "the cause" of a disease. The germ or virus, apparently, has to work in combination with other things that have already broken the body down in some way — such as the old adrenal hyperactivity. Dr. Hall would like to see some autopsy studies made to record the size of adrenal glands in New York, especially of people crowded into slums and people who go through the full rush-hour-work-rush-hour cycle every day. He is afraid that until there is some clinical, statistical data on how overcrowding actually ravages the human body, no one will be willing to do anything about it. Even in so obvious a thing as air pollution, the pattern is familiar. Until people can actually see the smoke or smell the sulphur or feel the sting in their eyes, politicians will not get excited about it, even through it is well known that many of the lethal substances polluting the air are invisible and odorless. For one thing, most politicians are like the aristocrat rats. They are insulated from The Sink by practically sultanic buffers — limousines, chauffeurs, secretaries, aides-de-camp, doormen, shuttered houses, high-floor apartments. They almost never ride subways, fight rush hours, much less live in the slums or work in the Pan-Am Building.

Meanings and Values

1a. Who are members of the "species Mediterranean"?
b. Who belong to the "species North European"?
c. What could account for their difference in space requirements (pars. 8–10)?

2. Is this writing primarily objective or subjective? (See Guide to Terms: *Objective/Subjective.*) Why?

3a. Do you get the impression that the author is being unkind, "making fun" of the harried New Yorkers?

b. How, if at all, does he prevent such an impression?

4a. Compare Wolfe's style, tone, and point of view with those of Catton (sec. 3), or King (sec. 4). (Guide: *Style/Tone, Point of View.*)

b. Do these features necessarily make one author less effective than the other in achieving his purposes? Explain.

Expository Techniques

1a. Using whatever criteria we have available for judging the success of analogy, appraise the effectiveness of this one.

b. Does the author work it *too* hard? Be prepared to defend your answer.

2. What are the benefits of the frequent return to what Dr. Hall is doing or saying (e.g., in pars. 3, 5, 7, 9, 11, 23)?

3. Paragraph 12 has a useful function beyond the simple information it imparts — a sort of organic relation to the coming development. Explain how this is accomplished.

4. How is the switch to Sika deer (par. 21) prepared for, and bumpy transition avoided?

5. The preceding three questions have been related in some manner to the problems of transition. How, if at all, are such problems also matters of coherence? (Guide: *Coherence.*)

6. Wolfe is adept at creating just the effect he wants, and the careful student of writing can detect a subtle change of style and pace with each change of subpurpose. (Guide: *Style/Tone.*)

a. Analyze stylistic differences, with resulting effects, between the description of chaos at Grand Central and the information about Dr. Hall in paragraph 7.

b. Analyze such differences between the Grand Central scene and the account of the laboratory experiment with rats.

c. Analyze the differences between the Grand Central scene and the final paragraph.

7. Explain how the style of the more descriptive portions is also a matter of emphasis. (Guide: *Emphasis.*)

8a. Illustrate as many as possible of the elements of effective syntax (itself a matter of style) by examples from this selection. (Guide: *Syntax.*)

b. What is gained or lost by the unusual length and design of the last sentence of paragraph 24? (We can be sure that it did not "just happen" to Wolfe — and equally sure that one of such length would be disastrous in most writing.)

Diction and Vocabulary

1. What is the significance of the word "Gotham"?
2a. Why do you think the author refers (deliberately, no doubt) to "my fellow New Yorkers" in the first sentence?
b. What soon could have been the effect if he had not taken such a step?
3. Why does he consistently, after paragraph 2, refer to the people as "poor white humans," "poor human animals," etc?
4. In paragraph 14 he refers to the connotations of the word "sink." What are its possible connotations? (Guide: *Connotation/Denotation.*)
5. Cite examples of verbal irony to be found in paragraphs 5, 8, 24. (Guide: *Irony.*)
6. Which of the elements of style mentioned in your answer to question 4a of "Meaning and Values" are also matters of diction?
7. Consult your dictionary as needed for full understanding of the following words: autistic, puling (par. 1); etiolate (4); effluvia, sebaceous (8); pathology (14); satyrism (16); senescent (17); decibel, thrombosis (24); lethal (25).

Suggestions for Writing and Discussion

1. Carrying Wolfe's analogy still further, trace the steps by which a rise in serious crime must result from the overcrowding of "poor human animals."
2. If you are familiar with another city, particularly during rush hours, which appears to you much like New York in this respect, describe it.
3. If you are familiar with some area of high density population that has solved its problem of overcrowding, explain the solution.
4. What practical steps can the *individual* take, if forced to live and/or work in overcrowded conditions, to avoid becoming the victim of his own adrenals?

(NOTE: Suggestions for topics requiring development by use of ANALOGY are on page 152, at the end of this section.)

Writing Suggestions for Section 4
Analogy

(In any normal situation, of course, the analogy is chosen to help explain a theme-idea that already exists — such as those in the first group below. But for classroom training, which even at best is bound to be somewhat artificial, it is sometimes permissible to work from the other direction, to develop a theme that fits some preselected analogy-symbol. Your instructor will indicate which of the groups he prefers you to use.)

1. State a central theme about one of the following general topics or a suitable one of your own, and develop it into a composition by use of an analogy of your own choosing.

    a. A well-organized school system or business establishment.
    b. Starting a new kind of business or other enterprise.
    c. The long-range value of programs for underprivileged children.
    d. The complexity of narcotics control.
    e. The need for cooperation between management and labor.
    f. Today's intense competition for success.
    g. Women's liberation in a "man's world."
    h. The results of ignorance.
    i. The dangers of propaganda.

2. Select an analogy-symbol from the following list and fashion a worthwhile theme that it can illustrate. Develop your composition as instructed.

    a. A freeway at commuting time.
    b. Building a road through a wilderness.
    c. Building a bridge across a river.
    d. A merry-go-round.
    e. A wedding.
    f. A car-wash.
    g. Flood-destruction of a levee.
    h. The tending of a young orchard.
    i. An animal predator stalking prey.
    j. A medical clinic.
    k. A juggling act.
    l. An oasis.

5

Explaining Through *Process Analysis*

Process analysis explains how the steps of an operation lead to its completion. Although in one narrow sense it may be considered a kind of narration, process analysis has an important difference in purpose, and hence in approach. Other narration is mostly concerned with the story itself, or with a general concept illustrated by it, but process tells of methods that end in specified results. We might narrate a story about a rifle — its purchase, its role in colorful episodes, perhaps its eventual retirement from active servce. (We could, for other purposes, *define* "rifle," or *classify* the types of rifles, no doubt *compare* and *contrast* these types and *illustrate* by examples.) But to show how a rifle works, or how it is manufactured, or how it should be cared for — this is process, and it sometimes becomes the basic pattern of an exposition.

Most writers are especially concerned with two kinds of process, both of them apparent in the preceding example of rifles: the directional, which explains how to *do* something (how to shoot a gun or how to clean it); and the informational, which explains how something is or was *done* (how guns are manufactured). The directional process can range from the instructions on a shampoo bottle to a detailed plan showing how to make the United Nations more effective, and will often contain detailed justification for individual steps or for the process itself. The informational process, on the other hand, might explain the steps of a wide variety of operations or actions, of mental or evolutionary processes, with no how-to-do-it purpose at all — how someone went about choosing a college or how the planet Earth was formed. Informational process analysis has been seen in earlier selections: Peter and Hull explained how the Peter Principle works, Wolfe how the experiment with Norway rats was conducted.

Most process analyses are explained in simple, chronological steps. Indeed, the exact order is sometimes of greatest importance, as in a recipe. But occasionally there are problems in organization. The step-by-step format may need to be interrupted for descriptions, definitions, or other explanatory asides. And, still more of a problem, some processes defy a strict chronological treatment, because several things occur simultaneously. To explain the operating process of a gasoline engine, for example, the writer would be unable to convey at once everything that happens at the same time. Some way must be found to present the material in *general* stages, organized as subdivisions, so that the reader can see the step-by-step process through the confusion of interacting relationships.

Another difficulty in explaining by process analysis is estimating what knowledge the reader may already have. Presuming too little background may quickly result in boredom or even irritation, with a resulting communication block; presuming too much will almost certainly leave him bewildered. Like a chain dependent on its weakest link for its strength, the entire process analysis can fail because of just one unclear point that makes the rest unintelligible.

LEWIS THOMAS

LEWIS THOMAS was born in 1913, attended private schools in New York and then Princeton University and Harvard Medical School. As a United States naval officer he took part in the invasion of Okinawa during World War II. After the war he advanced steadily in medical research, teaching, and administration. He has served in posts at the University of Minnesota and New York University Medical School; at Yale, Cornell, and Rockefeller universities. For several years Thomas has been president of Memorial Sloan-Kettering Cancer Center in New York. He remains active in committee work, frequently appears before Congressional hearings in Washington, and also serves on the Harvard Board of Overseers. A lifelong interest in literature and writing led Thomas in 1970 to begin writing a monthly column for the *New England Journal of Medicine* — a practice that has evolved into his two collections of essays: *The Lives of a Cell: Notes of a Biology Watcher* (1974), which has become a steady best-seller; and *The Medusa and the Snail* (1979).

Natural Man

"Natural Man" is one of the essays included in *The Lives of a Cell.* It illustrates Thomas's clear and characteristic style. Basically the essay develops by the simplest kind of process, showing the evolutionary steps of man in the way he regards his environment. But this essay is different from most other environmental pieces: it ends on a decidedly optimistic note.

The social scientists, especially the economists, are moving deeply into ecology and the environment these days, with disquieting results. It goes somehow against the grain to learn that cost-benefit analyses can be done neatly on lakes, meadows, nesting gannets, even whole oceans. It is hard enough to confront the environmental options ahead, and the hard choices, but even harder when the price 1 tags are so visible. Even the new jargon is disturbing: it hurts the spirit, somehow, to read the word *environments,* when the plural means that there are so many alternatives there to be sorted through, as in a market, and voted on. Economists need cool heads and cold hearts for this sort of work, and they must write in icy, often skiddy prose.

The degree to which we are all involved in the control of the earth's life is just beginning to dawn on most of us, and it means another revolution for human thought. 2

This will not come easily. We've just made our way through inconclusive revolutions on the same topic, trying to make up our minds how we feel about nature. As soon as we arrived at one kind of consensus, like an enormous committee, we found it was time to think it through all over, and now here we are, at it again. 3

The oldest, easiest-to-swallow idea was that the earth was man's personal property, a combination of garden, zoo, bank vault, and energy source, placed at our disposal to be consumed, ornamented, or pulled apart as we wished. The betterment of mankind was, as we understood it, the whole point of the thing. Mastery over nature, mystery and all, was a moral duty and social obligation. 4

In the last few years we were wrenched away from this way of looking at it, and arrived at something like general agreement that we had it wrong. We still argue the details, but it is conceded almost everywhere that we are not the masters of nature that we thought ourselves; we are as dependent on the rest of life as are the leaves or midges or fish. We are part of the system. One way to put it is that the earth is a loosely formed, spherical organism, with all its working parts linked in symbiosis. We are, in this view, neither owners nor operators; at best, we might see ourselves as motile tissue specialized for receiving information — perhaps, in the best of all possible worlds, functioning as a nervous system for the whole being. 5

There is, for some, too much dependency in this view, and they prefer to see us as a separate, qualitatively different, special species, unlike any other form of life, despite the sharing around of genes, enzymes, and organelles. No matter, there is still the underlying idea that we cannot have a life of our own without concern for the ecosystem in which we live, whether in majesty or not. This idea has been strong enough to launch the new movements for the sustenance of wilderness, the protection of wildlife, the turning off of insatiable technologies, the preservation of "whole earth." 6

But now, just when the new view seems to be taking hold, we may be in for another wrench, this time more dismaying and unsettling than anything we've come through. In a sense, we shall be obliged to swing back again, still believing in the new way but constrained by the facts of life to live in the old. It may be too late, as things have turned out. 7

We are, in fact, the masters, like it or not. 8

It is a despairing prospect. Here we are, practically speaking twenty-first-century mankind, filled to exuberance with our new understanding of kinship to all the family of life, and here we are, still nineteenth-century man, walking boot-shod over the open face of nature, subjugating and civilizing it. And we cannot stop this controlling, unless we vanish under the hill ourselves. If there were such a thing as a world mind, it should crack over this. 9

The truth is, we have become more deeply involved than we ever dreamed. The fact that we sit around as we do, worrying seriously about how best to preserve the life of the earth, is itself the sharpest measure of our involvement. It is not human arrogance that has taken us in this direction, but the most natural of natural events. We developed this way, we grew this way, we are this kind of species. 10

We have become, in a painful, unwished-for way, nature itself. We have grown into everywhere, spreading like a new growth over the entire surface, touching and affecting every other kind of life, *incorporating* ourselves. The earth risks being eutrophied by us. We are now the dominant feature of our own environment. Humans, large terrestrial metazoans, fired by energy from microbial symbionts lodged in their cells, instructed by tapes of nucleic acid stretching back to the earliest live membranes, informed by neurons essentially the same as all the other neurons on earth, sharing structures with mastodons and lichens, living off the sun, are now in charge, running the place, for better or worse. 11

Or is it really this way? It could be, you know, just the other way around. Perhaps we are the invaded ones, the subjugated, used. 12

Certain animals in the sea live by becoming part-animal, part-plant. They engulf algae, which then establish themselves as complex plant tissues, essential for the life of the whole company. I suppose the giant clam, if he had more of a mind, would have moments of dismay on seeing what he has done to the plant world, incorporating so much of it, enslaving green cells, living off the photosynthesis. But the plant cells would take a different view of it, having captured the 13 clam on the most satisfactory of terms, including the small lenses in his tissues that focus sunlight for their benefit; perhaps algae have bad moments about what they may collectively be doing to the world of clams.

With luck, our own situation might be similar, on a larger scale. This might turn out to be a special phase in the morphogenesis of the earth when it is necessary to have something like us, for a time anyway, to fetch and carry energy, look after new symbiotic arrangements, store up information for some future season, do a certain amount of ornamenting, maybe even carry seeds around the solar system. That kind of thing. Handyman for the earth. 14

I would much prefer this useful role, if I had any say, to the essentially unearthly creature we seem otherwise on the way to becoming. It would mean making some quite fundamental changes in our attitudes toward each other, if we were really to think of ourselves as indispensable elements of nature. We would surely become the environment to worry about the most. We would discover, in ourselves, the sources of wonderment and delight that we have discerned in all other manifestations of nature. Who knows, we might even acknowledge the fragility and vulnerability that always accompany high specialization in biology, and movements might start up for the protection of ourselves as a valuable, endangered species. We couldn't lose. 15

Meanings and Values

1a. How would you describe this author's attitude toward his subject?
b. Is the writing more nearly objective, or subjective? (See Guide to Terms: *Objective/Subjective.*)
c. What, if any, evidence of sentimentality do you find? (Guide: *Sentimentality.*)

2. In what basic ways does this selection differ from most writings on the environment?
3. What is a "cost-benefit analysis" (par. 1)?
4. Is it an exaggeration to claim that we are *all* involved in the control of earth's life (par. 2)? Why, or why not?
5. In what way, or ways, may it indeed be "too late" (par. 7)?
6. Why does Thomas prefer the role as "handyman for the earth" (pars. 14, 15)?

Expository Techniques

1a. Briefly outline the three broad stages of this evolutionary process.
 b. With which pargraph does discussion of each begin?
 c. In what ways does the third stage differ from the other two?

2a. One paragraph develops entirely by analogy. Which is it?
 b. How does it qualify as analogy?

3a. What seems to be the purpose of paragraphs 2 and 3?
 b. Is it a useful function?

4a. What is the actual relationship, if any, between the introduction and the overall subject?
 b. Is the relationship close enough for this to be an effective introduction?

5a. This essay is noteworthy for the syntax. (Guide: *Syntax.*) Cite the syntactic features that seem to make it different from most other writing.
 b. To what extent is this a matter of style? (Guide: *Style/Tone.*)

6. "Natural Man" employs almost entirely one of the standard techniques of closing. Which is it? (Guide: *Closings.*)

Diction and Vocabulary

1. What is the effect of the consistent use of "we" in this essay—instead, for instance, of the equally available "humans," "mankind," or "people"?
2. Cite the various uses of figurative language and note which kind each is. (Guide: *Figures of Speech.*)
3. You may have noticed a flair for coupling ordinary words in crisp and colorful ways, an important aspect of Thomas's style. (Guide: *Style/Tone.*) Cite several examples.
4. Does the large number of "dictionary-type" words in certain paragraphs damage the essay's overall effectiveness? Explain.
5. Use the dictionary as necessary to understand the meanings of the following words: midges, symbiosis, motile (par. 5); organelles, ecosystem (6); constrained (7); eutrophied, terrestrial, metazoans, neurons, mastodons, lichens (11); photosynthesis (13); morphogenesis (14); manifestations (15).

Suggestions for Writing and Discussion

1. Discuss the ways even the least "involved" of us is involved in the control of the earth's life (par. 2).

2. Illustrate by factual examples the turning off of one or more of the "insatiable technologies" (par. 6).
3. Do you agree with Thomas's assertion that it is not human arrogance that has involved us so, but merely that we are "this kind of species" (par. 10)? Why, or why not? (Perhaps human arrogance is one *characteristic* of this kind of species.)
4. Explore further the possibilities suggested by paragraph 14 — e.g., that it may be our job to "look after new symbiotic arrangements."
5. If we did have the obligations suggested by paragraph 14, why would we then "surely become the environment to worry about the most" (par. 15)?

(NOTE: Suggestions for topics requiring development by PROCESS ANALYSIS are on page 184, at the end of this section.)

ROBERT M. PIRSIG

ROBERT M. PIRSIG was born in Minneapolis in 1928. He received both B.A. and M.A. degrees at the University of Minnesota and has been a Guggenheim Fellow since 1974. His first important book, *Zen and the Art of Motorcycle Maintenance* (1974), was quickly acclaimed by most reviewers—e.g.,in *The New York Times:* "Profoundly important . . . full of insights into our most perplexing contemporary dilemmas . . . intellectual entertainment of the highest order." It was also rated on various best-seller lists, including those of college bookstores. Pirsig's next book, he says, will be about boats and sailing.

Mechanics' Logic

"Mechanics' Logic" (editor's title), from *Zen and the Art of Motorcycle Maintenance,* analyzes a much more complex process than that of the preceding selection. Although no doubt a worthwhile subject, it is also one that could easily be dry and uninteresting to more readers than not — perhaps even too "difficult" for the average nonlogician. The fact that it is readable and even interesting for many laymen is a tribute to the author's skill — and discovering the techniques by which he achieves this success can provide one of the most rewarding experiences of its study.

Two kinds of logic are used [in motorcycle maintenance], inductive and deductive. Inductive inferences start with observations of the machine and arrive at general conclusions. For example, if the cycle goes over a bump and the engine misfires, and then goes over another bump and the engine misfires, and then goes over another bump and the engine misfires, and then goes over a long smooth stretch of road and there is no misfiring, and then goes over a fourth bump and the engine misfires again, one can logically conclude that the misfiring is caused by the bumps. That is induction: reasoning from particular experiences to general truths. 1

Deductive inferences do the reverse. They start with general 2
knowledge and predict a specific observation. For example, if, from reading the hierarchy of facts about the machine, the mechanic knows the horn of the cycle is powered exclusively by electricity from the battery, then he can logically infer that if the battery is dead the horn will not work. That is deduction.

Solution of problems too complicated for common sense to solve 3
is achieved by long strings of mixed inductive and deductive inferences that weave back and forth between the observed machine and the mental hierarchy of the machine found in the manuals. The correct program for this interweaving is formalized as scientific method.

Actually I've never seen a cycle-maintenance problem complex 4
enough really to require full-scale formal scientific method. Repair problems are not that hard. When I think of formal scientific method an image sometimes comes to mind of an enormous juggernaut, a huge bulldozer — slow, tedious, lumbering, laborious, but invincible. It takes twice as long, five times as long, maybe a dozen times as long as informal mechanic's techniques, but you know in the end you're going to *get* it. There's no fault isolation problem in motorcycle maintenance that can stand up to it. When you've hit a really tough one, tried everything, racked your brain and nothing works, and you know that this time Nature has really decided to be difficult, you say, "Okay, Nature, that's the end of the *nice* guy," and you crank up the formal scientific method.

For this you keep a lab notebook. Everything gets written down, 5
formally, so that you know at all times where you are, where you've been, where you're going and where you want to get. In scientific work and electronics technology this is necessary because otherwise the problems get so complex you get lost in them and confused and forget what you know and what you don't know and have to give up. In cycle maintenance things are not that involved, but when confusion starts it's a good idea to hold it down by making everything formal and exact. Sometimes just the act of writing down the problems straightens out your head as to what they really are.

The logical statements entered into the notebook are broken 6
down into six categories: (1) statement of the problem, (2) hypotheses as to the cause of the problem, (3) experiments designed to test each hypothesis, (4) predicted results of the experiments, (5) observed results of the experiments and (6) conclusions from the results of the experiments. This is not different from the formal arrangement

of many college and high-school lab notebooks but the purpose here is no longer just busywork. The purpose now is precise guidance of thoughts that will fail if they are not accurate.

The real purpose of scientific method is to make sure Nature 7
hasn't misled you into thinking you know something you don't actually know. There's not a mechanic or scientist or technician alive who hasn't suffered from that one so much that he's not instinctively on guard. That's the main reason why so much scientific and mechanical information sounds so dull and so cautious. If you get careless or go romanticizing scientific information, giving it a flourish here and there, Nature will soon make a complete fool out of you. It does it often enough anyway even when you don't give it opportunities. One must be extremely careful and rigidly logical when dealing with Nature: one logical slip and an entire scientific edifice comes tumbling down. One false deduction about the machine and you can get hung up indefinitely.

In Part One of formal scientific method, which is the statement 8
of the problem, the main skill is in stating absolutely no more than you are positive you know. It is much better to enter a statement "Solve Problem: Why doesn't cycle work?" which sounds dumb but is correct, than it is to enter a statement "Solve Problem: What is wrong with the electrical system?" when you don't absolutely *know* the trouble is *in* the electrical system. What you should state is "Solve Problem: What is wrong with cycle?" and *then* state as the first entry of Part Two: "Hypothesis Number One: The trouble is in the electrical system." You think of as many hypotheses as you can, then you design experiments to test them to see which are true and which are false.

This careful approach to the beginning questions keeps you from 9
taking a major wrong turn which might cause you weeks of extra work or can even hang you up completely. Scientific questions often have a surface appearance of dumbness for this reason. They are asked in order to prevent dumb mistakes later on.

Part Three, that part of formal scientific method called experi- 10
mentation, is sometimes thought of by romantics as all of science itself because that's the only part with much visual surface. They see lots of test tubes and bizarre equipment and people running around making discoveries. They do not see the experiment as part of a larger intellectual process and so they often confuse experiments with demonstrations, which look the same. A man conducting a gee-whiz science show with fifty thousand dollars' worth of Frankenstein

equipment is not doing anything scientific if he knows beforehand what the results of his efforts are going to be. A motorcycle mechanic, on the other hand, who honks the horn to see if the battery works is informally conducting a true scientific experiment. He is testing a hypothesis by putting the question to Nature. The TV scientist who mutters sadly, "The experiment is a failure; we have failed to achieve what we had hoped for," is suffering mainly from a bad scriptwriter. An experiment is never a failure solely because it fails to achieve predicted results. An experiment is a failure only when it also fails adequately to test the hypothesis in question, when the data it produces don't prove anything one way or another.

Skill at this point consists of using experiments that test only the 11
hypothesis in question, nothing less, nothing more. If the horn honks, and the mechanic concludes that the whole electrical system is working, he is in deep trouble. He has reached an illogical conclusion. The honking horn only tells him that the battery and horn are working. To design an experiment properly he has to think very rigidly in terms of what directly causes what. This you know from the hierarchy. The horn doesn't make the cycle go. Neither does the battery, except in a very distinct way. The point at which the electrical system *directly* causes the engine to fire is at the spark plugs, and if you don't test here, at the output of the electrical system, you will never really know whether the failure is electrical or not.

To test properly the mechanic removes the plug and lays it 12
against the engine so that the base around the plug is electrically grounded, kicks the starter lever and watches the spark-plug gap for a blue spark. If there isn't any he can conclude one of two things: (a) there is an electrical failure or (b) his experiment is sloppy. If he is experienced he will try it a few more times, checking connections, trying every way he can think of to get that plug to fire. Then, if he can't get it to fire, he finally concludes that *a* is correct, there's an electrical failure, and the experiment is over. He has proved that his hypothesis is correct.

In the final category, conclusions, skill comes in stating no more 13
than the experiment has proved. It hasn't proved that when he fixes the electrical system the motorcycle will start. There may be other things wrong. But he does know that the motorcycle isn't going to run until the electrical system is working and he sets up the next formal question: "Solve Problem: what is wrong with the electrical system?"

He then sets up hypotheses for these and tests them. By asking the right questions and choosing the right tests and drawing the right conclusions the mechanic works his way down the echelons of the motorcycle hierarchy until he has found the exact specific cause or causes of the engine failure, and then he changes them so that they no longer cause the failure. 14

An untrained observer will see only physical labor and often get the idea that physical labor is mainly what the mechanic does. Actually the physical labor is the smallest and easiest part of what the mechanic does. By far the greatest part of his work is careful observation and precise thinking. That is why mechanics sometimes seem so taciturn and withdrawn when performing tests. They don't like it when you talk to them because they are concentrating on mental images, hierarchies, and not really looking at you or the physical motorcycle at all. They are using the experiment as part of a program to expand their hierarchy of knowledge of the faulty motorcycle and compare it to the correct hierarchy in their mind. They are looking at underlying form. 15

Meanings and Values

1. For even nonmechanics, what potential value can you see in understanding the "scientific method" and the importance of logic?
2. Where would you place this piece on an objective/subjective continuum? Why? (See Guide to Terms: *Objective/Subjective.*)

3a. Do you suppose most master mechanics realize they are using a time-honored scientific method?
 b. If many do not consciously take the six steps in solving their problems, would this fact make Pirsig's thesis less valid? Why, or why not?

4. Judge the success of "Mechanics' Logic" by applying our three-step evaluation method. (Guide: *Evaluation.*)
5. If you have read the Hall selection (Sec. 2) for what kinds of reading might differing people use "Mechanics' Logic"? Consider your answer carefully and explain your reasons for it.

Expository Techniques

1a. On first impression, which of the two basic types of process analysis did you assume this to be? Why?
 b. Considering the reader-audience Pirsig evidently had in mind, which of the two types would he have intended it to be? Why?

c. Has he made his exposition understandable, as nearly as you can tell, to most types of readers? If not, what would be the exceptions?
d. Should he have included more justification for his rather laborious process? Why, or why not?

2. Pirsig uses examples to make his general statements more specific. Select three of the best of these and explain why you think they are well chosen or well presented, or both.

3a. Cite one use of analogy, however minor.
b. Why is it not a simple metaphor? (Guide: *Figure of Speech.*)
c. How effective is it, in the job it has to do?

4a. How is paragraph 9, dealing as it does with two different parts of the process, saved from gross disunity? (Guide: *Unity.*)
b. Would it have been better divided into two paragraphs? Why, or why not?

Diction and Vocabulary

1a. Cite as many colloquial expressions as possible. (Guide: *Colloquial Expressions.*)
b. Does this informal usage damage or improve the general tone of the writing? Analyze your reasons for this answer. (Guide: *Style/Tone.*)

2a. Cite one example of allusion. (Guide: *Figures of Speech.*)
b. Is its choice appropriate? Why, or why not?

3a. In what sense does Pirsig use the word "Nature"?
b. Why is it capitalized?

4a. If you have read "The Peter Principle" (Sec. 1), differentiate between the meanings of "hierarchy," as used here and in that selection.
b. Are both used correctly?

5. If you are not familiar with the meanings of the following words, as used in this selection, consult your dictionary: hypothesis (pars. 6, 11, 12, 14); edifice (7); bizarre (10); echelons (14); taciturn (15).

Suggestions for Writing and Discussion

1. Show how to apply Pirsig's six-step method to some problem in another field of endeavor with which you are familiar. Keep your subject narrow enough that it can be developed thoroughly.

2. Is it true that some people simply are not practical enough (logical enough?) to be good mechanics? Is the deficiency, if any, a matter of natural talent or training, or both? Can it be overcome? Use any of the four patterns of exposition previously studied that will support your thesis.

3. If you have read *Zen and the Art of Motorcycle Maintenance,* you are no doubt aware that the book is only incidentally about motorcycles.

What then is it about? You may decide to prepare a critical review of the book, tailored to whatever aspects or length you and your instructor prefer.

(NOTE: Suggestions for topics requiring development by PROCESS ANALYSIS are on page 184, at the end of this section.)

ALEXANDER PETRUNKEVITCH

ALEXANDER PETRUNKEVITCH (1875–1964) was a Russian-born zoologist who taught at several leading American universities and received honors from others. He was one of the world's foremost authorities on spiders, and his first important book, published in 1911, was *Index Catalogue of Spiders of North, Central, and South America.* He later achieved distinction for his writings on zoological subjects as well as for his translations of English poetry into Russian and Russian poetry into English. Two of his other books are *Choice and Responsibility* (1947) and *Principles of Classification* (1952).

The Spider and the Wasp

"The Spider and the Wasp" was first published in the August 1952 issue of *Scientific American,* and is reproduced here almost in its entirety. This essay should be particularly interesting to students of composition because it demonstrates not only exposition of natural process but also semiscientific writing that has been made understandable, perhaps even fascinating, for completely nonscientific readers. It is also a good illustration of the successful interweaving of several expository techniques.

In the feeding and safeguarding of their progeny insects and spiders exhibit some interesting analogies to reasoning and some crass examples of blind instinct. The case I propose to describe here is that of the tarantula spiders and their archenemy, the digger wasps of the genus Pepsis. It is a classic example of what looks like intelligence pitted against instinct — a strange situation in which the victim, though fully able to defend itself, submits unwittingly to its destruction. 1

Most tarantulas live in the tropics, but several species occur in the temperate zone and a few are common in the southern U.S. Some varieties are large and have powerful fangs with which they can 2 inflict a deep wound. These formidable looking spiders do not, however, attack man; you can hold one in your hand, if you are gentle, without being bitten. Their bite is dangerous only to insects and small mammals such as mice; for man it is no worse than a hornet's sting.

Tarantulas customarily live in deep cylindrical burrows, from which they emerge at dusk and into which they retire at dawn. Mature males wander about after dark in search of females and occasionally stray into houses. After mating, the male dies in a few weeks, but a female lives much longer and can mate several years in succession. In a Paris museum is a tropical specimen which is said to have been living in captivity for 25 years. 3

A fertilized female tarantula lays from 200 to 400 eggs at a time; thus it is possible for a single tarantula to produce several thousand young. She takes no care of them beyond weaving a cocoon of silk to enclose the eggs. After they hatch, the young walk away, find convenient places in which to dig their burrows and spend the rest of their lives in solitude. The eyesight of tarantulas is poor, being limited to a sensing of change in the intensity of light and to the perception of moving objects. They apparently have little or no sense of hearing, for a hungry tarantula will pay no attention to a loudly chirping cricket placed in its cage unless the insect happens to touch one of its legs. 4

But all spiders, and especially hairy ones, have an extremely delicate sense of touch. Laboratory experiments prove that tarantulas can distinguish three types of touch: pressure against the body wall, stroking of the body hair, and riffling of certain very fine hairs on the legs called trichobothria. Pressure against the body, by the finger or the end of a pencil, causes the tarantula to move off slowly for a short distance. The touch excites no defensive response unless the approach is from above where the spider can see the motion, in which case it rises on its hind legs, lifts its front legs, opens its fangs and holds this threatening posture as long as the object continues to move. 5

The entire body of a tarantula, especially its legs, is thickly clothed with hair. Some of it is short and wooly, some long and stiff. Touching this body hair produces one of two distinct reactions. When the spider is hungry, it responds with an immediate and swift attack. At the touch of a cricket's antennae the tarantula seizes the insect so swiftly that a motion picture taken at the rate of 64 frames 6 per second shows only the result and not the process of capture. But when the spider is not hungry, the stimulation of its hairs merely causes it to shake the touched limb. An insect can walk under its hairy belly unharmed.

The trichobothria, very fine hairs growing from disklike mem- 7
branes on the legs, are sensitive only to air movement. A light breeze makes them vibrate slowly, without disturbing the common hair. When one blows gently on the trichobothria, the tarantula reacts with a quick jerk of its four front legs. If the front and hind legs are stimulated at the same time, the spider makes a sudden jump. This reaction is quite independent of the state of its appetite.

These three tactile responses — to pressure on the body wall, to 8
moving of the common hair, and to flexing of the trichobothria — are so different from one another that there is no possibility of confusing them. They serve the tarantula adequately for most of its needs and enable it to avoid most annoyances and dangers. But they fail the spider completely when it meets its deadly enemy, the digger wasp Pepsis.

These solitary wasps are beautiful and formidable creatures. 9
Most species are either a deep shiny blue all over, or deep blue with rusty wings. The largest have a wing span of about four inches. They live on nectar. When excited, they give off a pungent odor — a warning that they are ready to attack. The sting is much worse than that of a bee or common wasp, and the pain and swelling last longer. In the adult stage the wasp lives only a few months. The female produces but a few eggs, one at a time at intervals of two or three days. For each egg the mother must provide one adult tarantula, alive but paralyzed. The mother wasp attaches the egg to the paralyzed spider's abdomen. Upon hatching from the egg, the larva is many hundreds of times smaller than its living but helpless victim. It eats no other food and drinks no water. By the time it has finished its single Gargantuan meal and become ready for wasphood, nothing remains of the tarantula but its indigestible chitinous skeleton.

The mother wasp goes tarantula-hunting when the egg in her 10
ovary is almost ready to be laid. Flying low over the ground late on a sunny afternoon, the wasp looks for its victim or for the mouth of a tarantula burrow, a round hole edged by a bit of silk. The sex of the spider makes no difference, but the mother is highly discriminating as to species. Each species of Pepsis requires a certain species of tarantula, and the wasp will not attack the wrong species. In a cage

with a tarantula which is not its normal prey, the wasp avoids the spider and is usually killed by it in the night.

11 Yet when a wasp finds the correct species, it is the other way about. To identify the species the wasp apparently must explore the spider with her antennae. The tarantula shows an amazing tolerance to this exploration. The wasp crawls under it and walks over it without evoking any hostile response. The molestation is so great and so persistent that the tarantula often rises on all eight legs, as if it were on stilts. It may stand this way for several minutes. Meanwhile the wasp, having satisfied itself that the victim is of the right species, moves off a few inches to dig the spider's grave. Working vigorously with legs and jaws, it excavates a hole 8 to 10 inches deep with a diameter slightly larger than the spider's girth. Now and again the wasp pops out of the hole to make sure that the spider is still there.

12 When the grave is finished, the wasp returns to the tarantula to complete her ghastly enterprise. First she feels it all over once more with her antennae. Then her behavior becomes more aggressive. She bends her abdomen, protruding her sting, and searches for the soft membrane at the point where the spider's legs join its body — the only spot where she can penetrate the horny skeleton. From time to time, as the exasperated spider slowly shifts ground, the wasp turns on her back and slides along with the aid of her wings, trying to get under the tarantula for a shot at the vital spot. During all this maneuvering, which can last for several minutes, the tarantula makes no move to save itself. Finally the wasp corners it against some obstruction and grasps one of its legs in her powerful jaws. Now at last the harassed spider tries a desperate but vain defense. The two contestants roll over and over on the ground. It is a terrifying sight and the outcome is always the same. The wasp finally manages to thrust her sting into the soft spot and holds it there for a few seconds while she pumps in the poison. Almost immediately the tarantula falls paralyzed on its back. Its legs stop twitching; its heart stops beating. Yet it is not dead, as is shown by the fact that if taken from the wasp it can be restored to some sensitivity by being kept in a moist chamber for several months.

13 After paralyzing the tarantula, the wasp cleans herself by dragging her body along the ground and rubbing her feet, sucks a drop of blood oozing from the wound in the spider's abdomen, then grabs a leg of the flabby, helpless animal in her jaws and drags it down to the bottom of the grave. She stays there for many minutes, some-

times for several hours, and what she does all that time in the dark we do not know. Eventually she lays her egg and attaches it to the side of the spider's abdomen with a sticky secretion. Then she emerges, fills the grave with soil carried bit by bit in her jaws, and finally tramples the ground all around to hide any trace of the grave from prowlers. Then she flies away, leaving her descendant safely started in life.

In all this the behavior of the wasp evidently is qualitatively 14
different from that of the spider. The wasp acts like an intelligent animal. This is not to say that instinct plays no part or that she reasons as man does. But her actions are to the point; they are not automatic and can be modified to fit the situation. We do not know for certain how she identifies the tarantula — probably it is by some olfactory or chemo-tactile sense — but she does it purposefully and does not blindly tackle a wrong species.

On the other hand, the tarantula's behavior shows only confu- 15
sion. Evidently the wasp's pawing gives it no pleasure, for it tries to move away. That the wasp is not simulating sexual stimulation is certain because male and female tarantulas react in the same way to its advances. That the spider is not anesthetized by some odorless secretion is easily shown by blowing lightly at the tarantula and making it jump suddenly. What, then, makes the tarantula behave as stupidly as it does?

No clear, simple answer is available. Possibly the stimulation by 16
the wasp's antennae is masked by a heavier pressure on the spider's body, so that it reacts as when prodded by a pencil. But the explanation may be much more complex. Initiative in attack is not in the nature of tarantulas; most species fight only when cornered so that escape is impossible. Their inherited patterns of behavior apparently prompt them to avoid problems rather than attack them. For example, spiders always weave their webs in three dimensions, and when a spider finds that there is insufficient space to attach certain threads in the third dimension, it leaves the place and seeks another, instead of finishing the web in a single plane. This urge to escape seems to arise under all circumstances, in all phases of life, and to take the place of reasoning. For a spider to change the pattern of its web is as impossible as for an inexperienced man to build a bridge across a chasm obstructing his way.

In a way the instinctive urge to escape is not only easier but often 17
more efficient than reasoning. The tarantula does exactly what is

most efficient in all cases except in an encounter with a ruthless and determined attacker dependent for the existence of her own species on killing as many tarantulas as she can lay eggs. Perhaps in this case the spider follows its usual pattern of trying to escape, instead of seizing and killing the wasp, because it is not aware of its danger. In any case, the survival of the tarantula species as a whole is protected by the fact that the spider is much more fertile than the wasp.

Meanings and Values

1. Briefly summarize the "qualitative" differences between the behavior of the tarantula and that of the wasp.
2. What is the likelihood that some humans also have inherited patterns of behavior that "prompt them to avoid problems rather than attack them" (par. 16)? Use concrete examples, if possible, to support your view.
3. What parallels to the tarantula-wasp relationship can you find in the history of nations? Be specific and explain.

4a. Describe the type, or types, of readers to whom you think *Scientific American* is meant to appeal. (Do not jump to conclusions: if not familiar with the magazine, you may have to browse through a few issues.)

b. If you were the editor, why would you have chosen (or not chosen) to publish this piece?

Expository Techniques

1a. Where does the author state his central theme?

b. Is this a desirable location? Why, or why not?

2a. What is the primary function of the process analysis in relation to the central theme?

b. How successfully does it accomplish its purpose?

3. In paragraph 9 the author goes from pure description of the wasp into the narrative account that involves both wasp and spider. How does he arrange the content itself to provide smooth and natural transition, hence ensuring coherence? (See Guide to Terms: *Transition* and *Coherence.*)
4. The author also usually arranges his subject materials to help achieve effective *inter*paragraph transitions so that one gets an echo of the last part of one paragraph when reading the topic sentence of the next. List or mark the uses of this transitional device.
5. Effective coherence also depends to a great extent on smooth sentence-to-sentence transitions. In describing events in a time sequence,

it is sometimes hard to avoid a dull list that runs on "and then . . . and then . . . " List or mark the eight introductory devices showing time relationship in paragraph 12, and notice their variety.

6a. How many paragraphs constitute the closing?
b. What function do they serve in addition to concluding the selection?

7. This essay utilizes, to varying extents, the expository patterns of cause and effect, definition, induction, and description. It can also be used to illustrate three patterns we have already studied.
a. What are the patterns?
b. Explain their use in this essay.

Diction and Vocabulary

1. Do such informal expressions as "pops out of the hole" (par. 11), "for a shot at the vital spot," and "pumps in the poison" (12) help or hinder the essay's success? Why?

2. Consider such expressions as "beautiful and formidable creatures" (par. 9), "ghastly enterprise," and "terrifying sight" (12).
a. Are these expressions objective or subjective? (Guide: *Objective/Subjective.*) Explain why.
b. Why would they be, or not be, suitable in a scientific report?
c. What useful purpose, if any, do they serve here?

3a. What do your answers to questions 1 and 2 indicate about the author's tone? (Guide: *Style/Tone.*)
b. How would you describe his tone?
c. Explain why it is, or is not, suitable to his subject matter and to his audience.

4. Any specialist writing on a technical subject for a lay audience (as much of *Scientific American's* audience is) has a problem with professional terminology. Consider this author's use of "trichobothria" (par. 5), "chitinous" (9), "olfactory," and "chemo-tactile" (14).
a. Does there seem to be an excessive use of technical lauguage?
b. Do you think these words could have been avoided without weakening scientific exactness? If so, how?
c. Does their use create a communication block for the lay reader, or does the author succeed in avoiding this fault?
d. Why has he bothered to define "trichobothria" — even repeating his definition — but not the others?

5. The use of "Gargantuan" (par. 9) is an allusion. (Guide: *Figures of Speech.*) Find the source to which the author alludes and explain the word's meaning in this essay.

6. Consult the dictionary as needed for a full understanding of the following words, especially as used in this essay: progeny, archenemy, classic (par. 1); formidable (2); perception (4); riffling (5); disklike (7); tactile (8); pungent, chitinous (9); discriminating (10); evoking, moles-

tation (11); harassed (12); secretion (13); qualitatively, olfactory, chemo-tactile (14); ruthless (17).

Suggestions for Writing and Discussion

1. Use the tarantula-wasp relationship as the basis of an analogy to explain the relationship between two persons that you know.
2. Use analogy as suggested above to explain the historical relationship between two specific countries.
3. Using patterns of illustration and comparison, distinguish between intellectual and instinctive human behavior.
4. Compare or contrast man's motives for killing with those of animals. Some use of classification might also be helpful in this assignment.

(NOTE: Suggestions for topics requiring development by PROCESS ANALYSIS are on page 184, at the end of this section.)

JESSICA MITFORD

JESSICA MITFORD was born in 1917, the daughter of an English peer. Her brother was sent to Eton, but she and her six sisters were educated at home by their mother. At the age of nineteen Mitford left home, eventually making her way to the United States in 1939. Since 1944 she has been an American citizen, and is now living in San Francisco. She did not begin her writing career until she was thirty-eight. Her books are *Lifeitselfmanship* (1956); her autobiography, *Daughters and Rebels* (1960); the best-seller, *The American Way of Death* (1963); *The Trial of Dr. Spock* (1969); *Kind and Usual Punishment* (1973), a devastating study of the American penal system; *A Fine Old Conflict* (1977); and *Poison Penmanship* (1979). Mitford's articles have appeared in *The Atlantic Monthly, Harper's,* and *McCall's.*

To Dispel Fears of Live Burial

"To Dispel Fears of Live Burial" (editor's title) is a portion of *The American Way of Death,* a book described in *The New York Times* as a "savagely witty and well-documented exposé." The "savagely witty" style, evident in this selection, does not obscure the fact of its being a tightly organized, step-by-step process analysis.

Embalming is indeed a most extraordinary procedure, and one must wonder at the docility of Americans who each year pay hundreds of millions of dollars for its perpetuation, blissfully ignorant of what it is all about, what is done, how it is done. Not one in ten thousand has any idea of what actually takes place. Books on the subject are extremely hard to come by. They are not to be found in most libraries or bookshops. 1

In an era when huge television audiences watch surgical operations in the comfort of their living rooms, when, thanks to the animated cartoon, the geography of the digestive system has become 2 familiar territory even to the nursery school set, in a land where the satisfaction of curiosity about almost all matters is a national pastime, the secrecy surrounding embalming can, surely, hardly be attributed to the inherent gruesomeness of the subject. Custom in this regard has within this century suffered a complete reversal. In the early days of American embalming, when it was performed in the home of the deceased, it was almost mandatory for some relative to stay by the embalmer's side and witness the procedure. Today, family members who might wish to be in attendance would certainly be dissuaded by the funeral director. All others, except apprentices, are excluded by law from the preparation room.

A close look at what does actually take place may explain in large measure the undertaker's intractable reticence concerning a procedure that has become his major *raison d'être.* Is it possible he fears that public information about embalming might lead patrons to wonder if they really want this service? If the funeral men are loath to discuss the subject outside the trade, the reader may, understandably, be equally loath to go on reading at this point. For those who have the stomach for it, let us part the formaldehyde curtain. . . . 3

The body is first laid out in the undertaker's morgue — or rather, Mr. Jones is reposing in the preparation room — to be readied to bid the world farewell. 4

The preparation room in any of the better funeral establishments has the tiled and sterile look of a surgery, and indeed the embalmer-restorative artist who does his chores there is beginning to adopt the term "dermasurgeon" (appropriately corrupted by some mortician-writers as "demisurgeon") to describe his calling. His equipment, consisting of scalpels, scissors, augers, forceps, clamps, needles, pumps, tubes, bowls and basins, is crudely imitative of the surgeon's as is his technique, acquired in a nine- or twelve-month post-high-school course in an embalming school. He is supplied by an advanced chemical industry with a bewildering array of fluids, sprays, pastes, oils, powders, creams, to fix or soften tissue, shrink or distend it as needed, dry it here, restore the moisture there. There are cosmetics, waxes and paints to fill the cover features, even plaster of Paris to replace entire limbs. There are ingenious aids to prop and stabilize the cadaver: A Vari-Pose Head Rest, the Edwards Arm and Hand Positioner, the Repose Block (to support the shoulders during the embalming), and the Throop Foot Positioner, which resembles an old-fashioned stocks. 5

Mr. John H. Eckels, president of the Eckels College of Mortuary Science, thus describes the first part of the embalming procedure: "In the hands of a skilled practitioner, this work may be done in a comparatively short time and without multilating the body other than by slight incision — so slight that it scarcely would cause serious inconvenience if made upon a living person. It is necessary to remove the blood, and doing this not only helps in the disinfecting, but removes the principal cause of disfigurements due to discoloration." 6

Another textbook discusses the all-important time element: "The earlier this is done, the better, for every hour that elapses between death and embalming will add to the problems and complications encountered. . . ." Just how soon should one get going on the embalming? The author tells us, "On the basis of such scanty information made available to this profession through its rudimentary and haphazard system of technical research, we must conclude that the best results are to be obtained if the subject is embalmed before life is completely extinct — that is, before cellular death has occurred. In the average case, this would mean within an hour after somatic death." For those who feel that there is something a little rudimentary, not to say haphazard, about this advice, a comforting thought is offered by another writer. Speaking of fears entertained in early days of premature burial, he points out, "One of the effects of embalming by chemical injection, however, has been to dispel fears of live burial." How true; once the blood is removed, chances of live burial are indeed remote. 7

To return to Mr. Jones, the blood is drained out through the veins and replaced by embalming fluid pumped in through the arteries. As noted in *The Principles and Practices of Embalming,* "every operator has a favorite injection and drainage point — a fact which becomes a handicap only if he fails or refuses to forsake his favorites when conditions demand it." Typical favorites are the carotid artery, femoral artery, jugular vein, subclavian vein. There are various choices of embalming fluid. If Flextone is used, it will produce a "mild, flexible rigidity. The skin retains a velvety softness, the tissues are rubbery and pliable. Ideal for women and children." It may be blended with B. and G. Products Company's Lyf-Lyk tint, which is guaranteed to reproduce "nature's own skin texture . . . the velvety appearance of living tissue." Suntone comes in three separate tints: Suntan; Special Cosmetic Tint, a pink shade "especially indicated for young female subjects"; and Regular Cosmetic Tint, moderately pink. 8

About three to six gallons of a dyed and perfumed solution of 9
formaldehyde, glycerin, borax, phenol, alcohol and water is soon circulating through Mr. Jones, whose mouth has been sewn together with a "needle directed upward between the upper lip and gum and brought out through the left nostril," with the corners raised slightly "for a more pleasant expression." If he should be bucktoothed, his teeth are cleaned with Bon Ami and coated with colorless nail polish. His eyes, meanwhile, are closed with flesh-tinted eye caps and eye cement.

The next step is to have at Mr. Jones with a thing called a trocar. 10
His is a long, hollow needle attached to a tube. It is jabbed into the abdomen, poked around the entrails and chest cavity, the contents of which are pumped out and replaced with "cavity fluid." This done, and the hole in the abdomen sewn up, Mr. Jones's face is heavily creamed (to protect the skin from burns which may be caused by leakage of the chemicals), and he is covered with a sheet and left unmolested for a while. But not for long — there is more, much more, in store for him. He has been embalmed, but not yet restored, and the best time to start the restorative work is eight to ten hours after embalming, when the tissues have become firm and dry.

The object of all this attention to the corpse, it must be remem- 11
bered, is to make it presentable for viewing in an attitude of healthy repose. "Our customs require the presentation of our dead in the semblance of normality . . . unmarred by the ravages of illness, disease or mutilation," says Mr. J. Sheridan Mayer in his *Restorative Art.* This is rather a large order since few people die in the full bloom of health, unravaged by illness and unmarked by some disfigurement. The funeral industry is equal to the challenge: "In some cases the gruesome appearance of a mutilated or disease-ridden subject may be quite discouraging. The task of restoration may seem impossible and shake the confidence of the embalmer. This is the time for intestinal fortitude and determination. Once the formative work is begun and affected tissues are cleaned or removed, all doubts of success vanish. It is surprising and gratifying to discover the results which may be obtained."

The embalmer, having allowed an appropriate interval to elapse, 12
returns to the attack, but now he brings into play the skill and equipment of sculptor and cosmetician. Is a hand missing? Casting one in plaster of Paris is a simple matter. "For replacement purposes, only a cast of the back of the hand is necessary; this is within the ability of the average operator and is quite adequate." If a lip or two,

a nose or an ear should be missing, the embalmer has at hand a variety of restorative waxes with which to model replacements. Pores and skin texture are simulated by stippling with a little brush, and over this cosmetics are laid on. Head off? Decapitation cases are rather routinely handled. Ragged edges are trimmed, and head joined to torso with a series of splints, wires and sutures. It is a good idea to have a little something at the neck — a scarf or high collar — when time for viewing comes. Swollen mouth? Cut out tissue as needed from inside the lips. If too much is removed, the surface contour can easily be restored by padding with cotton. Swollen necks and cheeks are reduced by removing tissue through vertical incisions made down each side of the neck. "When the deceased is casketed, the pillow will hide the suture incisions . . . as an extra precaution against leakage, the suture may be painted with liquid sealer."

The opposite condition is more likely to present itself — that of emaciation. His hypodermic syringe now loaded with massage cream, the embalmer seeks out and fills the hollowed and sunken areas by injection. In this procedure the backs of the hands and fingers and the under-chin area should not be neglected. 13

Positioning the lips is a problem that recurrently challenges the ingenuity of the embalmer. Closed too tightly, they tend to give a stern, even disapproving expression. Ideally, embalmers feel, the lips should given the impression of being ever so slightly parted, the upper lip protruding slightly for a more youthful appearance. This takes some engineering, however, as the lips tend to drift apart. Lip drift can sometimes be remedied by pushing one or two straight pins through the inner margin of the lower lip and then inserting them between the two front upper teeth. If Mr. Jones happens to have no teeth, the pins can just as easily be anchored in his Armstrong Face Former and Denture Replacer. Another method to maintain lip closure is to dislocate the lower jaw, which is then held in its new position by a wire run through holes which have been drilled through the upper and lower jaws at the midline. As the French are fond of saying, *il faut souffrir pour être belle.*[1] 14

If Mr. Jones has died of jaundice, the embalming fluid will very likely turn him green. Does this deter the embalmer? Not if he has intestinal fortitude. Masking pastes and cosmetics are heavily laid on, burial garments and casket interiors are color-correlated with partic- 15

[1]You have to suffer if you want to be beautiful. (Editor's note)

ular care, and Jones is displayed beneath rose-colored lights. Friends will say, "How *well* he looks." Death by carbon monoxide, on the other hand, can be rather a good thing from the embalmer's viewpoint: "One advantage is the fact that this type of discoloration is an exaggerated form of a natural pink coloration." This is nice because the healthy glow is already present and needs but little attention.

The patching and filling completed, Mr. Jones is now shaved, washed and dressed. Cream-based cosmetic, available in pink, flesh, suntan, brunette and blond, is applied to his hands and face, his hair is shampooed and combed (and, in the case of Mrs. Jones, set), his hands manicured. For the horny-handed son of toil special care must be taken; cream should be applied to remove ingrained grime, and the nails cleaned. "If he were not in the habit of having them manicured in life, trimming and shaping is advised for better appearance — never questioned by kin." 16

Jones is now ready for casketing (this is the present participle of the verb "to casket"). In this operation, his right shoulder should be depressed slightly "to turn the body a bit to the right and soften the appearance of lying flat on the back." Positioning the hands is a matter of importance, and special rubber positioning blocks may be used. The hands should be cupped slightly for a more lifelike, relaxed appearance. Proper placement of the body requires a delicate sense of balance. It should lie as high as possible in the casket, yet not so high that the lid, when lowered, will hit the nose. On the other hand, we are cautioned, placing the body too low" creates the impression that the body is in a box." 17

Jones is next wheeled into the appointed slumber room where a few last touches may be added — his favorite pipe placed in his hand or, if he was a great reader, a book propped into position. (In the case of little Master Jones a Teddy bear may be clutched.) Here he will hold open house for a few days, visiting hours 10 A.M. to 9 P.M. 18

Meanings and Values

1a. What is the author's tone? (See Guide to Terms: *Style/Tone.*)
b. Try to analyze the effect this tone had, at first reading, on your impressions of the subject matter itself.
c. Form a specific comparision between this effect of tone and the effect of "tone of voice" in spoken language.

2. Why was it formerly "almost mandatory" for some relative to witness the embalming procedure (par. 2)?

3a. Do you believe that public information about this procedure would cost mortuaries much embalming business (par. 3)? Why, or why not?
b. Why *do* people subject their dead to such a process?

4. Use the three-part system of evaluation to judge the success of this process analysis. (Guide: *Evaluation.*)

Expository Techniques

1a. What is the central theme? (Guide: *Unity.*)
b. Which parts of the writing, if any, do not contribute to the theme, thus damaging unity?
c. What other elements of the writing contribute to, or damage unity?

2a. Beginning with paragraph 4, list or mark the transitional devices that help to bridge between paragraphs. (Guide: *Transition.*)
b. Briefly explain how coherence is aided by such interparagraph transitions.

3. In this selection, far more than in most, emphasis can best be studied in connection with style. In fact, the two are almost indistinguishable here, and few, if any, of the other methods of achieving emphasis are used at all. (Guide: *Emphasis* and *Style/Tone.*) Consider each of the following stylistic qualities (some may overlap; others are included in diction) and illustrate, by examples, how each does create emphasis.
a. Number and selection of details — e.g., the equipment and "aids" (par. 5).
b. Understatement — e.g., the chances of live burial" (par. 7).
c. Special use of quotations — e.g., "that the body is in a box" (par. 17).
d. Sarcasm and/or other forms of irony. (Guide: *Irony*) — e.g., "How *well* he looks" (par. 15).

Diction and Vocabulary

1. Much of the essay's unique style (with resulting emphasis) results from qualities of diction. Use examples to illustrate the following. (Some may be identical to those of the preceding answer, but they need not be.)
a. Choice of common, low-key words to achieve sarcasm through understatement — e.g., "This is nice . . ." (par. 15).
b. Terms of violence — e.g., "returns to the attack" (par. 12).
c. Terms of the living — e.g., "will hold open house" (par. 18).
d. The continuing use of "Mr. Jones."

2a. Illustrate the meaning of "connotation" with examples of quotations from morticians. (Guide: *Connotation/Denotation.*)
b. Are these also examples of "euphemism"?

c. Show how the author uses these facts to her own advantage — i.e., again, to achieve emphasis.

3a. Comment briefly on the quality and appropriateness of the metaphor that ends the introduction. (Guide: *Figures of Speech.*)

b. Is this, in any sense, also an allusion? Why, or why not?

4. Use the dictionary as needed to understand the meanings of the following words: docility, perpetuation (par. 1); inherent, mandatory (2); intractable, reticence, *raison d'être* (3); ingenious (5); rudimentary, cellular, somatic (7); carotid artery, femoral artery, subclavian vein (8); semblance (11); simulated, stippling, sutures (12); emaciation (13); dispel (7, title).

Suggestions for Writing and Dicussion

1. What evidence can you find that "the satisfaction of curiosity about almost all matters is a national pastime" (par 2)? Is this a good thing or not? Why?
2. Burial customs differ widely from country to country, sometimes from area to area in this country. If you can, describe one of the more distinctive customs and, if possible, show its sources — e.g., the climate, "old country" tradition.
3. What do you foresee as near and far-future trends or radical changes in American burial practices? Why?
4. You may wish to develop further your answers to question 3 of "Meanings and Values"; the rationale of a large majority of people who do use this mortuary "service" for their departed relatives.
5. If you like, explain your personal preferences and the reasons for them.

Writing Suggestions for Section 5

Process Analysis

1. From one of the following topics develop a central theme into an *informational* process analysis showing:

   a. How you selected a college.
   b. How you selected your future career or major field of study.
   c. How your family selected a home.
   d. How a potential riot was stopped.
   e. How religious faith is achieved.
   f. How gasoline is made.
   g. How the air in ________ becomes polluted.
   h. How lightening kills.
   i. How foreign policy is made.
   j. How political campaigns are financed.
   k. How ________ Church was rebuilt.
   l. How fruit blossoms are pollinated.

2. Select a specific reader-audience and write a *directional* process analysis on one of the following topics, showing:

   a. How to *do* any of the processes suggested by topics 1a–e. (This treatment will require a different viewpoint, completely objective, and may require a different organization.)
   b. How to overcome shyness.
   c. How to overcome stage fright.
   d. How to make the best use of study time.
   e. How to write a college composition.
   f. How to sell an ugly house.
   g. How to prepare livestock or any other entry for a fair.
   h. How to start a club (or some other kind of recurring activity).
   i. How to reduce the number of highway accidents in an area.
   j. How to survive a tornado (or other natural disaster).
   k. How to select a car.
   l. How to develop moral (or physical) courage.

6

Analyzing *Cause* and *Effect* Relationships

Unlike process analysis, which merely tells *how,* causal analysis seeks to explain *why.* The two may be combined, but they need not be — many people have driven a car successfully after being told how to do it, never knowing or caring why the thing moved when they turned a key and worked a pedal or two.

Some causes and effects are not very complicated; at least the need for their explanation requires only a simple statement. A car may sit in the garage for a while because its owner has no money for a license tag, and sometimes this is explanation enough. But frequently a much more thorough analysis is required, and this may even become the basic pattern of an exposition.

To explain fully the causes of a war or depression or election results the writer must seek not only *immediate* causes (the ones he encounters first) but also *ultimate* causes (the basic, underlying factors that help to explain the more apparent ones). The business or professional man, as well as the student, often has pressing need for this type of analysis. How else could he fully understand or report on a failing sales campaign, diminishing church membership, a local increase of traffic accidents, or teenage use of hard drugs? The immediate cause of a disastrous warehouse fire could be faulty electrical wiring, but this might be attributed in turn to the company's unwise economy measures, which might be traced even further to undue pressures on the management to show large profits. The written analysis might logically stop at any point, of course, depending entirely on its purpose and the reader-audience for which it is intended.

Similarly, both the immediate and ultimate *effects* of an action or situation may, or may not, need to be fully explored. If a 5 percent pay raise is granted, what will be the immediate effect on the cost of production, leading to what ultimate effects on prices and, in some cases, on the whole economy of a business, a town, or perhaps the entire nation?

In earlier selections of this book we have seen several examples of causal analysis. In Section 1, for instance, Peter and Hull are concerned with the ultimate causes of incompetence in public life, and, in Section 3, Toffler with both immediate and ultimate causes and effects of "future shock."

Causal analysis is one of the chief techniques of reasoning; and if the method is used at all, the reader must always have confidence in its thoroughness and logic. Here are some ways to avoid the most common faults in causal reasoning:

1. Never mistake the fact that something happens with or after another occurrence as evidence of a causal relationship — for example, that a black cat crossing the road caused the flat tire a few minutes later, or that a course in English composition caused a student's nervous breakdown that same semester.

2. Consider all possibly relevant factors before attributing causes. Perhaps studying English did result in a nervous breakdown, but the cause may also have been ill health, trouble at home, or the anguish of a love affair. (The composition course, by providing an "emotional" outlet, may even have helped *postpone* the breakdown!)

3. Support the analysis by more than mere assertions: offer evidence. It would not often be enough to *tell* why Shakespeare's wise Othello believed the villainous Iago — the dramatist's lines should be used as evidence, possibly supported by the opinions of at least one literary scholar. If explaining that capital punishment deters crime, do not expect the reader to take your word for it — give before-and-after statistics or the testimony of reliable authorities.

4. Be careful not to omit any links in the chain of causes or effects unless you are certain that the readers for whom the writing is intended will automatically make the right connections themselves — and this is frequently a dangerous assumption. To unwisely omit one or more of the links might leave the reader with only a vague, or even erroneous, impression of the causal connection, possibly invalidating all that follows and thus making the entire writing ineffective.

5. Be honest and objective. The writer (or thinker) who brings his old prejudices to the task of causal analysis, or who fails to see the probability of *multiple* causes or effects, is almost certain to distort his analysis or to make it so superficial, so thin, as to be almost worthless.

Ordinarily the method of causal analysis is either to work logically from the immediate cause (or effect) down toward the most basic, or to start with the basic and work up toward the immediate. But after he has at least analyzed the subject in his mind and decided what his purpose requires in the paragraph or entire composition, the writer will usually find that a satisfactory pattern suggests itself.

SISSELA BOK

SISSELA BOK born in 1934, is a lecturer on medical ethics at Harvard–MIT, Division of Health Sciences and Technology. She was educated at the Sorbonne in Paris; George Washington University; and Harvard University, where she received her Ph.D. Bok, who speaks French, German, the Scandinavian languages, Latin, and some Greek, has served on numerous advisory boards and committees, and helped to conduct many seminars. She is also the author of many articles in the broad field of ethics in medicine and in governmental affairs. She wrote the book *Lying: Moral Choice in Private and Public Life,* published in 1978, and was coauthor-editor of *The Dilemmas of Euthanasia* (1975). She is now working as coeditor on *The Teaching of Ethics,* soon to be published. Bok is married to Derek Bok, president of Harvard University; they have three children.

To Lie or Not to Lie

"To Lie or Not to Lie," first published in *The New York Times,* employs an uncomplicated cause-effect analysis. But before the author gets to either causes or effects, she develops almost as much of the essay by another pattern of exposition we have already studied.

No misconception is so dangerous, wrote the Marquis de Condorcet, the 18th-century social philosopher and revolutionist, as the view that Government lies can sometimes serve the public interest; no error gives rise to so many other delusions. 1

We have had a vivid demonstration of how lies undermine a political system. The webs of deceit from Vietnam and Watergate were of an intricacy and a scope that may not soon be surpassed. But most observers would agree that deception is also part and parcel of many everyday Government decisions. Government officials may sometimes look at lies as the only way to cope with what they take 2

Reprinted by permission of the publisher from *The New York Times* (April 20, 1978).

to be an unmanageable bureaucracy, a needlessly suspicious press, or an uncomprehending public.

In this way false rumors may be leaked by subordinates who 3
believe that unwise administrative action is about to be taken. Statistics may be presented in such a way as to diminish the gravity of embarrassing problems. Government officials may hotly deny rumors of policy changes one day only to implement the changes the next. And they may misrepresent altogether some policies — preparations for war, for example — that they take to be beyond the comprehension of citizens.

Public obtuseness is also invoked by candidates who make 4
promises they know they cannot keep, or take stands they plan to reverse if elected. And members of Congress may deny having made deals that led them to vote for measures they would otherwise have opposed.

The incentives to deceit are often strong. Consider the Adminis- 5
tration official who has worked long in the hope that Congress will enact new anti-poverty legislation. Should he lie to a Congressman he believes unable to understand the importance and urgency of the proposed bill, yet powerful enough to block its passage? Should he warn — contrary to fact — that the Administration will press for a far more extensive measure unless the present bill is enacted?

He may regard such a lie as a trifling concession for a pressing 6
goal, and have full confidence in his disinterested motives and in his ability to distinguish such lies from more harmful ones.

Such thinking is shortsighted. The most fundamental error that 7
people make when weighing lies is to evaluate the costs and benefits of a particular lie in an isolated case, and then to favor the lie if the benefits seem to outweigh the costs. In doing so, they overlook two factors. Bias, first of all, skews all judgment, but never more than in the search for good reasons to deceive. Liars tend to overestimate their own good will, high motives, and chances to escape detection, to underrate the intelligence of the deceived and to ignore their rights.

Second, in focusing on the isolated lie it is easy to ignore the 8
most significant costs of lying: to ignore what lying — even in a good cause — does to the standards of those who tell the lies as well as to their credibility; to overlook the effects of lies on the coworkers who witness them, and who may imitate them, or on others who learn about them and who may deceive in retaliation or merely to stay

even. Above all, such a narrow focus ignores the cumulative effects of lies — many told for what seemed at the time "good reasons" — as they build up into vast institutional practices. The long-range effects of the narrow and biased calculations that underlie each isolated lie are severe.

Lying by public officials is now so widely suspected that voters 9
are at a loss to know when they can and cannot believe what a Government spokesman reports, or what a candidate says in campaigning. The damage to trust has been immense. Two years ago, 69 percent of the respondents to a national poll agreed that this country's leaders have consistently lied to the people over the last 10 years. And over 40 percent agreed that most politicians are so similar that it does not really matter who is elected.

Many refuse to vote under such circumstances. Others look to 10
appearance or to personality factors for clues as to which candidate might be more trustworthy than the rest. Once trust has eroded to this extent, it is hard to regain. Even the most honest public officials then meet with suspicion. And in times of national stress when problems require joint efforts — problems, for example, of preparing for energy shortages or for inflation — the cynicism and apathy that greet Government calls to common sacrifice are crippling. Citizens and governments alike are the true losers when a political system has reached such a low level of trust.

Meanings and Values

1. Would you classify this writing as more nearly subjective, or objective? Why? (See Guide to Terms: *Objective/Subjective.*)
2. Is it a formal essay? Why, or why not? (Guide: *Essay.*)
3a. What qualifier is used frequently in the first half of this essay? (Guide: *Qualification.*)
 b. Does it always serve a worthwhile purpose? Discuss any exceptions.
4. What, if anything, is notable about the style of Bok's writing? (Guide: *Style/Tone.*)

Expository Techniques

1a. Cite the paragraphs in which are discussed the effects of lying by public officials.
 b. Which of these are immediate and which ultimate effects?

c. Is there always a clear distinction between the two?

2a. What other pattern of exposition is employed extensively in this essay?

b. What seems to be its primary purpose?

3a. Which of the standard introductory techniques are used in paragraph 1? (Guide: *Introductions.*)

b. Does the paragraph perform the three essential functions of a good introduction?

4. Comment on the manner in which this essay is concluded. (Guide: *Closings.*)

Diction and Vocabulary

1. Do you find any clichés in this writing? If so, are they justified? (Guide: *Clichés.*)
2. Explain precisely what happens when candidates invoke "public obtuseness" (par. 4).

Suggestions for Writing and Discussion

1. Are there any times when lying by government officials may be justified? Consider fully, for instance, what would happen if officials always told the truth during wartime, or just where the line should be drawn between justified and unjustified lying.
2. Show how personal lying may, or may not, be as harmful in private life as public lying is to the conduct of government.

(NOTE: Suggestions for topics requiring development by analysis of CAUSE and EFFECT are on page 209, at the end of this section.)

GAIL SHEEHY

GAIL SHEEHY (born 1937) is a native New Yorker. After graduating from the University of Vermont she was a department store consumer representative, a fashion coordinator, newspaper fashion editior, and women's feature writer for the New York *Herald Tribune.* Since 1968 Sheehy has been a contributing editor for *New York* magazine. Her articles have appeared in numerous magazines, including *McCall's, Cosmopolitan, Holiday, Glamour, Good Housekeeping,* and *The New York Times Magazine.* Her books are *Lovesounds* (1970), *Speed Is of the Essence* (1971), *Panthermania* (1971), *Hustling* (1973), and *Passages* (1976), which was on the nation's best-seller lists for many months.

$70,000 a Year, Tax Free

"$70,000 a Year, Tax Free" (editor's title) was written for NBC's "Comment" series, but the material was incorporated into *Hustling.* Its brevity, due to time limitations on the original presentation, obviously precluded a really thorough analysis of the topic. Observing how the author did use the time at her disposal provides some of the value of studying the selection here.

1 How many women do you know who can take home seventy thousand dollars a year? A psychiatrist? She might take home half that. A congresswoman? Shirley Chisholm's salary is forty-two-five.

2 No, the quickest way for a woman to get ahead in this country is to take up the oldest profession: prostitution.

3 As one veteran streetwalker explained to a runaway she was breaking in: "You have no status, no power, and no way to get it except by using your body. Why give it away? You're sitting on a gold mine."

4 And so, every summer, in New York City, the hue and cry goes up: Crack down on prostitution! Close the massage parlors! But why has New York become a boomtown for hustlers? Not because of the increased use of drugs, as most people assume. It began with a change

in New York's penal code four years ago. Loitering for the purpose of prostitution was reduced by former Police Commissioner Leary from a misdemeanor to a violation. Even girls found guilty on the more serious "pross collar" rarely go to jail. Most judges let them go for a twenty-five to fifty dollar fine — and a week to pay. It amounts to a license.

Word of this change spread with interest through the pimp 5
grapevine around the country: New York was wide open. Today, you'd hardly guess which four states have the largest pipeline shipping prostitutes to New York: in order, they are Minnesota, Massachusetts, Michigan, and Ohio. There are lots of fair haired girls from Minnesota with street names like Little Tiffany, and Marion the Librarian. But why do they come? It couldn't be a more American phenomenon: The prostitute's dream is the most upward mobile, middle class, American pie dream of all.

Number one: she wants money — high-style clothes, a model 6
apartment, candy color wigs and her teeth capped.

Number two: she's looking for a "family." Most of the girls have 7
one or two children — illegitimate. On top of that, the girl is often white and her illegitimate child is black. Back home in Minnneapolis, she was already a social pariah, and she couldn't make a go of living and working while dragging a baby from room to rented room. So she comes to New York, looking for a new kind of family — exactly what the pimp provides.

He puts up his stable of three or four girls in a high-rise apart- 8
ment, pays their rent, buys their clothes, foots their doctor bills. Top woman in this "family" — the pimp's favorite, who brings in the most money — is called his "wife." The rest are known as "wife-in-laws." Remarkably enough, they all get along quite well. The tie that really binds is the baby sitter — the girls share one for seventy-five dollars a week and this is what frees them to work.

As a midtown hooker from Virginia put it to me: "Most of the 9
girls are here doing it for their kids. I don't want my daughter to have the kind of childhood I had. She's going to have the best!"

So now the prostitute has money, a family, a baby sitter. The 10
other thing she craves is "glamour and excitement," things she probably dreamed of finding in a career as a model or actress. But those fields are fiercely competitive. Besides, as a prostitute sees it, models and actresses are treated like dress hangers or pieces of meat: they give their bodies away to advance their careers, while so-called straight women exchange sex for the financial security of marriage.

A "working girl," as the prostitute refers to herself, is the only honest one: She sets the price, delivers the goods, and concludes her business within the hour — no romantic nonsense about it.

And finally, after she is on the street for a few months, the pace of peeping and hiding, the game of stinging johns and ducking police vans becomes a way of life. It gets into the blood like gambler's fever. 11

The hooker with the heart of gold? That's a male myth. Many of our street girls can be as vicious and money mad as any corporation president. Moreover, they can be less emotional than men in conducting acts of personal violence. The bulk of their business is not the dispensation of pleasure: it is to mug, rob, swindle, knife and possibly, even murder their patrons. Police drags against them are about as effective as pacification programs in Vietnam. Apply police pressure to streetwalkers and robberies generally go up. If a girl doesn't bring in that fixed amount, two hundred and fifty a night, she'll go home to a beating from her pimp. 12

People are puzzled: why this boom in prostitution when young America is bursting with sexual freedom? They forget about men over forty, men who learned their sexual fantasies from nudie calendars in the gas station. To be fun, the bedmate must be a no-no. "You can't fantasize about your wife or girlfriend," one man explained. "The woman has to be an unknown." And where is this illicit thrill of forbidden flesh still to be found? On the black market of course. Furthermore, the prostitute makes no emotional demands. She would never call his office the next day. It is her stock in trade to encourage men's sexual fantasies and exploit them. How else can a girl make seventy thousand dollars a year, tax free? 13

Meanings and Values

1a. Briefly summarize the author's reasons for a girl's becoming a prostitute.

b. Do you consider these ultimate or immediate causes — or would you classify them somewhere in between? Why?

2a. Why does the author consider these motivations as an "American pie dream" (par. 5)?

b. To which of the causes, if any, does the description seem to you not to apply? Why?

3. Why does she assume that we'd "hardly guess" which four states have the largest pipelines into New York prostitution (par. 5)?

4. Do you see anything ironical in the prostitute's comments in paragraph 9? (See Guide to Terms: *Irony.*) If so, explain.

5a. How can perpetuation of the "male myth" (par. 12) be explained?
b. Why would it be more difficult to "fantasize" about one's wife or girlfriend (par. 13)?

6a. Where would you locate this selection on a objective-to-subjective continuum? (Guide: *Objective/Subjective.*)
b. Is the author guilty of any sentimentality? (Guide: *Sentimentality.*) If so, where?

Expository Techniques

1a In which paragraphs does the author explain why prostitution has increased greatly in New York City?
b. Does this seem to be a thorough cause-and-effect analysis?
c. Is it sufficient for the purpose? Why, or why not?

2a. In paragraphs 6–11 she outlines a different set of causes. Would they have been more effective for her purpose if she had gone deeper into the more ultimate causes?
b. Why do you think she did not?
c. What function is served by the first sentence of paragraph 10? Why would the author have considered it a useful device in this particular exposition?

3a. What is Sheehy's central theme? (Guide: *Unity.*)
b. Do all portions of the essay serve as tributaries into this theme, thus giving unity to the writing? If not, what are the exceptions?

4a. Which of the standard techniques of introduction does this author use? (Guide: *Introductions.*)
b. Why do they seem particularly well chosen, considering the basic purpose of this exposition?

5a. The last sentence is a good example of at least one standard technique of closing. (Guide: *Closings.*) What is it?
b. Suggest a different kind of closing and compare the relative effectiveness of the two.

6. Which of the patterns of exposition already studied does Sheehy employ in paragraph 10?

7. In your opinion, would any of her statements have benefited by further qualification? (Guide: *Qualification.*) If so, explain why.

Diction and Vocabulary

1. Illustrate the meaning of the following terms by use of one or more examples from this selection.

a. Colloquialism. (Guide: *Colloquial Expressions.*)
b. Simile. (Guide: *Figures of Speech.*)
c. Cliché. (Guide: *Clichés.*)

2. What is a "social pariah" (par. 7)?
3. Considering this exposition's original purpose, why do you think the author used few, if any, "dictionary-type" words?

Suggestions for Writing and Discussion

1. The author says most people assume that the increase of prostitution is related to an increased use of drugs. How logical does this assumption appear to you? Explain.
2. Explore parallels in other, more legitimate fields in which motivation may be provided by the "upward mobile, middle class, American pie dream" (par. 5).
3. In view of the five reasons for a girl's becoming a prostitute — all seeming to be fairly common desires — why is it that even more girls do not engage in prostitution?
4. Which of her five reasons do you think would also apply to the thriving business (in some cities especially) of male prostitution? Are there other reasons that apply here?
5. How logical and/or just do you consider the move in many areas toward "equal guilt" laws, whereby the male is considered as guilty as the prostitute he employs?
6. Should there even *be* laws prohibiting prostitution?
7. The word "prostitution" is often used with broader meaning than in Sheehy's analysis — e.g., "prostitution of talent" or "prostitution of science." Select one such usage and examine motivations in terms of this author's "upward mobility" theories.

(NOTE: Suggestions for topics requiring development by analysis of CAUSE and EFFECT are on page 209, at the end of this section.)

MARGARET HALSEY

MARGARET HALSEY was born in Yonkers, New York in 1910. A graduate of Skidmore College and Teachers College of Columbia University, she wrote her first book after living in England for a year. *With Malice Towards Some,* a comic study of the English, was a runaway bestseller in 1938. During World War II, she worked at the famous Stage Door Canteen in New York's Times Square, one of only two canteens in the country open to black servicemen as well as white. Her book about this experiment in racial integration, *Color Blind,* was published in 1946. The author of four other books, including *No Laughing Matter: The Autobiography of a WASP* (1977), Halsey now lives in London with her daughter.

What's Wrong with "Me, Me, Me"?

"What's Wrong with 'Me, Me, Me'?" was first published in *Newsweek.* Here Halsey is concerned with both immediate and ultimate effects, as she examines the popular cult of "Inner Wonderfulness." The author uses sarcasm as one subtle but important device by which to show the basic error of the "human-potential industry" and the "me" generation they attempt to help find themselves.

Tom Wolfe has christened today's young adults the "me" generation, and the 1970s—obsessed with things like consciousness expansion and self-awareness—have been described as the decade of the new narcissism. The cult of "I," in fact, has taken hold with the strength and impetus of a new religion. But the joker in the pack is that it is all based on a false idea. 1

The false idea is that inside every human being, however unprepossessing, there is a glorious, talented and overwhelmingly attractive personality. This personality — so runs the erroneous belief — will be revealed in all its splendor if the individual just forgets about courtesy, cooperativeness and consideration for others and proceeds to do exactly what he or she feels like doing. 2

Nonsense. 3

Inside each of us is a mess of unruly primitive impulses, and these can sometimes, under the strenuous self-discipline and dedication of art, result in notable creativity. But there is no such thing as a pure, crystalline and well-organized "native" personality, though a host of trendy human-potential groups trade on the mistaken assumption that there is. And backing up the human-potential industry is the advertising profession, which also encourages the idea of an Inner Wonderfulness that will be unveiled to a suddenly respectful world upon the purchase of this or that commodity. 4

However, an individual does not exist in a vacuum. A human being is not an isolated, independent thing-in-itself, but inevitably reflects the existence of others. The young adults of the "me" generation would never have lived to grow up if a great many parents, doctors, nurses, farmers, factory workers, teachers, policemen, firemen and legions of others had not ignored their human potential and made themselves do jobs they did not perhaps feel like doing in order to support the health and growth of children. 5

And yet, despite the indulgence of uninhibited expression, the "self" in self-awareness seems to cause many new narcissists and members of the "me" generation a lot of trouble. This trouble emerges in talk about "identity." We hear about the search for identity and a kind of distress called an identity crisis. 6

"I don't know who I am." How many bartenders and psychiatrists have stifled yawns on hearing that popular threnody for the thousandth time! 7

But this sentence has no meaning unless spoken by an amnesia victim, because many of the people who say they do not know who they are, actually *do* know. What such people really mean is that they are not satisfied with who they are. They feel themselves to be timid and colorless or to be in some way or other fault-ridden, but they have soaked up enough advertising and enough catch-penny ideas of self-improvement to believe in universal Inner Wonderfulness. So they turn their backs on their honest knowledge of themselves — which with patience and courage could start them on the road to genuine development — and embark on a quest for a will-o'-the-wisp called "identity." 8

But a *search* for identity is predestined to fail. Identity is not found, the way Pharaoh's daughter found Moses in the bulrushes. Identity is built. It is built every day and every minute throughout 9 the day. The myriad choices, small and large, that human beings make all the time determine identity. The fatal weakness of the currently fashionable approach to personality is that the "self" of the self-awareness addicts, the self of Inner Wonderfulness, is static. Being perfect, it does not need to change. But genuine identity changes as one matures. If it does not, if the 40-year-old has an identity that was set in concrete at the age of 18, he or she is in trouble.

The idea of a universal Inner Wonderfulness that will be appar- 10 ent to all beholders after a six-week course in self-expression is fantasy.

But how did this fantasy gain wide popular acceptance as a 11 realizable fact?

Every society tries to produce a prevalent psychological type 12 that will best serve its ends, and that type is always prone to certain emotional malfunctions. In early capitalism, which was a producing society, the ideal type was acquisitive, fanatically devoted to hard work and fiercely repressive of sex. The emotional malfunctions to which this type was liable were hysteria and obsession. Later capitalism, today's capitalism, is a consuming society, and the psychological type it strives to create, in order to build up the largest possible markets, is shallow, easily swayed and characterized much more by self-infatuation than self-respect. The emotional malfunction of this type is narcissism.

It will be argued that the cult of "I" has done some individuals 13 a lot of good. But at whose expense? What about the people to whom these "healthy" egotists are rude or even abusive? What about the people over whom they ride roughshod? What about the people they manipulate and exploit? And — the most important question of all — how good a preparation for inevitable old age and death is a deliberately cultivated self-love? The psychologists say that the full-blown classic narcissists lose all dignity and go mad with fright as they approach their final dissolution. Ten or fifteen years from now — when the young adults of the "me" generation hit middle age — will be the time to ask whether "self-awareness" really does people any good.

A long time ago, in a book called "Civilization and Its Discon- 14 tents," Freud pointed out that there is an unresolvable conflict between the human being's selfish, primitive, infantile impulses and the restraint he or she must impose on those impulses if a stable society is to be maintained. The "self" is not a handsome god or goddess waiting coyly to be revealed. On the contrary, its complexity, confusion and mystery have proved so difficult that throughout the ages men and women have talked gratefully about *losing* themselves. They *lose* the self in contemplating a great work of art, or in nature, or in scientific research, or in writing poetry, or in fashioning things with their hands or in projects that will benefit others rather than themselves.

The current glorification of self-love will turn out in the end to 15
be a no-win proposition, because in questions of personality or "identity," what counts is not who you are, but what you do. "By their fruits, ye shall know them." And by their fruits, they shall know themselves.

Meanings and Values

1a. What irony is involved in Halsey's comments on people's "search for identity"? (See Guide to Terms: *Irony.*)
b. Why is it ironical?
c. What kind of irony is it?

2a. What is the author's point of view? (Guide: *Point of View.*)
b. Is it too extreme to be most effective?

3a. Would the essay benefit by greater use of qualification? (Guide: *Qualification.*)
b. If so, how could the author have gone about it?
c. If not, explain why the writing is better as it is.

4. Is it really necessary for today's capitalism to create the psychological type described in paragraph 12? Use specific advertising examples to illustrate your points.

5. Use the three-point system by which to evaluate the success of this selection. (Guide: *Evaluation.*)

Expository Techniques

1a. Which of the standard techniques are used for the introduction? (Guide: *Introductions.*)
b. How successful are they in fulfilling the three basic requirements of a good introduction?

2. One of the most interesting aspects of this essay is the manner of alternating between a cause/effect analysis and other patterns of exposition.

a. What is the primary pattern used in paragraphs 2 and 3, and the first part of 4?
b. What pattern is used in the latter part of paragraph 4?
c. Are the effects considered in paragraphs 6–8 better classified as immediate or ultimate? Why?
d. What is the primary pattern of paragraph 9?
e. Paragraph 12 analyzes the causes of today's "fantasy," but it also makes good use of another basic pattern of exposition. What is it?
f. The real climax of the writing comes in paragraph 13. Do you think the author is more concerned here with immediate or ultimate effects? Why?

3a. Are the questions of paragraph 13 classifiable as "rhetorical"? (Guide: *Rhetorical Questions.*) Why, or why not?
b. Do they provide an effective way of presenting the climactic material of the paragraph?

4a. The closing consists of the last two paragraphs. What standard techniques are used? (Guide: *Closings.*)
b. Does it perform the basic function of a good closing?

Diction and Vocabulary

1a. Cite the figures of speech in paragraphs 1, 4, and 9.
b. Are they well chosen?

2. What are the rhetorical benefits of the one-word paragraph 3?

3. Explain the source and meaning of "narcissism" (or "narcissists"), as used in several paragraphs of this essay.

4. For various reasons Halsey's uses of "Inner Wonderfulness" gain much desired emphasis. (Guide *Emphasis.*) List all the factors that contribute to this effect.

5. Consult your dictionary as needed to determine meanings of the following words: impetus (par. 1); unprepossessing (2); crystalline (4); threnody (7); acquisitive (12).

Suggestions for Writing and Discussion

1. If you consider the "me generation" too broad a generalization, in view of the many obvious exceptions, explain why. Be as specific as possible.

2. Explore the possibility that a search for identity might *lead* one to be more considerate of and involved with others.

3. Discuss in depth the ideas suggested by one or more of the following quotations:

a. "Inside each of us is a mess of unruly primitive impulses" (par. 4).
b. Identity "is built every day and every minute throughout the day" (par. 9).
c. "Throughout the ages men and women have talked gratefully about *losing* themselves" (par. 14).

(NOTE: Suggestions for topics requiring development by analysis of CAUSE and EFFECT are on page 209, at the end of this section.)

JACQUES BARZUN

JACQUES BARZUN was born in France, in 1907, but received his A.B., M.A., and Ph.D. degrees at Columbia University. There he has also had a long and distinguished career as historian, professor, and author of innumerable books and articles published in such periodicals as *Harper's, Atlantic Monthly, Saturday Review, New Republic,* and *New York Times* Magazine. He has belonged to various distinguished societies and been the recipient of many honors and awards. His extensive list of published books includes *The Use and Abuse of Art* (1974); *Classic, Romantic, and Modern, The House of Intellect,* and *Simple and Direct: A Rhetoric for Writers,* all published in 1975.

The Professions Under Siege

"The Professions Under Siege" was first published in *Harper's* and later condensed for *Reader's Digest.* Here Barzun analyzes both causes and effects of the present crisis in the professions; but he also makes efficient use of various other patterns of exposition.

The status of any profession goes up and down like the stock market, in response to things other than net worth. And, for a decade or more, the public and the press have made it clear that the learned professions are not the splendid companies, held in awe and respect, that they once were. 1

Doctors, formerly worshiped as omniscient Good Samaritans, are now seen as profiteers, often of doubtful competence, who cover up one another's homicidal mistakes. Lawyers, once the defenders of private and civil rights, now are thought neglectful and extortionate, calculatedly deceiving the public through purposely mystifying language. The academics lost their prestige by their fecklessness in the campus troubles of 1965–1970. The scientists, demigods since Darwin, became objects of suspicion after Hiroshima. Latest on the car- 2 pet, the austere, unfathomable accountant is being shown up as a master of misrepresentation, a *cordon bleu*[1] at cooking the books.

Long ago, Bernard Shaw wrote that a self-governed profession is "a conspiracy against the laity." The epigram should not be dismissed as a joke or a needless exaggeration. The only overemphasis is in the word *conspiracy,* which implies a secret purpose to overreach the public. Yet it is that very imputation of making the most of closely held secrets that becomes the common man's idea of a profession when it begins to lose the public's faith and regard. And there lies the danger. For the obvious next idea that occurs to the aroused critics is to demand strong supervision from outside. 3

Yet better relations between layman and professional can hardly be brought about in mutual suspicion and hostility. Nor can there be improvement through collective bargaining. The essence of those relations is individual, from which it follows that some clearer idea of what a profession is must once again become common property among insiders and outsiders both. 4

According to Abraham Flexner, the famous reformer of medical education nearly 70 years ago, to be medically trained implies "the possession of certain portions of many sciences arranged and organized with a distinct practical purpose in view. That is what makes it a 'profession.' " Since the laity, by definition, has no such purposes and lacks special training, a profession is necessarily a monopoly. In modern societies this monopoly is made legal by a license to practice. Professionals justify the monopoly by calling it essential to the safety of the public. But between monopoly and conspiracy the line of demarcation is hard to fix and easy to step over. 5

The upshot is that a profession is by nature a vulnerable institution. It makes claims; it demands unique privileges; and it has to perform. But "it" of course does not exist as a single entity; it is a few hundred or many thousands of individuals, who differ as widely as all other human beings, yet who, as professionals, are expected to act in a standard manner and to be invariably successful in their art. 6

In fact, though, as a whole every profession is horribly average, mediocre. By definition it cannot be anything else. But the public expectation aims much higher than mediocrity, so that in a time of reckoning, when the laity is hot about its rights, general dismay and 7

[1]Any person highly distinguished in his field. Formerly the emblem worn by France's highest order of knighthood. (Editor's note)

recrimination are inevitable. What is more, although any art should be judged by its best results, a democratic nation, bent on equality in all things, is sure to judge a profession by its worst exemplars. That is the condition we are in now.

Consider the malpractice suit. From one point of view, it is just that a patient — or his heirs — should recover damages for careless or ignorant treatment. From another point of view, it is absurd that after the best professional efforts failure should be a cause of complaint. Yet a customer cannot tell whether he has had the best. He judges by gross results — kill or cure — and wants the reasons plain. 8

The subtleties of the predicament are even clearer in education, where the failure to "educate" a particular student is evident in the student, yet assigning blame is beyond human wit. Nor can our modern system follow the example of the old-time college president who said to the indignant parent: "Madam, we guarantee results — or we return the boy." 9

It is because of these intricacies behind the gross results — a cure, a good education, winning the lawsuit — that for centuries it has seemed best to let the professions police themselves. But the regulations of business came about because business did not regulate itself. It exploited labor and the buyer, under the motto "The public be damned." An alert professional today has the uneasy feeling that the professions are at the juncture where the same motto is being imputed to them. 10

There are other signs of a gradual demoting of the professions to the level of ordinary trades and businesses. The right of lawyers and physicians to advertise, which reintroduces money competition, has been granted. Architects are being allowed to act as contractors. Teachers have been unionized. Laymen demand the right to sit on various professional boards on the ground that internal management is unable to serve the public fairly without supervision. The great force of government money works to the same end, for bureaucracy follows the funds and while directing their use is bound to control the user. 11

Such moves, whether viewed as threats or reforms, signify one thing: The modern professions have enjoyed their monopoly so long that they have forgotten that it is a privilege given in exchange for a public benefit. Occasional complaints have been interpreted as envy or misunderstanding, instead of what they are: resentment at breach of faith, contempt of complacency. 12

It may be, of course, that we are witnessing the evolution of a drive toward a society collectivized through and through, the theory being that no individual *or* group can be trusted. That would mean the death of the very idea of a profession. 13

The message for the professions today is that their one hope of survival with anything like their present freedoms is the recovery of mental and moral force. *Moral* here does not mean merely honest; it refers to the nature of any encounter between two human beings. As soon as a person serves another, ethical issues spring to life and get settled well or badly. Such practices as experiments on poor patients, or operations by young residents while the patient thinks he is in the hands of the great surgeon, seem clear-cut matters that find their parallels in teaching and in the law. But more subtle situations arise from group practice, in any profession, where the client may be tossed about among several hands, losing confidence all the while, and in the end knowing that responsible attention has been denied him. 14

Moral sensitivity will not return to the individual practitioner by his guild's writing a fresh code. A code only sets the limits beyond which behavior will be condemned, and the moral level is not high when most of those living under it always act within a hairline of those limits. Codes, in fact, are for criminals and competitors, not for professions that want to be known as dedicated. No doubt the professional codes now in force can benefit from revision, but what the professions need first is the will to police themselves with no fraternal hand, with no thought of public relations. Any few scandals giving the group a bad name will soon convince the public that self-policing means what it says and confidence will return. Disciplining from within must continue, steady and firm, or it will be taken over by public bodies. 15

But policing, being negative, is not enough. Moral regeneration can come about only when the members of a group feel once more confident that ethical behavior *is* desirable, widely practiced, approved and admired. After a marked decline, it can only be a slow growth, and only one force can start it on its way: the force of moral and intellectuul leadership. All professions need critics from inside, men who know what conditions are and can offer their fellow practitioners a new vision of the profession as an institution. 16

For each profession, details will have to be spelled out and embedded in general principles. The aim is to lift the critique from a set of complaints to a set of purposes. That is what Flexner did when he 17 riddled medical education in 1910. He changed American medicine, having made it impossible for do-nothing schools to continue in being.

When the problem is a failure of competence and morality, nothing will solve it but the work of an individual mind and conscience, aided of course by the many scattered men of talent and good will who are only waiting for a lead. Without some such heroic effort, we professionals shall all go down — appropriately — as non-heroes together. 18

Meanings and Values

1. What kind of essay is this — formal, informal, or familiar? (See Guide to Terms: *Essay.*) Why would you so classify it?
2a. What is Barzun's point of view? (Guide: *Point of View.*)
 b. Explain why it is, or is not, a credible one.
3. Do you agree that Flexner's definition of a profession (par. 5) does not apply to the trades or business? Why, or why not?
4. Why must every profession, as a whole, be horribly average and mediocre "by definition" (par. 7)?
5. Do you agree that a democratic nation is sure to judge a profession by its worst exemplars (par. 7)? Why, or why not?
6. Do you agree that is is "beyond human wit" to assign blame for failure to educate a particular student (par. 9)? Discuss.
7. Reread paragraph 13 carefully and determine whether Barzun implies that medicine, for example, is not a profession in Russia or China — or, for that matter, in England or Sweden. Would you agree with him? Why, or why not?

Expository Techniques

1. Does the first paragraph successfully perform the three essential functions of an introduction? Point out any inadequacies. (Guide: *Introductions.*)
2a. Briefly, what does the author say are the causes of the state of the professions today?
 b. Are these immediate or ultimate causes?
 c. What does he say will be the ultimate effect, if something is not done?
 d. What will be the ultimate effects if the steps he suggests are followed?
 e. Is the cause/effect relationship clearly enough explained?
3a. Two paragraphs are devoted exclusively to examples. Which paragraphs are they?
 b. What is the generality illustrated by each?

4a. In paragraph 10 we can find still another of the patterns of exposition put to work. What is the pattern?
b. How effectively is it used?

Diction and Vocabulary

1a. What allusion do you find in paragraph 2? (Guide: *Figures of Speech.*)
b. Explain the reference.
c. Why is it not a literal reference?

2a. Why is *cordon bleu* italicized (par. 2)?
b. What kind of figure of speech is "cooking the books"? (Guide: *Figures of Speech.*)

3a. The author says that a profession is necessarily a monopoly (par. 5). How does the connotation of this word affect your reaction to that statement? (Guide: *Connotation/ Denotation.*)
b. What is its denotation?

4a. Paragraphs 16 and 18 use "men" in a way that has come to be regarded as bad manners, if not outright chauvinism. Is there any good reason why it is necessary here?
b. How, if at all, could the problem be avoided?

5. Consult your dictionary as needed to determine the meanings of the following words: omniscient, extortionate, fecklessness (par.2); laity, epigram, imputation (3); demarcation (5); recrimination, exemplars (7); regeneration (16).

Suggestions for Writing and Discussion

1. Barzun says (par 2), "The academics lost their prestige by their fecklessness in the campus troubles of 1965–1970." What other events have also cost teachers a considerable amount of their status as a profession?

2. Consider each of the examples listed in paragraph 11, and explain fully why you consider each a "threat" or "reform" (par. 12).

3. For each of the examples listed in paragraph 11, discuss whether or not there should be any use at all of "government money," with the resulting control.

4. What are some of the "parallels in teaching and the law" that compare with the unethical practices of some doctors, mentioned in paragraph 14?

5. Apparently the greatest threat to the professions, if they do not straighten up, is being "taken over by public bodies" (par. 15). Discuss the good and bad points of this concept and try to reach a conclusion about it.

Writing Suggestions for Section 6
Analysis of Cause and Effect

Analyze the immediate and ultimate causes and/or effects of one of the following subjects, or another suggested by them. (Be careful that your analysis does not develop into a mere listing of superficial "reasons.")

1. The ethnic makeup of a neighborhood.
2. Some *minor* discovery or invention.
3. The popularity of some modern singer or other celebrity admired especially by young people.
4. The popularity of some fad of clothing or hair style.
5. The widespread fascination for antique cars (or guns, furniture, dishes, etc.).
6. The widespread enjoyment of fishing or hunting.
7. Student cheating.
8. One person's decision to join a "hippie" commune.
9. Too much pressure (on you or an acquaintance) for good school grades.
10. Your being a member of some minority ethnic or religious group.
11. Your association, as an outsider, with members of such a group.
12. The decision of some close acquaintance to enter the religious life.
13. Some unreasonable fear or anxiety that afflicts you or someone you know well.
14. Your need to conform.
15. Your tendency toward individualism.

7

Using *Definition* to Help Explain

Few writing faults can cause a more serious communication block between writer and reader than using key terms that can have various meanings or shades of meaning. To be useful rather than detrimental, such terms must be adequately defined.

Of the two basic types of definition, only one is our special concern as a pattern of exposition. But the other, the simpler form, if often useful to clarify meanings of concrete or noncontroversial terms. This simple process is similar to that used most in dictionaries: either providing a synonym (for example, cinema: a motion picture), or placing the word in a class and then showing how it differs from others of the same class (for example, metheglin: an alcoholic liquor made of fermented honey — here the general class is "liquor," and the differences between metheglin and other liquors are that it is "alcoholic" and "made of fermented honey").

Berne, for instance, sees the need to define several of his key terms in the process of classifying — e.g., viscerotonic endormorph, somatotonic mesomorph, and cerebrotonic ectomorph; and Toffler, in contrasting "future shock" and "culture shock," must devote much of his essay to defining two of his key terms.

With many such abstract, unusual, or coined terms, typical readers are too limited by their own experiences and opinions (and no two sets are identical) for the writer to expect understanding of the exact sense in which he uses the terms. He has a right, of course, to use such abstract words any way he chooses — as long as his readers know what that way is. The importance of making this meaning clear becomes crucial when the term is used as a key element of the overall explanation. And sometimes the term being defined is even more than a key element: it may be the subject itself. For instance, to define "The Peter Principle" (Sec. 1) was really the primary purpose of writing, even though the authors use examples almost exclusively as a *means* of defining.

Extended definition, unlike the simple, dictionary type, follows no set and formal pattern. Often the reader is not even aware of the process. Because it is an integral part of the overall subject, extended definition is written in the same tone as the rest of the exposition, usually with an attempt to interest the reader, as well as to inform him.

There are some expository techniques peculiar to definition alone. The purpose may be served by giving the background of the term. Or the definition may be clarified by negation, sometimes called "exclusion" or "differentiation," by showing what is *not* meant by the term. Still another way is to enumerate the characteristics of what is defined, sometimes isolating an essential one for special treatment.

To demonstrate the possibilities in these patterns, we can use the term "juvenile delinquency," which might need defining in some contexts since it certainly means different things to different people. (Where do we draw the line, for instance, between "boyish pranks" and delinquency, or between delinquent and nondelinquent experimentation with sex or marijuana?) We might show how attitudes toward juvenile crime have changed: "youthful high spirits" was the label for some of our grandfathers' activities that would be called "delinquency" today. Or we could use negation, eliminating any classes of juvenile wrongdoing not considered delinquency in the current discussion. Or we could simply list characteristics of the juvenile delinquent or isolate one of these — disrespect for authority or lack of consideration for other people — as a universal.

But perhaps the most dependable techniques for defining are the basic expository patterns already studied. The writer could illustrate his meaning of "juvenile delinquency" by giving *examples* from his own experience, from newspaper accounts, or from other sources. (Every one of the introductions to the ten sections of this book, each a definition, relies greatly on illustration by example, as does the Peter/Hull selection.) He could analyze the subject by *classification* of types or degrees of delinquency. He could use the process of *compari-*

son and *contrast,* perhaps between delinquent and nondelinquent youth. Showing the *causes* and *effects* of juvenile crime could help explain his attitude toward it, and hence its meaning for him. He might choose to use *analogy,* perhaps comparing the child to a young tree growing grotesque because of poor care and attention. Or a step-by-step analysis of the *process* by which a child becomes delinquent might, in some cases, help explain the intended meaning.

Few extended definitions would use all these methods, but the extent of their use must always depend on three factors: (1) the term itself, since some are more elusive and subject to misunderstanding than others; (2) the function the term is to serve in the writing, since it would be foolish to devote several pages to defining a term that serves only a casual or unimportant purpose; and (3) the prospective reader-audience, since the writer wants to avoid insulting the intelligence or background of his readers, yet wants to go far enough to be sure of their understanding.

But this, of course, is a basic challenge in any good writing — analyzing the prospective reader and writing for the best effect on *him.*

RICHARD SELZER

RICHARD SELZER, son of a family doctor, was born in 1928 in Troy, New York, and educated at Union College, Schenectady (B.S. degree) and at Albany Medical College (M.D. degree). He did post-graduate studies at Yale University and also served two years in the United States Army. Selzer lives in Connecticut, where he has a private practice in general surgery, but he is a prolific writer, contributing steadily to such magazines as *Esquire, Harper's, Redbook, Mademoiselle,* and *American Review.* His books are *Rituals of Surgery* (1974) and *Mortal Lessons: Notes on the Art of Surgery* (1976).

"All Right, What Is a Laugh, Anyway?"

"All Right, What Is a Laugh, Anyway?" is the first part of an article by that title originally published in *Esquire.* As with most of Selzer's writing, this piece is a nice blend of humor and memorable message. In it he makes extensive use of another of the expository patterns as he defines his term.

Consider tickling. 1

Commotion! You are seized. It is a mauling that begins anywhere — the sole of the foot, your armpit, your thigh. Another person is present. Cunningly he strokes your skin, lightly, rhythmically, presses the soft tissues into your underlying bones. You try to pull away, wriggle free. He will not let you. He is stronger. He has friends who hold you down. What you feel is somewhere between pain and itch. Again and again he does his work. If he does not stop, you may die of it. In medieval Germany, in Rotenburg an der Fulda, people did. There, in that place, prisoners were trussed in metal or leather to restrict expansion of the chest. Salt was rubbed on feet; goats were invited to lick it off. 2

Up from your foot surges bolt after bolt of not-quite-pain, riding ever larger nerve trunks. Then up the spinal cord skittering to the 3 brain. At the very bottom of the brain there is a nubbin called the hypothalamus, the pituitary gland hard by. The tickling bursts upon the hypothalamus, and the electricity of it is passed through reverberating circuits. Some goes to the frontal lobes, which advise that laughing, and not, say, sneezing, is the appropriate response.

Thus are you tickled, and thus do you laugh. 4

5 Now you are listening to a man speak. All at once he says something wildly out of place, shocking. You are caught off guard. The news is sucked into your brain and goes to your hypothalamus. Once again into the reverberating circuitry. It is converted into electric impulses by still mysterious chemistries. Some of these are transferred to the frontal lobes for interpretation; the rest careen along the round-and-round, cars on a toy railroad, until the weighty verdict from the cortex has been announced. Then off the waves scatter to the motor centers of the brain to deliver the orders. To the breathing center first, and thence to the muscles of expiration. CONTRACT. And they obediently do, the muscles of the chest, back and belly, the neck and shoulders, all are thrown into strongest exercise. It is a rhythmic, mighty thing that rocks and wobbles the body, forcing air from the lungs toward the mouth. At the same time, electricity fires the larynx. RELAX. And the vocal cords back apart to let the gathering air be expelled, lest it bombard against the locked gate of the glottis with a pressure that would surely suffocate you. Out bellows the blast at seventy miles an hour. Tears are squeezed from the lacrimal glands, and there is coughing, too, as the rush of air flings mucus against the lining of the windpipe, a coughing that empurples the face, engorges the veins of head and neck, and makes of the words "to die laughing" not entirely hyperbole. Shaking, writhing, weeping, coughing, you laugh. It is a violent, risky affair, a seismic dislocation, a volcano blowing off.

6 Of the laughs most difficult to come by, surely the least accessible was observed by a (playful?) neurosurgeon during a brain operation. After removal of a tumor near the hypothalamus, he stroked the floor of the brain with a little brush. Whereupon the patient was seen to smile and shortly thereafter to burst into laughter. When the stroking was discontinued, laughter stopped, only to recur upon further stroking. But only for the most recalcitrant of depressions is it recommended that one volunteer for such a massage.

Equipped with an inherent sagacity, or some precognition of the inconvenience of extrauterine life, the newborn does not laugh. He does not even smile. With the advance of age, however, his natural gloom and testiness are replaced by a kind of go-to-hell blathery resignation to his predicament, and at the end of four weeks he might be seen to smile. Not until the third or fourth month can the baby bring himself to give what could be called an outright laugh. A further weakening in the infant's resolve to remain dignified and grave at all costs is noted as time goes by. The incidence of smiles, from one every six minutes at the age of eighteen months, increases to one every one and one third minutes at the age of four years. A smile a minute! At eighteen months there is one laugh for every ten smiles, while the fourth year hears one for every three smiles. The causes for this wholly unjustifiable merriment are, in fact, almost always the relief of unpleasant bodily sensations, as in the passage of gas, or the removal from the buttocks of a wet diaper. It is only much later, beginning with puberty and reaching full flower during adolescence, that we are reduced to laughter by the sight of someone falling down, the recognition of mental inferiority in another, the discovery of one's teacher in a compromised condition, or, worst of all, by puns. 7

Meanings and Values

1a. What, if anything, did you gain by reading this piece?
  b. What do you think were Selzer's objectives in writing it?
  c. Judging his reading audience by yourself and the fact that he was writing for *Esquire,* does it seem that he accomplished his objectives? Why, or why not?
  d. Do you think the benefits warrant the trouble of writing something like this? Explain your reasoning.

2a. Use this selection by which to illustrate the relationship between tone and point of view. (See Guide to Terms: *Style/Tone* and *Point of View.*)
  b. Is there any way, other than by reading the headnotes, that you might guess the author is also a surgeon? Explain.

Expository Techniques

1a. What pattern of exposition already studied do you find most pervasive in this selection?
  b. Cite the paragraphs in which this technique is used.

c. Is it an effective technique of definition? Why, or why not?

2. What generality is exemplified in paragraph 2?

3. In which paragraphs do we find several minor uses of cause/effect to aid in the definition?

4a. Is the two-word introduction effective? Why, or why not?
b. Which of the standard techniques does it represent? (Guide: *Introductions.*)

5a. Is the next to last sentence of paragraph 5 loose or periodic? Why? (Guide: *Emphasis.*)
b. Which kind of sentence is the first one of paragraph 7? Why?
c. What effect is gained by the use of such constructions?

6. Illustrate the meaning of "paradox" by using materials from this selection. (Guide: *Paradox.*)

7a. Analyze the writing in an attempt to determine the sources and characteristics of Selzer's style. (Guide: *Style/Tone.*)
b. Illustrate each trait by an example or two from the selection itself.

Diction and Vocabulary

1. Which of the traits listed in the answer to question 7 of "Expository Techniques" are also matters of diction or syntax? (Guide: *Diction* and *Syntax.*)

2a. Cite two uses of figurative language. (Guide: *Figures of Speech.*)
b. Which kind are they?

3a. How much, if at all, does the liberal use of rather heavy physiological terms bother you?
b. Is there any way they could — or should — have been avoided?

4. What is the "predicament" a baby eventually becomes reconciled to (par. 7)?

5. Use the dictionary as necessary to understand the meanings of the following words: trussed (par. 2); skittering, nubbin (3); reverberating (3, 5); engorges, hyperbole, seismic (5); recalcitrant (6); inherent, sagacity, extrauterine, blathery (7).

Suggestions for Writing and Discussion

1. How can you account for the fact that some people laugh a great deal whereas others almost never do?

2. Would you tend to trust a surgeon more, or less — or exactly the same — knowing that he sometimes wrote essays such as this in his spare time?

3. What are your impressions of the following quotation from one of

Lord Chesterfield's letters to his son: "Frequent and loud laughter is the characteristic of folly and ill manners: it is the manner in which the mob express their silly joy at silly things, and they call it being merry. In my mind there is nothing so illiberal and so ill-bred as audible laughter."

(NOTE: Suggestions for topics requiring development by use of DEFINITION are on page 239, at the end of this section.)

BARBARA LAWRENCE

BARBARA LAWRENCE was born in Hanover, New Hampshire. After receiving a B.A. in French literature from Connecticut College she worked for some time as an editor on *McCall's, Redbook, Harper's Bazaar,* and *The New Yorker.* During this period she also took an M.A. in philosophy from New York University. Currently an associate professor of humanities at the State University of New York's College at Old Westbury, Lawrence has published criticism, poetry, and fiction in *Choice, Commonweal, Columbia Poetry, The New York Times,* and *The New Yorker.*

Four-Letter Words Can Hurt You

"Four-Letter Words Can Hurt You" first appeared in *The New York Times* and was later published in *Redbook.* In explaining precisely why she is offended by the "earthy, gut-honest" language often preferred by her students, Lawrence also provides a thoughtful, even scholarly, extended definition of "obscenity" itself. To accomplish her purpose, the author employs several of the patterns of exposition we have already studied.

Why should any words be called obscene? Don't they all describe natural human functions? Am I trying to tell them, my students demand, that the "strong, earthy, gut-honest" — or, if they are fans of Norman Mailer, the "rich, liberating, existential" — language they use to describe sexual activity isn't preferable to "phony-sounding, middle-class words like 'intercourse' and 'copulate'?" "Cop You Late!" they say with fancy infections and gagging grimaces. "Now, what is *that* supposed to mean?" 1

Well, what is it supposed to mean? And why indeed should one group of words describing human functions and human organs be acceptable in ordinary conversation and another, describing presumably the same organs and functions, be tabooed — so much so, in fact, that some of these words still cannot appear in print in many parts of the English-speaking world? 2

The argument that these taboos exist only because of "sexual hangups" (middle-class, middle-age, feminist), or even that they are a result of class oppression (the contempt of the Norman conquerors for the language of their Anglo-Saxon serfs), ignores a much more likely explanation, it seems to me, and that is the sources and functions of the words themselves. 3

The best known of the tabooed sexual verbs, for example, comes from the German *ficken,* meaning "to strike"; combined according to Partridge's etymological dictionary *Origins,* with the Latin sexual verb *futuere:* associated in turn with the Latin *fustis,* "a staff or cudgel"; the Celtic *buc,* "a point, hence to pierce"; the Irish *bot,* "the male member"; the Latin *battuere,* "to beat"; the Gaelic *batair,* "a cudgeller"; the Early Irish *bualaim,* "I strike"; and so forth. It is one of what etymologists sometimes called "the sadistic group of words for the man's part in copulation." 4

The brutality of this word, then, and its equivalents ("screw," "bang," etc.), is not an illusion of the middle class or a crotchet of Women's Liberation. In their origins and imagery these words carry undeniably painful, if not sadistic, implications, the object of which is almost always female. Consider, for example, what a "screw" actually does to the wood it penetrates; what a painful, even mutilating, activity this kind of analogy suggests. "Screw" is particularly interesting in this context, since the noun, according to Partridge, comes from words meaning "groove," "nut," "ditch," "breeding sow," "scrofula" and "swelling," while the verb besides its explicit imagery, has antecedent associations to "write on," "scratch," "scarify," and so forth — a revealing fusion of a mechanical or painful action with an obviously denigrated object. 5

Not all obscene words, of course, are as implicitly sadistic or denigrating to women as these, but all that I know seem to serve a similar purpose: to reduce the human organism (especially the female organism) and human functions (especially sexual and procreative) to their least organic, most mechanical dimension; to substitute a trivializing or deforming resemblance for the complex human reality of what is being described. 6

Tabooed male descriptives, when they are not openly denigrating to women, often serve to divorce a male organ or function from any significant interaction with the female. Take the word "testes," for example, suggesting "witnesses" (from the Latin *testis*) to the sexual and procreative strengths of the male organ; and the obscene 7 counterpart of this word, which suggests little more than a mechanical shape. Or compare almost any of the "rich," "liberating" sexual verbs, so fashionable today among male writers, with that much-derided Latin word "copulate" ("to bind or join together") or even that Anglo-Saxon phrase (which seems to have had no trouble surviving the Norman Conquest) "make love."

How arrogantly self-involved the tabooed words seem in comparision to either of the other terms, and how contemptuous of the female partner. Understandably so, of course, if she is only a "skirt," a "broad," a "chick," a "pussycat" or a "piece." If she is, in other words, no more than her skirt, or what her skirt conceals; no more than a breeder, or the broadest part of her; no more than a piece of a human being or a "piece of tail." 8

The most severely tabooed of all the female descriptives, incidentally, are those like a "piece of tail," which suggest (either explicitly or through antecedents) that there is no significant difference between the female channel through which we are all conceived and born and the anal outlet common to both sexes — a distinction that pornographers have always enjoyed obscuring. 9

This effort to deny women their biological identity, their individuality, their humanness, is such an important aspect of obscene language that one can only marvel at how seldom, in an era preoccupied with definitions of obscenity, this fact is brought to our attention. One problem, of course, is that many of the people in the best position to do this (critics, teachers, writers) are so reluctant today to admit that they are angered or shocked by obscenity. Bored, maybe, unimpressed, aesthetically displeased, but — no matter how brutal or denigrating the material — never angered, never shocked. 10

And yet how eloquently angered, how piously shocked many of these same people become if denigrating language is used about any minority group other than women; if the obscenities are racial or ethnic, that is, rather than sexual. Words like "coon," "kike," "spic," "wop," after all, deform identity, deny individuality and humanness in almost exactly the same way that sexual vulgarisms and obscenities do. 11

No one that I know, least of all my students, would fail to question the values of a society whose literature and entertainment rested heavily on racial or ethnic pejoratives. Are the values of a society whose literature and entertainment rest as heavily as ours on sexual pejoratives any less questionable? 12

Meanings and Values

1a. Explain the meaning of "irony" by use of at least one illustration from the latter part of this essay. (See Guide to Terms: *Irony.*)
b. What kind of irony is it?

2a. Inasmuch as the writing itself includes many of the so-called "strong, earthy, gut-honest" words, could anyone logically call it obscene? Why, or why not?
b. To what extent, if at all does the author's point of view help determine your answer to "a"? (Guide: *Point of View.*)

3a. Compose, in your own words, a compact statement of Lawrence's central theme. (Guide: *Unity.*)
b. Are all parts of the essay completely relevant to this theme? Justify your answer.
c. Does the writing have unity?

4. Evaluate this composition by use of our three-question system. (Guide: *Evaluation.*)

Expository Techniques

1a. Where does the author first let us know what major term is to be defined?
b. Can the resulting treatment qualify as *extended* definition? Why, or why not?

2a. Which of the methods "peculiar to definition alone" (see the introduction to this section) does the author employ in developing her major definition?
b. Which of the regular patterns of exposition does she also use?
c. Explain your reasons and cite examples to justify your answers to "a" and "b."

3a. Cite five examples of the simpler, non-"extended" kind of definition.
b. Are these sufficiently documented to fulfill their funtion? Cite examples to justify your answer to "a."

4a. Illustrate the difference between "specific" and "general" by use of passages from this writing. (Guide: *Specific/General.*)
b. Does it seem to you that the author becomes too involved with achieving one or the other? Explain.

5a. Which of the standard techniques of introduction are used? (Guide: *Introductions.*)
b. Which methods are used to close it? (Guide: *Closings.*)

Diction and Vocabulary

1a. How, if at all, is this discussion of words related to "connotation"? (Guide: *Connotation/Denotation.*)

b. To what extent would connotations in this matter depend on setting and circumstances in which the words are used? Cite illustrations to clarify your answer.

2. In view of the fact that the author uses frankly many of the "gut-honest" words, why do you suppose she plainly avoids others, such as in paragraphs 4 and 7?

3. The author says that a "kind of analogy" is suggested by some of the words discussed (par. 5). If you have studied Section 4 of this book, does her use of the term "analogy" seem in conflict with what you believed it to mean? Explain.

4. Study the author's uses of the following words, consulting the dictionary as needed: existential, grimaces (par. 1); etymological, cudgel (4); sadistic (4–6); crotchet, scrofula, explicit, antecedent, scarify (5); denigrated (5–7, 10–11), aesthetically (10); pejoratives (12).

Suggestions for Writing and Discussion

1. What is the relationship, if any, between obscene language and pornography?

2. Why is it the so-called middle class that is so often accused of having sexual hangups — and hence all sorts of sex-related taboos?

3. Probably most people using obscene language (obscene, at least, by Lawrence's definition) are not aware of the etymology of the words. Can they, therefore, be accused of denigrating women — or, unlike in legal matters, is ignorance a suitable defense?

4. Does the author make a justifiable comparision between obscene words and ethnic pejoratives? Using illustrations for specificity, carry the comparison further to show why it is sound, or explain why you consider it a weak comparison.

(NOTE: Suggestions for topics requiring development by use of DEFINITION are on page 239, at the end of this section.)

D. H. LAWRENCE

DAVID HERBERT LAWRENCE (1885–1930), British novelist, poet, essayist, and playwright, was for many years a controversial literary figure because of his frank and, for his time, obsessive treatment of sex in some of his novels. The son of a coal miner, Lawrence began his career as a schoolmaster and with the success of his first novel, *The White Peacock* (1911), he decided to live by writing. His books include *Sons and Lovers* (1913), *The Rainbow* (1915), *Women in Love* (1921), and *Lady Chatterly's Lover* (1928). Lawrence has been admired by many for his insightful and artistic power in prose. E. M. Forster referred to him as "the greatest imaginative novelist of our generation."

Pornography

"Pornography" is excerpted from *Pornography and Obscenity,* first published in 1930. Providing us with one man's definition of a still highly controversial term, this selection also illustrates the naturalness and vivid spontaneity of style characteristic of Lawrence's writing. Also interesting should be a comparision of the way another Lawrence, from a different era and background, and with a different point of view, defines a term which is very close to the "obscenity" that concerns Barbara Lawrence.

What is pornography to one man is the laughter of genius to another. 1

The word itself, we are told, means "pertaining to harlots" — 2 the graph of the harlot. But nowadays, what is a harlot? If she was a woman who took money from a man in return for going to bed with him — really, most wives sold themselves, in the past, and plenty of harlots gave themselves, when they felt like it, for nothing. If a woman hasn't got a tiny streak of harlot in her, she's a dry stick as a rule. And probably most harlots had somewhere a streak of womanly generosity. Why be so cut and dried? The law is a dreary thing, and its judgments have nothing to do with life. . . .

One essay on pornography, I remember, comes to the conclusion 3 that pornography in art is that which is calculated to arouse sexual desire, or sexual excitement. And stress is laid on the fact, whether the author or artist *intended* to arouse sexual feelings. It is the old vexed question of intention, become so dull today, when we know how strong and influential our unconscious intentions are. And why a man should be held guilty of his conscious intentions, and innocent of his unconscious intentions, I don't know, since every man is more made up of unconscious intentions than of conscious ones. I am what I am, not merely what I think I am.

However! We take it, I assume, that *pornography* is something 4
base, something unpleasant. In short, we don't like it. And why don't we like it? Because it arouses sexual feelings?

I think not. No matter how hard we may pretend otherwise, 5
most of us rather like a moderate rousing of our sex. It warms us, stimulates us like sunshine on a grey day. After a century or two of Puritanism, this is still true of most people. Only the mob-habit of condemning any form of sex is too strong to let us admit it naturally. And there are, of course, many people who are genuinely repelled by the simplest and most natural stirrings of sexual feeling. But these people are perverts who have fallen into hatred of their fellow-men; thwarted, disappointed, unfulfilled people, of whom, alas, our civilisation contains so many. And they nearly always enjoy some unsimple and unnatural form of sex excitement, secretly.

Even quite advanced art critics would try to make us believe that 6
any picture or book which had "sex appeal" was *ipso facto* a bad book or picture. This is just canting hypocrisy. Half the great poems, pictures, music, stories, of the whole world are great by virtue of the beauty of their sex appeal. Titian or Renoir, the Song of Solomon or *Jane Eyre,* Mozart or "Annie Laurie," the loveliness is all interwoven with sex appeal, sex stimulus, call it what you will. Even Michelangelo, who rather hated sex, can't help filling the Cornucopia with phallic acorns. Sex is a very powerful, beneficial and necessary stimulus in human life, and we are all grateful when we feel its warm, natural flow through us, like a form of sunshine. . . .

Then what is pornography, after all this? It isn't sex appeal or 7
sex stimulus in art. It isn't even a deliberate intention on the part of the artist to arouse or excite sexual feelings. There's nothing wrong with sexual feelings in themselves, so long as they are straightforward and not sneaking or sly. The right sort of sex stimulus is invaluable to human daily life. Without it the world grows grey. I would give everybody the gay Renaissance stories to read, they would help

to shake off a lot of grey self-importance, which is our modern civilised disease.

But even I would censor genuine pornography, rigorously. It 8
would not be very difficult. In the first place, genuine pornography is almost always underworld, it doesn't come into the open. In the second, you can recognise it by the insult it offers, invariably, to sex and to the human spirit.

Pornography is the attempt to insult sex, to do dirt on it. This 9
is unpardonable. Take the very lowest instance, the picture postcard sold underhand, by the underworld, in most cities. What I have seen of them have been of an ugliness to make you cry. The insult to the human body, the insult to a vital human relationship! Ugly and cheap they make the human nudity, ugly and degraded they make the sexual act, trivial and cheap and nasty.

It is the same with the books they sell in the underworld. They 10
are either so ugly they make you ill, or so fatuous you can't imagine anybody but a cretin or a moron reading them, or writing them.

It is the same with the dirty limericks that people tell after 11
dinner, or the dirty stories one hears commercial travellers telling each other in a smoke-room. Occasionally there is a really funny one, that redeems a great deal. But usually they are just ugly and repellent, and the so-called "humour" is just a trick of doing dirt on sex.

Now the human nudity of a great many modern people is just 12
ugly and degraded, and the sexual act between modern people is just the same, merely ugly and degrading. But this is nothing to be proud of. It is the catastrophe of our civilisation. I am sure no other civilisation, not even the Roman, has showed such a vast proportion of ignominious and degraded nudity, and ugly, squalid dirty sex. Because no other civilisation has driven sex into the underworld, and nudity to the w.c.

The intelligent young, thank heaven, seem determined to alter 13
in these two respects. They are rescuing their young nudity from the stuffy, pornographical hole-and-corner underworld of their elders, and they refuse to sneak about the sexual relation. This is a change the elderly grey ones of course deplore, but it is in fact a very great change for the better, and a real revolution.

But it is amazing how strong is the will in ordinary, vulgar 14
people, to do dirt on sex. It was one of my fond illusions, when I was young, that the ordinary healthy-seeming sort of men in railway carriages, or the smoke-room of an hotel or a pullman, were healthy

in their feelings and had a wholesome rough devil-may-care attitude towards sex. All wrong! All wrong! Experience teaches that common individuals of this sort have a disgusting attitude towards sex, a disgusting contempt of it, a disgusting desire to insult it. If such fellows have intercourse with a woman, they triumphantly feel that they have done her dirt, and now she is lower, cheaper, more contemptible than she was before.

It is individuals of this sort that tell dirty stories, carry indecent 15 picture postcards, and know the indecent books. This is the great pornographical class — the really common men-in-the-street and women-in-the-street. They have as great a hate and contempt of sex as the greyest Puritan, and when an appeal is made to them, they are always on the side of the angels. They insist that a film-heroine shall be a neuter, a sexless thing of washed-out purity. They insist that real sex-feeling shall only be shown by the villain or villainess, low lust. They find a Titian or a Renoir really indecent, and they don't want their wives and daughters to see it.

Why? Because they have the grey disease of sex-hatred, coupled 16 with the yellow disease of dirt-lust. The sex functions and the excrementory functions in the human body work so close together, yet they are, so to speak, utterly different in direction. Sex is a creative flow, the excrementory flow is towards dissolution, de-creation, if we may use such a word. In the really healthy human being the distinction between the two is instant, our profoundest instincts are perhaps our instincts of opposition between the two flows.

But in the degraded human being the deep instincts have gone 17 dead, and then the two flows become identical. *This* is the secret of really vulgar and of pornographical people: the sex flow and the excrement flow is the same to them. It happens when the psyche deteriorates, and the profound controlling instincts collapse. Then sex is dirt and dirt is sex, and sexual excitement becomes a playing with dirt, and any sign of sex in a woman becomes a show of her dirt. This is the condition of the common, vulgar human being whose name is legion, and who lifts his voice and it is the *Vox populi, vox Dei.* And this is the source of all pornography.

Meanings and Values

1. Could this selection better serve to illustrate subjective or objective writing? (See Guide to Terms: *Objective/Subjective.*) Justify your answer, citing specific examples.

2. Would you classify it as formal or informal writing? (Guide: *Essay.*) Why?

3a. Do you think that a person should, in general, be held responsible for his "unconscious intentions" (par. 3)?
 b. Does the law do so?

4a. Does it seem to you that the author may be overgeneralizing in the last sentence of paragraph 5?
 b. If such forms of sex excitement are enjoyed "secretly," how could he know enough about the matter to make such a broad assertion?

5. What, if anything, is paradoxical in the fact that the type of men described early in paragraph 14 have the "grey disease" (par. 16)? (Guide: *Paradox.*)

Expository Techniques

1a. In developing his definition of pornography, Lawrence uses negation, or exclusion. What is negated?
 b. Which paragraphs are devoted to negation?
 c. Why do you suppose he considers them important enough for so much attention? Do you agree?

2a. Which of the other methods of extended definition does he use?
 b. In which paragraphs may they be found?

3. In your estimation, are rhetorical questions overused in this selection? (Guide: *Rhetorical Questions.*) Be prepared to justify your answer.

4a. Cite examples of as many as possible of the standard methods of achieving emphasis. (Guide: *Emphasis.*)
 b. What, to you, is the overall effect?

5. Several of the most noticeable features of Lawrence's style are also matters of syntax. (Guide: *Style/Tone* and *Syntax.*) Illustrate as many of these as possible by examples from the writing.

Diction and Vocabulary

1a. In the second paragraph is a metaphor that is also a cliché. (Guide: *Clichés.*) What is it?
 b. How, if at all, can we justify its use?

2. Cite at least two other examples of metaphor and one of simile. (Guide: *Figures of Speech.*)

3. What is the meaning of "w.c." (par 12)?

4a. What is the meaning of *ipso facto* (par. 6)?
 b. Why is it italicized?

5. What is the meaning of *Vox populi, vox Dei* (par. 17)?

6a. In at least five paragraphs Lawrence uses a euphemism. (Guide: *Connotation/Denotation*.) What is it?

b. In which paragraphs do you find it used?

c. If sex-hatred is the "grey disease," why do you suppose he chose "yellow" to describe the disease of "dirt-lust"?

7. Consult your dictionary as necessary for the meaning of the following words: canting, phallic (par. 6); fatuous, cretin (10); ignominious (12).

Suggestions for Writing and Discussion

1. Select one or more of the artists or works of art listed in paragraph 6, analyze, and explain fully why you agree or disagree that "the loveliness is all interwoven with sex appeal [or] sex stimulus."
2. The "intelligent young" of 1930 (par. 13) are now the grey "establishment" of parents and grandparents against whom the intelligent young of the 1960s and 1970s staged their so-called sexual revolution. Trace the process by which such an ironic reversal came about. Do you believe this is an inevitable result of generation-aging — e.g., will *your* children and grandchildren also be engaging in sexual revolution?
3. Both of the author's "negated" definitions have been used repeatedly in the attempt to get a fair and workable *legal* distinction between pornography and nonpornography. Usually these attempts failed, and no one felt that the problem had been really solved. How well would Lawrence's definition work as a legal definition — perhaps with some modificationyoucansuggest?
4. What, if anything, do you think should be done about "hard-core" pornography?

(NOTE: Suggestions for topics requiring development by use of DEFINITION are on page 239, at the end of this section.

CLAUDE BROWN

CLAUDE BROWN, a playwright and versatile author, was born in New York in 1937 and attended Howard University from 1961 to 1965. Some of his plays were performed by the American Afro-Negro Theater Guild in New York. Brown's autobiographical book, *Manchild in the Promised Land* (1965), was well received by readers and critics alike; his articles and essays have been published in numerous periodicals. *The Children of Ham* was published in 1976.

The Language of Soul

"The Language of Soul" was originally published in *Esquire* in April 1968. "Soul," Brown's key term, is extremely fluid and elusive, and he has extensively illustrated and explained in order to make its definition fully understood and appreciated.

Perhaps the most soulful word in the world is "nigger." Despite its very definite fundamental meaning (the Negro man), and disregarding the deprecatory connotation of the term, "nigger" has a multiplicity of nuances when used by soul people. Dictionaries define the term as being synonymous with Negro, and they generally point out that it is regarded as a vulgar expression. Nevertheless, to those of chitlins-and-neck-bones background the word nigger is neither a synonym for Negro nor an obscene expression. 1

"Nigger" has virtually as many shades of meaning in Colored English as the demonstrative pronoun "that," prior to application to a noun. To some Americans of African ancestry (I avoid using the term Negro whenever feasible, for fear of offending the Brothers X, a pressure group to be reckoned with), nigger seems preferable to Negro and has a unique kind of sentiment attached to it. This is exemplified in the frequent — and perhaps even excessive — usage of the term to denote either fondness or hostility. 2

3 It is probable that numerous transitional niggers and even established exsoul brothers can — with pangs of nostalgia — reflect upon a day in the lollipop epoch of lives when an adorable lady named Mama bemoaned her spouse's fastidiousness with the strictly secular utterance: "Lord, how can one nigger be so hard to please?" Others are likely to recall a time when that drastically lovable colored woman, who was forever wiping our noses and darning our clothing, bellowed in a moment of exasperation: "Nigger, you gonna be the death o' me." And some of the brethren who have had the precarious fortune to be raised up, wised up, thrown up or simply left alone to get up as best they could, on one of the nation's South Streets or Lenox Avenues, might remember having affectionately referred to a best friend as "My nigger."

4 The vast majority of "back-door Americans" are apt to agree with Webster — a nigger is simply a Negro or black man. But the really profound contemporary thinkers of this distinguished ethnic group — Dick Gregory, Redd Foxx, Moms Mabley, Slappy White, etc. — are likely to differ with Mr. Webster and define nigger as "something else" — a soulful "something else." The major difference between the nigger and the Negro, who have many traits in common, is that the nigger is the more soulful.

5 Certain foods, customs and artistic expressions are associated almost solely with nigger: collard greens, neck bones, hog maws, black-eyed peas, pigs' feet, etc. A nigger has no desire to conceal or disavow any of these favorite dishes or restrain other behavioral practices such as bobbing his head, patting his feet to funky jazz, and shouting and jumping in church. This is not to be construed that all niggers eat chitlins and shout in church, nor that only niggers eat the aforementioned dishes and exhibit this type of behavior. It is to say, however, that the soulful usage of the term nigger implies all of the foregoing and considerably more.

6 The Language of Soul — or, as it might also be called, Spoken Soul or Colored English — is simply an honest vocal portryal of black America. The roots of it are more than three hundred years old.

7 Before the Civil War there were numerous restrictions placed on the speech of slaves. The newly arrived Africans had the problem of learning to speak a new language, but also there were inhibitions placed on the topics of the slaves' conversation by slave masters and overseers. The slaves made up songs to inform one another of, say, the underground railroads' activity. When they sang *Steal Away* they

were planning to steal away to the North, not to heaven. Slaves who dared to speak of rebellion or even freedom usually were severely punished. Consequently, Negro slaves were compelled to create a semi-clandestine vernacular in the way that the criminal underworld has historically created words to confound law-enforcement agents. It is said that numerous Negro spirituals were inspired by the hardships of slavery, and that what later became songs were initally moanings and coded cotton-field lyrics. To hear these songs sung today by a talented soul brother or sister or by a group is to be reminded of an historical spiritual bond that cannot be satisfactorily described by the mere spoken word.

The American Negro, for virtually all of his history, has consti- 8
tuted a vastly disproportionate number of the country's illiterates. Illiteracy has a way of showing itself in all attempts at vocal expression by the uneducated. With the aid of colloquialisms, malapropisms, battered and fractured grammar, and a considerable amount of creativity, Colored English, the sound of soul, evolved.

The progess has been cyclical. Often terms that have been dis- 9
carded from the soul people's vocabulary for one reason or another are reaccepted years later, but usually with completely different meaning. In the Thirties and Forties "stuff" was used to mean vagina. In the middle Fifties it was revived and used to refer to heroin. Why certain expressions are thus reactivated is practically an indeterminable question. But it is not difficult to see why certain terms are dropped from the soul language. Whenever a soul term becomes popular with whites it is common practice for the soul folks to relinquish it. The reasoning is that "if white people can use it, it isn't hip enough for me." To many soul brothers there is just no such creature as a genuinely hip white person. And there is nothing more detrimental to anything hip than to have it fall into the square hands of the hopelessly unhip.

White Americans wrecked the expression "something else." It 10
was bad enough that they couldn't say "sump'n else," but they weren't even able to get out "somethin' else." They had to go around saying *something else* with perfect or nearly perfect enunciation. The while folks invariably fail to perceive the soul sound in soulful terms. They get hung up in diction and grammar, and when they vocalize the expression it's no longer a soulful thing. In fact, it can be asserted that spoken soul is more of a sound than a language. It generally possesses a pronounced lyrical quality which is frequently incompat-

ible to any music other than that ceaseless and relentlessly driving rhythm that flows from poignantly spent lives. Spoken soul has a way of coming out metered without the intention of the speaker to invoke it. There are specific phonetic traits. To the soulless ear the vast majority of these sounds are dismissed as incorrect usage of the English language and, not infrequently, as speech impediments. To those so blessed as to have had bestowed upon them at birth the lifetime gift of soul, these are the most communicative and meaningful sounds ever to fall upon human ears: the familiar "mah" instead of "my," "gonna" for "going to," "yo" for "your." "Ain't" is pronounced "ain' "; "bread" and "bed," "bray-ud" and "bay-ud"; "baby" is never "bay-bee" but "bay-buh"; Sammy Davis Jr. is not "Sammee" but a kind of "Sam-eh"; the same goes for "Eddeh" Jefferson. No matter how many "man's" you put into your talk, it isn't soulful unless the word has the proper plaintive, nasal "maee-yun."

Spoken soul is distinguished from slang primarily by the fact 11
that the former lends itself easily to conventional English, and the latter is diametrically opposed to adaptations within the realm of conventional English. Police (pronounced pō'lice) is a soul term, whereas "The Man" is merely slang for the same thing. Negroes seldom adopt slang terms from the white world and when they do the terms are usually given a different meaning. Such was the case with the term "bag." White racketeers used it in the Thirties to refer to the graft that was paid to the police. For the past five years soul people have used it when referring to a person's vocation, hobby, fancy, etc. And once the appropriate term is given the treatment (soul vocalization) it becomes soulful.

However, borrowings from spoken soul by white men's slang — 12
particularly teen-age slang — are plentiful. Perhaps because soul is probably the most graphic language of modern times, everybody who is excluded from Soulville wants to usurp it, ignoring the formidable fettering to the soul folks that has brought the langauge about. Consider "uptight," "strung-out," "cop," "boss," "kill 'em," all now widely used outside Soulville. Soul people never question the origin of a slang term; they either dig it and make it a part of their vocabulary or don't and forget it. The expression "uptight," which meant being in financial straits, appeared on the soul scene in the general vicinity of 1953. Junkies were very fond of the word and used it literally to describe what was a perpetual condition with them. The word was pictorial and pointed; therefore it caught on quickly in

Soulville across the country. In the early Sixties when "uptight" was on the move, a younger generation of soul people in the black urban communities along the Eastern Seaboard regenerated it with a new meaning: "everything is cool, under control, going my way." At present the term has the former meaning for the older generation and the latter construction for those under thirty years of age.

It is difficult to ascertain if the term "strung-out" was coined by junkies or just applied to them and accepted without protest. Like the term "uptight" in its initial interpretation, "strung-out" aptly described the constant plight of the junkie. "Strung-out" had a connotation of hopeless finality about it. "Uptight" implied a temporary situation and lacked the overwhelming despair of "strung-out." 13

The term "cop," (meaning "to get"), is an abbreviation of the word "copulation." "Cop," as originally used by soulful teen-agers in the early Fifties, was deciphered to mean sexual coition, nothing more. By 1955 "cop" was being uttered throughout national Soulville as a synonym for the verb "to get," especially in reference to illegal purchases, drugs, pot, hot goods, pistols, etc. ("Man, where can I cop now?") But by 1955 the meaning was all-encompassing. Anything that could be obtained could be "copped." 14

The word "boss," denoting something extraordinarily good or great, was a redefined term that had been popular in Soulville during the Forties and Fifties as a complimentary remark from one soul brother to another. Later it was replaced by several terms such as "groovy," "tough," "beautiful" and, most recently, "out of sight." This last expression is an outgrowth of the former term "way out," the meaning of which was equivocal. "Way out" had an ad hoc hickish ring to it which made it intolerably unsoulful and consequently it was soon replaced by "out of sight," which is also likely to experience a relatively brief period of popular usage. "Out of sight" is better than "way out," but it has some of the same negative, childish taint of its predecessor. 15

The expression, "kill 'em," has neither a violent nor a malicious interpretation. It means "good luck," "give 'em hell," or "I'm pulling for you," and originated in Harlem from six to nine years ago. 16

There are certain classic soul terms which, no matter how often borrowed, remain in the canon and are reactivated every so often, just as standard jazz tunes are continuously experiencing renaissances. Among the classical expressions are: "solid," "cool," "jive" (generally 17 as a noun), "stuff," "thing," "swing" (or "swinging"), "pimp," "dirt," "freak," "heat," "larcency," "busted," "okee doke," "piece," "sheet" (a jail record), "squat," "square," "stash," "lay," "sting," "mire," "gone," "smooth," "joint," "blow," "play," "shot," and there are many more.

Soul language can be heard in practically all communities 18
throughout the country, but for pure, undiluted spoken soul one must go to Soul Street. There are several. Soul is located at Seventh and "T" in Washington, D.C., on One Two Five Street in New York City; on Springfield Avenue in Newark; on South Street in Philadelphia; on Tremont Street in Boston; on Forty-seventh Street in Chicago, on Fillmore in San Francisco, and dozens of similar locations in dozens of other cities.

As increasingly more Negroes desert Soulville for honorary 19
membership in the Establishment clique, they experience a metamorphosis, the repercussions of which have a marked influence on the young and impressionable citizens of Soulville. The expatriates of Soulville are often greatly admired by the youth of Soulville, who emulate the behavior of such expatriates as Nancy Wilson, Ella Fitzgerald, Eartha Kitt, Lena Horne, Diahann Carroll, Billy Daniels, or Leslie Uggams. The result — more often than not — is a trend away from spoken soul among the young soul folks. This abandonment of the soul language is facilitated by the fact that more Negro youngsters than ever are acquiring college educations (which, incidentally, is not the best treatment for the continued good health and growth of soul); integration and television, too, are contributing significantly to the gradual demise of spoken soul.

Perhaps colleges in America should commence to teach a course 20
in spoken soul. It could be entitled the Vocal History of Black America, or simply Spoken Soul. Undoubtedly there would be no difficulty finding teachers. There are literally thousands of these experts throughout the country whose talents lie idle while they await the call to duty.

Meanwhile the picture looks dark for soul. The two extremities 21
in the Negro spectrum — the conservative and the militant — are both trying diligently to relinquish and repudiate whatever vestige they may still possess of soul. The semi-Negro — the soul brother intent on gaining admission to the Establishment even on an honorary basis — is anxiously embracing and assuming conventional English.

The other extremity, the Ultra-Blacks are frantically adopting everything from a Western version of Islam that would shock the Caliph right out of his snugly fitting shintiyan to anything that vaguely hints of that big, beautiful, bountiful black bitch lying in the arms of the Indian and Atlantic Oceans and crowned by the majestic Mediterranean Sea. Whatever the Ultra-Black is after, it's anything but soulful.

Meanings and Values

1a. Describe what seems to be the author's attitude toward his subject in general.
  b. What is his attitude toward the "Ultra-Black"? How can you tell?
  c. What is it toward the "semi-Negro"? How can you tell?
  d. Where do you suppose he would class himself from one soul "extremity" to the other? Why?

2a. Show the relation between Brown's attitude toward his subject in general and the general tone of the writing. (See Guide to Terms: *Style/Tone.*)
  b. Describe his tone when he refers to the "Ultra-Black."
  c. Does tone help or hinder the effectiveness of the writing? If either, explain the reason for your answer and cite any important exceptions.

3. How do you account for the fact that soul expressions spread so easily through the much larger white youth subculture?

4. What value do you see, if any, in reading about a highly colloquial "language" used by only a portion of a minority people — a language, at that, which even the author regards as dying?

Expository Techniques

1a. What are the hazards of using, without preliminaries or explanation, a developed example as an introduction? (Guide: *Introductions.*)
  b. How well, if at all, has Brown avoided these hazards?
  c. Show where, and how, the author achieves smooth transition into the basic definition, in this case also the central theme.

2. The introductory example itself is, of course, an extended definition. What methods are used in its development?

3a. Where else, if at all, are extended definitions used to develop the larger one?
  b. Cite two examples of the simpler, nonextended type of definition.

4a. Does the author handle the extensive use of examples well, or does he allow them to move in and take over the essay (perhaps really using a framework of definition merely for the purpose of the examples, rather than vice versa)? Be specific in justifying your answer.

b. How is this a matter of unity? (Guide: *Unity.*)

c. Does this essay have desirable unity?

5. Several other techniques are used in the major definition. Cite any uses you can find of the following methods:
   a. Giving historical background.
   b. Showing by negation.
   c. Enumerating characteristics.
   d. Comparing and/or contrasting.
   e. Analyzing causes and/or effects.

6. Demonstrate, by use of at least two well-chosen paragraphs, how the author makes his abstract statements concrete. (Guide: *Concrete/Abstract.*)

Diction and Vocabulary

1. Demonstrate, by using examples (other than "nigger") from this essay, the importance of connotation in differentiating soul language from standard English. (Guide: *Connotation/Denotation.*)

2. Undoubtedly, spoken soul includes more earthy expressions than any examples used. Is the author justified in ignoring these? Why, or why not?

3a. Select two sentences from this essay in which you think the syntax is notably either good or bad, and analyze them to determine why. (Guide: *Syntax.*)

b. Comment briefly on the quality of syntax in general.

4a. You may notice an unusually large proportion of difficult, or at least multisyllable, words in this selection. How, if at all, does this fact hurt, or help, the overall effectiveness?

b. If you find any words whose same precise function could have been served by simpler words, list or mark them and supply the substitutions.

c. Would such changes improve the style? (Guide: *Style/Tone.*) The readability for an average educated reader? Explain.

5. Use the dictionary as necessary to become familiar with the following words and their meanings: deprecatory, nuances (par. 1); feasible (2); nostalgia, fastidiousness, secular, precarious (3); profound (4); maws, funky, construed (5); clandestine, vernacular (7); malapropisms (8); cyclical (9); poignantly, phonetic, impediments, plaintive (10); diametrically (11); graphic, formidable, fettering, regenerated (12); ascertain (13); coition (14); equivocal, ad hoc (15); canon, renaissances (17); clique, metamorphosis, repercussions, expatriates, facilitated, demise (19); repudiate, vestige, caliph, shintiyan (21).

Suggestions for Writing and Discussion

1. Show why many soul brothers are correct, or incorrect, in their belief that there is "no such creature as a genuinely hip white person" (par. 9).
2. Objectively present the reasons for *and* against the offering of college courses in "Spoken Soul" (par. 20).
3. If you can do so with some degree of authority, explain what the "Ultra-Black" *is* after (par. 21).
4. You may wish to expand your answer to question 3 of "Meanings and Values." For example, explain the irony that at the very time when large numbers of young Negroes are deserting soul, the usage of soul-derived expressions has become widespread among white youths.
5. Explain how one can tell genuine soul music from the imitation and from other similar types of music.
6. Describe some other "spiritual bond" or bonds (par. 7), not necessarily pertaining to race, that are sometimes formed by hardship or tragedy.

Writing Suggestions for Section 7
Definition

Develop a composition for a specified purpose and audience, using whatever methods and expository patterns will help convey a clear understanding of your meaning of one of the following terms:

1. Country rock music.
2. Conscience.
3. Religion.
4. Bigotry.
5. Rationalization
6. Empathy.
7. Altruism.
8. Hypocrisy.
9. Humor.
10. Sophistication
11. Naiveté
12. Cowardice.
13. Wisdom.
14. Integrity.
15. Morality.
16. Sin.
17. Social poise.
18. Intellectual (the person).
19. Pornography (if your opinions differ appreciably from D. H. Lawrence's).

8

Explaining with the Help of *Description*

Although usually classed as one of the four basic forms of prose, description is used nearly always as a supporting device of one of the other three. Exposition, as well as argument and narration, can be made more vivid, and hence more understandable, with this support. Most exposition does contain some elements of description, and at times description carries almost the entire burden of the explanation, becoming a basic pattern for the expository purpose.

Description is most useful in painting a word-picture of something concrete, such as a scene or a person. Its use is not restricted, however, to what we can perceive with our senses; we can also describe (or attempt to describe) an abstract concept, such as an emotion or quality or mood. But most attempts to describe fear, for instance, still resort to the physical — a "coldness around the heart," perhaps — and in such concrete ways communicate the abstract to the reader.

In its extreme forms, description is either *objective* or *impressionistic* (subjective), but most of its uses are somewhere between these extremes. Objective description is purely factual, uncolored by any feelings of the author; it is the type used for scientific papers and most business reports. But impressionistic description, as the term implies, at least tinges the purely factual with the author's personal impressions; instead of describing how something *is,* objectively, he describes how it *seems,* subjectively. Such a description might refer to the "blazing heat" of an August day. Somewhat less impressionistic would be "extreme heat." But the scientist would describe it precisely as "115 degrees Fahrenheit," and this would be purely objective reporting, unaffected by the impressions of the author. (No examples of the latter are included in this section, but many textbooks for other courses utilize the technique of pure objective description, as do encyclopedias. The Petrunkevitch essay in Section 5 provides some good examples of objective description, although not entirely unmixed with colorful impressionistic details.)

The first and most important job in any descriptive endeavor is the selection of details to be included. There are usually many from which to choose, and the writer must constantly keep in mind the kind of picture he wants to paint with words — for *his* purpose and *his* audience. Such a word-picture need not be entirely visual; in this respect the writer has more freedom than the artist, for he can use strokes that will add the dimension of sound, smell, and even touch. Such "strokes," if made to seem natural enough, can help create a vivid and effective image in the reader's mind.

Most successful impressionistic description focuses on a single *dominant impression.* Of the many descriptive details ordinarily available for use, the author selects those which will help create a mood or atmosphere or emphasize a feature or quality. But more than the materials themselves are involved, for even diction can often assist in creating the desired dominant impression. Sometimes syntax is also an important factor, as in the use of short, hurried sentences to help convey a sense of urgency or excitement.

Actual structuring of passages is perhaps less troublesome in description than that in most of the other patterns. But some kind of orderliness is needed for the sake of both readability and a realistic effect. (Neither objective nor impressionistic description can afford not to be realistic, in one manner or another.) In visual description, orderliness is usually achieved by presenting details as the eye would find them — that is as arranged in space. We could describe a person from head to toe, or vice versa, or begin with his most noticeable feature and work from there. A scenic description might move from near to far or from far to near, from left to right or from right to left. It might also start with a broad, overall view, gradually narrowing to a focal point, probably the most significant feature of the scene. These are fairly standard kinds of description; but as the types and occasions for using description vary widely, so do the possibilities for interesting treatment. In many cases, the writer is limited only by his own ingenuity.

But ingenuity should not be allowed to produce *excessive* description, an amazingly certain path to reader boredom. A few well-chosen details are better than profusion. Economy of words is desirable in any writing, and description is no exception. Appropriate use of figurative language and careful choices of strong nouns and verbs will help prevent the need for strings of modifiers, which are wasteful and can seem amateurish.

Even for the experienced writer, however, achieving good description remains a constant challenge; the beginner should not expect to attain this goal without working at it.

SHARON CURTIN

SHARON CURTIN, a native of Douglas, Wyoming, was raised in a family of ranchers and craftsmen. Curtin, a women's liberationist and political leftist, has worked as a nurse in New York and California but now devotes most of her time to writing and to operating a small farm in Virginia. Her current projects include a book about industrial development in the western Great Plains.

Aging in the Land of the Young

"Aging in the Land of the Young" is the first part of Curtin's article by that title, as it appeared in *The Atlantic* in July 1972. It is largely a carefully restructured composite of portions of her book *Nobody Ever Died of Old Age,* also published in 1972. It illustrates the subjective form of description, generally known as impressionistic.

Old men, old women, almost 20 million of them. They constitute 10 percent of the total population, and the percentage is steadily growing. Some of them, like conspirators, walk all bent over, as if hiding some precious secret, filled with self-protection. The body seems to gather itself around those vital parts, folding shoulders, arms, pelvis like a fading rose. Watch and you see how fragile old people come to think they are. 1

Aging paints every action gray, lies heavy on every movement, imprisons every thought. It governs each decision with a ruthless and single-minded perversity. To age is to learn the feeling of no longer growing, of struggling to do old tasks, to remember familiar actions. The cells of the brain are destroyed with thousands of unfelt tiny strokes, little pockets of clotted blood wiping out memories and abilities without warning. The body seems slowly to give up, randomly stopping, sometimes starting again as if to torture and tease 2

Reprinted by permission of Little, Brown and Company in association with The Atlantic Monthly Press from *Nobody Ever Died of Old Age,* by Sharon R. Curtin. This material originally appeared in *The Atlantic Monthly.*

with the memory of lost strength. Hands become clumsy, frail transparencies, held together with knotted blue veins.

3 Sometimes it seems as if the distance between your feet and the floor were constantly changing, as if you were walking on shifting and not quite solid ground. One foot down, slowly, carefully force the other foot forward. Sometimes you are a shuffler, not daring to lift your feet from the uncertain earth but forced to slide hesitantly forward in little whispering movements. Sometimes you are able to "step out," but this effort — in fact the pure exhilaration of easy movement — soon exhausts you.

4 The world becomes narrower as friends and family die or move away. To climb stairs, to ride in a car, to walk to the corner, to talk on the telephone; each action seems to take away from the energy needed to stay alive. Everything is limited by the strength you hoard greedily. Your needs decrease, you require less food, less sleep, and finally less human contact; yet this little bit becomes more and more difficult. You fear that one day you will be reduced to the simple acts of breathing and taking nourishment. This is the ultimate stage you dread, the period of helplessness and hopelessness, when independence will be over.

5 There is nothing to prepare you for the experience of growing old. Living is a process, an irreversible progression toward old age and eventual death. You see men of eighty still vital and straight as oaks; you see men of fifty reduced to gray shadows in the human landscape. The cellular clock differs for each one of us, and is profoundly affected by our own life experiences, our heredity, and perhaps most important, by the concepts of aging encountered in society and in oneself.

6 The aged live with enforced leisure, on fixed incomes, subject to many chronic illnesses, and most of their money goes to keep a roof over their heads. They also live in a culture that worships youth.

7 A kind of cultural attitude makes me bigoted against old people; it makes me think young is best; it makes me treat old people like outcasts.

Hate that gray? Wash it away! 8
Wrinkle cream. 9
Monkey glands. 10
Face-lifting. 11
Look like a bride again. 12

Don't trust anyone over thirty. 13
I fear growing old. 14
Feel Young Again! 15

I am afraid to grow old — we're all afraid. In fact, the fear of growing old is so great that every aged person is an insult and a threat to the society. They remind us of our own death, that our body won't always remain smooth and responsive, but will someday betray us by aging, wrinkling, faltering, failing. The ideal way to age would be to grow slowly invisible, gradually disappearing, without causing worry or discomfort to the young. In some ways that does happen. Sitting in a small park across from a nursing home one day, I noticed that the young mothers and their children gathered on one side, and the old people from the home on the other. Whenever a youngster would run over to the "wrong" side, chasing a ball or just trying to cover all the available space, the old people would lean forward and smile. But before any communication could be established, the mother would come over, murmuring embarrassed apologies, and take her child back to the "young" side. 16

Now, it seemed to me that the children didn't feel any particular fear and the old people didn't seem to be threatened by the children. The division of space was drawn by the mothers. And the mothers never looked at the old people who lined the other side of the park like so many pigeons perched on the benches. These well-dressed young matrons had a way of sliding their eyes over, around, through the old people; they never looked at them directly. The old people may as well have been invisible; they had no reality for the youngsters, who were not permitted to speak to them, and they offended the aesthetic eye of the mothers. 17

My early experiences were somewhat different; since I grew up in a small town, my childhood had more of a nineteenth-century flavor. I knew a lot of old people, and considered some of them friends. There was no culturally defined way for me to "relate" to old people, except the rules of courtesy which applied to all adults. My grandparents were an integral and important part of the family and of the community. I sometimes have a dreadful fear that mine will be the last generation to know old people as friends, to have a sense of what growing old means, to respect and understand man's mortality and his courage in the face of death. Mine may be the last generation to have a sense of living history, of stories passed from generation to generation, of identity established by family history. 18

Meanings and Values

1. What is the general tone of this writing? (See Guide to Terms: *Style/Tone.*)
2. If you find it depressing to read about aging, try to analyze why (especially in view of the fact that you are very likely many years from the stage of "a fading rose").
3. Why do you suppose it is more likely to be the mothers than the children who shun old people (pars. 16–17)?

4a. Has this author avoided the excesses of sentimentality? (Guide: *Sentimentality.*)
 b. If not, where does she fail? If she does avoid them, try to discover how.

Expository Techniques

1a. Why should this writing be classed as primarily impressionistic, rather than objective?
 b. What is the dominant impression?

2a. Analyze the role that selection of details plays in creating the dominant impression.
 b. Provide examples of the type of details that could have been included but were not.
 c. Are such omissions justifiable?

3a. Paragraph 5 ends the almost pure description to begin another phase of the writing. What is it?
 b. How has the author provided for a smooth transition between the two? (Guide: *Transition.*)

4a. What particular method of gaining emphasis has been used effectively in one portion of the selection? (Guide: *Emphasis.*)
 b. How might the material have been presented if emphasis were not desired?

5. Which previously studied patterns of exposition are also used in this writing? Cite paragraphs where each may be found.

Diction and Vocabulary

1a. The author sometimes changes person — e.g., "they" to "you" after paragraph 2. Analyze where the changes occur.
 b. What justification, if any, can you find for each change?

2a. Which two kinds of figure of speech do you find used liberally to achieve this description? (Guide: *Figures of Speech.*)
 b. Cite three or more examples of each.
 c. As nearly as you can tell, are any of them clichés? (Guide: *Clichés.*)

Suggestions for Writing and Discussion

1. If Curtin is correct in her fears expressed in the last two sentences, what could be the consequences for society in general?
2. Discuss the pros and cons of placing senile old people in rest homes, rather than letting them live alone or taking them to live with the family. What other alternatives, if any, does the family have?
3. If you know some very old person who (apparently) is not as affected by aging as the ones the author describes, what seems to account for this difference?
4. If you are familiar with the Gray Power movement, or others like it, what exactly is it that they hope to accomplish?
5. If many people at age sixty to sixty-five are still efficient at their jobs, as is often argued, what practical reasons are there for forcing retirement at that age?

(NOTE: Suggestions for topics requiring development by use of DESCRIPTION are on page 272, at the end of this section.)

GEORGE SIMPSON

GEORGE SIMPSON, born in Virginia in 1950, received his B.A. degree in journalism from the University of North Carolina. He has been employed at *Newsweek* since 1972 and in 1978 became public affairs director for that magazine. Before joining *Newsweek,* Simpson worked for two years as a writer and editor for the *Carolina Financial Times* in Chapel Hill and as a reporter for the *News-Gazette* in Lexington, Virginia. He received the Best Feature Writing award from Sigma Delta Chi in 1972 for a five-part investigative series on the University of North Carolina football program. He has written freelance stories for *The New York Times, Sport, Glamour,* the *Winston-Salem Journal,* and *New York.*

The War Room at Bellevue

"The War Room at Bellevue" was first published in *New York* magazine. The author chose, for good reason, to stay strictly within a time sequence as he described the emergency ward. This essay is also noteworthy for the cumulative descriptive effect, which was accomplished almost entirely with objective details.

Bellevue. The name conjures up images of an indoor war zone: the wounded and bleeding lining the halls, screaming for help while harried doctors in blood-stained smocks rush from stretcher to stretcher, fighting a losing battle against exhaustion and the crushing number of injured. "What's worse," says a longtime Bellevue nurse, "is that we have this image of being a hospital only for . . . " She pauses, then lowers her voice; "for crazy people." 1

Though neither battlefield nor Bedlam is a valid image, there is something extraordinary about the monstrous complex that spreads for five blocks along First Avenue in Manhattan. It is said best by the head nurse in Adult Emergency Service: "If you have any chance for survival, you have it here." Survival — that is why they come. Why do injured cops drive by a half-dozen other hospitals to be treated at Bellevue? They've seen the Bellevue emergency team in action. 2

9:00 P.M. It is a Friday night in the Bellevue emergency room. The after-work crush is over (those who've suffered through the day, only to come for help after the five-o'clock whistle has blown) and it is nearly silent except for the mutter of voices at the admitting desk, where administrative personnel discuss who will go for coffee. Across the spotless white-walled lobby, ten people sit quietly, passively, in pastel plastic chairs, waiting for word of relatives or to see doctors. In the past 24 hours, 300 people have come to the Bellevue Adult Emergency Service. Fewer than 10 percent were true emergencies. One man sleeps fitfully in the emergency ward while his heartbeat, respiration, and blood pressure are monitored by control consoles mounted over his bed. Each heartbeat trips a tiny bleep in the monitor, which attending nurses can hear across the ward. A half hour ago, doctors in the trauma room withdrew a six-inch stiletto blade from his back. When he is stabilized, the patient will be moved upstairs to the twelve-bed Surgical Intensive Care Unit. 3

9:05 P.M. An ambulance backs into the receiving bay, its red and yellow lights flashing in and out of the lobby. A split second later, the glass doors burst open as a nurse and an attendant roll a mobile stretcher into the lobby. When the nurse screams, "Emergent!" the lobby explodes with activity as the way is cleared to the trauma room. Doctors appear from nowhere and transfer the bloodied body of a black man to the treatment table. Within seconds his clothes are stripped away, revealing a tiny stab wound in his left side. Three doctors and three nurses rush around the victim, each performing a task necessary to begin treatment. Intravenous needles are inserted into his arms and groin. A doctor draws blood for the lab, in case surgery is necessary. A nurse begins inserting a catheter into the victim's penis and continues to feed in tubing until the catheter reaches the bladder. Urine flows through the tube into a plastic bag. Doctors are glad not to see blood in the urine. Another nurse records pulse and blood pressure. 4

The victim is in good shape. He shivers slightly, although the trauma room is exceedingly warm. His face is bloodied, but shows no major lacerations. A third nurse, her elbow propped on the treatment table, asks the man a series of questions, trying to quickly outline his medical history. He answers abruptly. He is drunk. His left side is swabbed with yellow disinfectant and a doctor injects a local anesthetic. After a few seconds another doctor inserts his finger into the wound. It sinks in all the way to the knuckle. He begins to 5 rotate his finger like a child trying to get a marble out of a milk bottle. The patient screams bloody murder and tries to struggle free.

Meanwhile in the lobby, a security guard is ejecting a derelict 6 who has begun to drink from a bottle hidden in his coat pocket. "He's a regular, was in here just two days ago," says a nurse. "We checked him pretty good then, so he's probably okay now. Can you believe those were clean clothes we gave him?" The old man, blackened by filth, leaves quietly.

9:15 P.M. A young Hispanic man interrupts, saying his pregnant 7 girl friend, sitting outside in his car, is bleeding heavily from her vagina. She is rushed into an examination room, treated behind closed doors, and rolled into the observation ward, where, much later in the night, a gynecologist will treat her in a special room — the same one used to examine rape victims. Nearby, behind curtains, the neurologist examines an old white woman to determine if her headaches are due to head injury. They are not.

9:45 P.M. The trauma room has been cleared and cleaned merci- 8 lessly. The examination rooms are three-quarters full — another overdose, two asthmatics, a young woman with abdominal pains. In the hallway, a derelict who has been sleeping it off urinates all over the stretcher. He sleeps on while attendants change his clothes. An ambulance — one of four that patrol Manhattan for Bellevue from 42nd Street to Houston, river to river — delivers a middle-aged white woman and two cops, the three of them soaking wet. The woman has escaped from the psychiatric floor of a nearby hospital and tried to drown herself in the East River. The cops fished her out. She lies on a stretcher shivering beneath white blankets. Her eyes stare at the ceiling. She speaks clearly when an administrative worker begins routine questioning. The cops are given hospital gowns and wait to receive tetanus shots and gamma globulin — a hedge against infection from the befouled river water. They will hang around the E.R. for another two hours, telling their story to as many as six other policemen who show up to hear it. The woman is rolled into an examination room, where a male nurse speaks gently: "They tell me you fell into the river." "No," says the woman, "I jumped. I have to commit suicide." "Why?" asks the nurse. "Because I'm insane and I can't help [it]. I have to die." The nurse gradually discovers the woman has a history of psychological problems. She is given dry bedclothes and placed under guard in the hallway. She lies on her side, staring at the wall.

The pace continues to increase. Several more overdose victims arrive by ambulance. One, a young black woman, had done a strip-tease on the street just before passing out. A second black woman is semiconscious and spends the better part of her time at Bellevue alternately cursing at and pleading with the doctors. Attendants find a plastic bottle coated with methadone in the pocket of a Hispanic O.D. The treatment is routinely the same, and sooner or later involves vomiting. Just after doctors begin to treat the O.D., he vomits great quantities of wine and methadone in all directions. "Lovely business, huh?" laments one of the doctors. A young nurse confides that if there were other true emergencies, the overdose victims would be given lower priority. "You can't help thinking they did it to themselves," she says, "while the others are accident victims." 9

10:30 P.M. A policeman who twisted his knee struggling with an "alleged perpetrator" is examined and released. By 10:30, the lobby is jammed with friends and relatives of patients in various stages of treatment and recovery. The attendant who also functions as a translator for Hispanic patients adds chairs to accommodate the overflow. The medical walk-in rate stays steady — between eight and ten patients waiting. A pair of derelicts, each with battered eyes, appear at the admitting desk. One has a dramatically swollen face laced with black stitches. 10

11:00 P.M. The husband of the attempted suicide arrives. He thanks the police for saving his wife's life, then talks at length with doctors about her condition. She continues to stare into the void and does not react when her husband approaches her stretcher. 11

Meanwhile, patients arrive in the lobby at a steady pace. A young G.I. on leave has lower-back pains; a Hispanic man complains of pains in his side; occasionally parents hurry through the adult E.R. carrying children to the pediatric E.R. A white woman of about 50 marches into the lobby from the walk-in entrance. Dried blood covers her right eyebrow and upper lip. She begins to perform. "I was assaulted on 28th and Lexington, I was," she says grandly, "and I don't have to take it *anymore.* I was a bride 21 years ago and, God, I was beautiful then." She has captured the attention of all present. "I was there when the boys came home — on Memorial Day — and I don't have to take this kind of treatment." 12

As midnight approaches, the nurses prepare for the shift change. They must brief the incoming staff and make sure all reports are up-to-date. One young brunet says, "Christ, I'm gonna go home and take a shower — I smell like vomit." 13

11:50 P.M. The triage nurse is questioning an old black man about 14
chest pains, and a Hispanic woman is having an asthma attack, when an ambulance, its sirens screaming full tilt, roars into the receiving bay. There is a split-second pause as everyone drops what he or she is doing and looks up. Then all hell breaks loose. Doctors and nurses are suddenly sprinting full-out toward the trauma room. The glass doors burst open and the occupied stretcher is literally run past me. Cops follow. It is as if a comet has whooshed by. In the trauma room it all becomes clear. A half-dozen doctors and nurses surround the lifeless form of a Hispanic man with a shotgun hole in his neck the size of your fist. Blood pours from a second gaping wound in his chest. A respirator is slammed over his face, making his chest rise and fall as if he were breathing. "No pulse," reports one doctor. A nurse jumps on a stool and, leaning over the man, begins to pump his chest with her palms. "No blood pressure," screams another nurse. The ambulance driver appears shaken. "I never thought I'd get here in time," he stutters. More doctors from the trauma team upstairs arrive. Wrappings from syringes and gauze pads fly through the air. The victim's eyes are open yet devoid of life. His body takes on a yellow tinge. A male nurse winces at the gunshot wound. "This guy really pissed off somebody," he says. This is no ordinary shooting. It is an execution. IV's are jammed into the body in the groin and arms. One doctor has been plugging in an electrocardiograph and asks everyone to stop for a second so he can get a reading. "Forget it," shouts the doctor in charge. "No time." "Take it easy, Jimmy," someone yells at the head physician. It is apparent by now that the man is dead, but the doctors keep trying injections and finally they slit open the chest and reach inside almost up to their elbows. They feel the extent of the damage and suddenly it is all over. "I told 'em he was dead," says one nurse, withdrawing. "They didn't listen." The room is very still. The doctors are momentarily disgusted, then go on about their business. The room clears quickly. Finally there is only a male nurse and the still-warm body, now waxy-yellow, with huge ribs exposed on both sides of the chest and giant holes in both sides of the neck. The nurse speculates that this is yet another murder in a Hispanic political struggle that has brought many such victims to Bellevue. He marvels at the extent of the wounds and repeats, "This guy was really blown away."

Midnight. A hysterical woman is hustled through the lobby into 15
an examination room. It is the dead man's wife, and she is nearly delirious. "I know he's dead, I know he's dead," she screams over and

over. Within moments the lobby is filled with anxious relatives of the victim waiting for word on his condition. The police are everywhere asking questions, but most people say they saw nothing. One young woman says she heard six shots, two louder than the other four. At some point, word is passed that the man is, in fact, dead. Another woman breaks down in hysterics; everywhere young Hispanics are crying and comforting each other. Plainclothes detectives make a quick examination of the body, check on the time of pronouncement of death, and begin to ask questions, but the bereaved are too stunned to talk. The rest of the uninvolved people in the lobby stare dumbly, their injuries suddenly paling in light of a death.

12:30 A.M. A black man appears at the admissions desk and says 16
he drank poison by mistake. He is told to have a seat. The ambulance brings in a young white woman, her head wrapped in white gauze. She is wailing terribly. A girl friend stands over her, crying, and a boyfriend clutches the injured woman's hands, saying, "I'm here, don't worry, I'm here." The victim has fallen downstairs at a friend's house. Attendants park her stretcher against the wall to wait for an examination room to clear. There are eight examination rooms and only three doctors. Unless you are truly an emergency, you will wait. One doctor is stitching up the eyebrow of a drunk who's been punched out. The friends of the woman who fell down the stairs glance up at the doctors anxiously, wondering why their friend isn't being treated faster.

1:10 A.M. A car pulls into the bay and a young Hispanic asks if 17
a shooting victim has been brought here. The security guard blurts out, "He's dead." The young man is stunned. He peels his tires leaving the bay.

1:20 A.M. The young woman of the stairs is getting stitches in a 18
small gash over her left eye when the same ambulance driver who brought in the gunshot victim delivers a man who has been stabbed in the back on East 3rd Street. Once again the trauma room goes from 0 to 60 in five seconds. The patient is drunk, which helps him endure the pain of having the catheter inserted through his penis into his bladder. Still he yells, "That hurts like a bastard," then adds sheepishly, "Excuse me, ladies." But he is not prepared for what comes next. An X ray reveals a collapsed right lung. After just a shot of local anesthetic, the doctor slices open his side and inserts a long plastic tube. Internal bleeding had kept the lung pressed down and prevented it from reinflating. The tube releases the pressure. The ambu-

lance driver says the cops grabbed the guy who ran the eight-inch blade into the victim's back. "That's not the one," says the man. "They got the wrong guy." A nurse reports that there is not much of the victim's type blood available at the hospital. One of the doctors says that's okay, he won't need surgery. Meanwhile blood pours from the man's knife wound and the tube in his side. As the nurses work they chat about personal matters, yet they respond immediately to orders from either doctor. "How ya doin'?" the doctor asks the patient. "Okay," he says. His blood spatters on the floor.

So it goes into the morning hours. A Valium overdose, a woman who fainted, a man who went through the windshield of his car. More overdoses. More drunks with split eyebrows and chins. The doctors and nurses work without complaint. "This is nothing, about normal, I'd say," concludes the head nurse. "No big deal." 19

Meanings and Values

1a. What is the author's point of view? (See Guide to Terms: *Point of View.*)
 b. How is this reflected by the tone? (Guide: *Style/Tone.*)

2a. Does Simpson ever slip into sentimentality — a common failing when describing the scenes of death and tragedy? (Guide: *Sentimentality.*)
 b. If so, where? If not, how does he avoid it?

3a. Cite at least six facts learned from reading this piece that are told, not in general terms, but by specific, concrete details — e.g., that a high degree of cleanliness is maintained at Bellevue, illustrated by "spotless, white-walled lobby" (par. 3) and "the trauma room has been cleared and cleaned mercilessly" (par. 8).
 b. What are the advantages of having facts presented in this way?

4. If you have read Barzun's "The Professions Under Siege" (Sec. 6), show how the professionals of Bellevue probably do, or do not, share the problem of many of their colleagues, as described by Barzun.

5. If you have read the Halsey selection in Section 6, tell how the Bellevue staff members (many of them undoubtedly young) apparently avoided the "new narcissism" that afflicts so many of their generation.

Expository Techniques

1. How do you think the author went about selecting details, from among the thousands that must have been available to him?

2a. Do you consider the writing to be primarily objective, or impressionistic?
b. Clarify any apparent contradictions.
c. What is the dominant impression, if any?

3. What is the value of using a timed sequence in such a description?

4. Does it seem to you that any of this description is excessive — i.e., unnecessary to the task at hand?

5a. List, in skeletal form, the facts learned about the subject from reading the two-paragraph introduction.
b. How well does it perform the three basic purposes of an introduction? (Guide: *Introductions.*)

6a. What is the significance of the rhetorical question in paragraph 2? (Guide: *Rhetorical Questions.*)
b. Why is it rhetorical?

7. Is the short closing effective? (Guide: *Closings.*) Why, or why not?

Diction and Vocabulary

1a. Cite the clichés in paragraphs 4, 5, 8, and 14. (Guide: *Clichés.*)
b. What justification, if any, can you offer for their use?

2. Cite the allusion in paragraph 2, and explain its meaning and source. (Guide: *Figures of Speech.*)

3a. Simpson uses some slang and other colloquialisms. Cite as many of these as you can find. (Guide: *Colloquial Expressions.*)
b. Is their use justified? Why, or why not?

4. Why is "alleged perpetrator" placed in quotation marks (par. 10)?

Suggestions for Writing and Discussion

1. Explain why "neither battlefield nor Bedlam is a valid image" of the emergency room at Bellevue (pars. 1, 2).

2. Do you think it is right and/or understandable that ODs should be given lower priorities than "true emergencies" (par. 9)? Defend your views.

3. If you have had a job that to the outsider might seem hectic or hazardous, or both, were the personnel also able to "chat about personal matters" while the work was in progress? What were the circumstances?

(NOTE: Suggestions for topics requiring development by use of DESCRIPTION are on page 272, at the end of this section.)

BOB GREENE

BOB GREENE is a columnist for the *Chicago Tribune.* His daily reports and commentary are syndicated to more than 120 other newspapers in the United States, Canada, Latin America, and Japan. He is the winner of the 1977 National Headliner Award as best columnist in the United States. His articles have appeared in *Newsweek, Harper's, Rolling Stone, Sport, New Times,* and *The New York Times,* and his commentary has been featured on the CBS television and radio networks. Greene has written four books: *We Didn't Have None of Them Fat Funky Angels on the Wall of Heartbreak Hotel, and Other Reports from America* (1971); *Running: A Nixon-McGovern Campaign Journal* (1973); *Billion Dollar Baby* (1974); and *Johnny Deadline, Reporter: The Best of Bob Greene* (1976).

Hef's

"Hef's" was written for the *Chicago Sun-Times* and later published in the collection *Johnny Deadline, Reporter.* It is an extremely informal and basically descriptive piece that, without ever becoming blatant, still manages to convey a vivid impression of what life is really like in Hefner's mansion. Many of the stylistic characteristics are also worthy of study by serious students of composition.

My first secret fantasy in this life started when I was ten years old and used to sneak into my father's shirt drawer. Under a pile of white shirts I would find his latest copy of *Playboy.* In the late '50s, in Columbus, Ohio, you couldn't buy the magazine over the counter at most stores, and no family would think of keeping a copy out on a living room table. I would take my father's copy into my room, lock the door, and stay for hours. The naked girls were fine, they were great, but that wasn't the fantasy. The fantasy was much bigger than that. What I really wanted to do was to grow up, get myself to Chicago, and live in Hef's pad. 1

God, what a life! *Playboy* would run all these stories about the 2 parties Hugh Hefner gave for his celebrity friends in his mansion in Chicago. Every issue for years, it seemed, had full-color shots of that dark living room with the suit of armor in the corner and the LeRoy Neiman paintings on the walls; and the steam room with the girls sitting there with towels around their bottoms; and the firepole with cool-looking men wearing Italian suits and holding their drinks in one hand while sliding down to yet another level; and spiral staircases where people would kind of lounge around and make brilliant small talk.

Most of all I would think of something the caption writers called Woo Grotto, which was a small cranny of the swimming pool that seemed private, but that was actually visible through a trap door in a little room in the mansion, so that Hef and his fun-loving pals could peek at what was going on down there. Or so I recall. 3

Wherever I went during the years that followed, however much I was enjoying myself, I understood implicitly that they were having a better time at the Playboy Mansion. During high school, when my 16-year-old friends and I would get older guys to buy us six-packs of beer and we would drive off to drink it in someone's back seat, my thoughts were on the mansion. I knew that Hef was in the living room with some Bunny or Playmate, doing the frug while he clamped down on his pipe and butlers circulated with drinks. And in college, while the Revolution was forming in the fraternities and dorms, I was thinking of the mansion on a Saturday night, with girls stretched out and cuddled up in armchairs while Hefner had private showings of movies I would like to see. 4

It was also in college that I first read the Playboy Philosophy. This was Hefner's rambling, dull explanation of the changes of morality taking place in the country. The philosophy ran on for thousands upon thousands of words, but what it came down to was this: if something feels good and doesn't really hurt anybody, then go ahead and do it. 5

I had never read any philosophy before, but to a college freshman, the Playboy Philosophy didn't sound so bad. 6

At the time it was considered pretty daring stuff, and I dimly remember Hefner printing a load of letters in the magazine from clergymen and theologians and the like, saying Hefner had a point. And then of course came the explosion of the late '60s in the way people lived in America. 7

By the beginning of the '70s no one talked about the Playboy Philosophy anymore. That is because the Playboy Philosophy had become the American way of life. If you don't believe that, consider the fact that, in the spring of 1968, it was front-page news all over the country when a male college student and a female college student in New York admitted they were sharing an apartment. In the years since then, we have come to the point where Linda Lovelace can tour America's talk-show circuit on the strength of how good she is with her mouth, and where the women on Michigan Avenue in the summertime often approach the state of undress that was pictured in Hefner's magazine in the early days. 8

Sometime between then and now, the philosophy of *Playboy* magazine stopped being a point of national controversy and began being the way we live. You don't buy *Playboy* under the counter anymore. It sells more copies than *Time,* or *Newsweek,* or the *Atlantic,* or *Harper's,* or *Rolling Stone*—seven million copies every issue. 9

During the years of *Playboy's* growth, though, the revolution in sexuality and morality in the country ended any reason for a ten-year-old to sneak into his father's shirt drawer in order to fantasize about living at Hefner's. You don't have to go to a mansion on North State Parkway in Chicago to live a life where feeling good is reason enough to do what you want to do. You can do that in any high school in the country now. 10

So when I read somewhere that *Playboy* was about to celebrate its 20th anniversary of publishing, I decided to satisfy a curiosity that had started 15 years ago. I would live in Hef's pad. What better setting for thinking about the Playboy Philosophy, 20 years after Hefner had come up with it? 11

I made a phone call and inquired about living in the mansion for a week or so, and it didn't take long for an affirmative answer to be returned. Easy as that. They said to just let them know when I would like to check in. 12

I arrived on a Sunday afternoon. A butler let me in. We walked upstairs. The living room was empty. Hefner and most of his staff at the mansion keep night hours, and 3:00 P.M. was too early for them to be stirring. In preparation for a buffet that evening, a platoon of waiters and butlers was forming in a side room. One waiter was looking at the latest issue of *Oui,* Hefner's new magazine, and pointed to a picture of a man and woman in a difficult-to-achieve 13 sexual position. "Would you look at that!" the waiter said. "Whooooo!" Another waiter turned to him and said, "That's for younger men."

I was shown to my room, which was just off the living room. 14
Called the Blue Room, it was comparable in size to a room in a nice hotel, and done all in blue. After the butler had given me the key and left, I started to look around. I walked into the bathroom, only to find three women in bathrobes. "We thought we heard someone come in there," one of them said.

The tallest of the women, a blonde, was a prospective Playmate 15
of the Month, and it turned out that she was staying in the Red Room, right next door to the Blue Room, and that we shared the bathroom. The other two women had stayed with her the night before. We all allowed as to how it was nice to know each other.

I walked around the mansion. Early years of reading *Playboy* had 16
left a lasting impression. In every room—the swimming pool room, the steambath room, the underwater bar, the winding staircases—I felt as if I had spent hours there before. Perhaps because the house had been photographed so much, it actually seemed small to me, almost like a movie set of the Playboy Mansion. I kept waiting to see a part of the house that I had never seen in the magazine, but there was no such area. I sat by the swimming pool for 45 minutes. No one appeared.

That evening, *Westworld* was shown on a full-width screen in 17
the living room. Several of the 25 or so Bunnies who pay $50 a month to live in a dormitory section of the mansion came to see the movie.

When it was over, a Bunny named Joyce asked if I would like 18
to see a bar where the Bunnies go on nights they don't work at the Chicago Playboy Club. I said sure, and we took a cab to a place called The Bistro. The Bistro is a gay bar that features a dance floor and music. "Hey," I said to Joyce, "there's guys dancing with guys in here." "You're very observant," she said.

I asked why Bunnies liked to go to The Bistro, and she said that 19
it was a place where they could relax and have a drink and listen to music without worrying about men hitting on them and grabbing at them and trying to pick them up. "We get enough of that all the time," Joyce said. "In here, you usually don't have to deal with that."

We didn't stay long. As we were walking back to the mansion, 20 we talked about the changes in American culture in the years since Hugh Hefner started his magazine. Joyce is in her early 20s; she had been a child when Hefner was designing the pages of Vol. 1, No. 1 of *Playboy.*

Now, in 1973, she was living in his house. She is a striking- 21
looking girl with a perfect body that she shows off to her best advantage. I said that so much of what we had seen in the past hour could be traced back to Hefner—her, for instance, a young woman physically beautiful and thus drawn, naturally enough, to a job as a Playboy Bunny; and the homosexual bar where we had just been, a place that would only have been whispered about 20 years ago, but now, in the age of anything's OK, a well-known, legitimate, hip, popular spot in downtown Chicago; and Rush Street, where we were now walking, with its singles out for the one-night stands that had become an acceptable part of being unattached and alone in the modern city.

We talked about this for a while, and about how it all seems 22
natural anymore, but that it grew in a climate that was mainly nurtured by one man, Hugh Hefner. And we agreed that it did seem a little strange to be going back to Hefner's home in light of all these thoughts — that it was odd, when you thought about it, to realize that the man who started the loosening of sexual attitudes in America was in fact still fairly young himself, and still living in Chicago.

When we got to the mansion we walked into the living room. 23
The movie screen had been rolled up. The guests had gone home. And there was Hefner, wearing green pajamas. A song by the Carpenters was on the stereo. It was not yet midnight. Hefner was with his girl friend, Karen Christy, and two of his associates in Playboy Enterprises. While the wicked city did its stuff outside, Hefner was here with three friends. They were sitting around a Monopoly board, and Hefner was rolling the dice. He looked like a suburban father killing time, waiting for his teenage daughter to come home from a date.

The Monopoly routine was not unusual, I found out. Hefner 24
divides his time between the mansion in Chicago and another one in California, and most of his late evenings are devoted to playing Monopoly or backgammon with friends.

One night I sat in on the game. "New Hampshire!" Hefner 25
shouted as someone's token landed on his property and he was able

to collect a new pile of play money. "That's $200," he said to the rival player, who was being slow to pay off.

Maybe because of Hefner's close identity with his magazine, to me he always has been kind of a lecherous uncle figure, and I found it impossible to dislike him. He has been criticized for his glorification of material possessions, and for his, quote, treatment of women as sexual objects, unquote. But he has never hidden his liking for a certain style of life, and if he is ostentatious and showy about it at times, well, there have been a lot of people just like me who grew up getting a kick out of Hefner's fantasy life. Besides, allowances should be made for special cases, and Hugh Hefner happens to be the Citizen goddamn Kane of our age, and his mansion happens to be San Simeon. 26

Among the things he has done, in an era of electronic communications, is to prove once again that the printed page is capable not only of being immensely profitable, but also of creating an image, an aura, that can be presented in no other way. Hefner knows that the printed page can act as a medium of suggestion, a seductive invitation to a way of life, that breeds most heartily in the imagination. Television cannot do that; it is too graphic, too stark. Say the word "Playboy," and a picture of a whole way of living forms in the mind of just about every person in America. The printed page has done that. Say the words "Tonight Show," or "Wide World of Sports," or whatever, and the image is much more limited. Hefner understands why. 27

"Come on," Hefner said to Karen Christy, "get your mind on the game. It's your turn to roll." While she rolled the dice, Hefner studied a list he had compiled of all properties on the Monopoly board—which ones are the most profitable, which ones are likely to be a waste of money. The board itself was somewhat different from most Monopoly boards. Instead of standard tokens, each person played with a ceramic figure sculptured to look just like the player; a stack of these personalized tokens was kept by Hefner for friends who frequently played. And instead of standard hotel pieces, Hefner's board featured models of his Playboy Plaza in Miami Beach. 28

The stero clicked off. Hefner walked over and punched two buttons. He has a huge collection of records to choose from, but insisted on playing the same two albums over and over. One was a collection of old ballads by Harry Nilsson, the other a collection of 29

old ballads by Peggy Lee. He never seemed to tire of these two
records. "Maybe I'm right, and maybe I'm wrong . . . ," Hefner sang
along with Nilsson. "You can love me like I am, or goodby . . . ,"
Hefner sang with Peggy Lee. As he sang and played Monopoly, he
drank an endless supply of Pepsi Cola. As soon as he had finished
half a bottle, he would ring for a butler to bring a fresh one.

He examined his supply of paper money. "You can't lose too 30
much in Monopoly," he said. "That's one of the nice things about
this game."

Hefner was deadly serious about winning the game. He prided 31
himself on being the household champion. At one point Victor
Lownes, who runs Playboy's operations in Europe for Hefner, looked
as if he were going to dominate this particular contest. Lownes, in
Chicago on business, was staying in a guest room at the mansion. As
he acquired yet another property on the board, Hefner turned to him.
"The lock on your room and the outside lock on the house will be
changed," Hefner said.

It was getting late. Watching the game was a kind of a kick for 32
awhile, but before long it became immensely boring, especially when
it became obvious that this was what Hefner would be doing for the
rest of the night, probably until dawn. I thought of all the cars in all
the small towns of America, with the famous rabbit decal stuck to
the back windows, and the young men behind the wheels looking for
action, for good times and fast women.

"Maybe I'm right, and maybe I'm wrong . . . ," Hefner sang along 33
with Nilsson.

There was a rustling over in the corner of the living room. An 34
unlikely scenario was unfolding. Hefner's dog was unquestionably
trying to form a sexual union with Hefner's cat.

"Now look at that," Hefner said, "This *is* a house of love." 35

The thing about living in the mansion, I discovered after the first 36
few days, is that you soon learn that there is no good reason to leave,
ever. Each guest room has a room-service menu so comprehensive,
so enticing, that it is possible to do nothing but plan your days
around the next meal. With the staff of butlers and waiters and maids
actually there on a genuine 24-hour basis, it is as easy to have a steak
and a milkshake at 4:00 A.M., and then to go for a swim and have a
few drinks, as it is at 2:00 P.M., or 7:00 P.M.

The movies are the usual way of passing idle hours in the man- 37 sion. In the living room there is an oversized card file, and in the file is a list of the motion pictures that Hefner has on hand. There are hundreds, and they are all good—*The Godfather, Casablanca, The Graduate, Goldfinger*—and all you have to do is tell a butler what you'd like to see, and within five minutes the projector in the living room is set up, the screen is lowered, the lights are switched off, and you are watching.

For me, the hardest thing was to get used to dealing with butlers 38
on those terms. While I was staying at the mansion, I usually got the urge to see a movie somewhere in the middle of the night, and my natural inclination is not to bother other people at so late an hour. But the all-night crew would *rather* be doing something—the alternative for them is to sit around until dawn looking at old copies of *Playboy*—so they welcomed the chance to show a movie, just to break the boredom.

The other time-killer is the game room, just off the swimming 39
pool. Here Hefner has installed bank upon bank of pinball machines, electronic tennis machines, shooting-gallery machines, electric hockey machines. All of them are wired for free play.

On my first day in the mansion, I spent about five minutes in 40
the game room before becoming restless. But by the end of the week, I could spend two or three hours at a shot there, drinking vodka and trying to better my record scores on each machine. Once you realize there is no reason to rush around, that the services of the mansion are there for you all day and all night, and that it is unnecessary to hurry or rush or glance at your watch in order to meet some schedule that doesn't exist, it becomes very easy to play the pins for a couple of hours, or to order up three movies in a row.

Life in the house isn't an orgy day-and-night; rather, it is just 41
so pleasant and easy in a low-key way that it provides a hypnotic kind of soothing pleasure that becomes increasingly magnetic. Little things: your shirts are dirty, you go out to play the pins and take a swim, and when you come back to your room, the shirts have been laundered and hung in the closet. Each edition of the newspapers appears regularly in the living room and the breakfast area where the Bunnies take their meals, and where you can go for a snack if you are tired of room service. The telephone rings, and a voice tells you that a buffet will be served in the living room at 7:00 P.M. if you would like to attend.

It doesn't take long before you begin to make excuses to avoid 42
going outside the mansion. It is all just so much *easier* there. Have to meet someone for an appointment? Call them and tell them to meet you at the mansion instead. They'll be there.

It is not suprising that, among the people who live in the man- 43
sion, stories have arisen concerning the evil things that can befall you if you go outside. The Bunnies talk about the time that Victor Lownes went to Old Town and was mugged; he learned his lesson, and now whenever he is in Chicago, he seldom leaves the house. Johnny Crawford, the star of *The Naked Ape,* a Playboy movie production, was staying in the house while I was there, and he told me that he had gone outside, and that a drunk on the street had harrassed him and the Bunny he was with. He learned his lesson, too; he would think twice before going outside again.

One morning I went to the breakfast-room area and ordered 44
eggs. Thirty minutes later they had not come, which seemed odd because I was the only person at the table, so I asked the waiter what the delay was.

"The boss woke up and was hungry," he said. "When he orders, 45
everything else stops."

I checked this out later. It was true: When Hefner places a food 46
order, everything else is scrapped. One man cracks the eggs, another puts bread in the toaster, another greases the frying pan. Every butler, cook, and waiter is put to work on the order, so that Hefner receives his food quickly.

"We try to anticipate," one of the waiters told me. "If we know 47
that Hefner is up, and we get a feeling that he's getting hungry, we make up a whole batch of the things he likes to eat and hope he chooses one of them. That way, it's ready as soon as he calls."

Over the years hundred, probably thousands, of famous people 48
have stayed at the mansion at Hefner's invitation. But Hefner has chosen to commemorate only one of these visits. In the game room is a framed poster. It features a drawing of an airplane with a familiar lapping tongue logo on the tail. There are five signatures on the poster: Charlie Watts, Keith Richards, Mick Taylor, Bill Wyman. And, over to the left, "To Hugh Hefner, for his warm hospitality—from Mick Jagger and the Stones."

One night, after watching Hefner play backgammon with Victor Lownes for an hour or so, I went to my room to go to bed. It was about 1:00 A.M., and Hefner was drinking his Pepsi and singing along with Nilsson on the stereo. The next morning, at 10:30, I walked through the living room on my way to order breakfast. Hefner and Lownes were still at it, still sitting in the same chairs. Hefner was drinking his Pepsi and singing along with Nilsson on the stereo. 49

On another evening Hefner had a screening of the movie *Cops and Robbers.* Only a dozen or so people were in the living room for the picture. Hefner was in his pajamas, his girl friend Karen in a bathrobe. 50

When the movie ended, Hefner began discussing its merits. Because he tends to become the center of attention when he is out and about in the mansion, everyone in the room looked at him and listened. Then, in the middle of a sentence, he began to nuzzle Karen, and within a minute, was laughingly simulating what used to be referred to, in the days before Hugh Hefner, as an "unnatural act." 51

The other people in the living room fell silent. Despite all the connotations of unrestricted sex attached to the word "Playboy," it was still slightly awkward to be sitting in the living room watching Hefner play with his girl friend. 52

Finally Gene Siskel, the movie critic for the *Chicago Tribune* and a friend of Hefner's, broke the quiet. He motioned at Hefner and said, "Take pornography away from people, and see what happens? They go wild." 53

In the middle of my week at the mansion, Hefner announced that he would be flying to the California mansion. He said he would be leaving the next afternoon and asked if I would like to come along. 54

I had to say no, because I had commitments in Chicago that I could not postpone. And it was just as well; California would undoubtedly be fun, but this way I would have the Chicago mansion to myself, which wouldn't be all that bad either. 55

The evening after Hefner left, I took a slow walk around the house. In the game room I noticed that several scoreboards were attached to the wall, posting Hefner's all-time best efforts on the pinball machines. I stopped at each of the bars throughout the house and poured myself a fresh drink whenever I needed one. I walked down a corridor to Hefner's bowling alley, punched a button to 56 turn on the automatic pinsetting machine, and bowled until I tired of it.

I had no idea what time it was, but by this point in the week it didn't matter. I took my drink to the underwater bar and leaned back on a padded deck next to a big window that looked into the pool. On the walls were large color transparencies of past Playmates. 57

I attempted to do some serious thinking about What It All Meant, as that was ostensibly why I had come to the mansion. Several times during the week I had begun to try such thinking, but every time I had put it off for a few hours. My original theory, before I had come to the mansion, was that the Playboy Philosophy, 20 years later, was an anachronism—that Hefner was living in a self-contained harem based on the principle of easy pleasure when, in reality, he didn't have to, when he could have the same thing just by going out on the street, just like anyone else. 58

But that theory didn't seem quite right. The whole idea of the Playboy Mansion as a harem isn't even right. Yes, Hefner has the 25 Bunnies living in the house, and they are around all the time. But that idea, to the millions of American men who know about it through the magazine, is far more exciting in the imagination than it is in reality. 59

It's not that "the mansion is more sexless than a convent," as one writer put it. That isn't true, either. Rather a house with 25 attractive young girls in it is no more a monolithic entity than the 25 Bunnies; they are all different, and they are all there for different reasons, and most of them have been living there for so long that they don't even consider it unusual that their home is the Playboy Mansion. A few are so shy that they hesitate to ring the waiter to bring lunch, and instead wait for someone else to come in and beckon the waiter. Others more perfectly fit the image of the Bunny as a free-and-easy woman. (One Bunny was at breakfast one morning looking through an advance copy of a new issue of *Playboy.* She stopped at a survey of sexual activities among Americans, running her fingers down the list of pratices as if she were looking for something in particular. Finally she found it. "All RIGHT!" she said. "Anal intercourse.") 60

So it's nice that the girls are around, and maybe, in an earlier year of *Playboy's* history, it was even a great turnon. But if that were the only reason for the mansion's existence, then my original theory would be right. Life in the mansion would indeed be an anachronism, if it depended on the availability of 25 women for its lure. If that were 61 the only criterion, then Hefner would not have a monopoly on his particular way of life.

That is not the case, of course. The appeal of the Playboy Mansion comes from the one thing that Hefner has been able to give himself that is so rare in America these days—a way to lock out the troubles. In that mansion Hugh Hefner has devised a little world that is carefree and completely self-contained. There are people paid to make sure that the master of the house never wants for anything. In the United States in the '70s, it is often true that nothing works anymore. In the Playboy Mansion, everything works, always. There are electricians and technicians in the house around the clock to fix up anything that should go wrong—to replace the bulb in the movie projector, to repair the knob on the electronic tennis game, to secure the beaded curtains by the swimming pool. There are plain-clothes guards posted around the house to make sure that no one gets in who is not wanted. There are men assigned to keeping Hefner's movies and records up to date. There are butlers whose duty is to make sure the master's supply of Pepsi never dwindles below the danger point. Everything has been thought of. 62

For years, Hefner has been criticized for living this way. The Playboy way of life, epitomized by Hefner's personal way of life, has been called shallow and meaningless and plastic. But almost all the people who scorn Hefner, who mock his values and the way he chooses to live, are people whom Hefner has never met, and will never know. Hefner has done the one thing that sounds so simple: he has thought about the way he would like to live and then has gone ahead and lived that way. 63

My last night in the Playboy Mansion, I went into the living room and asked one of the butlers to show me a movie print of the first "Frank Sinatra: A Man and His Music" television special. Another butler brought me some drinks while I was watching Sinatra sing, and then I asked to see *Midnight Cowboy,* and while that was showing I had dinner. 64

When the movies were over, I looked around the room. Here it was, Hefner's house. There were the LeRoy Neiman paintings, and there was the suit of armor, and over there was the spiral staircase leading down to the swimming pool. Some of the Bunnies were just beginning to come in from work, and they were sitting around the living room with nothing to do on a Saturday night. I gave some 65 thought to those days of sneaking *Playboy* out of my father's shirt drawer, and then a butler came up and asked me if I would like another drink. I laughed out loud; this was just crazy, and too funny. Hefner was out of town, and I had the run of the mansion. Too much.

In the morning I got out of bed early, packed my bag, gave the 66
key to my room back to a butler, and left. I didn't even stay for breakfast. As I walked out the front gate, a middle-aged man and woman were stopped on the sidewalk, looking at the house. The man asked me if this wasn't Hugh Hefner's Playboy Mansion, and I said it sure was. He rolled his eyes, I winked at him. I thought about hailing a cab, but I walked home instead.

Meanings and Values

1a. What basic irony do you find in this selection? (See Guide to Terms: *Irony.*)
 b. What kind of irony is it?

2. What is the dominant impression of the visit itself?

3a. What justification, if any, can you see for Greene's apparent exaggeration from time to time (e.g., in paragraph 4 and in his comment to Joyce in paragraph 18)?
 b. List all paragraphs that seem to you to contain exaggerations, and briefly state whether or not each serves some purpose.
 c. Is any harm done by them?

4. From your own experience or knowledge, do you agree with the last sentence of paragraph 10? Explain.

5a. For what was the author really waiting by the pool (par. 16)?
 b. This paragraph serves a key function structurally. What is it?

6a. In your opinion, is the fact that many people have gotten a kick out of Hefner's fantasy life justification enough for "his glorification of material possessions and treatment of women as sexual objects" (par. 26)?
 b. Exactly why, if you agree, should allowance be made for "special cases" like Hefner? If you do not agree, explain your viewpoint.

7a. Do you agree that sexual attitudes have become as loose as Greene implies?
 b. Does it seem likely that the revolution "grew in a climate that was mainly nurtured by one man"? Why, or why not?

8. Cite any passages that tended to convince you that the inhabitants of Hefner's mansion lead boring lives.

9a. If you have read the Halsey selection in Section 6, what might that author say is the widespread contemporary disease that has made Hefner rich? Explain.

b. Do you think he may have become afflicted with it himself? Why, or why not?

Expository Techniques

1a. Where would you place "Hef's" on an impressionistic–objective continuum?
b. Is there a dominant impression in the first part of the essay? If so, what is it?
c. What is the dominant impression, if any, of the major portion?
d. Why is it not surprising that that dominant impression is less pronounced in this writing that it is in the work of some other descriptive authors?

2. After twenty years (more or less) of fantasizing and one week of on-the-scene impressions, the author must have had thousands of details from which to choose. Examine the following passages and briefly state why Greene might have chosen these particular details:
a. Paragraphs 2 and 3.
b. Paragraph 8.
c. The last sentence of paragraph 15.
d. Paragraph 9.
e. The example of Johnny Crawford (par. 43).
f. Paragraphs 44–49.

3a. Explain why the noticeably loose organization of "Hef's" is justified, or why it is not.
b. Do the frequent divisions such as that between paragraphs 43 and 44 seem to fragment the writing? Why, or why not?
c. Explain how this is, or would be, a matter of coherence. (Guide: *Coherence.*)

4. Decide on another possible way to have introduced this composition, and state why it is more, or less, effective than Greene's beginning. (Guide: *Introductions.*)

5a. The author's closing consists of two paragraphs. What standard techniques are used? (Guide: *Closings.*)
b. What subtle effect is achieved by the brief anecdote of the last paragraph?
c. What is strongly implied by the last sentence?

Diction and Vocabulary

1a. Would you consider colorful diction an important element of this author's style? (Guide: *Diction.*)
b. Cite three examples of colloquial usage or slang in the first four paragraphs. Does their use damage the writing? (Guide: *Colloquial Expressions.*)

2. How would the author say the connotation of the word "playboy" has changed in the last twenty years? (Guide: *Connotation/Denotation.*)
3. What "revolution" was forming in the fraternities and dorms when Greene was in college (par. 4)?
4. What effect, if any, is achieved by the use of the four short sentences to begin paragraph 13?
5. Explain the allusion in paragraph 26. (Guide: *Figures of Speech.*)
6. If you are unfamiliar with any of the following words, consult your dictionary as necessary: implicitly (par. 4); lecherous, ostentatious (26); aura (27); ostensibly (58); anachronism (58, 61); monolithic (60); criterion (61); epitomized (63).

Suggestions for Writing and Discussion

1. Do you believe that sexual permissiveness has become as all-pervasive as the author seems to think? Why, or why not?
2. Discuss the charge that Hefner treats women as sexual objects—e.g., who gets hurt if the accusation is true?
3. Would the world be better, or worse, if we all adopted the Hefner philosophy (par. 5), which some people call "shallow and meaningless and plastic" (par. 63)? Defend your answer.
4. If you have read the Simpson selection, you might like to contrast the apparent personal philosophies of the staff at Bellevue emergency room and the inhabitants of Hef's mansion. Which do you think are more likely to find their self-identity? (A familiarity with the Halsey essay in Section 6 would also be helpful.) Which place would you rather be?

(NOTE: Suggestions for topics requiring development by use of DESCRIPTION are on page 272, at the end of this section.)

Writing Suggestions for Section 8
Description

1. Primarily by way of impressionistic description that focuses on a single dominant impression, show and explain the mood, or atmosphere of one of the following:

    a. A county fair.
    b. A ball game.
    c. A rodeo.
    d. A wedding.
    e. A funeral.
    f. A riot.
    g. A ghost town.
    h. A cave.
    i. A mine.
    j. An antique shop.
    k. A party.
    l. A family dinner.
    m. A traffic jam.
    n. Reveille.
    o. An airport (or bus depot).
    p. A drag race (or horse race).
    q. A home during one of its rush hours.
    r. The last night of Christmas shopping.
    s. A natural scene at a certain time of day.
    t. The campus at examination time.
    u. A certain person at a time of great emotion — e.g., joy, anger, grief.

2. Using objective description as your basic pattern, explain the functional qualities or the significance of one of the following:

    a. A house for sale.
    b. A public building.
    c. A dairy barn.
    d. An ideal workshop (or hobby room).
    e. An ideal garage.
    f. A commune.
    g. The layout of a town (or airport).
    h. The layout of a farm.
    i. A certain type of boat.

9

Using *Narration* as an Expository Technique

Attempts to classify the functions of narration seem certain to develop difficulties and end in arbitrary and sometimes fuzzy distinctions. These need not distress us, however, if we remember that narration remains narration — a factual or fictional report of a sequence of events — and that our only reason for trying to divide it into categories is to find some means of studying its uses.

In a sense, as we have already seen in Section 5, exposition by process analysis makes one important, if rather narrow, use of narration, since it explains in sequence how specific steps lead to completion of some process. But at the other extreme is narration that has very little to do with exposition: the story itself is the important thing, and instead of a series of steps leading obviously to a completed act, events *develop* out of each other and build suspense, however mild, through some kind of conflict. Here narration assumes importance in its own right as one of the four basic forms of prose, and it includes the novel and short story, as well as some news and sports reporting. Because we are studying exposition, however, we must avoid getting too involved with these uses of narration; they require special techniques, the study of which would require a whole course or, in fact, several courses.

Between the extremes of a very usable analysis of process and a very intriguing narration for the story's sake — and often seeming to blur into one or the other — is narration for *explanation's* sake, to explain a concept that is more than process and that might have been explained by one of the other patterns of exposition. Here only the form is narrative; the function is expository.

Fortunately, the average student seldom needs to use narration for major explanatory purposes, as it has been used in each of the following selections. But to learn the handling of even minor or localized narration, the best procedure (short of taking several college courses, or at least one that concentrates on the narrative form) is simply to observe how successful writers use it to perform various functions. Localized narration can sometimes be helpful as an aid in developing any of the other major patterns of exposition — e.g., as in the writings of Peter/Hull (Section 1), or Catton (Section 3).

The most common problems can be summarized as follows:

1. *Selection of details.* As in writing description, the user of narration always has far more details available than he can or should use. Good unity demands that he select only those which are most relevant to his purpose and the effect he wants to create.

2. *Time order.* The writer can use straight chronology, relating events as they happen (the usual method in minor uses of narration); or he can use the flashback method, leaving the sequence temporarily in order to go back and relate some now-significant happening of a time prior to the main action. If flashback is used, it should be deliberate and for a valid reason — not merely because the episode was neglected at the beginning.

3. *Transitions.* The lazy writer of narration is apt to resort to the transitional style of a three-year-old: " . . . and then we . . . and then she . . . and then we . . . ." Avoiding this style may tax his ingenuity, but invariably the result is worth the extra investment of time and thought.

4. *Point of view.* This is a large and complex subject if dealt with fully, as a course in narration would do. Briefly, however, the writer should decide at the beginning whether the reader is to experience the action through a character's eyes (and ears and brain), or from an overall, objective view. This decision makes a difference in how much can be told, whose thoughts or secret actions can be included. The writer must be consistent throughout the narrative and include only information that could logically be known through the adopted point of view.

5. *Dialogue.* Presumably the writer already knows the mechanics of using quotations. Beyond these, his problems are to make

conversation as natural-sounding as possible and yet to keep it from rambling through many useless details — to keep the narrative moving forward by *means* of dialogue.

As in most patterns of writing, the use of expository narration is most likely to be successful if the writer constantly keeps his purpose and his audience in mind, remembering that the only reason for using the method in the first place — for doing *any* writing — is to communicate ideas. Soundness, clarity, and interest are the best means of attaining this goal.

MARTIN GANSBERG

MARTIN GANSBERG, born in Brooklyn, N.Y., in 1920, received a Bachelor of Social Sciences degree from St. John's University. He has been an editor and reporter on *The New York Times* since 1942, including a three-year period as editor of its international edition in Paris. He also served on the faculty of Fairleigh Dickinson University for fifteen years. Gansberg has written for many magazines, including *Diplomat, Catholic Digest, Facts,* and *U.S. Lady.*

38 Who Saw Murder Didn't Call the Police

"38 Who Saw Murder . . . " was written for *The New York Times* in 1964, and for obvious reasons it has been anthologized frequently since then. Cast in a deceptively simple news style, it still provides material for serious thought, as well as a means of studying the use and technique of narration.

For more than half an hour 38 respectable, law-abiding citizens in Queens watched a killer stalk and stab a woman in three separate attacks in Kew Gardens. 1

Twice their chatter and the sudden glow of their bedroom lights interrupted him and frightened him off. Each time he returned, sought her out, and stabbed her again. Not one person telephoned the police during the assault; one witness called after the woman was dead. 2

That was two weeks ago today. 3

Still shocked is Assistant Chief Inspector Frederick M. Lussen, in charge of the borough's detectives and a veteran of 25 years of homicide investigations. He can give a matter-of-fact recitation on many murders. But the Kew Gardens slaying baffles him — not because it is a murder, but because the "good people" failed to call the police. 4

Reprinted by permission of the publisher from *The New York Times* (March 17, 1964).

"As we have reconstructed the crime," he said, "the assailant had three chances to kill this woman during a 35 minute period. He returned twice to complete the job. If we had been called when he first attacked, the woman might not be dead now." 5

This is what the police say happened beginning at 3:20 A.M. in the staid, middle-class, tree-lined Austin Street area: 6

Twenty-eight-year-old Catherine Genovese, who was called Kitty by almost everyone in the neighborhood, was returning home from her job as manager of a bar in Hollis. She parked her red Fiat in a lot adjacent to the Kew Gardens Long Island Rail Road Station, facing Mowbray Place. Like many residents of the neighborhood, she had parked there day after day since her arrival from Connecticut a year ago, although the railroad frowns on the practice. 7

She turned off the lights of her car, locked the door, and started to walk the 100 feet to the entrance of her apartment at 82–70 Austin Street, which is in a Tudor building, with stores in the first floor and apartments on the second. 8

The entrance to the apartment is in the rear of the building because the front is rented to retail stores. At night the quiet neighborhood is shrouded in the slumbering darkness that marks most residential areas. 9

Miss Genovese noticed a man at the far end of the lot, near a seven-story apartment house at 82–40 Austin Street. She halted. Then, nervously, she headed up Austin Street toward Lefferts Boulevard, where there is a call box to the 102nd Police Precinct in nearby Richmond Hill. 10

She got as far as a street light in front of a bookstore before the man grabbed her. She screamed. Lights went on in the 10-story apartment house at 82–67 Austin Street, which faces the bookstore. Windows slid open and voices punctuated the early-morning stillness. 11

Miss Genovese screamed: "Oh, my God, he stabbed me! Please help me! Please help me!" 12

From one of the upper windows in the apartment house, a man called down: "Let that girl alone!" 13

The assailant looked up at him, shrugged and walked down Austin Street toward a white sedan parked a short distance away. Miss Genovese struggled to her feet. 14

Lights went out. The killer returned to Miss Genovese, now trying to make her way around the side of the building by the parking lot to get to her apartment. The assailant stabbed her again. 15

"I'm dying!" she shrieked. "I'm dying!" 16

Windows were opened again, and lights went on in many apartments. The assailant got into his car and drove away. Miss Genovese staggered to her feet. A city bus, O–10, the Lefferts Boulevard line to Kennedy International Airport, passed. It was 3:35 A.M. 17

The assailant returned. By then, Miss Genovese had crawled to the back of the building, where the freshly painted brown doors to the apartment house held out hope for safety. The killer tried the first door; she wasn't there. At the second door, 82–62 Austin Street, he saw her slumped on the floor at the foot of the stairs. He stabbed her a third time — fatally. 18

It was 3:50 by the time the police received their first call, from a man who was a neighbor of Miss Genovese. In two minutes they were at the scene. The neighbor, a 70-year-old woman, and another woman were the only persons on the street. Nobody else came forward. 19

The man explained that the had called the police after much deliberation. He had phoned a friend in Nassau County for advice and then he had crossed the roof of the building to the apartment of the elderly woman to get her to make the call. 20

"I didn't want to get involved," he sheepishly told the police. 21

Six days later, the police arrested Winston Moseley, a 29-year-old business-machine operator, and charged him with homicide. Moseley had no previous record. He is married, has two children and owns a home at 133–19 Sutter Avenue, South Ozone Park, Queens. On Wednesday, a court committed him to Kings County Hospital for psychiatric observation. 22

When questioned by the police, Moseley also said that he had slain Mrs. Annie May Johnson, 24 of 146–12 133d Avenue, Jamaica, on Feb. 29 and Barbara Kralik, 15, of 174–17 140th Avenue, Springfield Gardens, last July. In the Kralik case, the police are holding Alvin L. Mitchell, who is said to have confessed that slaying. 23

The police stressed how simple it would have been to have gotten in touch with them. "A phone call," said one of the detectives, "would have done it." The police may be reached by dialing "O" for operator or SPring 7–3100. 24

Today witnesses from the neighborhood, which is made up of 25
one-family homes in the $35,000 to $60,000 range with the exception of the two apartment houses near the railroad station, find it difficult to explain why they didn't call the police.

A housewife, knowingly if quite casually, said, "We thought it 26
was a lover's quarrel." A husband and wife both said, "Frankly, we were afraid." They seemed aware of the fact that events might have been different. A distraught woman, wiping her hands in her apron, said, "I didn't want my husband to get involved."

One couple, now willing to talk about that night, said they heard 27
the first screams. The husband looked thoughtfully at the bookstore where the killer first grabbed Miss Genovese.

"We went to the window to see what was happening," he said, 28
"but the light from our bedroom made it difficult to see the street." The wife, still apprehensive, added: "I put out the light and we were able to see better."

Asked why they hadn't called the police, she shrugged and re- 29
plied: "I don't know."

A man peeked out from a slight opening in the doorway to his 30
apartment and rattled off an account of the killer's second attack. Why hadn't he called the police at the time? "I was tired," he said without emotion. "I went back to bed."

It was 4:25 A.M. when the ambulance arrived to take the body 31
of Miss Genovese. It drove off. "Then," a solemn police detective said, "the people came out."

Meanings and Values

1a. What is Gansberg's central (expository) theme?
 b. How might he have developed this theme without using narration at all? Specify what patterns of exposition he could have used instead.
 c. Would any of them have been as effective as narration *for the purpose?* Why, or why not?

2. Show how this selection could be used as an illustration in an explanatory discussion of abstract and concrete writing. (See Guide to Terms: *Concrete/Abstract.)*

3a. Why has this narrative account of old news (the murder made its only headlines in 1964) retained its significance to this day?
 b. Are you able to see in this event a paradigm of any larger condition or situation? If so, explain, using examples as needed to illustrate your ideas.

4. If you have read Wolfe's essay (Sec. 4), do you think Dr. Hall would have been very surprised at this New York case of noninvolvement? Why, or why not?

Expository Techniques

1a. What standard introductory technique is exemplified in paragraph 1? (Guide: *Introductions.*)
b. How effective do you consider it?
c. If you see anything ironic in the fact stated there, explain the irony. (Guide: *Irony.*)

2a. Where does the main narration begin?
b. What, then, is the function of the preceding paragraphs?

3a. Study several of the paragraph transitions within the narration itself to determine Gansberg's method of advancing the time sequence (to avoid overuse of "and then"). What is the technique?
b. Is another needed? Why, or why not?

4a. What possible reasons do you see for the predominant use of short paragraphs in this piece?
b. Does this selection lose any effectiveness because of the short paragraphs?

5. Undoubtedly, the author selected with care the few quotations from witnesses that he uses. What principle or principles, do you think applied to his selection?

6. Explain why you think the quotation from the "solemn police detective" was, or was not, deliberately and carefully chosen to conclude the piece. (Guide: *Closings.*)

7a. Briefly identify the point of view of the writing. (Guide: *Point of View.*)
b. Is it consistent throughout?
c. Show the relation, as you see it, between this point of view and the author's apparent attitude toward his subject matter.

8a. Does he permit himself any sentimentality? If so, where? (Guide: *Sentimentality.*)
b. If not, specifically what might he have included that would have slipped into melodrama or sentimentality?

Diction and Vocabulary

1a. Why do you think the author used no difficult words in this narration?
b. Do you find the writing at all belittling to college people because of this fact? Why, or why not?

Suggestions for Writing and Discussion

1. Use both developed and undeveloped examples to show the prevalence, among individuals, of an anti-involvement attitude today. Or, if you prefer, show that this accusation is unjustified.
2. If this narration can be regarded as a paradigm (see question 3b of "Meanings and Values"), select one example from the larger subject and develop it on whatever theme you choose. Your example could be from international affairs, if you like (and if you don't mind becoming the center of a controversy) — e.g., the recent cries of "murder!" from numerous small countries. If you prefer, go into more distant (and therefore less controversial) history for your example.
3. If such a crime as the Genovese murder were happening in an area or a situation where police were not so instantly available, what do you think an observer should do about it? What would *you* do? Justify your stand fully.

(NOTE: Suggestions for topics requiring development by NARRATION are on page 296, at the end of this section.)

GEORGE ORWELL

GEORGE ORWELL (1903–1950), whose real name was Eric Blair, was a British novelist and essayist, well known for his satire. He was born in India and educated at Eton in England; he was wounded while fighting in the Spanish Civil War. Later he wrote the books *Animal Farm* (1945), a satire on Soviet history, and *1984* (1949), a vivid picture of life in a projected totalitarian society. He was, however, also sharply aware of injustices in democratic societies and was consistently socialistic in his views. Many of Orwell's essays are collected in *Critical Essays* (1946), *Shooting an Elephant* (1950), and *Such, Such Were the Joys* (1953).

A Hanging

"A Hanging" is typical of Orwell's essays in its setting — Burma — and in its subtle but biting commentary on colonialism, on capital punishment, even on one aspect of human nature itself. Although he is ostensibly giving a straightforward account of an execution, the author masterfully uses descriptive details and dialogue to create atmosphere and sharply drawn characterizations. The essay gives concrete form to a social message that is often delivered much less effectively in abstract generalities.

It was in Burma, a sodden morning of the rains. A sickly light, like 1
yellow tinfoil, was slanting over the high walls into the jail yard. We were waiting outside the condemned cells, a row of sheds fronted with double bars, like small animal cages. Each cell measured about ten feet by ten and was quite bare within except for a plank bed and a pot for drinking water. In some of them brown, silent men were squatting at the inner bars, with their blankets draped round them. These were the condemned men, due to be hanged within the next week or two.

2 One prisoner had been brought out of his cell. He was a Hindu, a puny wisp of a man, with a shaven head and vague liquid eyes. He had a thick, sprouting mustache, absurdly too big for his body, rather like the moustache of a comic man on the films. Six tall Indian warders were guarding him and getting him ready for the gallows. Two of them stood by with rifles and fixed bayonets, while the others handcuffed him, passed a chain through his handcuffs and fixed it to their belts, and lashed his arms tight to his sides. They crowded very close about him, with their hands always on him in a careful, caressing grip, as though all the while feeling him to make sure he was there. It was like men handling a fish which is still alive and may jump back into the water. But he stood quite unresisting, yielding his arms limply to the ropes, as though he hardly noticed what was happening.

3 Eight o'clock struck and a bugle call, desolately thin in the wet air, floated from the distant barracks. The superintendent of the jail, who was standing apart from the rest of us, moodily prodding the gravel with his stick, raised his head at the sound. He was an army doctor, with a grey toothbrush moustache and a gruff voice. "For God's sake hurry up, Francis," he said irritably. "The man ought to have been dead by this time. Aren't you ready yet?"

4 Francis, the head jailer, a fat Dravidian in a white drill suit and gold spectacles, waved his black hand. "Yes sir, yes sir," he bubbled. "All iss satisfactorily prepared. The hangman iss waiting. We shall proceed."

5 "Well, quick march, then. The prisoners can't get their breakfast till this job's over."

6 We set out for the gallows. Two warders marched on either side of the prisoner, with their rifles at the slope; two others marched close against him, gripping him by arm and shoulder, as though at once pushing and supporting him. The rest of us, magistrates and the like, followed behind. Suddenly, when we had gone ten yards, the procession stopped short without any order or warning. A dreadful thing had happened — a dog, come goodness knows whence, had appeared in the yard. It came bounding among us with a loud volley of barks and leapt round us wagging its whole body, wild with glee at finding so many human beings together. It was a large woolly dog, half Airedale, half pariah. For a moment it pranced round us, and then, before anyone could stop it, it had made a dash for the prisoner, and jumping up tried to lick his face. Everybody stood aghast, too taken aback even to grab the dog.

"Who let that bloody brute in here?" said the superintendent angrily. "Catch it, someone!" 7

A warder detached from the escort, charged clumsily after the dog, but it danced and gambolled just out of his reach, taking everything as part of the game. A young Eurasian jailer picked up a handful of gravel and tried to stone the dog away, but it dodged the stones and came after us again. Its yaps echoed from the jail walls. The prisoner, in the grasp of the two warders, looked on incuriously, as though this was another formality of the hanging. It was several minutes before someone managed to catch the dog. Then we put my handkerchief through its collar and moved off once more, with the dog still straining and whimpering. 8

It was about forty yards to the gallows. I watched the bare brown back of the prisoner marching in front of me. He walked clumsily with his bound arms, but quite steadily, with that bobbing gait of the Indian who never straightens his knees. At each step his muscles slid neatly into place, the lock of hair on his scalp danced up and down, his feet printed themselves on the wet gravel. And once, in spite of the men who gripped him by each shoulder, he stepped lightly aside to avoid a puddle on the path. 9

It is curious; but till that moment I had never realized what it means to destroy a healthy, conscious man. When I saw the prisoner step aside to avoid the puddle I saw the mystery, the unspeakable wrongness, of cutting a life short when it is in full tide. This man was not dying, he was alive just as we are alive. All the organs of his body were working — bowels digesting food, skin renewing itself, nails growing, tissues forming — all toiling away in solemn foolery. His nails would still be growing when he stood on the drop, when he was falling through the air with a tenth-of-a-second to live. His eyes saw the yellow gravel and the grey walls, and his brain still remembered, foresaw, reasoned — even about puddles. He and we were a party of men walking together, seeing, hearing, feeling, understanding the same world; and in two minutes, with a sudden snap, one of us would be gone — one mind less, one world less. 10

The gallows stood in a small yard, separate from the main grounds of the prison, and overgrown with tall prickly weeds. It was a brick erection like three sides of a shed, with planking on top, and above that two beams and a crossbar with the rope dangling. The hangman, a greyhaired convict in the white uniform of the prison, was waiting beside his machine. He greeted us with a servile crouch 11 as we entered. At a word from Francis the two warders, gripping the prisoner more closely than ever, half led, half pushed him to the gallows and helped him clumsily up the ladder. Then the hangman climbed up and fixed the rope round the prisoner's neck.

We stood waiting, five yards away. The warders had formed in a rough circle round the gallows. And then, when the noose was fixed, the prisoner began crying out to his god. It was a high, reiterated cry of "Ram! Ram! Ram! Ram!" not urgent and fearful like a prayer or cry for help, but steady, rhythmical, almost like the tolling of a bell. The dog answered the sound with a whine. The hangman, still standing on the gallows, produced a small cotton bag like a flour bag and drew it down over the prisoner's face. But the sound, muffled by the cloth, still persisted, over and over again: "Ram! Ram! Ram! Ram! Ram!" 12

The hangman climbed down and stood ready, holding the lever. Minutes seemed to pass. The steady, muffled crying from the prisoner went on and on, "Ram! Ram! Ram!" never faltering for an instant. The superintendent, his head on his chest, was slowly poking the ground with his stick; perhaps he was counting the cries, allowing the prisoner a fixed number — fifty, perhaps, or a hundred. Everyone had changed colour. The Indians had gone grey like bad coffee, and one or two of the bayonets were wavering. We looked at the lashed, hooded man on the drop, and listened to his cries — each cry another second of life; the same thought was in all our minds; oh, kill him quickly , get it over, stop that abominable noise! 13

Suddenly the superintendent made up his mind. Throwing up his head he made a swift motion with his stick. "Chalo!" he shouted almost fiercely. 14

There was a clanking noise, and then dead silence. The prisoner had vanished, and the rope was twisting on itself. I let go of the dog, and it galloped immediately to the back of the gallows; but when it got there it stopped short, barked, and then retreated into a corner of the yard, where it stood among the weeds, looking timorously out at us. We went round the gallows to inspect the prisoner's body. He was dangling with his toes pointed straight downwards, very slowly revolving, as dead as a stone. 15

The superintendent reached out with his stick and poked the bare brown body; it oscillated slightly. "*He's* all right," said the superintendent. He backed out from under the gallows, and blew out a deep breath. The moody look had gone out of his face quite sud- 16 denly. He glanced at his wrist-watch. "Eight minutes past eight. Well, that's all for this morning, thank God."

The warders unfixed bayonets and marched away. The dog, sobered and conscious of having misbehaved itself, slipped after them. We walked out of the gallows yard, past the condemned cells with their waiting prisoners, into the big central yard of the prison. The convicts, under the command of warders armed with lathis, were already receiving their breakfast. They squatted in long rows, each man holding a tin pannikin, while two warders with buckets marched round ladling out rice; it seemed quite a homely, jolly scene, after the hanging. An enormous relief had come upon us now that the job was done. One felt an impulse to sing, to break into a run, to snigger. All at once everyone began chattering gaily. 17

The Eurasian boy walking beside me nodded towards the way we had come, with a knowing smile: "Do you know, sir, our friend (he meant the dead man) when he heard his appeal had been dismissed, he pissed on the floor of his cell. From fright. Kindly take one of my cigarettes, sir. Do you not admire my new silver case, sir? From the boxwallah, two rupees eight annas. Classy European style." 18

Several people laughed — at what, nobody seemed certain. 19

Francis was walking by the superintendent, talking garrulously: "Well, sir, all has passed off with the utmost satisfactoriness. It was all finished — flick! Like that. It iss not always so — oah, no! I have known cases where the doctor wass obliged to go beneath the gallows and pull the prissoner's legs to ensure decease. Most disagreeable!" 20

"Wriggling about, eh? That's bad," said the superintendent. 21

"Arch, sir, it iss worse when they become refractory! One man, I recall, clung to the bars of hiss cage when we went to take him out. You will scarcely credit, sir, that it took six warders to dislodge him, three pulling at each leg. We reasoned with him, 'My dear fellow,' we said, 'think of all the pain and trouble you are causing to us!' But no, he would not listen! Ach, he wass very troublesome!" 22

I found that I was laughing quite loudly. Everyone was laughing. Even the superintendent grinned in a tolerant way. "You'd better all come out and have a drink," he said quite genially. "I've got a bottle of whisky in the car. We could do with it." 23

We went through the big double gates of the prison into the road. "Pulling at his legs!" exclaimed a Burmese magistrate suddenly, and burst into a loud chuckling. We all began laughing again. At that moment Francis' anecdote seemed extraordinarily funny. We all had 24 a drink together, native and European alike, quite amicably. The dead man was a hundred yards away.

Meanings and Values

1. What was the real reason for the superintendent's impatience?
2. On first impression it may have seemed that the author gave undue attention to the dog's role in this narrative.
   a. Why was the episode such a "dreadful thing" (par. 6)?
   b. Why did the author think it worth noting that the dog was excited at "finding so many human beings together"?
   c. Of what significance was the dog's trying to lick the prisoner's face?
3. Explain how the prisoner's stepping around a puddle could have given the author a new insight into what was about to happen (par. 10).
4. Why was there so much talking and laughing after the hanging was finished?
5. What is the broadest meaning of Orwell's last sentence?

Expository Techniques

1. Cite examples of both objective and impressionistic description in the first paragraph.

2a. What time order is used primarily in this narrative?
 b. If there are any exceptions, state where.

3. Considering the relatively few words devoted to them, several of the characterizations in this essay are remarkably vivid—a result, obviously, of highly discriminating selection of details from the multitude of those that must have been available to the author. For each of the following people, list the character traits that we can observe, and state whether these impressions come to us through details of description, action, and/or dialogue.
   a. The prisoner.
   b. The superintendent.
   c. Francis.
   d. The Eurasian boy

4a. Why do you think the author included so many details of the preparation of the prisoner (par. 2)?
 b. Why did he include so many details about the dog and his actions?
 c. What is gained by the assortment of details in paragraph 10?

5. The tone of a writing such as this can easily slip into sentimentality or even melodrama without the author's realizing what is happening. (See Guide to Terms: *Sentimentality.*) Select three places in this narrative where a less-skilled writer might have had such trouble, and note by what restraints Orwell prevented sentimentality.

Diction and Vocabulary

1. A noteworthy element of Orwell's style is his occasional use of figurative language. Cite six metaphors and similes, and comment on their choice and effectiveness.
2. Orwell was always concerned with the precise effects that words could give to meaning and style.
   a. Cite at least six nonfigurative words that seem to you particularly well chosen for their purpose.
   b. Show what their careful selection contributes to the description of atmosphere or to the subtle meanings of the author.
   c. How is this attention to diction a matter of style? (Guide: *Style/Tone.*)

Suggestions for Writing and Discussion

1. Select *one* of the points of controversy over capital punishment and present both sides with equal objectivity.
2. Consider the dilemma of a person whose "duty" seems to require one course of action and "conscience" just the opposite course. Use concrete illustrations to show how serious such dilemmas can be.
3. Examine the moral right, or lack of it, of the people of one country to impose their laws on the people of another country.
4. Discuss one benefit of colonialism to the people colonized. Use specific illustrations.
5. Explain how, in your own experience, a seemingly minor incident led to much deeper insight into a matter not fully understood before.

(NOTE: Suggestions for topics requiring development by NARRATION are on page 296, at the end of this section.)

MAYA ANGELOU

MAYA ANGELOU, born Marguerita Johnson in 1928 in St. Louis, spent the greater part of her childhood in rural Stamps, Arkansas, and later studied dance in San Francisco. She toured Europe and Africa for the State Department in *Porgy and Bess,* and taught dance in Rome and Tel Aviv. In collaboration with Godfrey Cambridge she produced, directed, and starred in *Cabaret for Freedom,* and also starred in Genet's *The Blacks.* At the request of the late Martin Luther King, Jr., Angelou became northern coordinator for the Southern Christian Leadership Conference. From this position she went to Africa to write for newspapers in Cairo and Ghana. She has written and produced a ten-part TV series on the positive traditions in American life. Her autobiography thus far consists of three books: *I Know Why the Caged Bird Sings* (1970), *Gather Together in My Name* (1974), and *Singin' and Swingin' and Gettin' Merry Like Christmas* (1976). She has also written several books of poetry: *Just Give Me a Cool Drink of Water . . . 'Fore I Diiie* (1971), *Oh Pray My Wings Are Gonna Fit Me Well* (1975), and *And Still I Rise* (1978). Angelou speaks French, Spanish, Italian, Arabic, and Fanti. She is now married and lives in Sonoma, California.

Momma's Private Victory

"Momma's Private Victory" (editor's title) is the fifth chapter of Angelou's book *I Know Why the Caged Bird Sings.* Since early childhood she and her brother, who was a year older, had lived with their grandmother ("Momma" of the narrative), who operated a store in the front room of her home in the black section of their small Arkansas town.

"Thou shall not be dirty" and "Thou shall not be impudent" were 1
the two commandments of Grandmother Henderson upon which hung our total salvation.

Each night in the bitterest winter we were forced to wash faces, 2
arms, necks, legs and feet before going to bed. She used to add, with

a smirk that unprofane people can't control when venturing into profanity, "and wash as far as possible, then wash possible."

We would go to the well and wash in the ice-cold, clear water, grease our legs with the equally cold stiff Vaseline, then tiptoe into the house. We wiped the dust from our toes and settled down for schoolwork, cornbread, clabbered milk, prayers and bed, always in that order. Momma was famous for pulling the quilts off after we had fallen asleep to examine our feet. If they weren't clean enough for her, she took the switch (she kept one behind the bedroom door for emergencies) and woke up the offender with a few aptly placed burning reminders. 3

The area around the well at night was dark and slick, and boys told about how snakes love water, so that anyone who had to draw water at night and then stand there alone and wash knew that moccasins and rattlers, puff adders and boa constrictors were winding their way to the well and would arrive just as the person washing got soap in her eyes. But Momma convinced us that not only was cleanliness next to Godliness, dirtiness was the inventor of misery. 4

The impudent child was detested by God and a shame to its parents and could bring destruction to its house and line. All adults had to be addressed as Mister, Missus, Miss, Auntie, Cousin, Unk, Uncle, Buhbah, Sister, Brother and a thousand other appellations indicating familial relationship and the lowliness of the addressor. 5

Everyone I knew respected these customary laws, except for the powhitetrash children. 6

Some families of powhitetrash lived on Momma's farm land behind the school. Sometimes a gaggle of them came to the Store, filling the whole room, chasing out the air and even changing the well-known scents. The children crawled over the shelves and into the potato and onion bins, twanging all the time in their sharp voices like cigar-box guitars. They took liberties in my Store that I would never dare. Since Momma told us that the less you say to white-folks (or even powhitetrash) the better, Bailey and I would stand, solemn, quiet, in the displaced air. But if one of the playful apparitions got close to us, I pinched it. Partly out of angry frustration and partly because I didn't believe in its flesh reality. 7

They called my uncle by his first name and ordered him around the Store. He, to my crying shame, obeyed them in his limping dip-straight-dip fashion. 8

My grandmother, too, followed their orders, except that she didn't seem to be servile because she anticipated their needs. 9

"Here's sugar, Miz Potter, and here's baking powder. You didn't buy soda last month, you'll probably be needing some." 10

Momma always directed her statements to the adults, but sometimes, Oh painful sometimes, the grimy, snotty-nosed girls would answer her. 11

"Naw, Annie . . . "—to Momma? Who owned the land they lived on? Who forgot more than they would ever learn? If there was any justice in the world, God should strike them dumb at once!—"Just give us some extra sody crackers, and some more mackerel." 12

At least they never looked in her face, or I never caught them doing so. Nobody with a smidgen of training, not even the worst roustabout, would look right in a grown person's face. It meant the person was trying to take the words out before they were formed. The dirty little children didn't do that, but they threw their orders around the Store like lashes from a cat-o'-nine-tails. 13

When I was around ten years old, those scruffy children caused me the most painful and confusing experience I had ever had with my grandmother. 14

One summer morning, after I had swept the dirt yard of leaves, spearmint-gum wrappers and Vienna-sausage labels, I raked the yellow-red dirt, and made half-moons carefully, so that the design stood out clearly and mask-like. I put the rake behind the Store and came through the back of the house to find Grandmother on the front porch in her big, wide white apron. The apron was so stiff by virtue of the starch that it could have stood alone. Momma was admiring the yard, so I joined her. It truly looked like a flat redhead that had been raked with a big-toothed comb. Momma didn't say anything but I knew she liked it. She looked over toward the school principal's house and to the right at Mr. McElroy's. She was hoping one of those community pillars would see the design before the day's business wiped it out. Then she looked upward to the school. My head had swung with hers, so at just about the same time we saw a troop of the powhitetrash kids marching over the hill and down by the side of the school. 15

I looked to Momma for direction. She did an excellent job of sagging from her waist down, but from the waist up she seemed to be pulling for the top of the oak tree across the road. Then she began to moan a hymn. Maybe not to moan, but the tune was so slow and the meter so strange that she could have been moaning. She didn't look at me again. When the children reached halfway down the hill, halfway to the Store, she said without turning, "Sister, go on inside." 16

I wanted to beg her, "Momma, don't wait for them. Come on inside with me. If they come in the Store, you go to the bedroom and let me wait on them. They only frighten me if you're around. Alone I know how to handle them." But of course I couldn't say anything, so I went in and stood behind the screen door. 17

Before the girls got to the porch I heard their laughter crackling and popping like pine logs in a cooking stove. I suppose my lifelong paranoia was born in those cold, molasses-slow minutes. They came finally to stand on the ground in front of Momma. At first they pretended seriousness. Then one of them wrapped her right arm in the crook of her left, pushed out her mouth and started to hum. I realized that she was aping my grandmother. Another said, "Naw, Helen, you ain't standing like her. This here's it." Then she lifted her chest, folded her arms and mocked that strange carriage that was Annie Henderson. Another laughed, "Naw, you can't do it. Your mouth ain't pooched out enough. It's like this." 18

I thought about the rifle behind the door, but I knew I'd never be able to hold it straight, and the .410, our sawed-off shotgun, which stayed loaded and was fired every New Year's night, was locked in the trunk and Uncle Willie had the key on his chain. Through the fly-specked screen-door, I could see that the arms of Momma's apron jiggled from the vibrations of her humming. But her knees seemed to have locked as if they would never bend again. 19

She sang on. No louder than before, but no softer either. No slower or faster. 20

The dirt of the girls' cotton dresses continued on their legs, feet, arms and faces to make them all of a piece. Their greasy uncolored hair hung down, uncombed, with a grim finality. I knelt to see them better, to remember them for all time. The tears that had slipped down my dress left unsurprising dark spots, and made the front yard blurry and even more unreal. The world had taken a deep breath and was having doubts about continuing to revolve. 21

The girls had tired of mocking Momma and turned to other means of agitation. One crossed her eyes, stuck her thumbs in both sides of her mouth and said, "Look here, Annie." Grandmother hummed on and the apron strings trembled. I wanted to throw a handful of black pepper in their faces, to throw lye on them, to scream that they were dirty, scummy peckerwoods, but I knew I was as clearly imprisoned behind the scene as the actors outside were confined to their roles. 22

One of the smaller girls did a kind of puppet dance while her fellow clowns laughed at her. But the tall one, who was almost a woman, said something very quietly, which I couldn't hear. They all moved backward from the porch, still watching Momma. For an awful second I thought they were going to throw a rock at Momma, who seemed (except for the apron springs) to have turned into stone herself. But the big girl turned her back, bent down and put her hands flat on the ground—she didn't pick up anything. She simply shifted her weight and did a hand stand. 23

Her dirty bare feet and long legs went straight for the sky. Her dress fell down around her shoulders, and she had on no drawers. The slick pubic hair made a brown triangle where her legs came together. She hung in the vacuum of that lifeless morning for only a few seconds, then wavered and tumbled. The other girls clapped her on the back and slapped their hands. 24

Momma changed her song to "Bread of Heaven, bread of Heaven, feed me till I want no more." 25

I found that I was praying too. How long could Momma hold out? What new indignity would they think of to subject her to? Would I be able to stay out of it? What would Momma really like me to do? 26

Then they were moving out of the yard, on their way to town. They bobbed their heads and shook their slack behinds and turned, one at a time: 27

"'Bye, Annie." 28

"'Bye, Annie." 29

"'Bye, Annie." 30

Momma never turned her head or unfolded her arms, but she stopped singing and said, "'Bye, Miz Helen, 'bye, Miz Ruth, 'bye, Miz Eloise." 31

I burst. A firecracker July-the-Fourth burst. How could Momma call them Miz? The mean nasty things. Why couldn't she have come inside the sweet, cool store when we saw them breasting the hill? What did she prove? And then if they were dirty, mean and impudent, why did Momma have to call them Miz? 32

She stood another whole song through and then opened the screen door to look down on me crying in rage. She looked until I looked up. Her face was a brown moon that shone on me. She was beautiful. Something had happened out there, which I couldn't completely understand, but I could see that she was happy. Then she bent 33 down and touched me as mothers of the church "lay hands on the sick and afflicted" and I quieted.

"Go wash your face, Sister." And she went behind the candy counter and hummed, "Glory, glory, hallelujah, when I lay my burden down." 34

I threw the well water on my face and used the weekday handkerchief to blow my nose. Whatever the contest had been out front, I knew Momma had won. 35

I took the rake back to the front yard. The smudged footprints were easy to erase. I worked for a long time on my new design and laid the rake behind the wash pot. When I came back in the Store, I took Momma's hand and we both walked outside to look at the pattern. 36

It was a large heart with lots of hearts growing smaller inside, and piercing from the outside rim to the smallest heart was an arrow. Momma said, "Sister, that's right pretty." Then she turned back to the Store and resumed, "Glory, glory, hallelujah, when I lay my burden down." 37

Meanings and Values

1. Where would you place this narrative on an objective to subjective continuum? Why? (See Guide to Terms: *Objective/Subjective.*)

2a. Is the point of view consistent throughout the narrative?
 b. Cite the limitations and the special advantages inherent in this point of view.

3. Demonstrate how this narrative would have differed if written from one of the other potential points of view.

4a. Explain how it was that these characters were all imprisoned in their own roles (par. 22).
 b. Show how it would have been an entirely different narration if one of them had performed her role with any radical difference.

Expository Techniques

1. Explain carefully why the first paragraph is, or is not, an effective introduction for this *whole* narration.

2a. What is the structural function of paragraph 6?
 b. Of paragraph 14?

3a. Why do you think so many of Angelou's descriptive details have to do, one way or another, with dirtiness? (Another writer might have described the children once as "dirty," and let it go at that.)

b. How different would the narrative have been if Momma had held different concepts of cleanliness and impudence?

Diction and Vocabulary

1. Demonstrate the significance of connotation by use of the apparently differing views of "dirtiness" held by the characters of this narrative. (Guide: *Connotation/Denotation.*)
2. Select several distinctive examples of Angelou's style — figurative and nonfigurative — and show what makes them distinctive. (Guide: *Style/Tone.*)

Suggestions for Writing and Discussion

1. Write a character study of Momma, using no narration and only the information you have available from this selection.
2. What *had* been the contest out front (par. 35)? Do you agree that Momma had won?

Writing Suggestions for Section 9
Narration

Use narration as at least a partial pattern (e.g., in developed examples or in comparison) for one of the following expository themes or another suggested by them. You should avoid the isolated personal account that has little broader significance. Remember, too, that development of the essay should itself make your point, without excessive moralizing.

1. People can still succeed without a college education.
2. The frontiers are not all gone.
3. When people succeed in communicating, they can learn to get along with each other.
4. Even with "careful" use of capital punishment, innocent people can be executed.
5. Homosexuals can't always be recognized by appearance and mannerisms.
6. True courage is different from boldness in time of sudden danger.
7. Conditioning to the realities of his job is an important to the policeman as professional training.
8. It is possible for the employee himself to determine when he has reached his highest level of competence.
9. Wartime massacres are not a new development.
10. Worn-out land can be restored without chemicals to its original productivity.
11. Back-to-the-earth, "family" style communes can be made to work.
12. Such communes (as in 11 above) are a good (or poor) place to raise children.
13. Both heredity and environment shape personality.

10

Reasoning by Use of *Induction* and *Deduction*

Induction and deduction, important as they are in argumentation, may also be useful methods of exposition. They are often used simply to explain a stand or conclusion, without any effort or need to win converts.

Induction is the process by which we accumulate evidence until, at some point, we can make the "inductive leap" and thus reach a useful *generalization.* The science laboratory employs this technique; hundreds of tests and experiments and analyses may be required before the scientist will generalize, for instance, that polio is caused by a certain virus. It is also the primary technique of the prosecuting attorney who presents pieces of inductive evidence, asking the jury to make the inductive leap and conclude that the accused did indeed kill the victim. On a more personal level, of course, we all learned to use induction at a very early age. We may have disliked the taste of orange juice, winter squash, and carrots, and we were not too young to make a generalization: orange-colored food tastes bad.

Whereas induction is the method of reaching a potentially useful generalization (for example, Professor Melville always gives an "F" to students who cut his class three times), *deduction* is the method of *using* such a generality, now accepted as a fact (for example, if we cut this class again today, we will get an "F"). Working from a generalization already formulated — by ourselves, by someone else, or by tradition — we may deduce that a specific thing or circumstance that fits into the generality will act the same. Hence, if convinced that orange-colored food tastes bad, we will be reluctant to try pumpkin pie.

A personnel manager may have discovered over the years that electronics majors from Central College are invariably well trained in their field. His induction may have been based on the evidence of observations, records, and the opinions of fellow Rotary members; and, perhaps without realizing it, he has made the usable generalization about the training of Central College electronics majors. Later, when he has an application from Nancy Poe, a graduate of Central College, his *de*ductive process will probably work as follows: Central College turns out well-trained electronics majors; Poe was trained at Central; therefore, Poe must be well trained. Here he has used a generalization to apply to a specific case. (We can also see both kinds of reasoning at work in Pirsig's "Mechanics' Logic" in Section 5.)

Put in this simplified form (which, in writing, it seldom is),[1] the deductive process is also called a "syllogism" — with the beginning generality known as the "major premise" and the specific that fits into the generality known as the "minor premise." For example:

Major premise — Orange-colored food is not fit to eat.
Minor premise — Pumpkin pie is orange-colored.
Conclusion — Pumpkin pie is not fit to eat.

Frequently, however, the validity of one or both of the premises may be questionable, and here is one of the functions of *in*duction: to give needed support — with evidence such as opinions of experts, statistics, and results of experiments or surveys — to the *de*ductive syllogism, whether stated or implied. Deductive reasoning, in whatever form presented, is only as sound as both its premises. The child's conviction that orange-colored food is not fit to eat was not necessarily true; therefore his conclusion about pumpkin pie is not very trustworthy. The other conclusions, that we will automatically get an "F" by cutting Melville's class and that Poe is well trained in elec-

[1]Neither induction nor deduction is confined even to a particular order of presentation. If we use specific evidence to *reach* a generalization, it is induction regardless of which part is stated first in a written or spoken account. (Very likely, both the prosecutor's opening remarks and Dr. Salk's written reports first presented their generalizations and then the inductive evidence by which they had been reached.) But if we use a generality in which to *place* a specific, it is still deduction, however stated. (Hence, the reasoning of the personnel manager might be: "Poe must be well trained because she was educated at C.C., and there's where they really know how to do it.")

tronics, can be only as reliable as the original generalizations that were used as deductive premises. If the generalizations themselves were based on flimsy or insufficient evidence, any future deduction using them is likely to be erroneous.

These two faults are common in induction: (1) the use of *flimsy* evidence — mere opinion, hearsay, or analogy, none of which can support a valid generalization — instead of verified facts or opinions of reliable authorities; and (2) the use of *too little* evidence, leading to a premature inductive leap.

The amount of evidence needed in any situation depends, of course, on purpose and audience. The success of two Central College graduates might be enough to convince some careless personnel director that all Central electronics graduates would be good employees, but two laboratory tests would not have convinced Dr. Salk, or any of his colleagues, that he had learned anything worthwhile about the polio virus. The authors of the Declaration of Independence, in explaining to a wide variety of readers and listeners why they considered the king tyrannical, listed twenty-eight despotic acts of his government, each of which was a verifiable fact, a matter of public record.

Induction and deduction are highly logical processes, and any trace of weakness can seriously undermine an exposition that depends on their reasonableness. (Such weakness can, of course, be even more disastrous in argument.) Although no induction or deduction ever reaches absolute, 100 per cent certainty, we should try to get from these methods as high a degree of *probability* as possible. (We can never positively prove, for instance, that the sun will rise in the east tomorrow, but thousands of years of inductive observation and theorizing make the fact extremely probable — and certainly sound enough for any working generalization.)

The student using induction and deduction in compositions, essay examinations, or term papers — showing that Stephen Crane was a naturalistic writer, or that our national policies are unfair to revolutionary movements — should always assume that he will have a skeptical audience that wants to know the logical basis for *all* generalizations and conclusions.

NORMAN COUSINS

NORMAN COUSINS, longtime editor of *Saturday Review,* was born in Union Hill, New Jersey, in 1915. He attended Columbia University before becoming editor of *Current History* in 1935. Cousins edited *Saturday Review* almost without interruption from 1942 to 1978. He has many honorary degrees and has received several awards for his essays and books. Among his latest books are *The Improbable Triumvirate* (1972), *The Celebration of Life* (1974), and *The Quest for Immortality* (1974).

How to Make People Smaller Than They Are

"How to Make People Smaller Than They Are" was first published in *Saturday Review* in 1978. Here Cousins deals with a current and extremely relevant matter — the balance of curricula between the humanities and "vocational" subjects. His conclusions are supported by a web of almost entirely inductive reasoning.

One of the biggest problems confronting American education today is the increasing vocationalization of our colleges and universities. Throughout the country, schools are under pressure to become job-training centers and employment agencies. 1

The pressure comes mainly from two sources. One is the growing determination of many citizens to reduce taxes — understandable and even commendable in itself, but irrational and irresponsible when connected to the reduction or dismantling of vital public services. The second source of pressure comes from parents and students who tend to scorn courses of study that do not teach people how to become attractive to employers in a rapidly tightening job market. 2

It is absurd to believe that the development of skills does not also require the systematic development of the human mind. Education is being measured more by the size of the benefits the individual can extract from society than by the extent to which the individual can 3 come into possession of his or her full powers. The result is that the life-giving juices are in danger of being drained out of education.

Emphasis on "practicalities" is being characterized by the subordination of words to numbers. History is seen not as essential experience to be transmitted to new generations, but as abstractions that carry dank odors. Art is regarded as something that calls for indulgence or patronage and that has no place among the practical realities. Political science is viewed more as a specialized subject for people who want to go into politics than as an opportunity for citizens to develop a knowledgeable relationship with the systems by which human societies are governed. Finally, literature and philosophy are assigned the role of add-ons — intellectual adornments that have nothing to do with "genuine" education. 4

Instead of trying to shrink the liberal arts, the American people ought to be putting pressure on colleges and universities to increase the ratio of the humanities to the sciences. Most serious studies of medical-school curricula in recent years have called attention to the stark gaps in the liberal education of medical students. The experts agree that the schools shouldn't leave it up to students to close those gaps. 5

We must not make it appear, however, that nothing is being done. In the past decade, the National Endowment for the Humanities has been a prime mover in infusing the liberal arts into medical education and other specialized schools. During this past year alone, NEH has given 108 grants to medical schools and research organizations in the areas of ethics and human values. Some medical schools, like the one at Pennsylvania State University, have led the way in both the number and the depth of courses offered in the humanities. Penn State has been especially innovative in weaving literature and philosophy into the full medical course of study. It is ironical that the pressure against the humanities should be manifesting itself at precisely the time when so many medical schools are at long last moving in this direction. 6

The irony of the emphasis being placed on careers is that nothing is more valuable for anyone who has had a professional or vocational education than to be able to deal with abstractions or complexities, or to feel comfortable with subtleties of thought or language, or to think sequentially. The doctor who knows only disease is at a disadvantage alongside the doctor who knows at least as much about people as he does about pathological organisms. The lawyer who 7 argues in court from a narrow legal base is no match for the lawyer who can connect legal precedents to historical experience and who employs wide-ranging intellectual resources. The business executive whose competence in general management is bolstered by an artistic ability to deal with people is of prime value to his company. For the technologist, the engineering of consent can be just as important as the engineering of moving parts. In all these respects, the liberal arts have much to offer. Just in terms of career preparation, therefore, a student is shortchanging himself by shortcutting the humanities.

But even if it could be demonstrated that the humanities con- 8
tribute nothing directly to a job, they would still be an essential part of the educational equipment of any person who wants to come to terms with life. The humanities would be expendable only if human beings didn't have to make decisions that affect their lives and the lives of others; if the human past never existed or had nothing to tell us about the present; if thought processes were irrelevant to the achievement of purpose; if creativity was beyond the human mind and had nothing to do with the joy of living; if human relationships were random aspects of life; if human beings never had to cope with panic or pain, or if they never had to anticipate the connection between cause and effect; if all the mysteries of mind and nature were fully plumbed; and if no special demands arose from the accident of being born a human being instead of hen or a hog.

Finally, there would be good reason to eliminate the humanities 9
if a free society were not absolutely dependent on a functioning citizenry. If the main purpose of a university is job training, then the underlying philosophy of our government has little meaning. The debates that went into the making of American society concerned not just institutions or governing principles but the capacity of humans to sustain those institutions. Whatever the disagreements were over other issues at the American Constitutional Convention, the fundamental question sensed by everyone, a question that lay over the entire assembly, was whether the people themselves would understand what it meant to hold the ultimate power of society, and whether they had enough of a sense of history and destiny to know where they had been and where they ought to be going.

Jefferson was prouder of having been the founder of the Univer- 10
sity of Virginia than of having been President of the United States. He knew that the educated and developed mind was the best assurance that a political system could be made to work — a system based

on the informed consent of the governed. If this idea fails, then all the saved tax dollars in the world will not be enough to prevent the nation from turning on itself.

Meanings and Values

1. How can this essay best be classified — as formal, informal, or familiar? Why? (See Guide to Terms: *Essay.*)
2. Would the writing have been more, or less, effective with greater use of qualification? (Guide: *Qualification.*) Clarify and, if necessary, defend your answer.
3. Explain the concept that emphasis on "practicalities" is being characterized by the subordination of words to numbers (par. 4). Do you agree?

4a. Precisely what is it that happens to a free society without the "educated and developed mind" (par. 10)?
b. In what way can a nation turn on itself?

Expository Techniques

1a. A generalization is stated in the last sentence of paragraph 3. Where does the author give us the inductive evidence that supports it?
b. How many pieces of such evidence does he supply?
c. Are they well chosen for the purpose?

2. A study of the remaining inductive reasoning, which provides the real heart of the essay, shows a sort of two-stage but closely integrated system. If we see that the main generalization of the essay concerns the relative value of the humanities in the curriculum, we should look for the evidence that led to Cousins's conclusion, or generalization. This evidence is basically in three parts, first of which is the importance of the job itself.
a. What are the other two?
b. Why is the mere statement of these three inductive pieces not sufficient by itself?

3a. What four inductive pieces *support* the author's allegation that humanities are important to the job?
b. What is the function of the nine inductive pieces given (in rather unusual form) in paragraph 8? List this evidence.
c. Instead of supporting the third basic allegation by induction, on what does the author rely? Is it sufficient?

4a. How should this induction have differed if written as logical *argument* — e.g., to convince a school board?
b. Is it adequate for Cousins's purpose and audience? Why, or why not?

5. Are paragraphs 5 and 6 closely enough related to the central theme (as the tributary to the river) to maintain good unity? (Guide: *Unity.*) Why, or why not?
6. What is gained (stylistically and otherwise) by the long sentence of paragraph 8? (Guide: *Parallel Structure* and *Style/Tone.*)

7a. Which of the standard techniques do you find in this closing? (Guide: *Closings.*)
 b. Is it an effective closing? Why, or why not?

Diction and Vocabulary

1a. What are the ironies referred to in paragraphs 6 and 7? (Guide: *Irony.*) Why are they ironies?
 b. What kind are they?

2a. Comment on the meanings and implications of the following phrases:
i. "to think sequentially" (par. 7)
ii. "artistic ability" to deal with people (par. 7)
iii. "engineering of consent" (par. 7)
iv. "come to terms with life" (par. 8)
v. the "informed consent" of the governed (par. 10)
 b. Such matters of diction also help to distinguish an author's style. (Guide: *Style/Tone.*) Compare this aspect of Cousins's style with that of two other authors previously studied.

Suggestions for Writing and Discussion

1. Do you consider the various taxpayers' revolts against increasing school budgets as "irrational and irresponsible"? For instance, are they even directed against the humanities? If not, what are they against?
2. Are you more interested in the size of the benefits you "can extract from society," or the extent to which you "can come into possession of [your] full powers" (par. 3)? Explain.
3. Discuss any one of the "practicalities" listed in paragraph 4, particularly as it applies to you or to those you know.
4. If you have read the Barzun selection (Section 6), how does Cousins help explain what may be responsible for the present state of the professions?

(NOTE: Suggestions for topics requiring development by INDUCTION and DEDUCTION are on page 319, at the end of this section.)

THOMAS JEFFERSON

THOMAS JEFFERSON (1743–1826) was born in Virginia, where he lived during his childhood and later attended William and Mary College. He became a lawyer, a member of the Virginia House of Burgesses and of the Continental Congress in 1775. His influence as a liberal democrat was always aided by his prolific and forceful writing. During the Revolutionary War he became Governor of Virginia. After the war he served the new government in various capacities, including those of special minister to France, Secretary of State under Washington, Vice-President, and, for two terms, the country's third President. He died on July 4, the fiftieth anniversary of the signing of the Declaration of Independence.

The Declaration of Independence

The Declaration of Independence, written and revised by Jefferson, was later further revised by the Continental Congress, meeting then in Philadelphia. In this way, as Jefferson later remarked, it drew its authority from "the harmonizing sentiments of the day"; it was, when signed on July 4, 1776, "an expression of the American mind." However, the document still retained much of the form and style of Jefferson's writing, and as literature it has long been admired for its lean and forthright prose. We can find no clearer example of the practical combination of deductive and inductive writing.

When in the course of human events, it becomes necessary for one people to dissolve the political bands which have connected them with another, and to assume among the Powers of the earth, the separate and equal station to which the Laws of Nature and of Nature's God entitle them, a decent respect to the opinions of mankind requires that they should declare the causes which impel them to the separation. 1

We hold these truths to be self-evident, that all men are created equal, that they are endowed by their Creator with certain unalienable Rights, that among these are Life, Liberty and the pursuit of Happiness. That to secure these rights, Governments are instituted 2 among Men, deriving their just powers from the consent of the governed. That whenever any Form of Government becomes destructive of these ends, it is the Right of the People to alter or to abolish it, and to institute new Government, laying its foundation on such principles and organizing its powers in such form, as to them shall seem most likely to effect their Safety and Happiness. Prudence, indeed, will dictate that Governments long established should not be changed for light and transient causes; and accordingly all experience hath shown, that mankind are more disposed to suffer, while evils are sufferable, than to right themselves by abolishing the forms to which they are accustomed. But when a long train of abuses and usurpations pursuing invariably the same Object evinces a design to reduce them under absolute Despotism, it is their right, it is their duty, to throw off such government, and to provide new Guards for their future security. Such has been the patient sufferance of these Colonies; and such is now the necessity which constrains them to alter their former Systems of Government. The history of the present King of Great Britain is a history of repeated injuries and usurpations, all having in direct object the establishment of an absolute Tyranny over these States. To prove this, let Facts be submitted to a candid world.

He has refused his Assent to Laws, the most wholesome and 3
necessary for the public good.

He has forbidden his Governors to pass Laws of immediate and 4
pressing importance, unless suspended in their operation till his Assent should be obtained; and when so suspended, he has utterly neglected to attend to them.

He has refused to pass other Laws for the accommodation of 5
large districts of people, unless those people would relinquish the right of Representation in the Legislature, a right inestimable to them and formidable to tyrants only.

He has called together legislative bodies at places unusual, un- 6
comfortable, and distant from the depository of their Public Records, for the sole purpose of fatiguing them into compliance with his measures.

He has dissolved Representative Houses repeatedly, for oppos- 7
ing with manly firmness his invasions on the rights of the people.

He has refused for a long time, after such dissolutions, to cause 8
others to be elected; whereby the Legislative Powers, incapable of Annihilation, have returned to the People at large for their exercise;

the State remaining in the mean time exposed to all the dangers of invasion from without, and convulsions within.

He has endeavoured to prevent the population of these States; 9
for that purpose obstructing the Laws of Naturalization of Foreigners; refusing to pass others to encourage their migration hither, and raising the conditions of new Appropriations of Lands.

He has obstructed the Administration of Justice, by refusing his 10
Assent to Laws for establishing Judiciary Powers.

He has made Judges dependent on his Will alone, for the tenure 11
of their offices, and the amount and payment of their salaries.

He has erected a multitude of New Offices, and sent hither 12
swarms of Officers to harass our People, and eat out their substance.

He has kept among us, in time of peace, Standing Armies with- 13
out the Consent of our Legislature.

He has affected to render the Military independent of and supe- 14
rior to the Civil Power.

He has combined with others to subject us to jurisdictions for- 15
eign to our constitution, and unacknowledged by our laws; giving his Assent to their acts of pretended Legislation:

For quartering large bodies of armed troops among us: 16

For protecting them, by a mock Trial, from Punishment for any 17
Murders which they should commit on the Inhabitants of these States:

For cutting off our Trade with all parts of the world: 18

For imposing Taxes on us without our Consent: 19

For depriving us in many cases, of the benefits of Trial by Jury: 20

For transporting us beyond Seas to be tried for pretended 21
offenses:

For abolishing the free System of English Laws in a Neighbour- 22
ing Province, establishing therein an Arbitrary government, and enlarging its boundaries so as to render it at once an example and fit instrument for introducing the same absolute rule into these Colonies:

For taking away our Charters, abolishing our most valuable 23
Laws, and altering fundamentally the Forms of our Governments:

For suspending our own Legislatures, and declaring themselves 24
invested with Power to legislate for us in all cases whatsoever.

He has abdicated Government here, by declaring us out of his 25
Protection and waging War against us.

26 He has plundered our seas, ravaged our Coasts, burnt our towns and destroyed the Lives of our people.

27 He is at this time transporting large Armies of foreign Mercenaries to compleat the works of death, desolation and tyranny, already begun with circumstances of Cruelty & perfidy scarcely paralleled in the most barbarous ages, and totally unworthy the Head of a civilized nation.

28 He has constrained our fellow Citizens taken Captive on the high Seas to bear Arms against their Country, to become the executioners of their friends and Brethren, or to fall themselves by their Hands.

29 He has excited domestic insurrections amongst us, and has endeavoured to bring on the inhabitants of our frontiers, the merciless Indian Savages, whose known rule of warfare, is an undistinguished destruction of all ages, sexes and conditions.

30 In every stage of these Oppressions We Have Petitioned for Redress in the most humble terms: Our repeated petitions have been answered only by repeated injury. A Prince, whose character is thus marked by every act which may define a Tyrant, is unfit to be the ruler of a free People.

31 Not have We been wanting in attention to our British brethren. We have warned them from time to time of attempts by their legislature to extend an unwarrantable jurisdiction over us. We have reminded them of the circumstances of our emigration and settlement here. We have appealed to their native justice and magnanimity and we have conjured them by the ties of our common kindred to disavow these usurpations, which would inevitably interrupt our connections and correspondence. They too have been deaf to the voice of justice and of consanguinity. We must, therefore acquiesce in the necessity, which denounces our Separation, and hold them, as we hold the rest of mankind, Enemies in War, in Peace Friends.

32 We, therefore, the Representatives of the United States of America, in General Congress, Assembled, appealing to the Supreme Judge of the world for the rectitude of our intentions, do, in the Name, and by Authority of the good People of these Colonies, solemnly publish and declare, That these United Colonies are, and of Right ought to be Free and Independent States; that they are Absolved from all Allegiance to the British Crown, and that all political connection between them and the State of Great Britain, is and ought to be totally dissolved; and that as Free and Independent States, they have

full power to levy War, conclude Peace, contract Alliances, establish Commerce, and to do all other Acts and Things which Independent States may of right do. And for the support of this Declaration, with a firm reliance on the protection of Divine Providence, we mutually pledge to each other our lives, our Fortunes and our sacred Honor.

Meaning and Values

1. For what practical reasons (other than the "decent respect to the opinions of mankind") did the Founding Fathers need to explain so carefully their reasons for declaring independence?

2a. By what justification can this selection be considered expository?

b. Why might it also be classified as argument? (See Guide to Terms: *Argument.*)

c. Except for study purposes, is there any reason to categorize it at all? Explain.

3. Many American colonials opposed the break with England and remained loyal to the Crown throughout the struggle for independence. What do you suppose could inspire such loyalty to a king whom most of them had never seen and who had shown little concern for their welfare?

Expository Techniques

1. The basis of the Declaration of Independence is deduction and can therefore be stated as a logical syllogism. The major premise, stated twice in the second paragraph, may be paraphrased as follows: When a government proves to be despotic, it is the people's right and duty to get rid of it.

a. What, then, is the minor premise of the syllogism?

b. Where is the syllogism's conclusion set forth? Restate it concisely in your own words.

c. Write this resulting syllogism in standard form.

2. Twenty-eight pieces of inductive evidence are offered as support for one of the deductive premises.

a. Which premise is thus supported?

b. Demonstrate the meaning of "inductive leap" by use of materials from this selection. (Remember that the order of presentation in inductive or deductive writing is merely an arrangement for *telling,* not necessarily that of the original reasoning.)

3a. Why, according to the document itself, is the other premise not supported by any inductive reasoning?

b. Would everyone agree with this premise? If not, why do you suppose the Founding Fathers did not present inductive evidence to support it?

4. What benefits are gained in the Declaration by the extensive use of parallel structures? (Guide: *Parallel Structure.*)

5. Show as specifically as possible the effects that a "decent respect to the opinions of mankind" apparently had on the selection and use of materials in the Declaration of Independence.

Diction and Vocabulary

1. Select five words or phrases from the Declaration of Independence to demonstrate the value of an awareness of connotation. (Guide: *Connotation/Denotation.*)

2. If not already familiar with the following words as they are used in this selection, consult your dictionary for their meanings: impel (par. 1); transient, usurpations, evinces, sufferance, constrains (2); inestimable (5); depository (6); dissolutions (8); mercenaries, perfidy (27); redress (30); magnanimity, conjured, consanguinity, acquiesce (31); rectitude, absolved (32).

Suggestions for Writing and Discussion

1. George Santayana, an American writer and expatriate, called the Declaration of Independence "a salad of illusion." Develop this metaphor into a full-scale analogy to explain his meaning. Without arguing the matter, attempt to assess the truth of his allegation.

2. Select one important similarity or difference between the rebellion of the American colonials and that of some other country in recent history. Use comparison or contrast to develop a theme on this subject.

3. Compare or contrast any of the Declaration signers with one of the leaders of some other country's more recent severance of ties with a colonial power.

4. Give evidence from your knowledge of history to support, or to negate, the following statement by Patrick Henry, one of the signers of the Declaration: "It is impossible that a nation of infidels or idolators should be a nation of freemen. It is when a people forget God, that tyrants forge their chains. A vitiated state of morals, a corrupted public conscience, is incompatible with freedom."

(NOTE: Suggestions for topics requiring development by INDUCTION and DEDUCTION are on page 319, at the end of this section.)

MARGARET MEAD

Margaret Mead (1901–1978) was a widely respected anthropologist and author. She was educated at Barnard College (B.A., 1923) and Columbia University (Ph.D., 1929). In the course of a distinguished career she served in responsible positions, among them as associate curator and director of research programs at the American Museum of Natural History at Columbia University, where she was also professor of anthropology. Mead was in government service during World War II and served as president of the American Anthropological Association and of the World Federation for Mental Health. She wrote almost innumerable books and articles for both popular and professional magazines. One of her best-known and still-popular books is *Male and Female* (1949), but most of her writing was anthropological, based on many years of extensive field research in the Pacific islands.

UFOs: Visitors from Outer Space?

"UFOs: Visitors from Outer Space?" is reprinted from Redbook. Mead thinks there is no question of the existence of UFOs, but the bulk of her essay is devoted to the plausibility of their being from outer space. To accomplish this she uses various patterns of exposition but relies primarily on the inductive process.

"Do you believe in UFOs?" 1

Again and again over the years, I have been asked this extraordinary question, at times by people everywhere I go, at other times only by the few people whose passionate curiosity is sustained even when no new spectacular sightings are publicly reported in the press, in popular books or by serious scientists gathered at a meeting to discuss the problem. 2

Interest in unidentified flying objects always fluctuates as the number of reports of sightings rises and falls. But few people realize that in recent years masses of sightings seem to have come in waves, 3 now in one part of the world and now in another — from the Far North to Antarctica, from North and South America, from Europe to the Orient, even from remote Papua, New Guinea. In 1939 and 1946 Scandinavia seemed to be a center of UFO activity. In 1947, 1950 and again in 1952 the largest number of reports were made in the United States. In 1954 a wave spread from France across Western Europe and into Africa. The next wave, in 1957, began in South America and appeared to spread all over the world, reaching a climax of sightings in the United States.

Then there was a pause. News stories died down, flying saucer jokes faded away and people forgot — until 1967, when the waves of sightings began again and continued, now here and now there, almost up to the present. 4

In spite of all this, people still ask each other: "Do you believe in UFOs?" 5

I think this is a silly question, born of confusion. Belief has to do with matters of faith. It has nothing to do with the kind of knowledge that is based on scientific inquiry. We should not bracket UFOs with angels and archangels, devils and demons. But this is just what we are doing when we ask whether people "believe" in UFOs — as if their existence were an article of faith. Do people believe in the sun or the moon or the changing seasons or the chairs they are sitting on? 6

When we want to understand something strange, something previously unknown to anyone, we have to begin with an entirely different set of questions: What is it? How does it work? Are there recurrent regularities? 7

Beginning in this way with an open mind, people can take a hard look at all the evidence. They sift out the vague rumors, the tall tales, the obvious mistaken judgments, the fanciful embroidery of detail, the hoaxes and the distortions introduced both by those who are overeager to believe and by those who are determined to discredit everything. 8

Beginning in this way we can answer the question most people really have in mind: Yes, there are unidentified flying objects. There are phenomena that, even after the most cautious and painstaking investigations, cannot be explained away. This much, at least, we must accept. 9

Thousands of sightings have been reported, and not only by individuals faced, alone at night, by the terrifying spectacle of a 10 shining disk hovering soundlessly over the trees or apparently coming at them as they are driving down a road or touching the ground and then suddenly taking off vertically in a tremendous burst of speed. Pilots have continually reported sightings, and sometimes several planes have given chase — always unsuccessfully. Persons unknown to one another have described the same phenomenon seen in the same night — or daytime — sky.

Occasionally many people have watched, stunned, the same UFO event. In 1954, during the great wave of sightings in Europe, thousands of people in Rome watched while a cigar-shaped object — which simultaneously was tracked on the airport radar — performed acrobatic feats over the city for more than an hour. Radar tracings are not uncommon, and very occasionally fleeting views have been captured by cameras. 11

Sightings seem to become more numerous at those times when we on earth are taking a forward step into space. In 1897, four years before the first dirigible was successfully flown in France, sightings of phantom airships — never satisfactorily explained — raised excitement to fever pitch in America in the 20 states where they occurred. Late in World War II, crews of bomber squadrons in several war theaters described disturbing "blobs of light," which came to be known as "foo fighters." Intelligence services, ours and others', conjectured that they must be secret devices invented by the enemy; when it turned out that this was not the case, no new explanation was forthcoming. 12

Again there was the world-wide wave of sightings in 1957 when Russia and the United States launched the first satellites. And most recently, in the autumn of 1973, just before the unmanned U.S. spacecraft Pioneer Ten was to fly past Jupiter and out of our solar system, a new wave of sightings began. 13

Many explanations are possible. The simplest — and the most likely — explanation of the coincidence of sightings and events on earth is our own growing awareness. With each increase in expectation of what human beings could invent to lift themselves off the surface of the earth, more people accepted the evidence of their own eyes when they saw unidentifiable objects crossing the sky. And quite reasonably some of them related what they saw to objects they had heard or read about — airships at the turn of the century and, in 1957, satellites that might one day carry men to the moon or even, by a great stretch of imagination, beyond our Milky Way galaxy to 14 the Andromeda galaxy hundreds of thousands of light-years away. And what one man saw, others could accept with their own eyes.

That there are waves of "visits" by UFOs seems uncontestable. 15
But that sightings are much more massive just when we are entering some new phase of space exploration may be due to our own heightened interest in and greater sophistication about what is possible.

The late Carl Jung, in his book *Flying Saucers,* published in 1959, 16
added another dimension. He neither rejected nor accepted the reality of UFOs. What he suggested was that there is also a psychological component — what he called a living myth or a visionary rumor that is potentially shared by all human beings in a period of great change and deep anxiety about the future. UFOs, he speculated, might be a world-wide visualized projection of this uneasy psychic state. But he also speculated that the two unknowns — UFOs and our human visualized projections — may simply "coincide in a meaningful manner."

A very different explanation is that UFOs, in spite of world- 17
wide sightings, are no more than a gigantic hoax. Not long ago a huge crowd watched a "UFO" float over a stadium. This was indeed a hoax — a balloon lighted by a candle. So it has been argued that if one sighting is a hoax, all sightings must be hoaxes.

In this view all the accumulated supporting evidence is denied. 18
It has often been reported that UFO sightings have been accompanied by interference with and sometimes the temporary failure of car and airplane motors, communication devices and power lines. But if a great, luminous object speeding across the sky can be simulated, can't some device for bringing about electromagnetic disturbances be part of the hoax?

Arguments of this kind directed against UFOs are no more valid 19
than the hoax arguments intended to demolish the evidence of psychic phenomena. Just because fake mediums sitting in darkened rooms can induce gullible dupes to shake hands with cold, sand-filled rubber gloves, there is no reason to deny the reality of psychic phenomena we cannot yet explain.

Undeniably, such arguments have a seductive power. The temp- 20
tation to produce hoaxes and the temptation to believe that what is strange and not understood must be a hoax are equally human vulnerabilities. And so in exactly those fields in which human beings are exploring possibilities that boggle the mind it is most likely that some people will perpetrate hoaxes and that others, as one way of protecting themselves from anxiety, will suspect that they are being hood-

winked. But this does not mean that the whole thing is a hoax. It means only that one recurrent response to fear of the unknown is insistence that it's all some kind of trick.

Certainly a great many people are frightened by the idea that somewhere in outer space (we once thought somewhere in our own solar system) there are beings who are technologically more advanced than we are. Today, apparently, it is precisely those who are best informed about out technological capabilities — some government officials, scientists and members of the armed forces — who are most disturbed by the idea that technologically superior beings from some other, unknown planet are taking an interest — an unexplained interest — in our planet earth. 21

Consequently, from time to time we have official reports from groups such as Project Grudge, Project Blue Book, or the Colorado UFO project headed by Dr. Edward Condon that play down the evidence. UFO sightings are said to be really fireballs, lightning, flights of geese, the evening or the morning star, weather inversions that cause strange reflections, artificial satellites, hoaxes, the visions of disturbed individuals, and so on. These are, or may be, the explanations of many sightings. But in the end even such reports — usually based on samples of sightings from only a few areas, so that information about world-wide regularities is lost — always come to the same conclusion: There *are* unidentified flying objects. That is, there is a hard core of cases — perhaps 20 to 30 per cent in different studies — for which there is no explanation. 22

Yet the denials continue. While some scientists are probing space for evidence of extraterrestrial intelligence, others deny that any creature could build a vehicle that could arrive here from anywhere in space. But a little quiet thought ought to convince us that, knowing what we now know about space technology, the capability of reaching earth from somewhere else depends only on others having taken further steps into the unknown that are beyond our present ability. 23

Of course, there have always been those who have insisted that nothing further is possible. Trains, cars, airplanes, voyages to the moon . . . But other scientists and inventors have gone ahead and made feasible what once had been demonstrably impossible. 24

The next questions are the most facinating ones. If UFOs — the genuinely unexplained, unidentified but well-authenticated ones — are in fact vehicles that have come from a great distance, with or 25 without intelligent life aboard, *What are they doing? Why don't they declare themselves?*

These questions introduce a suspense element that is almost unbearable to us. If these creatures — whoever they are — have been coming here or have been sending unmanned vehicles here for a hundred years (or, as some investigators claim, for thousands of years), what are they doing it for? There is, of course, not the slightest evidence that "they" have ever done anything. There is some possible evidence of occasional landings. There is a giant crater in the Soviet Union that cannot be explained by any existing meteorological or geological knowledge. And there are unexplained accounts of brief landings. But that is all. 26

For the rest we can only imagine what purpose lies behind the activities of these quiet, harmlessly cruising objects that time and again approach the earth. The most likely explanation, it seems to me, is that they are simply watching what we are up to — that a responsible society outside our solar system is keeping an eye on us to see that we don't set in motion a chain reaction that might have repercussions far outside our solar system. This is a plausible way of thinking to attribute to such living extraterrestrial creatures — as plausible as any that we ourselves at present are capable of imagining. 27

But there is no evidence one way or the other, I think, whether or not UFOs have intelligent life aboard. They may well be unmanned vehicles controlled from elsewhere in space. We ourselves are learning very rapidly how to control and how to obtain increasingly sophisticated information from space probes. 28

And there is one UFO that we know about in the greatest detail. Pioneer Ten, which is forging its way into deep space, will, after all, someday be an unidentified flying object to the intelligent beings on some other planet in some other solar system. 29

Meanings and Values

1. Restate in your own language — in clearer fashion, if you can — the ideas attributed to Carl Jung in paragraph 16.

2a. How can suspicion of being hoodwinked *protect* one from anxiety (par. 20)?

b. Do you think it would protect you? Why, or why not?

3a. What is the irony implied in paragraphs 21 and 23? (See Guide to Terms: *Irony.*)

b. Why is it ironical?
c. What kind of irony is it?

4. What could be another reason why sightings of UFOs seem to come in waves?

5. Evaluate this essay, using our three-question system. (Guide: *Evaluation.*)

Expository Techniques

1. Is the primary means of development in paragraphs 3 and 4 that of induction or deduction? Why?

2. Analyze paragraphs 9–13 to determine the method, or methods, of development.
 a. By what method does the author conclude that there are, indeed, unidentified flying objects?
 b. Which paragraphs contain the supporting evidence?
 c. What is the function of the first sentence of paragraph 12?
 d. Where will we find the evidence that supports it?
 e. What kind of evidence is it?

3. Analyze the following paragraphs to determine the chief patterns of exposition used in each: paragraphs 6, 14, 17, 19, 24, and the latter part of 26.

4a. The organization might be improved by relocating paragraphs 3–4. If doing so, where would you put them?
 b. What benefit, or benefits, have you accomplished?

5a. Where would you place this essay on a specific–general continuum? (Guide: *Specific/General.*)
 b. Demonstrate how the essay could be made more specific if being expanded into a book or an argumentative piece.

Diction and Vocabulary

1. What are "light-years" (par. 14)?

2a. Compare the style of Mead's writing, in respect to diction and syntax, with that of Thomas or Mitford (Sec. 5), or Halsey (Sec. 6). (Guide: *Style/Tone, Diction,* and *Syntax.*)
 b. Is one style "better" than the other — i.e., more effective for the job the author has to do?

Suggestions for Writing and Discussion

1. Are you "frightened" by the idea that in space there may be creatures who are more advanced than we are (par. 21)? Is the suspense "almost unbearable" to you (par. 26)? Explain.

2. In view of any reading you have done on the subject, do you agree with Mead's assertion that there is not the slightest evidence that "they" have ever done anything (par. 26)? Why, or why not?
3. Do you agree that there is no evidence whether or not UFOs have intelligent life aboard (par. 27)? Discuss any seemingly sound evidence you may know about.
4. What type of chain reaction might worldlings set in motion that could have "repercussions far outside our solar system" (par. 27)?

Writing Suggestions for Section 10
Induction and Deduction

Choose one of the following unformed topics and shape your central theme from it. This could express the view you prefer or an opposing view. Develop your composition primarily by use of induction, alone or in combination with deduction. But unless otherwise directed by your instructor, be completely objective and limit yourself to exposition, rather than engaging in argumentation.

1. Little League Baseball (or the activities of 4-H clubs, Boy Scouts, Girl Scouts, etc.) as a molder of character.
2. Conformity as an expression of insecurity.
3. The display of *non*conformity as an expression of insecurity.
4. The status symbol as a motivator to success.
5. The liberal arts curriculum and its relevance to "real life."
6. Student opinion as the guide to better educational institutions.
7. College education as a prerequisite for worldly success.
8. The values of education, beyond dollars and cents.
9. Knowledge and its relation to wisdom.
10. The right of the individual to select the laws he obeys.
11. Television commercials as a molder of morals.
12. The "other" side of one ecological problem.
13. The value of complete freedom from worry.
14. Decreased effectiveness of the home as an influence in adolescent development.

Further Readings

PLATO

PLATO (about 427–347 B.C.), an early Greek philosopher, was a younger friend and perhaps student of Socrates. In Athens Plato founded and administered the first university, the Academy, which continued operation until A.D. 529. One of the most brilliant figures in the history of Western philosophy, his ideas are still reflected in much modern thought. He was a prolific writer (his works include *The Symposium, Phaedrus,* and *The Republic*), and frequently employed dialogue to reproduce conversations between Socrates (who had written nothing himself) and his students. While Plato was still a young man, Socrates had been condemned to death for "impiety" and "corruption of youth," trumped-up political charges brought by a hostile new democratic regime which feared that he was teaching his students disrespect for state authority and religious dogma. At the trial he defended himself, but his "defense" amounted more to avowal and justification, and he was executed — i.e., he "drank the hemlock" in the traditional manner. Plato later recorded his friend's defense as "The Apology of Socrates," of which the following is an excerpt.

Socrates "Defends" Himself

Someone will say: And are you not ashamed, Socrates, of a course of life which is likely to bring you to an untimely end? To him I may fairly answer: There you are mistaken: a man who is good for anything ought not to calculate the chance of living or dying; he ought only to consider whether in doing anything he is doing right or wrong — acting the part of a good man or of a bad. . . . 1

Strange, indeed, would be my conduct, O men of Athens, if I, who when I was ordered by the generals whom you chose to command me at Potidaea[1] and Amphipolis and Delium, remained where they placed me, like any other man, facing death — if now, when, as I conceive and imagine, God orders me to fulfill the philosopher's mission of searching into myself and other men, I were to desert my post through fear of death, or any other fear; that would indeed be strange, and I might justly be arraigned in court for denying the existence of the gods, if I disobeyed the oracle because I was afraid 2

[1]Socrates had served in the Athenian infantry during some of the northern campaigns of the Peloponnesian War.

of death, fancying that I was wise when I was not wise. For the fear of death is indeed the pretense of wisdom, and not real wisdom, being a pretense of knowing the unknown; and no one knows whether death, which men in their fear apprehend to be the greatest evil, may not be the greatest good. Is not this ignorance of a disgraceful sort, the ignorance which is the conceit that a man knows what he does not know? And in this respect only I believe myself to differ from men in general, and may perhaps claim to be wiser than they are: that whereas I know but little of the world below, I do not suppose that I know: but I do know that injustice and disobedience to a better, whether God or man, is evil and dishonorable, and I will never fear or avoid a possible good rather than a certain evil. And therefore if you let me go now, and are not convinced by Anytus,[2] who said that since I had been prosecuted I must be put to death (or if not, that I ought never to have been prosecuted at all); and that if I escape now, your sons will all be utterly ruined by listening to my words — if you say to me, Socrates, this time we will not mind Anytus, and you shall be let off, but upon one condition, that you are not to inquire and speculate in this way any more, and that if you are caught doing so again you shall die; if this was the condition on which you let me go, I should reply: Men of Athens, I honor and love you; but I shall obey God rather than you, and while I have life and strength I shall never cease from the practice and teaching of philosophy, exhorting anyone whom I meet and saying to him after my manner: "You my friend — a citizen of the great and mighty and wise city of Athens — are you not ashamed of heaping up the greatest amount of money and honor and reputation, and caring so little about wisdom and truth and the greatest improvement of the soul, which you never regard or heed at all?" And if the person with whom I am arguing, says: "Yes, but I do care"; then I do not leave him or let him go at once; but I proceed to interrogate and examine and cross-examine him, and if I think that he has no virtue in him, but only says that he has, I reproach him with undervaluing the greater and overvaluing the less. And I shall repeat the same words to everyone whom I meet, young and old, citizen and alien, but especially to the citizens, inasmuch as they are my brethren. For know that this is the command of God; and I believe that no greater good has ever happened in the state than my service to the God. For I do nothing

[2]Instigator of the proceedings.

but go about persuading you all, old and young alike, not to take thought for your persons or your properties, but first and chiefly to care about the greatest improvement of the soul. I tell you that virtue is not given by money, but that from virtue comes money and every other good of man, public as well as private. This is my teaching, and if this is the doctrine which corrupts the youth, I am a mischievous person. But if anyone says that this is not my teaching, he is speaking an untruth. Wherefore, O men of Athens, I say to you, do as Anytus bids or not as Anytus bids, and either acquit me or not; but whichever you do, understand that I shall never alter my ways, not even if I have to die many times.

Men of Athens, do not interrupt, but hear me; there was an 3
understanding between us that you should hear me to the end; I have something more to say, at which you may be inclined to cry out; but I believe that to hear me will be good for you, and therefore I beg that you will not cry out. I would have you know that if you kill such an one as I am, you will injure yourselves more than you will injure me. Nothing will injure me, not Meletus[3] nor yet Anytus — they cannot, for a bad man is not permitted to injure a better than himself. I do not deny that Anytus may, perhaps, kill him, or drive him into exile, or deprive him of civil rights; and he may imagine, and others may imagine, that he is inflicting a great injury upon him: but there I do not agree. For the evil of doing as he is doing — the evil of unjustly taking away the life of another — is greater far.

And now, Athenians, I am not going to argue for my own sake, 4
as you may think, but for yours, that you may not sin against the God by condemning me, who am his gift to you. For if you kill me you will not easily find a successor to me, who, if I may use such a ludicrous figure of speech, am a sort of gadfly, given to the state by God; and the state is a great and noble steed who is tardy in his motions owing to his very size, and requires to be stirred into life. I am that gadfly which God has attached to the state, and all day long and in all places am always fastening upon you, arousing and persuading and reproaching you. You will not easily find another like me, and therefore I would advise you to spare me. I dare say that you may feel out of temper (like a person who is suddenly awakened from sleep), and you think that you might easily strike me dead as Anytus advises, and then you would sleep on for the remainder of

[3]The prosecutor.

your lives, unless God in his care of you sent you another gadfly. When I say that I am given to you by God, the proof of my mission is this: if I had been like other men, I should not have neglected all my concerns or patiently seen the neglect of them during all these years, and have been doing yours, coming to you individually like a father or elder brother, exhorting you to regard virtue; such conduct, I say, would be unlike human nature. If I had gained anything, or if my exhortations had been paid, there would have been some sense in my doing so; but now, as you will perceive, not even the impudence of my accusers dares to say that I have ever exacted or sought pay of anyone; of that they have no witness. And I have a sufficient witness to the truth of what I say — my poverty.

Someone may wonder why I go about in private giving advice 5
and busying myself with the concerns of others, but do not venture to come forward in public and advise the state. I will tell you why. You have heard me speak at sundry times and in divers places of an oracle or sign which comes to me, and is the divinity which Meletus ridicules in the indictment. This sign, which is a kind of voice, first began to come to me when I was a child; it always forbids but never commands me to do anything which I am going to do. This is what deters me from being a politician. And rightly, as I think. For I am certain, O men of Athens, that if I had engaged in politics, I should have perished long ago, and done no good either to you or to myself. And do not be offended at my telling you the truth: for the truth is, that no man who goes to war with you or any other multitude, honestly striving against the many lawless and unrighteous deeds which are done in a state, will save his life; he who will fight for the right, if he would live even for a brief space, must have a private station and not a public one . . . .

JONATHAN SWIFT

JONATHAN SWIFT (1667–1745), an Anglican clergyman whose English family were long-time residents of Ireland, was Dean of Saint Patrick's in Dublin and also a poet and political pamphleteer. The greatest satirist of his period, Swift was noted for his clear, sharp prose and his effective indignation at social injustices of the day. His best-known works are *The Battle of the Books, Gulliver's Travels, The Tale of a Tub,* and *A Modest Proposal.* The last, written in 1729, remains one of the world's greatest satires[1] and is almost certainly the most vitriolic, grotesque in its details. It was aimed directly at his fellow Englishmen for their oppression of the Irish people. Writing students should remember, however, that effective as satire can be as a rouser of emotions (i.e., as persuasion), it is not a reliable tool of logic (e.g., as in argument).

A Modest Proposal

FOR PREVENTING THE CHILDREN OF POOR PEOPLE IN IRELAND FROM BEING A BURDEN TO THEIR PARENTS OR COUNTRY, AND FOR MAKING THEM BENEFICIAL TO THE PUBLIC

It is a melancholy object to those who walk through this great town[2] 1
or travel in the country, when they see the streets, the roads, and cabin doors, crowded with beggars of the female sex, followed by three, four, or six children, all in rags and importuning every passenger for an alms. These mothers, instead of being able to work for their honest livelihood, are forced to employ all their time in strolling to beg sustenance for their helpless infants, who, as they grow up, either turn thieves for want of work, or leave their dear native country to fight for the Pretender in Spain, or sell themselves to the Barbadoes.[3]

I think it is agreed by all parties that this prodigious number of 2
children in the arms, or on the backs, or at the heels of their mothers, and frequently of their fathers, is in the present deplorable state of the kingdom a very great additional grievance; and therefore whoever could find out a fair, cheap, and easy method of making these

[1]See Guide to Terms: *Satire.*

[2]Dublin.

[3]That is, bind themselves to work for a period of years, in order to pay for their transportation to a colony.

children sound, useful members of the commonwealth would deserve so well of the public as to have his statue set up for a preserver of the nation.

But my intention is very far from being confined to provide only 3
for the children of professed beggars; it is of a much greater extent, and shall take in the whole number of infants at a certain age who are born of parents in effect as little able to support them as those who demand our charity in the streets.

As to my own part, having turned my thoughts for many years 4
upon this important subject, and maturely weighed the several schemes of other projectors, I have always found them grossly mistaken in their computation. It is true, a child just dropped from its dam may be supported by her milk for a solar year, with little other nourishment; at most not above the value of two shillings, which the mother may certainly get, or the value in scraps, by her lawful occupation of begging; and it is exactly at one year old that I propose to provide for them in such a manner as instead of being a charge upon their parents or the parish, or wanting food and raiment for the rest of their lives, they shall on the contrary contribute to the feeding, and partly to the clothing, of many thousands.

There is likewise another great advantage in my scheme, that it 5
will prevent those voluntary abortions, and that horrid practice of women murdering their bastard children, alas, too frequent among us, sacrificing the poor innocent babes, I doubt, more to avoid the expense than the shame, which would move tears and pity in the most savage and inhuman breast.

The number of souls in this kingdom being usually reckoned one 6
million and a half, of these I calculate there may be about two hundred thousand couples whose wives are breeders; from which number I subtract thirty thousand couples who are able to maintain their own children, although I apprehend there cannot be so many under the present distress of the kingdom; but this being granted, there will remain an hundred and seventy thousand breeders. I again subtract fifty thousand for those women who miscarry, or whose children die by accident or disease within the year. There only remain an hundred and twenty thousand children of poor parents annually born. The question therefore is, how this number shall be reared and provided for, which, as I have already said, under the present situation of affairs, is utterly impossible by all the methods hitherto proposed. For we can neither employ them in handicraft or agricul-

ture; we neither build houses (I mean in the country) nor cultivate land. They can very seldom pick up a livelihood by stealing till they arrive at six years old, except where they are of towardly parts; although I confess they learn the rudiments much earlier, during which time they can however be looked upon only as probationers, as I have been informed by a principal gentleman in the country of Cavan, who protested to me that he never knew above one or two instances under the age of six, even in a part of the kingdom so renowned for the quickest proficiency in that art.

I am assured by our merchants that a boy or a girl before twelve 7
years old is no salable commodity; and even when they come to this age they will not yield above three pounds, or three pounds and half a crown at most on the Exchange; which cannot turn to account either to the parents or the kingdom, the charge of nutriment and rags having been at least four times that value.

I shall now therefore humbly propose my own thoughts, which 8
I hope will not be liable to the last objection.

I have been assured by a very knowing American of my ac- 9
quaintance in London, that a young healthy child well nursed is at a year old a most delicious, nourishing, and wholesome food, whether stewed, roasted, baked, or boiled; and I make no doubt that it will equally serve in a fricassee or a ragout.

I do therefore humbly offer it to public consideration that of the 10
hundred and twenty thousand children, already computed, twenty thousand may be reserved for breed, whereof only one fourth part to be males, which is more than we allow to sheep, black cattle, or swine; and my reason is that these children are seldom the fruits of marriage, a circumstance not much regarded by our savages, therefore one male will be sufficient to serve four females. That the remaining hundred thousand may at a year old be offered in sale to the persons of quality and fortune through the kingdom, always advising the mother to let them suck plentifully in the last month, so as to render them plump and fat for a good table. A child will make two dishes at an entertainment for friends; and when the family dines alone, the fore or hind quarter will make a reasonable dish, and seasoned with a little pepper or salt will be very good boiled on the fourth day, especially in winter.

I have reckoned upon a medium that a child just born will weigh 11
twelve pounds, and in a solar year if tolerably nursed increaseth to twenty-eight pounds.

I grant this food will be somewhat dear, and therefore very proper for landlords, who, as they have already devoured most of the parents, seem to have the best title to the children. 12

Infant's flesh will be in season throughout the year, but more plentiful in March, and a little before and after. For we are told by a grave author, an eminent French physician,[4] that fish being a prolific diet, there are more children born in Roman Catholic countries about nine months after Lent than at any other season; therefore, reckoning a year after Lent, the markets will be more glutted than usual, because the number of popish infants is at least three to one in this kingdom; and therefore it will have one other collateral advantage, by lessening the number of Papists among us. 13

I have already computed the charge of nursing a beggar's child (in which list I reckon all cottagers, laborers, and four fifths of the farmers) to be about two shillings per annum, rags included; and I believe no gentleman would repine to give ten shillings for the carcass of a good fat child, which, as I have said, will make four dishes of excellent nutritive meat, when he hath only some particular friend or his own family to dine with him. Thus the squire will learn to be a good landlord, and grow popular among the tenants; the mother will have eight shillings net profit, and be fit for work till she produces another child. 14

Those who are more thrifty (as I must confess the times require) may flay the carcass; the skin of which artifically dressed will make admirable gloves for ladies, and summer boots for fine gentlemen. 15

As to our city of Dublin, shambles may be appointed for this purpose in the most convenient parts of it, and butchers we may be assured will not be wanting; although I rather recommend buying the children alive, and dressing them hot from the knife as we do roasting pigs. 16

A very worthy person, a true lover of his country, and whose virtues I highly esteem, was lately pleased in discoursing on this matter to offer a refinment upon my scheme. He said that many gentlemen of his kingdom, having of late destroyed their deer, he conceived that the want of venison might be well supplied by the bodies of young lads and maidens, not exceeding fourteen years of age nor under twelve, so great a number of both sexes in every county being now ready to starve for want of work and service; and these 17

[4]François Rabelais.

to be disposed of by their parents, if alive, or otherwise by their nearest relations. But with due deference to so excellent a friend and so deserving a patriot, I cannot be altogether in his sentiments; for as to the males, my American acquaintance assured me from frequent experience that their flesh was generally tough and lean, like that of our schoolboys, by continual exercise, and their taste disagreeable; and to fatten them would not answer the charge. Then as to the females, it would, I think with humble submission, be a loss to the public, because they soon would become breeders themselves; and besides, it is not improbable that some scrupulous people might be apt to censure such a practice (although indeed very unjustly) as a little bordering upon cruelty; which, I confess, hath always been with me the strongest objection against any project, how well soever intended.

But in order to justify my friend, he confessed that this expedi- 18
ent was put into his head by the famous Psalmanazar, a native of the island Formosa, who came from thence to London above twenty years ago, and in conversation told my friend that in his country when any young person happened to be put to death, the executioner sold the carcass to the persons of quality as a prime dainty; and that in his time the body of a plump girl of fifteen, who was crucified for an attempt to poison the emperor, was sold to his Imperial Majesty's prime minister of state, and other great mandarins of the court, in joints from the gibbet, at four hundred crowns. Neither indeed can I deny that if the same use were made of several plump young girls in this town, who without one single groat to their fortunes cannot stir abroad without a chair, and appear at the playhouse and assemblies in foreign fineries which they never will pay for, the kingdom would not be the worse.

Some persons of a desponding spirit are in great concern about 19
that vast number of poor people who are aged, diseased, or maimed, and I have been desired to employ my thoughts what course may be taken to ease the nation of so grievous an encumbrance. But I am not in the least pain upon that matter, because it is very well known that they are every day dying and rotting by cold and famine, and filth and vermin, as fast as can be reasonably expected. And as to the younger laborers, they are now in almost as hopeful a condition. They cannot get work, and consequently pine away for want of nourishment to a degree that if any time they are accidentally hired

to common labor, they have not strength to perform it; and thus the country and themselves are happily delivered from the evils to come.

I have too long digressed, and therefore shall return to my subject. I think the advantages by the proposal which I have made are obvious and many, as well as of the highest importance. 20

For first, as I have already observed, it would greatly lessen the number of Papists, with whom we are yearly overrun, being the principal breeders of the nation as well as our most dangerous enemies; and who stay at home on purpose to deliver the kingdom to the Pretender, hoping to take their advantage by the absence of so many good Protestants, who have chosen rather to leave their country than to stay at home and pay tithes against their conscience to an Episcopal curate. 21

Secondly, the poorer tenants will have something valuable of their own, which by law may be made liable to distress, and help to pay their landlord's rent, their corn and cattle being already seized and money a thing unknown. 22

Thirdly, whereas the maintenance of an hundred thousand children, from two years old and upwards, cannot be computed at less than ten shillings a piece per annum, the nation's stock will be thereby increased fifty thousand pounds per annum, besides the profit of a new dish introduced to the tables of all gentlemen of fortune in the kingdom who have any refinement in taste. And the money will circulate among ourselves, the goods being entirely of our own growth and manufacture. 23

Fourthly, the constant breeders, besides the gain of eight shillings sterling per annum by the sale of their children, will be rid of the charge of maintaining them after the first year. 24

Fifthly, this food would likewise bring great custom to taverns, where the vintners will certainly be so prudent as to procure the best receipts for dressing it to perfection, and consequently have their houses frequented by all the fine gentlemen, who justly value themselves upon their knowledge in good eating; and a skillful cook, who understands how to oblige his guests, will contrive to make it as expensive as they please. 25

Sixthly, this would be a great inducement to marriage, which all wise nations have either encouraged by rewards or enforced by laws and penalties. It would increase the care and tenderness of mothers toward their children, when they were sure of a settlement for life 26 to the poor babes, provided in some sort by the public, to their annual profit instead of expense. We should see an honest emulation among the married women, which of them could bring the fattest child to the market. Men would become as fond of their wives during the time of their pregnancy as they are now of their mares in foal, their cows in calf, or sows when they are ready to farrow; nor offer to beat or kick them (as is too frequent a practice) for fear of a miscarriage.

Many other advantages might be enumerated. For instance, the 27
addition of some thousand carcasses in our exportation of barreled beef, the propagation of swine's flesh, and improvements in the art of making good bacon, so much wanted among us by the great destruction of pigs, too frequent at our tables, which are no way comparable in taste or magnificence to a well-grown, fat, yearling child, which roasted whole will make a considerable figure at a lord mayor's feast or any other public entertainment. But this and many others I omit, being studious of brevity.

Supposing that one thousand families in this city would be 28
constant customers for infants' flesh, besides others who might have it at merry meetings, particularly weddings and christenings, I compute that Dublin would take off annually about twenty thousand carcasses, and the rest of the kingdom (where probably they will be sold somewhat cheaper) the remaining eighty thousand.

I can think of no one objection that will possibly be raised 29
against this proposal, unless it should be urged that the number of people will be thereby much lessened in the kingdom. This I freely own, and it was indeed one principal design in offering it to the world. I desire the reader will observe, that I calculate my remedy for this one individual kingdom of Ireland and for no other that ever was, is, or I think ever can be upon earth. Therefore let no man talk to me of other expedients: of taxing our absentees at five shillings a pound: of using neither clothes nor household furniture except what is of our own growth and manufacture: of utterly rejecting the materials and instruments that promote foreign luxury: of curing the expensiveness of pride, vanity, idleness, and gaming in our women: of introducing a vein of parsimony, prudence, and temperance: of learning to love our country, in the want of which we differ even from Laplanders and the inhabitants of Topinamboo[5]: of quitting our animosities and factions, nor acting any longer like the Jews, who were murdering

[5]A district in Brazil.

one another at the very moment their city was taken: of being a little cautious not to sell our country and conscience for nothing: of teaching landlords to have at least one degree of mercy toward their tenants: lastly, of putting a spirit of honesty, industry, and skill into our shopkeepers; who, if a resolution could now be taken to buy only our native goods, would immediately unite to cheat and exact upon us in the price, the measure, and the goodness, nor could ever yet be brought to make one fair proposal of just dealing, though often and earnestly invited to it.[6]

Therefore I repeat, let no man talk to me of these and the like 30
expedients, till he hath at least some glimpse of hope that there will ever be some hearty and sincere attempt to put them in practice.

But as to myself, having been wearied out for many years with 31
offering vain, idle, visionary thoughts, and at length utterly despairing of success, I fortunately fell upon this proposal, which, as it is wholly new, so it hath something solid and real, of no expense and little trouble, full in our own power, and whereby we can incur no danger in disobliging England. For this kind of commodity will not bear exportation, the flesh being of too tender a consistence to admit a long continuance in salt, although perhaps I could name a country which would be glad to eat up our whole nation without it.

After all, I am not so violently bent upon my own opinion as to 32
reject any offer proposed by wise men, which shall be found equally innocent, cheap, easy, and effectual. But before something of that kind shall be advanced in contradiction to my scheme, and offering a better, I desire the author or authors will be pleased maturely to consider two points. First, as things now stand, how they will be able to find food and raiment for an hundred thousand useless mouths and backs. And secondly, there being a round million of creatures in human figure throughout this kingdom, whose sole subsistence put into a common stock would leave them in debt two millions of pounds sterling, adding those who are beggars by profession to the bulk of farmers, cottagers, and laborers, with their wives and children who are beggars in effect; I desire those politicians who dislike my overture, and may perhaps be so bold to attempt an answer, that they will first ask the parents of these mortals whether they would not at this day think it a great happiness to have been sold for food at a year old in this manner I prescribe, and thereby have avoided such a

[6]Swift himself has made these various proposals in previous works.

perpetual scene of misfortunes as they have since gone through by the oppression of landlords, the impossibility of paying rent without money or trade, the want of common sustenance, with neither house nor clothes to cover them from the inclemencies of the weather, and the most inevitable prospect of entailing the like or greater miseries upon their breed forever.

I profess, in the sincerity of my heart, that I have not the least 33
personal interest in endeavoring to promote this necessary work, having no other motive than the public good of my country, by advancing our trade, providing for infants, relieving the poor, and giving some pleasure to the rich. I have no children by which I can propose to get a single penny; the youngest being nine years old, and my wife past childbearing.

HENRY DAVID THOREAU

HENRY DAVID THOREAU (1817–1862) lived all but one year of his life in Concord, Massachusetts, where he was known as a nonconformist, an eccentric. He did some teaching and lecturing, and gained a sound reputation as a naturalist, and, of course, as an author, contributing both verse and prose to magazines and newspapers of the day. In *Walden,* his book of essays, Thoreau leaves us an account of his "experiment in living" (alone in the woods at Walden Pond), but he also gives us a careful study of nature, a critical view of then-modern society, and a work of much artistic merit. But probably none of his work has had such far-reaching effects as the essay "Civil Disobedience." It has been read, pondered, and acted upon in various parts of the world — e.g., by Mahatma Ghandi in his long and nonviolent struggle for a free India. Following is a portion of that essay.

From "Civil Disobedience"

I heartily accept the motto, — "That government is best which governs least"; and I should like to see it acted up to more rapidly and systematically. Carried out, it finally amounts to this, which also I believe, — "That government is best which governs not at all"; and when men are prepared for it, that will be the kind of government which they will have. Government is at best but an expedient; but most governments are usually, and all governments are sometimes, inexpedient. The objections which have been brought against a standing army, and they are many and weighty, and deserve to prevail, may also at last be brought against a standing government. The standing army is only an arm of the standing government. The government itself, which is only the mode which the people have chosen to execute their will, is equally liable to be abused and perverted before the people can act through it. Witness the present Mexican war, the work of comparatively a few individuals using the standing government as their tool; for, in the outset, the people would not have consented to this measure. 1

This American government, — what is it but a tradition, though a recent one, endeavoring to transmit itself unimpaired to posterity, but each instant losing some of its integrity? It has not the vitality and force of a single living man; for a single man can bend it to his 2 will. It is a sort of wooden gun to the people themselves. But it is not the less necessary for this; for the people must have some complicated machinery or other, and hear its din, to satisfy that idea of government which they have. Governments show thus how successfully men can be imposed on, even impose on themselves, for their own advantage. It is excellent, we must all allow. Yet this government never of itself furthered any enterprise, but by the alacrity with which it got out of its way. *It* does not keep the country free. *It* does not settle the West. *It* does not educate. The character inherent in the American people has done all that has been accomplished; and it would have done somewhat more, if the government had not sometimes got in its way. For government is an expedient by which men would fain succeed in letting one another alone; and, as has been said, when it is most expedient, the governed are most let alone by it. Trade and commerce, if they were not made of India-rubber, would never manage to bounce over the obstacles which legislators are continually putting in their way; and, if one were to judge these men wholly by the effects of their actions and not partly by their intentions, they would deserve to be classed and punished with those mischievous persons who put obstructions on the railroads.

But, to speak practically and as a citizen, unlike those who call 3
themselves no-government men, I ask for, not at once no government, but *at once* a better government. Let every man make known what kind of government would command his respect, and that will be one step toward obtaining it.

After all, the practical reason why, when the power is once in 4
the hands of the people, a majority are permitted, and for a long period continue, to rule is not because they are most likely to be in the right, nor because this seems fairest to the minority, but because they are physically the strongest. But a government in which the majority rule in all cases cannot be based on justice, even as far as men understand it. Can there not be a government in which majorities do not virtually decide right and wrong, but conscience? — in which majorities decide only those questions to which the rule of expediency is applicable? Must the citizen ever for a moment, or in the least degree, resign his conscience to the legislator? Why has every man a conscience, then? I think that we should be men first, and subjects afterward. It is not desirable to cultivate a respect for the law, so much as for the right. The only obligation which I have a right to assume is to do at any time what I think right. It is truly enough

said, that a corporation has no conscience; but a corporation of conscientious men is a corporation *with* a conscience. Law never made men a whit more just; and, by means of their respect for it, even the well-disposed are daily made the agents of injustice. A common and natural result of an undue respect for law is, that you may see a file of soldiers, colonel, captain, corporal, privates, powder-monkeys, and all, marching in admirable order over hill and dale to the wars, against their wills, ay, against their common sense and consciences, which makes it very steep marching indeed, and produces a palpitation of the heart. They have no doubt that it is a damnable business in which they are concerned; they are all peaceably inclined. Now, what are they? Men at all? or small movable forts and magazines, at the service of some unscupulous man in power? Visit the Navy-Yard, and behold a marine, such a man as an American government can make, or such as it can make a man with its black arts, — a mere shadow and reminiscence of humanity, a man laid out alive and standing, and already, as one may say, buried under arms with funeral accompaniments, though it may be, —

> Not a drum was heard, not a funeral note,
>   As his corse to the rampart we hurried;
> Not a soldier discharged his farewell shot
>   O'er the grave where our hero we buried.

The mass of men serve the state thus, not as men mainly, but 5
as machines, with their bodies. They are the standing army, and the militia, jailors, constables, posse comitatus, etc. In most cases there is no free exercise whatever of the judgment or of the moral sense; but they put themselves on a level with wood and earth and stones; and wooden men can perhaps be manufactured that will serve the purpose as well. Such command no more respect than men of straw or a lump of dirt. They have the same sort of worth only as horses and dogs. Yet such as these even are commonly esteemed good citizens. Others — as most legislators, politicians, lawyers, ministers, and office-holders — serve the state chiefly with their heads; and, as they rarely make any moral distinctions, they are as likely to serve the Devil, without *intending* it, as God. A very few, as heroes, patriots, martyrs, reformers in the great sense, and *men,* serve the state with their consciences also, and so necessarily resist it for the most part; and they are commonly treated as enemies by it. A wise man

will only be useful as a man, and will not submit to be "clay," and "stop a hole to keep the wind away," but leave that office to his dust at least:

> I am too high-born to be propertied,
> To be a secondary at control,
> Or useful serving-man and instrument
> To any sovereign state throughout the world.

He who gives himself entirely to his fellow-men appears to them useless and selfish; but he who gives himself partially to them is pronounced a benefactor and philanthropist. 6

How does it become a man to behave toward this American government to-day? I answer, that he cannot without disgrace be associated with it. I cannot for an instant recognize that political organization as *my* government which is the *slave's* government also. 7

All men recognize the right of revolution; that is, the right to refuse allegiance to, and to resist, the government, when its tyranny or its inefficiency are great and unendurable. But almost all say that such is not the case now. But such was the case, they think, in the Revolution of '75. If one were to tell me that this was a bad government because it taxed certain foreign commodities brought to its ports, it is most probable that I should not make an ado about it, for I can do without them. All machines have their friction; and possibly this does enough good to counterbalance the evil. At any rate, it is a great evil to make a stir about it. But when the friction comes to have its machine, and oppression and robbery are organized, I say, let us not have such a machine any longer. In other words, when a sixth of the population of a nation which has undertaken to be the refuge of liberty are slaves, and a whole country is unjustly overrun and conquered by a foreign army, and subjected to military law, I think that it is not too soon for honest men to rebel and revolutionize. What makes this duty the more urgent is the fact that the country so overrun is not our own, but ours is the invading army. . . . 8

Practically speaking, the opponents to a reform in Massachusetts are not a hundred thousand politicians at the South, but a hundred thousand merchants and farmers here, who are more interested in commerce and agriculture than they are in humanity, and are not prepared to do justice to the slave and to Mexico, *cost what it may.* I quarrel not with far-off foes, but with those who, near at home, 9 coöperate with, and do the bidding of, those far away, and without whom the latter would be harmless. We are accustomed to say, that the mass of men are unprepared, but improvement is slow, because the few are not materially wiser or better than the many. It is not so important that many should be as good as you, as that there be some absolute goodness somewhere; for that will leaven the whole lump. There are thousands who are *in opinion* opposed to slavery and to the war, who yet in effect do nothing to put an end to them; who, esteeming themselves children of Washington and Franklin, sit down with their hands in their pockets, and say that they know not what to do, and do nothing; who even postpone the question of freedom to the question of free-trade, and quietly read the prices-current along with the latest advices from Mexico, after dinner, and, it may be, fall asleep over them both. What is the price-current of an honest man and patriot to-day? They hesitate, and they regret, and sometimes they petition; but they do nothing in earnest and with effect. They will wait, well disposed, for others to remedy the evil, that they may no longer have it to regret. At most, they give only a cheap vote, and a feeble countenance and Godspeed, to the right, as it goes by them. There are nine hundred and ninety-nine patrons of virtue to one virtuous man. But it is easier to deal with the real possessor of a thing than with the temporary guardian of it.

All voting is a sort of gaming, like checkers or backgammon, 10
with a slight moral tinge to it, a playing with right and wrong, with moral questions; and betting naturally accompanies it. The character of the voters is not staked. I cast my vote, perchance, as I think right; but I am not vitally concerned that that right should prevail. I am willing to leave it to the majority. Its obligation, therefore, never exceeds that of expediency. Even voting *for the right* is *doing* nothing for it. Is is only expressing to men feebly your desire that it should prevail. A wise man will not leave the right to the mercy of chance, nor wish it to prevail through the power of the majority. There is but little virtue in the action of masses of men. When the majority shall at length vote for the abolition of slavery, it will be because they are indifferent to slavery, or because there is but little slavery left to be abolished by their vote. *They* will then be the only slaves. Only *his* vote can hasten the abolition of slavery who asserts his own freedom by his vote.

I hear of a convention to be held at Baltimore, or elsewhere, for 11
the selection of a candidate for the Presidency, made up chiefly of

editors, and men who are politicians by profession; but I think, what is it to any independent, intelligent, and respectable man what decision they may come to? Shall we not have the advantage of his wisdom and honesty, nevertheless? Can we not count upon some independent votes? Are there not many individuals in the country who do not attend conventions? But no: I find that the respectable man, so called, has immediately drifted from his position, and despairs of his country, when his country has more reason to despair of him. He forthwith adopts one of the candidates thus selected as the only *available* one, thus proving that he is himself *available* for any purposes of the demagogue. His vote is of no more worth than that of any unprincipled foreigner or hireling native, who may have been bought. O for a man who is a *man,* and, as my neighbor says, has a bone in his back which you cannot pass your hand through! Our statistics are at fault: The population has been returned too large. How many *men* are there to a square thousand miles in this country? Hardly one. Does not America offer any inducement for men to settle here? The American has dwindled into an Odd Fellow, — one who may be known by the development of his organ of gregariousness, and a manifest lack of intellect and cheerful self-reliance; whose first and chief concern, on coming into the world, is to see that the Almshouses are in good repair; and, before yet he has lawfully donned the virile garb, to collect a fund for the support of the widows and orphans that may be; who, in sort, ventures to live only by the aid of the Mutual Insurance company, which has promised to bury him decently.

It is not a man's duty, as a matter of course, to devote himself 12
to the eradication of any, even the most enormous wrong; he may still properly have other concerns to engage him; but it is his duty, at least, to wash his hands of it, and, if he gives it no thought longer, not to give it practically his support. If I devote myself to other pursuits and contemplations, I must first see, at least, that I do not pursue them sitting upon another man's shoulders. I must get off him first, that he may pursue his contemplations too. See what gross inconsistency is tolerated. I have heard some of my townsmen say, "I should like to have them order me out to help put down an insurrection of the slaves, or to march to Mexico; — see if I would go"; and yet these very men have each, directly by their allegiance, and so indirectly, at least, by their money, furnished a substitute. The soldier is applauded who refuses to serve in an unjust war by those

who do not refuse to sustain the unjust government which makes the war; is applauded by those whose own act and authority he disregards and sets at naught; as if the state were penitent and to that degree that it hired one to scourge it while it sinned, but not to that degree that it left off sinning for a moment. Thus, under the name of Order and Civil Government, we are all made at last to pay homage to and support our own meanness. After the first blush of sin comes its indifference, and from immoral it becomes, as it were, *un*moral, and not quite unnecessary to that life which we have made.

The broadest and most prevalent error requires the most disin- 13
terested virtue to sustain it. The slight reproach to which the virtue of patriotism is commonly liable, the noble are most likely to incur. Those who, while they disapprove of the character and measures of a government, yield to it their allegiance and support are undoubtedly its most conscientious supporters, and so frequently the most serious obstacles to reform. Some are petitioning the state to dissolve the Union, to disregard the requisitions of the President. Why do they not dissolve it themselves, — the union between themselves and the state, — and refuse to pay their quota into its treasury? Do not they stand in the same relation to the state that the state does to the Union? And have not the same reasons prevented the state from resisting the Union which have prevented them from resisting the state?

How can a man be satisfied to enertain an opinion merely, and 14
enjoy *it?* Is there any enjoyment in it, if his opinion is that he is aggrieved? If you are cheated out of a single dollar by your neighbor, you do not rest satisfied with knowing that you are cheated, or with saying that you are cheated, or even with petitioning him to pay you your due; but you take effectual steps at once to obtain the full amount, and see that you are never cheated again. Action from principle, the perception and the performance of right, changes things and relations; it is essentially revolutionary, and does not consist wholly with anything which was. It not only divides states and churches, it divides families; ay, it divides the *individual,* separating the diabolical in him from the divine.

Unjust laws exist: shall we be content to obey them, or shall we 15
endeavor to amend them, and obey them until we have succeeded, or shall we transgress them at once? Men generally, under such a government as this, think that they ought to wait until they have persuaded the majority to alter them. They think that, if they should

resist, the remedy would be worse than the evil. But it is the fault of the government itself that the remedy *is* worse than the evil. *It* makes it worse. Why is it not more apt to anticipate and provide for reform? Why does it not cherish its wise minority? Why does it cry and resist before it is hurt? Why does it not encourage its citizens to be on the alert to point out its faults and *do* better than it would have them? Why does it always crucify Christ, and excommunicate Copernicus and Luther, and pronounce Washington and Franklin rebels? . . .

I meet this American government, or its representative, the state 16
government, directly, and face to face, once a year — no more — in the person of its tax-gatherer; this is the only mode in which a man situated as I am necessarily meets it; and it then says distinctly, Recognize me; and the simplest, most effectual, and, in the present posture of affairs, the indispensablest mode of treating with it on this head, of expressing your little satisfaction with and love for it, is to deny it then. My civil neighbor, the tax-gatherer, is the very man I have to deal with, — for it is, after all, with men and not with parchment that I quarrel, — and he has voluntarily chosen to be an agent of the government. How shall he ever know well what he is and does as an officer of the government, or as a man, until he is obliged to consider whether he shall treat me, his neighbor, for whom he has respect, as a neighbor and well-disposed man, or as a maniac and disturber of the peace, and see if he can get over this obstruction to his neighborliness without a ruder and more impetuous thought or speech corresponding with his action. I know this well, that if one thousand, if one hundred, if ten men whom I could name, — if ten *honest* men only, — ay, if *one* HONEST man, in this State of Massachusetts, *ceasing to hold slaves,* were actually to withdraw from this copartnership, and be locked up in the county jail therefor, it would be the abolition of slavery in America. For it matters not how small the beginning may seem to be: what is once well done is done forever. But we love better to talk about it: that we say is our mission. Reform keeps many scores of newspapers in its service, but not one man. If my esteemed neighbor, the State's ambassador, who will devote his days to the settlement of the question of human rights in the Council Chamber, instead of being threatened with the prisons of Carolina, were to sit down the prisoner of Massachusetts, that State which is so anxious to foist the sin of slavery upon her sister, — though at present she can discover only an act of inhospitality to be the ground

of a quarrel with her, — the Legislature would not wholly waive the subject the following winter.

Under a government which imprisons any unjustly, the true place for a just man is also a prison. The proper place to-day, the only place which Massachusetts has provided for her freer and less desponding spirits, is in her prisons, to be put out and locked out of the State by her own act, as they have already put themselves out by their principles. It is there that the fugitive slave, and the Mexican prisoner on parole, and the Indian come to plead the wrongs of his race should find them; on that separate, but more free and honorable ground, where the State places those who are not *with* her, but *against* her, — the only house in a slave State in which a free man can abide with honor. If any think that their influence would be lost there, and their voices no longer afflict the ear of the State, that they would not be as an enemy within its walls, they do not know by how much truth is stronger than error, nor how much more eloquently and effectively he can combat injustice who has experienced a little in his own person. Cast your whole vote, not a strip of paper merely, but your whole influence. A minority is powerless while it conforms to the majority; it is not even a minority then; but it is irresistible when it clogs by its whole weight. If the alternative is to keep all just men in prison, or give up war and slavery, the State will not hesitate which to choose. If a thousand men were not to pay their tax bills this year, that would not be a violent and bloody measure, as it would be to pay them, and enable the State to commit violence and shed innocent blood. This is, in fact, the definition of a peaceable revolution, if any such is possible. If the tax-gatherer, or any other public officer, asks me, as one has done, "But what shall I do?" my answer is, "If you really wish to do anything, resign your office." When the subject has refused allegiance, and the officer has resigned his office, then the revolution is accomplished. But even suppose blood should flow. Is there not a sort of blood shed when the conscience is wounded? Through this wound a man's real manhood and immortality flow out, and he bleeds to an everlasting death. I see this blood flowing now. . . . 17

I have paid no poll-tax for six years. I was put into a jail once on this account, for one night; and, as I stood considering the walls of solid stone, two or three feet thick, the door of wood and iron, a foot thick, and the iron grating which strained the light. I could not help being struck with the foolishness of that institution which 18 treated me as if I were mere flesh and blood and bones, to be locked up. I wondered that it should have concluded at length that this was the best use it could put me to, and had never thought to avail itself of my services in some way. I saw that, if there was a wall of stone between me and my townsmen, there was a still more difficult one to climb or break through before they could get to be as free as I was. I did not for a moment feel confined, and the walls seemed a great waste of stone and mortar. I felt as if I alone of all my townsmen had paid my tax. They plainly did not know how to treat me, but behaved like persons who are underbred. In every threat and in every compliment there was a blunder; for they thought that my chief desire was to stand the other side of that stone wall. I could not but smile to see how industriously they locked the door on my meditations, which followed them out again without let or hindrance, and *they* were really all that was dangerous. As they could not reach me, they had resolved to punish my body; just as boys, if they cannot come at some person against whom they have a spite, will abuse his dog. I saw that the State was half-witted, that it was timid as a lone woman with her silver spoons, and that it did not know its friends from its foes, and I lost all my remaining respect for it, and pitied it.

Thus the State never intentionally confronts a man's sense, in- 19
tellectual or moral, but only his body, his senses. It is not armed with superior wit or honesty, but with superior physical strength. I was not born to be forced. I will breathe after my own fashion. Let us see who is the strongest. What force has a multitude? They only can force me who obey a higher law than I. They force me to become like themselves. I do not hear of *men* being *forced* to live this way or that by masses of men. What sort of life were that to live? When I meet a government which says to me, "Your money or your life," why should I be in haste to give it my money? It may be in a great strait, and not know what to do: I cannot help that. It must help itself: do as I do. It is not worth the while to snivel about it. I am not responsible for the successful working of the machinery of society. I am not the son of the engineer. I perceive that, when an acorn and a chestnut fall side by side, the one does not remain inert to make way for the other, but both obey their own laws, and spring and grow and flourish as best they can, till one, perchance, overshadows and destroys the other. If a plant cannot live according to its nature, it dies; and so a man.

GEORGE ORWELL

GEORGE ORWELL published "Politics and the English Language" in 1945. It became one of his most famous essays. (A biographical sketch of Orwell appears on page 282 in Section 9.)

Politics and the English Language

Most people who bother with the matter at all would admit that the English language is in a bad way, but it is generally assumed that we cannot by conscious action do anything about it. Our civilization is decadent and our language — so the argument runs — must inevitably share in the general collapse. It follows that any struggle against the abuse of language is a sentimental archaism, like preferring candles to electric light or hansom cabs to aeroplanes. Underneath this lies the half-conscious belief that language is a natural growth and not an instrument which we shape for our own purpose. 1

Now, it is clear that the decline of a language must ultimately have political and economic causes: it is not due simply to the bad influence of this or that individual writer. But an effect can become a cause, reinforcing the original cause and producing the same effect in an intensified form, and so on indefinitely. A man may take to drink because he feels himself to be a failure, and then fail all the more completely because he drinks. It is rather the same thing that is happening to the English language. It becomes ugly and inaccurate because our thoughts are foolish, but the slovenliness of our language makes it easier for us to have foolish thoughts. The point is that the process is reversible. Modern English, especially written English, is full of bad habits which spread by imitation and which can be avoided if one is willing to take the necessary trouble. If one gets rid of these habits one can think more clearly, and to think clearly is a necessary first step towards political regeneration: so that the fight against bad English is not frivolous and is not the exclusive concern of professional writers. I will come back to this presently, and I hope 2 that by that time the meaning of what I have said here will have become clearer. Meanwhile, here are five specimens of the English language as it is now habitually written.

These five passages have not been picked out because they are 3
especially bad — I could have quoted far worse if I had chosen — but because they illustrate various of the mental vices from which we now suffer. They are a little below the average, but are fairly representative samples. I number them so that I can refer back to them when necessary:

(1) I am not, indeed, sure whether it is not true to say that the Milton who once seemed not unlike a seventeenth-century Shelley had not become, out of an experience ever more bitter in each year, more alien [*sic*] to the founder of that Jesuit sect which nothing could induce him to tolerate.

Professor Harold Laski (Essay in *Freedom of Expression*).

(2) Above all, we cannot play ducks and drakes with a native battery of idioms which prescribes such egregious collocations of vocables as the Basic *put up with* for *tolerate* or *put at a loss* for *bewilder.*

Professor Lancelot Hogben *(Interglossa).*

(3) On the one side we have the free personality: by definition it is not neurotic, for it has neither conflict nor dream. Its desires, such as they are, are transparent, for they are just what institutional approval keeps in the forefront of consciousness; another institutional pattern would alter their number and intensity; there is little in them that is natural, irreducible, or culturally dangerous. But *on the other side,* the social bond itself is nothing but the mutual reflection of these self-secure integrities. Recall the definition of love. Is not this the very picture of a small academic? Where is there a place in this hall of mirrors for either personality or fraternity?

Essay on psychology in *Politics* (New York).

(4) All the "best people" from the gentlemen's clubs, and all the frantic fascist captains, united in common hatred of Socialism and bestial horror of the rising tide of the mass revolutionary movement, have turned to acts of provocation, to foul incendiarism, to medieval legends of poisoned wells, to legalize their own destruction of proletarian organizations, and rouse the agitated petty-bourgeoisie to chauvinistic fervour on behalf of the fight against the revolutionary way out of the crisis.

Communist pamphlet.

(5) If a new spirit *is* to be infused into this old country, there is one thorny and contentious reform which must be tackled, and that is the humanization and galvanization of the B.B.C. Timidity here will bespeak cancer

and atrophy of the soul. The heart of Britain may be sound and of strong beat, for instance, but the British lion's roar at present is like that of Bottom in Shakespeare's *Midsummer Night's Dream* — as gentle as any sucking dove. A virile new Britain cannot continue indefinitely to be traduced in the eyes or rather ears, of the world by the effete languors of Langham Place, brazenly masquerading as "standard English." When the Voice of Britain is heard at nine o'clock, better far and infinitely less ludicrous to hear aitches honestly dropped than the present priggish, inflated, inhibited, school-ma'amish arch braying of blameless bashful mewing maidens!

Letter in *Tribune.*

Each of these passages has faults of its own, but, quite apart from avoidable ugliness, two qualities are common to all of them. The first is staleness of imagery: the other is lack of precision. The writer either has a meaning and cannot express it, or he inadvertently says something else, or he is almost indifferent as to whether his words mean anything or not. The mixture of vagueness and sheer incompetence is the most marked characteristic of modern English prose, and especially of any kind of political writing. As soon as certain topics are raised, the concrete melts into the abstract and no one seems to think of turns of speech that are not hackneyed: prose consists less and less of *words* chosen for the sake of their meaning, and more and more of *phrases* tacked together like the sections of a prefabricated hen-house. I list below, with notes and examples, various of the tricks by means of which the work of prose-construction is habitually dodged: 4

DYING METAPHORS

A newly invented metaphor assists thought by evoking a visual image, while on the other hand a metaphor which is technically "dead" (e.g. *iron resolution*) has in effect reverted to being an ordinary word and can generally be used without loss of vividness. But in between these two classes there is a huge dump of worn-out metaphors which have lost all evocative power and are merely used because they save people the trouble of inventing phrases for themselves. Examples are: *Ring the changes on, take up the cudgels for, toe the line, ride roughshod over, stand shoulder to shoulder with, play into the hands of, no axe to grind, grist to the mill, fishing in troubled waters, on the order of the day, Achilles' heel, swan song, hotbed.* Many of these are used without knowledge of their meaning (what is a "rift", for instance?), and incompatible metaphors are frequently mixed, a sure 5 sign that the writer is not interested in what he is saying. Some metaphors now current have been twisted out of their original meaning without those who use them even being aware of the fact. For example, *toe the line* is sometimes written *tow the line.* Another example is *the hammer and the anvil,* now always used with the implication that the anvil gets the worst of it. In real life it is always the anvil that breaks the hammer, never the other way about: a writer who stopped to think what he was saying would be aware of this, and would avoid perverting the original phrase.

OPERATORS OR VERBAL FALSE LIMBS

These save the trouble of picking out appropriate verbs and nouns, 6
and at the same time pad each sentence with extra syllables which give it an appearance of symmetry. Characteristic phrases are: *render inoperative, militate against, make contact with, be subjected to, give rise to, give grounds for, have the effect of, play a leading part (role) in, make itself felt, take effect, exhibit a tendency to, serve the purpose of, etc., etc.* The keynote is the elimination of simple verbs. Instead of being a single word, such as *break, stop, spoil, mend, kill,* a verb becomes a *phrase,* made up of a noun or adjective tacked on to some general-purpose verb such as *prove, serve, form, play, render.* In addition, the passive voice is wherever possible used in preference to the active, and noun constructions are used instead of gerunds (*by examination of* instead of *by examining*). The range of verbs is further cut down by means of the *-ize* and *de-* formation, and the banal statements are given an appearance of profundity by means of the *not un-* formation. Simple conjunctions and prepositions are replaced by such phrases as *with respect to, having regard to, the fact that, by dint of, in view of, in the interests of, on the hypothesis that;* and the ends of sentences are saved from anticlimax by such resounding commonplaces as *greatly to be desired, cannot be left out of account, a development to be expected in the near future, deserving of serious consideration, brought to a satisfactory conclusion,* and so on and so forth.

PRETENTIOUS DICTION

Words like *phenomenon, element, individual* (as noun), *objective, categor-* 7
ical, effective, virtual, basic, primary, promote, constitute, exhibit, exploit, utilize, eliminate, liquidate, are used to dress up simple statements and give an air of scientific impartiality to biased judgments. Adjectives

like *epoch-making, epic, historic, unforgettable, triumphant, age-old, inevitable, inexorable, veritable,* are used to dignify the sordid processes of international politics, while writing that aims at glorifying war usually takes on an archaic color, its characteristic words being: *realm, throne, chariot, mailed fist, trident, sword, shield, buckler, banner, jackboot, clarion.* Foreign words and expressions such as *cul de sac, ancien régime, deus ex machina, mutatis mutandis, status quo, gleichshaltung, weltanschauung,* are used to give an air of culture and elegance. Except for the useful abbreviations *i.e., e.g.,* and *etc.,* there is no real need for any of the hundreds of foreign phrases now current in English. Bad writers, and especially scientific, political and sociological writers, are nearly always haunted by the notion that Latin or Greek words are grander than Saxon ones, and unnecessary words like *expedite, ameliorate, predict, extraneous, deracinated, clandestine, subaqueous* and hundreds of others constantly gain ground from their Anglo-Saxon opposite numbers.[1] The jargon peculiar to Marxist writing (*hyena, hangman, cannibal, petty bourgeois, these gentry, lacquey, flunkey, mad dog, White Guard,* etc.) consists largely of words and phrases translated from Russian, German or French; but the normal way of coining a new word is to use a Latin or Greek root with the appropriate affix and, where necessary, the *-ize* formation. It is often easier to make up words of this kind (*deregionalize, impermissible, extramarital, nonfragmentatory* and so forth) than to think up the English words that will cover one's meaning. The result, in general, is an increase in slovenliness and vagueness.

MEANINGLESS WORDS

In certain kinds of writing, particularly in art criticism and literary criticism, it is normal to come across long passages which are almost completely lacking in meaning.[2] Words like *romantic, plastic, values,* 8

[1]An interesting illustration of this is the way in which the English flower names which were in use till very recently are being ousted by Greek ones, *snapdragon* becoming *antirrhinum, forget-me-not* becoming *myosotis,* etc. It is hard to see any practical reason for this change of fashion: it is probably due to an instinctive turning-away from the more homely word and a vague feeling that the Greek word is scientific.

[2]Example: "Comfort's catholicity of perception and image, strangely Whitmanesque in range, almost the exact opposite in aesthetic compulsion, continues to evoke that trembling atmospheric accumulative hinting at a cruel, an inexorably serene timelessness . . . Wrey Gardiner scores by aiming at simple bull's-eyes with precision. Only they are not so simple, and through this contented sadness runs more than the surface bitter-sweet of resignation." (*Poetry Quarterly.*)

human, dead, sentimental, natural, vitality, as used in art criticism, are strictly meaningless in the sense that they not only do not point to any discoverable object, but are hardly ever expected to do so by the reader. When one critic writes, "The outstanding feature of Mr. X's work is its living quality", while another writes, "The immediately striking thing about Mr. X's work is its peculiar deadness", the reader accepts this as a simple difference of opinion. If words like *black* and *white* were involved, instead of the jargon words *dead* and *living,* he would see at once that language was being used in an improper way. Many political words are similarly abused. The word *Fascism* has now no meaning except in so far as it signifies "something not desirable." The words *democracy, socialism, freedom, patriotic, realistic, justice,* have each of them several different meanings which cannot be reconciled with one another. In the case of a word like *democracy,* not only is there no agreed definition, but the attempt to make one is resisted from all sides. It is almost universally felt that when we call a country democratic we are praising it: consequently the defenders of every kind of régime claim that it is a democracy, and fear that they might have to stop using the word if it were tied down to any one meaning. Words of this kind are often used in a consciously dishonest way. That is, the person who uses them has his own private definition, but allows his hearer to think he means something quite different. Statements like *Marshal Pétain was a true patriot, The Soviet Press is the freest in the world, The Catholic Church is opposed to persecution,* are almost always made with intent to deceive. Other words used in variable meanings, in most cases more or less dishonestly, are: *class, totalitarian, science, progressive, reactionary, bourgeois, equality.*

Now that I have made this catalogue of swindles and perver- 9
sions, let me give another example of the kind of writing that they lead to. This time it must of its nature be an imaginary one. I am going to translate a passage of good English into modern English of the worst sort. Here is a well-known verse from *Ecclesiastes:*

> I returned and saw under the sun, that the race is not to the swift, nor the battle to the strong, neither yet bread to the wise, nor yet riches to men of understanding, nor yet favour to men of skill; but time and chance happeneth to them all.

Here it is in modern English:

> Objective consideration of contemporary phenomena compels the conclusion that success or failure in competitive activities exhibits no tendency

to be commensurate with innate capacity, but that a considerable element of the unpredictable must invariably be taken into account.

This is a parody, but not a very gross one. Exhibit (3), above, for 10
instance, contains several patches of the same kind of English. It will be seen that I have not made a full translation. The beginning and ending of the sentence follow the original meaning fairly closely, but in the middle the concrete illustrations — race, battle, bread — dissolve into the vague phrase "success or failure in competitive activities." This had to be so, because no modern writer of the kind I am discussing — no one capable of using phrases like "objective consideration of contemporary phenomena" — would ever tabulate his thoughts in that precise and detailed way. The whole tendency of modern prose is away from concreteness. Now analyze these two sentences a little more closely. The first contains forty-nine words but only sixty syllables, and all its words are those of everyday life. The second contains thirty-eight words of ninety syllables: eighteen of its words are from Latin roots, and one from Greek. The first sentence contains six vivid images, and only one phrase ("time and chance") that could be called vague. The second contains not a single fresh, arresting phrase, and in spite of its ninety syllables it gives only a shortened version of the meaning contained in the first. Yet without a doubt it is the second kind of sentence that is gaining ground in modern English. I do not want to exaggerate. This kind of writing is not yet universal, and outcrops of simplicity will occur here and there in the worst-written page. Still, if you or I were told to write a few lines on the uncertainty of human fortunes, we should probably come much nearer to my imaginary sentence than to the one from *Ecclesiastes.*

As I have tried to show, modern writing at its worst does not 11
consist in picking out words for the sake of their meaning and inventing images in order to make the meaning clearer. It consists in gumming together long strips of words which have already been set in order by someone else, and making the results presentable by sheer humbug. The attraction of this way of writing is that it is easy. It is easier — even quicker once you have the habit — to say *In my opinion it is a not unjustifiable assumption that* than to say *I think.* If you use ready-made phrases, you not only don't have to hunt about for words; you also don't have to bother with the rhythms of your sentences, since these phrases are generally so arranged as to be more or less euphonious. When you are composing in a hurry — when you

are dictating to a stenographer, for instance, or making a public speech — it is natural to fall into a pretentious, Latinized style. Tags like *a consideration which we should do well to bear in mind* or *a conclusion to which all of us would readily assent* will save many a sentence from coming down with a bump. By using stale metaphors, similes and idioms, you save much mental effort, at the cost of leaving your meaning vague, not only for your reader but for yourself. This is the significance of mixed metaphors. The sole aim of a metaphor is to call up a visual image. When these images clash — as in *The Fascist octopus has sung its swan song, the jackboot is thrown into the melting pot* — it can be taken as certain that the writer is not seeing a mental image of the objects he is naming; in other words he is not really thinking. Look again at the examples I gave at the beginning of this essay. Professor Laski (1) uses five negatives in fifty-three words. One of these is superfluous, making nonsense of the whole passage, and in addition there is the slip *alien* for akin, making further nonsense, and several avoidable pieces of clumsiness which increase the general vagueness. Professor Hogben (2) plays ducks and drakes with a battery which is able to write prescriptions, and, while disapproving of the everyday phrase *put up with,* is unwilling to look *egregious* up in the dictionary and see what it means. (3), if one takes an uncharitable attitude towards it, is simply meaningless: probably one could work out its intended meaning by reading the whole of the article in which it occurs. In (4), the writer knows more or less what he wants to say, but an accumulation of stale phrases chokes him like tea leaves blocking a sink. In (5), words and meaning have almost parted company. People who write in this manner usually have a general emotional meaning — they dislike one thing and want to express solidarity with another — but they are not interested in the detail of what they are saying. A scrupulous writer, in every sentence that he writes, will ask himself at least four questions, thus: What am I trying to say? What words will express it? What image or idiom will make it clearer? Is this image fresh enough to have an effect? And he will probably ask himself two more: Could I put it more shortly? Have I said anything that is avoidably ugly? But you are not obliged to go to all this trouble. You can shirk it by simply throwing your mind open and letting the ready-made phrases come crowding in. They will construct your sentences for you — even think your thoughts for you, to a certain extent — and at need they will perform the important service of partially concealing your meaning even from yourself.

It is at this point that the special connection between politics and the debasement of language becomes clear.

In our times it is broadly true that political writing is bad writing. 12
Where it is not true, it will generally be found that the writer is some kind of rebel, expressing his private opinions and not a "party line." Orthodoxy, of whatever color, seems to demand a lifeless, imitative style. The political dialects to be found in pamphlets, leading articles, manifestos, White Papers and the speeches of under-secretaries do, of course, vary from party to party, but they are all alike in that one almost never finds in them a fresh, vivid, home-made turn of speech. When one watches some tired hack on the platform mechanically repeating the familiar phrases — *bestial atrocities, iron heel, bloodstained tyranny, free peoples of the world, stand shoulder to shoulder* — one often has a curious feeling that one is not watching a live human being but some kind of dummy; a feeling which suddenly becomes stronger at moments when the light catches the speaker's spectacles and turns them into blank discs which seem to have no eyes behind them. And this is not altogether fanciful. A speaker who uses that kind of phraseology has gone some distance towards turning himself into a machine. The appropriate noises are coming out of his larynx, but his brain is not involved as it would be if he were choosing his words for himself. If the speech he is making is one that he is accustomed to make over and over again, he may be almost unconscious of what he is saying, as one is when one utters the responses in church. And this reduced state of consciousness, if not indispensable, is at any rate favorable to political conformity.

In our time, political speech and writing are largely the defense 13
of the indefensible. Things like the continuance of British rule in India, the Russian purges and deportations, the dropping of the atom bombs on Japan, can indeed be defended, but only by arguments which are too brutal for most people to face, and which do not square with the professed aims of political parties. Thus political language has to consist largely of euphemism, question-begging and sheer cloudy vaguness. Defenseless villages are bombarded from the air, the inhabitants driven out into the countryside, the cattle machine-gunned, the huts set on fire with incendiary bullets: this is called *pacification.* Millions of peasants are robbed of their farms and sent trudging along the roads with no more than they can carry: this is called *transfer of population* or *rectification of frontiers.* People are imprisoned for years without trial, or shot in the back of the neck or sent

to die of scurvy in Arctic lumber camps: this is called *elimination of unreliable elements.* Such phraseology is needed if one wants to name things without calling up mental pictures of them. Consider for instance some comfortable English professor defending Russian totalitarianism. He cannot say outright, "I believe in killing off your opponents when you can get good results by doing so." Probably, therefore, he will say something like this:

"While freely conceding that the Soviet régime exhibits certain features which the humanitarian may be inclined to deplore, we must, I think, agree that a certain curtailment of the right to political opposition is an unavoidable concomitant of transitional periods, and that the rigors which the Russian people have been called upon to undergo have been amply justified in the sphere of concrete achievement." 14

The inflated style is itself a kind of euphemism. A mass of Latin words falls upon the facts like soft snow, blurring the outlines and covering up all the details. The great enemy of clear language is insincerity. When there is a gap between one's real and one's declared aims, one turns as it were instinctively to long words and exhausted idioms, like a cuttlefish squirting out ink. In our age there is no such thing as "keeping out of politics." All issues are political issues, and politics itself is a mass of lies, evasions, folly, hatred and schizophrenia. When the general atmosphere is bad, language must suffer. I should expect to find — this is a guess which I have not sufficient knowledge to verify — that the German, Russian and Italian languages have all deteriorated in the last ten or fifteen years, as a result of dictatorship. 15

But if thought corrupts language, language can also corrupt thought. A bad usage can spread by tradition and imitation, even among people who should and do know better. The debased language that I have been discussing is in some ways very convenient. Phrases like *a not unjustifiable assumption, leaves much to be desired, would serve no good purpose, a consideration which we should do well to bear in mind,* are a continuous temptation, a packet of aspirins always at one's elbow. Look back through this essay, and for certain you will find that I have again and again committed the very faults I am protesting against. By this morning's post I have received a pamphlet dealing with conditions in Germany. The author tells me that he "felt impelled" to write it. I open it at random, and here is almost the first sentence that I see: "(The Allies) have an opportunity not only of 16 achieving a radical transformation of Germany's social and political structure in such a way as to avoid a nationalistic reaction in Germany itself, but at the same time of laying the foundations of a co-operative and unified Europe." You see, he "feels impelled" to write — feels, presumably, that he has something new to say — and yet his words, like cavalry horses answering the bugle, group themselves automatically into the familiar dreary pattern. This invasion of one's mind by ready-made phrases (*lay the foundations, achieve a radical transformation*) can only be prevented if one is constantly on guard against them, and every such phrase anaesthetizes a portion of one's brain.

I said earlier that the decadence of our language is probably 17
curable. Those who deny this would argue, if they produced an argument at all, that language merely reflects existing social conditions, and that we cannot influence its development by any direct tinkering with words and constructions. So far as the general tone or spirit of a language goes, this may be true, but it is not true in detail. Silly words and expressions have often disappeared, not through any evolutionary process but owing to the conscious action of a minority. Two recent examples were *explore every avenue* and *leave no stone unturned,* which were killed by the jeers of a few journalists. There is a long list of flyblown metaphors which could similarly be got rid of if enough people would interest themselves in the job; and it should also be possible to laugh the *not un-* formation out of existence,[3] to reduce the amount of Latin and Greek in the average sentence, to drive out foreign phrases and strayed scientific words, and, in general, to make pretentiousness unfashionable. But all these are minor points. The defense of the English language implies more than this, and perhaps it is best to start by saying what it does *not* imply.

To begin with it has nothing to do with archaism, with the 18
salvaging of obsolete words and turns of speech, or with the setting up of a "standard English" which must never be departed from. On the contrary, it is especially concerned with the scrapping of every word or idiom which has outworn its usefulness. It has nothing to do with correct grammar and syntax, which are of no importance so long as one makes one's meaning clear, or with the avoidance of Americanisms, or with having what is called a "good prose style." On

[3]One can cure oneself of the *not un-* formation by memorizing this sentence: *A not unblack dog was chasing a not unsmall rabbit across a not ungreen field.*

the other hand it is not concerned with fake simplicity and the attempt to make written English colloquial. Nor does it even imply in every case preferring the Saxon word to the Latin one, though it does imply using the fewest and shortest words that will cover one's meaning. What is above all needed is to let the meaning choose the word, and not the other way about. In prose, the worst thing one can do with words is to surrender to them. When you think of a concrete object, you think wordlessly, and then, if you want to describe the thing you have been visualizing you probably hunt about till you find the exact words that seem to fit. When you think of something abstract you are more inclined to use words from the start, and unless you make a conscious effort to prevent it, the existing dialect will come rushing in and do the job for you, at the expense of blurring or even changing your meaning. Probably it is better to put off using words as long as possible and get one's meaning as clear as one can through pictures or sensations. Afterwards one can choose — not simply *accept* — the phrases that will best cover the meaning, and then switch round and decide what impression one's words are likely to make on another person. This last effort of the mind cuts out all stale or mixed images, all prefabricated phrases, needless repetitions, and humbug and vagueness generally. But one can often be in doubt about the effect of a word or a phrase, and one needs rules that one can rely on when instinct fails. I think the following rules will cover most cases:

(i) Never use a metaphor, simile or other figure of speech which you are used to seeing in print.

(ii) Never use a long word where a short one will do.

(iii) If it is possible to cut a word out, always cut it out.

(iv) Never use the passive where you can use the active.

(v) Never use a foreign phrase, a scientific word or a jargon word if you can think of an everyday English equivalent.

(vi) Break any of these rules sooner than say anything outright barbarous.

These rules sound elementary, and so they are, but they demand a deep change in attitude in anyone who has grown used to writing in the style now fashionable. One could keep all of them and still write bad English, but one could not write the kind of stuff that I quoted in those five specimens at the beginning of this article.

I have not here been considering the literary use of language, but 19 merely language as an instrument for expressing and not for concealing or preventing thought. Stuart Chase and others have come near to claiming that all abstract words are meaningless, and have used this as a pretext for advocating a kind of political quietism. Since you don't know what Fascism is, how can you struggle against Fascism? One need not swallow such absurdities as this, but one ought to recognize that the present political chaos is connected with the decay of language, and that one can probably bring about some improvement by starting at the verbal end. If you simplify your English, you are freed from the worst follies of orthodoxy. You cannot speak any of the necessary dialects, and when you make a stupid remark its stupidity will be obvious, even to yourself. Political language — and with variations this is true of all political parties, from Conservatives to Anarchists — is designed to make lies sound truthful and murder respectable, and to give an appearance of solidity to pure wind. One cannot change this all in a moment, but one can at least change one's own habits, and from time to time one can even, if one jeers loudly enough, send some worn-out and useless phrase — some *jackboot, Achilles' heel, hotbed, melting pot, acid test, veritable inferno* or other lump of verbal refuse — into the dustbin where it belongs.

E. B. WHITE

E. B. White, distinguished essayist, was born in Mount Vernon, New York, in 1899. A graduate of Cornell University, White has worked as reporter and advertising copywriter, and in 1926 he joined the staff of *The New Yorker* magazine. Since 1937 he has done most of the writing at his farm in Maine, for many years contributing a regular column, "One Man's Meat," for *Harper's* magazine and free-lance editorials for the "Notes and Comments" column of *The New Yorker.* White has also written children's books, two volumes of verse, and, with James Thurber, *Is Sex Necessary?* (1929). With his wife he compiled *A Subtreasury of American Humor* (1941). Collections of his own essays include *One Man's Meat* (1942), *The Second Tree from the Corner* (1953), *The Points of My Compass* (1962) and *Essays of E. B. White* (1977). In 1959 he revised and enlarged William Strunk's *The Elements of Style,* a textbook still widely used in college classrooms. White has been recipient of many honors and writing awards as he gained renown for his crisp, highly individual style and his sturdy independence of thought. These qualities are evident in the following unit, complete with editorial notations, from *Letters of E. B. White* (collected and edited by Dorothy Lobrano Guth, 1976), in which he starts (and wins) a controversy over what he could see, as few others had at the time, a serious threat to an independent press in America.

Letters on the"Xerox–Esquire–Salisbury Axis"

To the editor of the Ellsworth (Maine) American

[North Brooklin, Me.]
January 1, 1976

To the Editor:

1 I think it might be useful to stop viewing fences for a moment and take a close look at Esquire magazine's new way of doing business. In February, Esquire will publish a long article by Harrison E. Salisbury, for which Mr. Salisbury will receive no payment from

From *Letters of E. B. White,* collected and edited by Dorothy Lobrano Guth: "Letter to the Editor of the Ellsworth (Maine) *American* — North Brooklin, January 1, 1976," "Letter to W. B. Jones — North Brooklin, January 30, 1976," (pp. 657–661).

Esquire but will receive $40,000 from the Xerox Corporation — plus another $15,000 for expenses. This, it would seem to me, is not only a new idea in publishing, it charts a clear course for the erosion of the free press in America. Mr. Salisbury is a former associate editor of the New York Times and should know better. Esquire is a reputable sheet and should know better. But here we go — the Xerox–Salisbury–Esquire axis in full cry!

A news story about this amazing event in the December 14th issue of the Times begins: "Officials of Esquire magazine and of the Xerox Corporation report no adverse reactions, so far, to the announcement that Esquire will publish a 23-page article [about travels through America] in February 'sponsored' by Xerox." Herewith I am happy to turn in my adverse reaction even if it's the first one across the line. 2

Esquire, according to the Times story, attempts to justify its new payment system (get the money from a sponsor) by assuring us that Mr. Salisbury will not be tampered with by Xerox; his hand and his pen will be free. If Xerox likes what he writes about America, Xerox will run a "low keyed full-page ad preceding the article" and another ad at the end of it. From this advertising, Esquire stands to pick up $115,000 and Mr. Salisbury has already picked up $40,000, traveling, all expenses paid, through this once happy land. . . . 3

Apparently Mr. Salisbury had a momentary qualm about taking on the Xerox job. The Times reports him as saying, "At first I thought, gee whiz, should I do this?" But he quickly conquered his annoying doubts and remembered that big corporations had in the past been known to sponsor "cultural enterprises," such as opera. The emergence of a magazine reporter as a cultural enterprise is as stunning a sight as the emergence of a butterfly from a cocoon. Mr. Salisbury must have felt great, escaping from his confinement. 4

Well, it doesn't take a giant intellect to detect in all this the shadow of disaster. If magazines decide to farm out their writers to advertisers and accept the advertiser's payment to the writer and to the magazine, then the periodicals of this country will be far down the drain and will become so fuzzy as to be indistinguishable from the controlled press in other parts of the world. 5

E. B. White

[Some weeks after his letter on the Xerox–Esquire–Salisbury arrangement was published, White received a letter of inquiry from W. B. Jones, Director of Communications Operations at Xerox Corporation, outlining the ground rules of the corporation's sponsorship of the Salisbury piece and concluding: "With these ground rules, do you still see something sinister in the sponsorship? The question is put seriously, because if a writer of your achievement and insight — after considering the terms of the arrangement — still sees this kind of corporate sponsorship as leading the periodicals of this country toward the controlled press of other parts of the world, then we may well reconsider our plans to underwrite similar projects in the future." White's reply follows.] 6

TO W. B. JONES

North Brooklin
January 30, 1976

Dear Mr. Jones:

In extending my remarks on sponsorship, published in the Ellsworth *American,* I want to limit the discussion to the press — that is, to newspapers and magazines. I'll not speculate about television, as television is outside my experience and I have no ready opinion about sponsorship in the medium. 7

In your recent letter to me, you ask whether, having studied your ground rules for proper conduct in sponsoring a magazine piece, I still see something sinister in the sponsorship. Yes, I do. Sinister may not be the right word, but I see something ominous and unhealthy when a corporation underwrites an article in a magazine of general circulation. This is not, essentially, the old familiar question of an advertiser trying to influence editorial content; almost everyone is acquainted with that common phenomenon. Readers are aware that it is always present but usually in a rather subdued or non-threatening form. Xerox's sponsoring of a specific writer on a specific occasion for a specific article is something quite different. No one, as far as I know, accuses Xerox of trying to influence editorial opinion. But many people are wondering why a large corporation placed so much money on a magazine piece, why the writer of the piece was willing to get paid in so unusual a fashion, and why Esquire was ready and willing to have an outsider pick up the tab. These are reasonable questions. 8

The press in our free country is reliable and useful not because of its good character but because of its great diversity. As long as there are many owners, each pursuing his own brand of truth, we the people have the opportunity to arrive at the truth and to dwell in the light. The multiplicity of ownership is crucial. It's only when there are few owners, or, as in a government-controlled press, one owner, that the truth becomes elusive and the light fails. For a citizen in our free society, it is an enormous privilege and a wonderful protection to have access to hundreds of periodicals, each peddling its own belief. There is safety in numbers: the papers expose each other's follies and peccadillos, correct each other's mistakes, and cancel out each other's biases. The reader is free to range around in the whole editorial bouillabaisse and explore it for the one clam that matters — the truth. 9

When a large corporation or a rich individual underwrites an article in a magazine, the picture changes: the ownership of that magazine has been diminished, the outline of the magazine has been blurred. In the case of the Salisbury piece, it was as though Esquire had gone on relief, was accepting its first welfare payment, and was not its own man anymore. The editor protests that he accepts full responsibility for the text and that Xerox had nothing to do with the whole business. But the fact remains that, despite his full acceptance of responsibility, he somehow did not get around to paying the bill. This is unsettling and I think unhealthy. Whenever money changes hands, something goes along with it — an intangible something that varies with the circumstances. It would be hard to resist the suspicion that Esquire feels indebted to Xerox, that Mr. Salisbury feels indebted to both, and that the ownership, or sovereignty, of Esquire has been nibbled all around the edges. 10

Sponsorship in the press is an invitation to corruption and abuse. The temptations are great, and there is an opportunist behind every bush. A funded article is a tempting morsel for any publication — particularly for one that is having a hard time making ends meet. A funded assignment is a tempting dish for a writer, who may pocket a much larger fee than he is accustomed to getting. And sponsorship is attractive to the sponsor himself, who, for one reason or another, feels an urge to penetrate the editorial columns after being so long pent up in the advertising pages. These temptations are real, and if the barriers were to be let down I believe corruption and abuse would 11 soon follow. Not all corporations would approach subsidy in the immaculate way Xerox did or in the same spirit of benefaction. There are a thousand reasons for someone's wishing to buy his way into print, many of them unpalatable, all of them to some degree self-serving. Buying and selling space in news columns could become a serious disease of the press. If it reached epidemic proportions, it could destroy the press. I don't want IBM or the National Rifle Association providing me with a funded spectacular when I open my paper. I want to read what the editor and the publisher have managed to dig up on their own — and paid for out of the till. . . .

My affection for the free press in a democracy goes back a long 12
way. My love for it was my first and greatest love. If I felt a shock at the news of the Salisbury–Xerox–Esquire arrangement, it was because the sponsorship principle seemed to challenge and threaten everything I believe in: that the press must not only be free, it must be fiercely independent — to survive and to serve. Not all papers are fiercely independent, God knows, but there are always enough of them around to provide a core of integrity and an example that others feel obliged to steer by. The funded article is not in itself evil, but it is the beginning of evil and it is an invitation to evil. I hope the invitation will not again be extended, and, if extended, I hope it will be declined.

About a hundred and fifty years ago, Tocqueville wrote: "The 13
journalists of the United States are generally in a very humble position, with a scanty education and a vulgar turn of mind." Today, we chuckle at this antique characterization. But about fifty years ago, when I was a young journalist, I had the good fortune to encounter an editor who fitted the description quite closely. Harold Ross, who founded the *New Yorker,* was deficient in education and had — at least to all outward appearances — a vulgar turn of mind. What he did possess, though, was the ferocity of independence. He was having a tough time finding money to keep his floundering little sheet alive, yet he was determined that neither money nor influence would ever corrupt his dream or deflower his text. His boiling point was so low as to be comical. The faintest suggestion of the shadow of advertising in his news and editorial columns would cause him to erupt. He would explode in anger, the building would reverberate with his wrath, and his terrible swift sword would go flashing up and down the corridors. For a young man, it was an impressive sight and a memorable one. Fifty years have not dimmed for me either the spec-

tacle of Ross's ferocity or my own early convictions — which were identical with his. He has come to my mind often while I've been composing this reply to your inquiry.

I hope I've clarified by a little bit my feelings about the anatomy of the press and the dangers of sponsorship of articles. Thanks for giving me the chance to speak my piece. 14

Sincerely,
E. B. White

[Mr. Jones wrote and thanked White for "telling me what I didn't want to hear." In May another letter arrived from Jones saying that Xerox had decided not to underwrite any more articles in the press and that they were convinced it was "the right decision."] 15

A Guide to Terms

Abstract (See *Concrete/Abstract.*)
Allusion (See *Figures of Speech.*)
Analogy (See *Section 4.*)
Argument is one of the four basic forms of prose. It usually employs one or all of the other forms—exposition, narration, description —sometimes becoming difficult to distinguish from them. The difference is in its basic motivation: argument assumes that there are two sides to the matter under discussion, but it aims to resolve the conflict by influencing the reader to favor one side.

A distinction is ordinarily made between *logical argument* (usually called simply "argument") and *persuasive argument* (usually termed "persuasion"). Whereas logical argument appeals to reason, persuasion appeals to the emotions. The aim of both, however, is to convince, and they are nearly always blended into whatever mixture seems most likely to do the convincing. After all, reason and emotion are both important human elements—and we may have to persuade someone even to listen to our logic. The emphasis on one or the other, of course, should depend on the subject and the audience.

Some authorities make a somewhat different distinction: we argue merely to get someone to change his mind; we use persuasion to get him to *do* something about it—e.g., to vote a Republican ticket, not just agree with the party platform. But this view is not entirely inconsistent with the other. We can hardly expect to change a *mind* by emotional appeal, but we can hope to get someone to *act* because of it, whether or not his mind has been changed.

Cause (See *Section 6.*)

Central Theme (See *Unity.*)

Classification (See *Section 2.*)

Clichés are tired expressions, perhaps once fresh and colorful, that have been overused until they have lost most of their effectiveness and become trite or hackneyed. The term is also applied, less commonly, to trite ideas or attitudes.

We may need to use clichés in conversation, of course, where the quick and economical phrase is an important and useful tool of expression—and where no one expects us to be constantly original. We are fortunate, in a way, to have a large accumulation of clichés from which to draw. To describe someone, without straining our originality very much, we can always declare that he is *as innocent as a lamb, as thin as a rail,* or *as fat as a pig;* that he is *as dumb as an ox, as sly as a fox,* or *as wise as an owl;* that he is *financially embarrassed* or *has a fly in the ointment* or *his ship has come in;* or that, *last but not least, in this day and age,* the *Grim Reaper* has taken him to *his eternal reward.* There is indeed *a large stockpile* from which we can draw for ordinary conversation.

But the trite expression, written down on paper, is a permanent reminder that the writer is either lazy or not aware of the dullness of stereotypes—or, even more damaging, it is a clue that his ideas themselves may be threadbare, and therefore can be adequately expressed in threadbare language.

Occasionally, of course, a writer can use obvious clichés deliberately, for his own purposes (See Roiphe, par. 4; Sheehy, par. 12; B. Lawrence, par. 1.) But usually to be fully effective, writing must be fresh and should seem to have been written specifically for the occasion. Clichés, however fresh and appropriate at one time, have lost these qualities.

Closings are almost as much of a problem as introductions, and they are fully as important. The function of a closing is simply "to close," of course; but this implies somehow tying the entire writing into a neat package, giving the final sense of unity to the whole endeavor, and thus leaving the reader with a sense of satisfaction instead of an uneasy feeling that he ought to be looking around for another page. There is no standard length for closings. A short composition may be effectively completed with one sentence—or even without any real closing at all, if the last point discussed is a strong or climactic one. A longer piece of writing, however, may end more slowly, perhaps through several paragraphs.

A few types of weak endings are so common that warnings are in order here. The careful writer will avoid these faults: (1) giving the effect of having suddenly become tired and quit; (2) ending on a minor detail or an apparent afterthought; (3) bringing up a new point in the closing; (4) using any new qualifying remark in the closing (if he wants his opinions to seem less dogmatic or generalized, he should go back to do his qualifying where the damage was done); (5) ending with an apology of any kind (if the author is not interested enough to become at least a minor expert in his subject, he should not be wasting the reader's time).

Of the several acceptable ways of giving the sense of finality to a paper, the easiest is the *summary,* but it is also the least desirable for most short papers. If the reader has read and understood something only a page or two before, he probably does not need to have it reviewed for him. It is apt to seem merely repetitious. Longer writings, of course, such as research or term papers, may require thorough summaries.

Several other closing techniques are available to the writer. The following, which do not represent all the possibilities, are useful in many situations, and they can frequently be employed in combination:

1. *Using word signals*—e.g., *finally, at last, thus, and so, in conclusion,* as well as more original devices suggested by the subject itself. (See Thurber, Halsey, Simpson.)

2. *Changing the tempo*—usually a matter of sentence length or pace. This is a very subtle indication of finality, and it is difficult to achieve. (For examples of modified use, see Hall, Simpson.)

3. *Restating the central idea* of the writing—sometimes a "statement" so fully developed that it practically becomes a summary itself. (See Catton.)

4. *Using climax*—a natural culmination of preceding points or, in some cases, the last major point itself. This is suitable, however, only if the materials have been so arranged that the last point is outstanding. (See Catton, Rettie, Bok, Selzer, B. Lawrence, Mead.)

5. *Making suggestions,* perhaps mentioning a possible solution to the problem being discussed—a useful technique for exposition as well as for argument, and a natural signal of the end. (See Peter/Hull, Gregory, Highet.)

6. *Showing the topic's significance,* its effects, or the universality of its meaning—a commonly used technique that, if carefully handled, is an excellent indication of closing. (See Baker, Gregory, Morris, Rettie, Thomas, Halsey, Barzun, B. Lawrence, Cousins.)

7. *Echoing the introduction*—a technique that has the virtue of improving the effect of unity by bringing the development around full circle, so to speak. The echo may be a reference to a problem posed or a significant expression, quotation, analogy, or symbol used in the introduction or elsewhere early in the composition. (See Thurber, Greene, Cousins.)

8. *Using some rhetorical device*—a sort of catchall category, but a good supply source that includes several very effective techniques: pertinent quotations, anecdotes and brief dialogues, metaphors, allusions, ironic comments, and various kinds of witty or memorable remarks. All, however, run the risk of seeming forced, and hence amateurish; but properly handled they make for an effective closing. (See Baker, Gregory, Rettie, Sheehy, Halsey, B. Lawrence, Simpson, Greene.)

Coherence is the quality of good writing that results from the presentation of all parts in logical and clear relations.

Coherence and unity are usually studied together and, indeed, are almost inseparable. But whereas unity refers to the relation of parts to the central theme (see *Unity)*, coherence refers to their relations with each other. In a coherent piece of writing, each sentence, each paragraph, each major division seems to grow out of those preceding it.

Several transitional devices (see *Transition*) help to make these relations clear, but far more fundamental to coherence is the sound organization of materials. From the moment he first begins to visualize his subject materials in pattern, the writer's goal must be clear and logical development. If it is, coherence is almost ensured.

Colloquial Expressions are characteristic of conversation and informal writing, and they are normally perfectly appropriate in those contexts. However, most writing done for college, business, or professional purposes is considered "formal" writing; and for such usage colloquialisms are too informal, too *folksy* (a word itself which most dictionaries label "colloq.").

Some of the expressions appropriate only for informal usage are *kid* (for child), *boss* (for employer), *flunk, buddy, snooze, gym, a lot of, phone, skin flicks, porn.* In addition, contractions such as *can't* and *I'd* are usually regarded as colloquialisms and are never permissible in, for instance, a research or term paper.

Slang is defined as a low level of colloquialism, but it is sometimes placed "below" colloquialism in respectability; even standard dictionaries differ as to just what the distinction is. (Some of the examples in the preceding paragraph, if included in dictionaries at all, are identified both ways.) At any rate, slang generally comprises words either coined or given novel meanings in an attempt at colorful or humorous expression. Slang soon becomes limp with overuse, however, losing whatever vigor it first had. In time, slang expressions either disappear completely or graduate to more acceptable colloquial status and thence, possibly, into standard usage. (That is one way in which our language is constantly changing.) But until their "graduations," slang and colloquialism have an appropriate place in formal writing only if used sparingly and for special effect. Because dictionaries frequently differ in matters of usage, the student should be sure he is using a standard edition approved by his instructor. (For further examples, see Morgan, par. 2; Gregory, Roiphe, Wolfe, Pirsig, Sheehy, Brown; Simpson, pars. 8, 16, 17; Greene, pars. 2, 4.)

Comparison (See *Section 3.*)

Conclusions (See *Closings.*)

Concrete and **Abstract** words are both indispensable to the language, but a good rule in most writing is to use the concrete whenever possible. This policy also applies, of course, to sentences that express only abstract ideas, which can often be made clearer, more effective, by use of concrete examples. Many expository paragraphs are constructed with an abstract topic sentence and its concrete support. (See *Unity.*)

A concrete word names something that exists as an entity in itself, something that can be perceived by the human senses. We can see, touch, hear, and smell a horse—hence *horse* is a concrete word. But a horse's *strength* is not. We have no reason to doubt that strength exists, but it does not have an independent existence: something else must *be* strong or there is no strength. Hence, *strength* is an abstract word.

Purely abstract reading is difficult for the average reader; with no concrete images provided for him, he is constantly forced to make his own. Concrete writing helps the reader to visualize and is therefore easier and faster to read.

(See *Specific/General* for further discussion.)

Connotation and **Denotation** both refer to the meanings of words. Denotation is the direct, literal meaning as it would be found in a dictionary, whereas connotation refers to the response a word *really* arouses in the reader or listener. (See Wolfe, par. 14; B. Lawrence.)

There are two types of connotation: personal and general. Personal connotations vary widely, depending on the experiences and moods that an individual associates with the word. (This corresponds with personal symbolism; see *Symbol.*) *Waterfall* is not apt to have the same meaning for the happy young honeymooners at Yosemite as it has for the grieving mother whose child has just drowned in a waterfall. But general connotations are those shared by many people. *Fireside,* far beyond its obvious dictionary definition, generally connotes warmth and security and good companionship. *Mother,* which denotatively means simply "female parent," means much more connotatively.

A word or phrase considered less distasteful or offensive than a more direct expression is called a *euphemism,* and this is also a matter of connotation. (See Mitford.) The various expressions used instead of the more direct "four-letter words" referring to daily bathroom events are examples of euphemisms. (See Wolfe's "mounting" or D. H. Lawrence's "dirt.") *Remains* is often used instead of *corpse,* and a few newspapers still have people *passing away* and being *laid to rest,* rather than *dying* and being *buried.*

But a serious respect for the importance of connotations goes far beyond euphemistic practices. The young writer can hardly expect to know all the different meanings of words for all his potential readers, but he can at least be aware that they do *have* different meanings. Of course, this is most important in persuasive writing—in political speeches, in advertising copywriting, and in any endeavor where some sort of public image is being created. When President Franklin Roosevelt began his series of informal radio talks, he called them "fireside chats," thus putting connotation to work. An advertising copywriter trying to evoke the feeling of love and tenderness associated with motherhood is not seriously tempted to use *female parent* instead of *mother.*

In exposition, however, where the primary purpose is to explain, the writer ordinarily tries to avoid words that may have emotional overtones, unless these can somehow be used to increase understanding.

Contrast (See *Section 3.*)

Deduction (See *Section 10.*)

Denotation (See *Connotation/Denotation.*)

Description (See *Section 8.*)

Diction refers simply to "choice of words," but, not so simply, it involves many problems of usage, some of which are explained under several other headings in this guide, e.g., *Clichés, Colloquial Expressions, Connotation/Denotation, Concrete/Abstract*—anything, in fact, that pertains primarily to word choices. But the characteristics of good diction may be more generally classified as follows:

1. *Accuracy*—the choice of words that mean exactly what the author intends.

2. *Economy*—the choice of the simplest and fewest words that will convey the exact shade of meaning intended.

3. *Emphasis*—the choice of fresh, strong words, avoiding clichés and unnecessarily vague or general terms.

4. *Appropriateness*—the choice of words that are appropriate to the subject matter, to the prospective reader-audience, and to the purpose of the writing.

(For contrasts of diction see Baker, Thurber, Gregory, Highet, Thomas, Greene.)

Division (See *Section 2.*)

Effect (See *Section 6.*)

Emphasis is almost certain to fall *somewhere,* and the author should be the one to decide where. He should make certain that a major point, not some minor detail, is emphasized.

Following are the most common ways of achieving emphasis. Most of them apply to the sentence, the paragraph, or the overall writing—all of which can be seriously weakened by emphasis in the wrong places.

1. By *position.* The most emphatic position is usually at the end, the second most emphatic at the beginning. (There are a few exceptions, including news stories and certain kinds of scientific reports.) The middle, therefore, should be used for materials that do not deserve special emphasis. (See Peter/Hull, for the order of examples; Catton, par. 16; and Rettie, for the long withheld revelation of real central theme.)

A sentence in which the main point is held until the last is called a *periodic sentence,* e.g., "After a long night of suspense and horror, the cavalry arrived." In a *loose sentence,* the main point is disposed of earlier and followed by dependencies, e.g., "The cavalry arrived after a long night of suspense and horror."

2. By *proportion.* Ordinarily, but not necessarily, important elements are given the most attention and thus automatically achieve a certain emphasis. (See Baker, for his disproportionate attention to names; Hall, for his special treatment of the narcotic type of reading; and Rettie, for a unique kind of *reverse* application of this method.)

3. By *repetition.* Words and ideas may sometimes be given emphasis by reuse, usually in a different manner. If not cautiously handled, however, this method can seem merely repetitious, not emphatic. (See Thurber, Peter/Hull, Gregory, D. H. Lawrence.)

4. By *flat statement.* Although an obvious way to achieve emphasis is simply to *tell* the reader what is most important, it is often least effective, at least when used as the only method. Readers have a way of ignoring such pointers as "most important of all" and "especially true." (See Gregory, Catton, par. 16; Toffler, frequently.)

5. By *mechanical devices.* Emphasis can be achieved by using italics (underlining), capital letters, or exclamation points. But too often these devices are used, however unintentionally, to cover deficiencies of content or style. Their employment can quickly be overdone and their impact lost. (For very limited and therefore especially emphatic use of italics and capitalization, see D. H. Lawrence and the "Inner Wonderfulness" of Halsey. Notice that Mitford, with a more emphatic style than most, uses none of these devices.)

6. By *distinctiveness of style.* The author can emphasize subtly with fresh and concrete words or figures of speech, crisp or unusual structures, and careful control of paragraph or sentence lengths. (These methods are used in many essays in this book: see Baker; Morgan; Twain, who changes style radically for the second half of his essay; Catton; Rettie, par. 19; Wolfe; Thomas; and Curtin, pars. 7–15.) *Verbal irony* (see *Irony*), including *sarcasm* (see Hall) and the rather specialized form known as *understatement,* if handled judiciously, is another valuable means of achieving distinctiveness of style and increasing emphasis. (See Wolfe, Mitford, D. H. Lawrence.)

Essay refers to a brief prose composition on a single topic, usually, but not always, communicating the author's personal ideas and impressions. Beyond this, because of the wide and loose application of the term, no really satisfactory definition has been arrived at.

Classifications of essay types have also been widely varied and sometimes not very meaningful. One basic and useful distinction, however, is between *formal* and *informal* essays, although many defy classification even in such broad categories as these. It is best to regard the two types as opposite ends of a continuum, along which most essays may be placed.

The formal essay usually develops an important theme through a logical progression of ideas, with full attention to unity and coherence, and in a serious tone. Although the style is seldom completely impersonal, it is literary rather than colloquial. (For examples of essays that are somewhere near the "formal" end of the continuum, see Highet, Catton, Barzun, B. Lawrence, Cousins. The Declaration of Independence, a completely formal document, is not classifiable as an "essay" at all.)

The informal, or personal, essay is less elaborately organized and more chatty in style. First-person pronouns, contractions, and other colloquial or even slang expressions are often freely used. Informal essays are less serious in apparent purpose than formal essays. Although most do contain a worthwhile message or observation of some kind, an important purpose of many is to entertain. (See Baker, Thurber, Wolfe, Brown.)

The more personal and intimate informal essays may be classifiable as *familiar* essays, although, again, there is no well-established boundary. Familiar essays pertain to the author's own experience, ideas, or prejudices, frequently in a light and humorous style. (See Roiphe, Curtin, Greene, Angelou.)

Evaluation of a literary piece, like that of any other creative endeavor, is meaningful only when based somehow on the answers to three questions: (1) What was the author's purpose? (2) How successfully does he fulfill it? (3) How worthwhile was it?

An architect could hardly be blamed for designing a poor gymnasium if his commission had been to design a library. Similarly, if an author is trying to explain for us the difference between Chicanos and Anglos, as is Campa, he cannot be faulted for failing to make the reader laugh. However, if his purpose is simply to amuse (a worthy enough goal, by the way), he should not be condemned for teaching little about trichobothria, as did Petrunkevitch. (Nothing prevents his trying to explain pornography through the use of humor, or trying to amuse by comparing two Civil War generals, but in these situations his purpose has changed—and grown almost unbearably harder to achieve.)

If the architect was commissioned to design a gymnasium, however, he could be justifiably criticized on whether the building is successful and attractive *as a gymnasium.* If an author is trying to show why the "me" generation is headed the opposite direction from happiness (as is Halsey), the reader has a right to expect sound reasoning and clear expository prose.

Many things are written and published that succeed very well in carrying out the author's intent—but simply are not worthwhile. Although this is certainly justifiable ground for unfavorable criticism, the reader should first make full allowance for his own limitations and perhaps his narrow range of interests, evaluating the work as nearly as possible from the standpoint of the average reader for whom the writing was intended.

Figures of Speech are short, vivid comparisons, either stated or implied; but they are not literal comparisons (e.g., "Your car is like my car," which is presumably a plain statement of fact). Figures of speech are more imaginative. They imply analogy but, unlike analogy, are used less to inform than to make quick and forceful impressions. All figurative language is a comparison of unlikes, but the unlikes do have some interesting point of likeness, perhaps one never noticed before.

A *metaphor* merely suggests the comparison and is worded as if the two unlikes are the same thing—e.g., "the language of the river" and "was turned to blood" (Twain, par. 1) and "a great chapter in American life" (Catton, par. 1). (For some of the many other examples in this book, see Baker, Highet, Roiphe, Toffler, Thomas, Halsey, Barzun, Selzer.)

A *simile* (which is sometimes classified as a special kind of metaphor) expresses a similarity directly, usually with the word *like* or *as*—e.g., "like a kaleidoscope run wild" (Toffler, par. 4). (For further illustrations, see Barber, par. 2; Rettie, par. 6; Thomas, par. 11; Halsey, par. 9; Angelou, par. 33.)

A *personification,* which is actually a special type either of metaphor or simile, is usually classified as a "figure" in its own right. In personification, inanimate things are treated as if they had the qualities or powers of a person. (Baker does this throughout his essay; Hall refers to "concepts clothed in character," par. 5; and Brown concludes with "that big, beautiful, bountiful black bitch.") Some people would also label as personification any characterization of inanimate objects as animals, or of animals as humans—as in the descriptions and "love displays" of the Thurber piece.

An *allusion* is literally any casual reference, any alluding, to something; but rhetorically it is limited to a figurative reference to a famous or literary person, event, or quotation, and it should be distinguished from the casual reference that has a literal function in the subject matter. Hence, casual mention of Judas Iscariot's betrayal of Jesus is merely a reference, but calling a modern traitor a "Judas" is an allusion. A rooster might be referred to as "the Hitler of the barnyard," or a lover as a "Romeo." Many allusions refer to mythological or biblical persons or places (See Baker, par. 4; Barber, par. 16; Rettie, title; Wolfe, title and par. 1; Petrunkevitch, par. 9; Barzun, par. 2; and Simpson, par. 2.)

Irony and paradox (both discussed under their own headings) and analogy (see *Section 4*) are also frequently classed as figures of speech, and there are several other, less common types that are really subclassifications of those already discussed.

General (See *Specific/General*.)

Illustration (See *Section 1.*)

Impressionistic Description (See *Section 8.*)

Induction (See *Section 10.*)

Introductions give readers their first impressions, which often turn out to be the lasting ones. In fact, unless an introduction succeeds in somehow attracting a reader's interest, he probably will go no further. Its importance is one reason that writing it is nearly always difficult.

Sometimes, when the writer remains at a loss to know how to begin, he should forget about the introduction for a while and go ahead with the main body of his writing. Later he may find that a suitable introduction has suggested itself or even that the way he did start is actually introduction enough.

Introduction may vary in length from one sentence in a short composition to several paragraphs or even several pages in longer and more complex expositions, such as research papers and reports of various kinds.

Good introductions in expository writing have at least three and sometimes four functions:

1. *To identify the subject and set its limitations,* thus building a solid foundation for unity. This function usually includes some indication of the central theme, letting the reader know what point is to be made about the subject. Unlike the other forms of prose, which can often benefit by some degree of mystery, exposition has the primary purpose of explaining, so the reader has a right to know from the beginning just *what* is being explained.

2. *To interest the reader,* and thus ensure his attention. To be sure of doing this, the writer must analyze his prospective readers and their interest in his subject. The account of a new X-ray technique would need an entirely different kind of introduction if written for doctors than if written for the campus newspaper.

3. *To set the tone* of the rest of the writing. (See *Style/Tone.*) Tone varies greatly in writing, just as the tone of a person's voice

varies with his mood. One function of the introduction is to let the reader know the author's attitude since it may have a subtle but important bearing on the communication.

4. *Frequently,* but not always, *to indicate the plan of organization.* Although seldom important in short, relatively simple compositions and essay examinations, this function of introductions can be especially valuable in more complex papers.

These are the necessary functions of an introduction. For best results, keep these guidelines in mind: (1) Avoid referring to the title, or even assuming that the reader has seen it. Make the introduction do all the introducing. (2) Avoid crude and uninteresting beginnings, such as "This paper is about . . . ." (3) Avoid going too abruptly into the main body—smooth transition is at least as important here as anywhere else. (4) Avoid overdoing the introduction, either in length or in extremes of style.

Fortunately, there are many good ways to introduce expository writing, and several of the most useful are illustrated by the selections in this book. Many writings, of course, combine two or more of the following techniques for interesting introductions.

1. *Stating the central theme,* which is sometimes fully enough explained in the introduction to become almost a preview-summary of the exposition to come. (See Baker, Thurber, Morris, Petrunkevitch.)

2. *Showing the significance of the subject,* or stressing its importance. (See Catton, Wolfe, Bok, Simpson.)

3. *Giving the background of the subject,* usually in brief form, in order to bring the reader up to date as early as possible for a better understanding of the matter at hand. (See Peter/Hull, Hall, Halsey.)

4. *"Focusing down" to one aspect of the subject,* a technique similar to that used in some movies, showing first a broad scope (of subject area, as of landscape) and then progressively narrowing views until the focus is on one specific thing (perhaps the name "O'Grady O'Connor" on a mailbox by a gate—or Greene's actual visit to Hef's place). (See also Rettie, Thomas.)

5. *Using a pertinent rhetorical device* that will attract interest as it leads into the main exposition—e.g., an anecdote, anal-

ogy, allusion, quotation, or paradox. (See King, Bok, Sheehy, Halsey, Simpson.)

6. *Using a short but vivid comparison or contrast* to emphasize the central idea. (See Thurber, Petrunkevitch, Halsey, Barzun.)

7. *Posing a challenging question,* the answering of which the reader will assume to be the purpose of the writing. (See B. Lawrence, Mead.)

8. *Referring to the writer's experience with the subject,* perhaps even giving a detailed account of that experience. Some writings, of course, especially descriptive or narrative essays, are simply continuations of experience so introduced, perhaps with the expository purpose of making the telling entirely evident only at the end or slowly unfolding it as the account progresses. (See Peter/Hull, Roiphe, Greene.)

9. *Presenting a startling statistic or other fact* that will indicate the nature of the subject to be discussed. (See Thurber, Gregory.)

10. *Making an unusual statement* that can intrigue as well as introduce. (See Baker, Thurber, Roiphe, Berne, Wolfe, Sheehy, Selzer, Brown, Gansberg.)

11. *Making a commonplace remark* that can draw interest because of its very commonness in sound or meaning. (See Peter/Hull, Berne, King.)

Irony, in its verbal form sometimes classed as a figure of speech, consists of saying one thing on the surface but meaning exactly (or nearly) the opposite—e.g., "this beautiful neighborhood of ours" may mean that it is a dump. (For other illustrations, see Thurber, Wolfe, Mitford.)

Verbal irony has a wide range of tones, from the gentle, gay, or affectionate to the sharpness of outright *sarcasm* (see Hall), which is always intended to cut. It may consist of only a word or phrase (see Halsey's "Inner Wonderfulness"), it may be a simple *understatement* (see Mitford, or Selzer's last sentence of par. 6), or it may be sustained as one of the major components of satire.

Irony can be an effective tool of exposition if its tone is consistent with the overall tone and if the writer is sure that his audience is bright enough to recognize it. In speech, a person usually indicates by voice or eye-expression that he is not to be taken literally; in writing, the words on the page have to speak for themselves.

In addition to verbal irony, there is also an *irony of situation,* in which there is a sharp contradiction between what is logically expected to happen and what does happen—e.g., a man sets a trap for an obnoxious neighbor and then gets caught in it himself. Or the ironic situation may simply be some discrepancy that an outsider can see while those involved cannot. (The principle itself in "The Peter Principle" can illustrate irony of situation, as can the "situation" discussed in many of the other essays: e.g., Baker, par. 11; Thurber; Gregory, par. 12; Sheehy, par. 9; B. Lawrence, pars. 11–12; Greene; Mead, par. 21).

Logical Argument (See *Argument.*)

Loose Sentences (See *Emphasis.*)

Metaphor (See *Figures of Speech.*)

Narration (See *Section 9.*)

Objective writing and **Subjective** writing are distinguishable by the extent to which they reflect the author's personal attitudes or emotions. The difference is usually one of degree, as few writing endeavors can be completely objective or subjective.

Objective writing, seldom used in its pure form except in business or scientific reports, is impersonal and concerned almost entirely with straight narration, with logical analysis, or with the description of external appearances. (For somewhat objective writing, see Berne, Barber, Morris, Simpson.)

Subjective writing (in description called "impressionistic"—see *Section 8*) is more personalized, more expressive of the beliefs, ideals, or impressions of the author. Whereas in objective writing the emphasis is on the object being written about, in subjective writing the emphasis is on the way the author sees and interprets the object. (For some of the many examples in this book, see Baker, Morgan, Thurber, Gregory, Hall, Twain, King, Wolfe, Thomas, Mitford, Halsey, Selzer, B. Lawrence, D. H. Lawrence, Greene, Angelou.)

Paradox is a statement or remark that, although seeming to be contradictory or absurd, actually contains some truth. Many are also ironical. Toffler introduces several paradoxes into his paragraph 2 (e.g. "anarchists, who . . . are outrageous conformists," and "atheist ministers"), and Highet strongly implies paradox when he says that with luck it is possible for the human mind to survive wealth (par. 4).

Paragraph Unity (See *Unity.*)

Parallel Structure refers in principle to the same kind of "parallelism" that is studied in grammar: the principle that coordinate elements should have coordinate presentation, as in a pair of a series of verbs, prepositional phrases, gerunds. It is often as much a matter of "balance" as it is of parallelism.

But the principle of parallel structure, far from being just a negative "don't mix" set of rules, is also a positive rhetorical device. Many writers use it as an effective means of stressing variety or profusion in a group of nouns or modifiers, or of emphasizing parallel ideas in sentence parts, in two or more sentences, or even in two or more paragraphs. At times it can also be useful stylistically, to give a subtle poetic quality to the prose.

(For illustrations of parallel parts within a sentence: see Morgan, par. 17; Berne, 5; King, 1; Wolfe, 1, 4; Thomas, 4, 11. Of sentences themselves: Peter/Hull; Berne, par. 4; Catton, 14; Toffler, 15; Jefferson. Of both parts and sentences: Twain; Toffler, par. 2; King, 4, 5, 12. Of paragraphs: the beginnings of Rettie's paragraphs 6–14; Jefferson.)

Periodic Sentence (See *Emphasis.*)

Personification (See *Figures of Speech.*)

Point of view is simply the position of the author in relation to his subject matter. Rhetorical point of view, our only concern here, has little in common with the grammatical sort and differs somewhat from point of view in fiction.

A ranch in a mountain valley is seen differently by the practical stockman working at the corral, by his wife deciding where to plant her petunias, by the artist or poet viewing the ranch from the mountainside, and by the careful geographer in a plane above, map-sketching the valley in relation to the entire range. It is the same ranch, but the positions and attitudes of the viewers are varied.

So it is with expository prose. The position and attitude of the author are the important lens through which the reader sees the subject. Consistency is important, because if the lens is changed without sufficient cause and explanation, the reader will become disconcerted, if not annoyed.

Obviously, since the point of view is partially a matter of attitude, the tone and often the style of writing are closely linked to it. (See *Style/Tone.*)

The selections in this book provide examples of numerous points of view. Highet's and Twain's are those of authority in their own fields of experience; Mitford is the debunking prober. In each of these (and the list could be extended to include all the selections in the book), the subject would seem vastly different if seen from some other point of view.

Process Analysis (See *Section 5.*)

Purpose that is clearly understood by the author before he starts to write is essential to both unity and coherence. A worthwhile practice, certainly in the training stages, is to write down the controlling purpose before even beginning to outline. Some instructors require both a statement of purpose and a statement of central theme. (See *Unity.*)

The most basic element of a statement of purpose is the commitment to "explain," or perhaps for some assignments to "convince" (argument), to "relate" (narration), or to "describe." But the statement of purpose, whether written down or only decided upon, goes further—e.g., "to explain that most employees are promoted until they are on their level of incompetence, where they remain" (Peter/Hull) or "to explain that 'dirty words' are logically offensive because of the sources and connotations of the words themselves" (B. Lawrence.).

Qualification is the tempering of broad statements to make them more valid and acceptable, the author himself admitting the probability of exceptions. This qualifying can be done inconspicuously, to whatever degree needed, by the use of *possibly, nearly always* or *most often, usually* or *frequently, sometimes* or *occasionally.* Instead of saying, "Chemistry is the most valuable field of study," it would probably be more accurate and defensible to say that it is for *some* people, or that it *can* be the most valuable.

Bok uses such qualifiers throughout at least two of her paragraphs (2, 3), and Peter/Hull's "principle" states that "every employee *tends* to rise to his level of incompetence." (You may decide that some of the authors should have made greater use of qualification than they did.)

Rhetorical Questions are posed with no expectation of receiving an answer; they are merely structural devices to launch or further a discussion, or to achieve emphasis. (See Morgan; Berne's title; Roiphe, pars. 4, 6; Rettie's last sentence; Sheehy; B. Lawrence; D. H. Lawrence.)

Sarcasm (See *Irony.*)

Satire, sometimes called "extended irony," is a literary form that brings wit and humor to the serious task of pointing out frailties or evils of human institutions. It has thrived in Western literature since the time of the ancient Greeks, and English literature of the eighteenth century was particularly noteworthy for the extent and quality of its satire. Broadly, two types are recognized: *Horatian satire* that is gentle, smiling, and aims to correct by invoking laughter and sympathy; and *Juvenalian satire,* which is sharper and which points with anger, contempt, moral indignation, to corruption and evil. (Swift's "A Modest Proposal" belongs in the latter category.)

Sentimentality, also called *sentimentalism,* is an exaggerated show of emotion, whether intentional or caused by lack of restraint. An author can oversentimentalize almost any situation, but the trap is most dangerous when he writes of timeworn emotional symbols or scenes—e.g., a broken heart, mother love, a lonely death, the conversion of a sinner. However sincere the author may be, if his reader is not fully oriented to the worth and uniqueness of the situation described, he may be either resentful or amused at any attempt to play on his emotions. Sentimentality is, of course, one of the chief characteristics of melodrama. (For examples of writing that, less adeptly handled, could easily have slipped into sentimentality, see Gregory, Twain, Catton, King, Curtin, Simpson, or Gansberg.)

Simile (See *Figures of Speech.*)

Slang (See *Colloquial Expressions.*)

Specific and **General** terms, and the distinctions between the two, are similar to concrete and abstract terms (as discussed under their own heading), and for our purpose there is no real need to keep the two sets of categories separated. Whether *corporation* is thought of as "abstract" and *Ajax Motor Company* as "concrete," or whether they are assigned to "general" and "specific" categories, the principle is the same: in most writing, *Ajax Motor Company* is better.

But "specific" and "general" are relative terms. For instance, the word *apple* is more specific than *fruit* but less so than *Winesap.* And *fruit,* as general as it certainly is in one respect, is still more specific than *food.* Such relationships are shown more clearly in a series, progressing from general to specific: *food, fruit, apple, Winesap;* or *vehicle, automobile, Ford, Mustang.* Modifiers and verbs can also have degrees of specificity: *bright, red, scarlet;* or *moved, sped, careened.* It is not difficult to see the advantages to the reader—and, of course, to the writer who needs to communicate an idea clearly: in "the scarlet Mustang careened through the pass," instead of "the bright-colored vehicle moved through the pass."

Obviously, however, there are times when the general or the abstract term or statement is essential—e.g., "a balanced diet includes some fruit," or "there was no vehicle in sight." But the use of specific language whenever possible is one of the best ways to improve diction and thus clarity and forcefulness in writing.

(Another important way of strengthening general, abstract writing is, of course, to use examples of other illustrations. See *Section 1.*)

Style and **Tone** are so closely linked and so often even elements of each other, that it is best to consider them together.

But there is a difference. Think of two young men, each with his girl friend on separate moonlight dates, whispering in nearly identical, tender and loving tones of voice. One young man says, "Your eyes, dearest, reflect a thousand sparkling candles of heaven," and the other says, "Them eyes of yours—in this light—they sure do turn me on." Their *tones* were the same; their *styles* considerably different.

The same distinction exists in writing. But naturally, with more complex subjects than the effect of moonlight on a maiden's eyes, there are more complications in separating the two qualities, even for the purpose of study.

The tone is determined by the *attitude* of the writer toward his subject and toward his audience. He, too, may be tender and loving, but he may be indignant, solemn, playful, enthusiastic, belligerent, contemptuous—the list could be as long as a list of the many "tones of voice." (In fact, wide ranges of tone may be illustrated by essays of this book. Compare, e.g., those of the two parts of Twain; Cousins, and Mitford; or B. Lawrence and Hall.)

Style, on the other hand, expresses the author's individuality through his choices of word (see *Diction*), his sentence patterns (see *Syntax*), and his selection and arrangement of details and basic materials. (All these elements of style are illustrated in the contrasting statements of the moonstruck lads.) These matters of style are partially prescribed, of course, by the adopted tone, but they are still bound to reflect the writer's personality and mood, his education and general background.

(Some of the more distinctive styles—partially affected by and affecting tone—represented by selections in this book are those of Baker, Thurber, Gregory, Hall, Rettie, Wolfe, Thomas, Pirsig, D. H. Lawrence.)

Subjective Writing (See *Objective/Subjective.*)

Symbol refers to anything that, although real itself, also suggests something broader or more significant—not just in greater numbers, however, as a man would not symbolize a group or even mankind itself, although he might be typical or representative in one or more abstract qualities. On the most elementary level, even words are symbols—e.g., *bear* brings to mind the furry beast itself. But more important is that things, persons, or even acts may also be symbolic, if they invoke abstract concepts, values, or qualities apart from themselves or their own kind. Such symbols, in everyday life as well as in literature and the other arts, are generally classifiable according to three types, which, although terminology differs, we may label *natural, personal,* and *conventional.*

In a natural symbol, the symbolic meaning is inherent in the thing itself. The sunrise naturally suggests new beginnings to most people, an island is almost synonymous with isolation, a cannon automatically suggests war; hence these are natural symbols. It does not matter that some things, by their nature, can suggest more than one concept; although a valley may symbolize security to one person and captivity to another, both meanings, contradictory as they might seem, are inherent, and in both respects the valley is a natural symbol.

The personal symbol, depending as it does on private experience or perception, is meaningless to others unless they are told about it or allowed to see its significance in context (as in literature). Although the color green may symbolize the outdoor life to the farm boy trapped in the gray city (in this respect perhaps a natural symbol), it can also symbolize romance to the girl proposed to while wearing her green blouse, or dismal poverty to the woman who grew up in a weathered green shanty; neither of these meanings is suggested by something *inherent* in the color green, so they are personal symbols. Anything at all could take on private symbolic meaning, even the odor of marigolds or the sound of a lawnmower. The sunrise itself could mean utter despair, instead of fresh opportunities, to the man who has long despised his daily job and cannot find another.

Conventional symbols usually started as personal symbols, but continued usage in life or art permits them to be generally recognized for their broader meanings, which depend on custom rather than any inherent quality—e.g., the olive branch for peace, the flag for love of country, the cross for Christianity, the raised fist for black power.

Symbols are used less in expository writing than in fiction and poetry, but a few authors represented in this book have either referred to the subtle symbolism of others or made use of it in developing their own ideas. Without mentioning the term, Hall theorizes that in earlier and harder-working days, reading came to symbolize wealth and leisure; and Morris mentions "symbolic battle" and says that the human animal "cocks its leg symbolically all over his home base."

Syntax is a very broad term—too broad, perhaps, to be very useful —referring to the arrangement of words in a sentence. Good syntax implies the use not only of correct grammar but also of effective patterns. These patterns depend on sentences with good unity, coherence, and emphasis, on the use of subordination and parallel construction as appropriate, on economy, and on a consistent and interesting point of view. A pleasing variety of sentence patterns is also important in achieving effective syntax.

Theme (See *Unity.*)

Thesis (See *Unity.*)

Tone (See *Style/Tone.*)

Transition is the relating of one topic to the next, and smooth transition is an important aid to the coherence of a sentence, a paragraph, or an entire piece of writing. (See *Coherence.*)

The most effective coherence, of course, comes about naturally with sound development of ideas, one growing logically into the next—and that virtue depends on sound organization. But sometimes beneficial even in this situation, particularly in going from one paragraph to the next, is the use of appropriate transitional devices.

Readers are apt to be sensitive creatures, easy to lose. (And, of course, the writer is the real loser since he is the one who presumably has something he wants to communicate.) If the reader gets into a new paragraph and the territory seems familiar, chances are that he will continue. But if there are no identifying landmarks, he will often begin to feel uneasy and will either start worrying about his slow comprehension or take a dislike to the author and subject matter. Either way, a communication block arises, and very likely the author will soon have one less reader.

A good policy, then, unless the progression of ideas is exceptionally smooth and obvious, is to provide some kind of familiar identification early in the new paragraph, to keep the reader feeling at ease with the different ideas. The effect is subtle but important. These familiar landmarks or transitional devices are sometimes applied deliberately but more often come naturally, especially when the prospective reader is kept constantly in mind at the time of writing.

An equally important reason for using some kinds of transitional devices, however, is a logical one: while functioning as bridges between ideas, they also assist the basic organization by pointing out the *relationship* of the ideas—and thus contributing still further to readability.

Transitional devices useful for bridging paragraph changes (and, some of them, to improve transitional flow within paragraphs) may be roughly classified as follows:

1. *Providing an "echo"* from the preceding paragraph. This may be the repetition of a key phrase or word, or a pronoun referring back to such a word, or a casual reference to an idea. (See Thurber; Highet, from par. 12 to par. 13; Wolfe, especially from 1 to 2, and 4 to 5; Mitford; and Halsey, 1 to 2, and 8 to 9.) Such an echo cannot be superimposed on new ideas, but must, by careful planning, be made an organic part of them.

2. *Devising a whole sentence or paragraph* to bridge between other important paragraphs or major divisions. (See Morgan, par. 5; Peter/Hull, 30; Gregory, 4; Thomas, 8; Pirsig, 3; Halsey, 3; Selzer, 4.)

3. *Using parallel structure* between an important sentence of one paragraph and the first sentence of the next. This is a subtle means of making the reader feel at ease in the new surroundings, but it is seldom used because it is much more limited in its potential than the other methods of transition. (See B. Lawrence, pars. 1 to 2.)

4. *Using standard transitional expressions,* most of which have the additional advantage of indicating relationship of ideas. Only a few of those available are classified below, but nearly all the reading selections of this book can amply illustrate such transitional expressions:

Time—soon, immediately, afterward, later, meanwhile, after a while.

Place—nearby, here, beyond, opposite.

Result—as a result, therefore, thus, consequently, hence.

Comparison—likewise, similarly, in such a manner.

Contrast—however, nevertheless, still, but, yet, on the other hand, after all, otherwise.

Addition—also, too, and, and then, furthermore, moreover, finally, first, third.

Miscellaneous—for example, for instance, in fact, indeed, on the whole, in other words.

Trite (See *Clichés.*)

Unity in writing is the same as unity in anything else—in a picture, a musical arrangement, a campus organization—and that is a *one*-ness, in which all parts contribute to an overall effect.

Many elements of good writing contribute in varying degrees to the effect of unity. Some of these are properly designed introductions and closings; consistency of point of view, tone, and style; sometimes the recurring use of analogy or thread of symbolism; occasionally the natural time boundaries of an experience or event, as in the selections of Rettie, Pirsig, Mitford, Simpson, Greene, Gansberg, Orwell ("A Hanging"), or Angelou.

But in most expository writing the only dependable unifying force is the *central theme,* which every sentence, every word, must somehow help to support. (The central theme is also called the *central idea* or the *thesis* when pertaining to the entire writing. In an expository paragraph it is the same as the *topic sentence,* which may be implied or, if stated, may be located anywhere in the paragraph, but is usually placed first.) As soon as anything appears which is not related to the central idea, then there are *two* units instead of one. Hence, unity is basic to all other virtues of good writing, even to coherence and emphasis, the other two organic essentials. (See *Coherence* and *Emphasis*.)

An example of unity may be found in a single river system (for a practical use of analogy), with all its tributaries, big or little, meandering or straight, flowing into the main stream and making it bigger — or at least flowing into another tributary that finds its way to the main stream. This is *one* river system, an example of unity. But now also picture another, nearby stream that does not empty into the river but goes off in some other direction. There are now two systems, not one, and there is no longer unity.

It is the same way with writing. The central theme is the main river, flowing along from the first capital letter to the very last period. Every drop of information must find its way into this theme-river, or it is not a part of the system at all. It matters not even slightly if the water is good, the idea-stream perhaps deeper and finer than any of the others: if it is not a tributary, it has no business pretending to be relevant to *this* theme of writing.

And that is why most students are required to state their central idea, usually in solid sentence form, before even starting to organize their ideas. If the writer can use only tributaries, it is very important to know from the start just what the river is.

To the Student:

Part of our job as educational publishers is to try to improve the textbooks we publish. Thus, when revising, we take into account the experience of both instructors and students with the previous edition. At some time your instructor will be asked to comment extensively on *Patterns of Exposition 7,* but right now we want to hear from you. After all, though your instructor assigned this book, you are the one who paid for it.

Please help us by completing this questionnaire and returning it to College English Developmental Group, Little, Brown and Company, 34 Beacon Street, Boston, Mass. 02106.

School ________________ Course title ________________

Instructor's Name ______________________________

Other books assigned ______________________________

Please give us your reaction to the selections:	Liked best				Liked least	Didn't read
Baker, The Trouble with Baseball	5	4	3	2	1	_____
Morgan, The Murderous Species	5	4	3	2	1	_____
Thurber, Courtship Through the Ages	5	4	3	2	1	_____
Peter & Hull, The Peter Principle	5	4	3	2	1	_____
Gregory, The Ghetto Cop	5	4	3	2	1	_____
Berne, Can People Be Judged by Their Appearance?	5	4	3	2	1	_____
Highet, The Pleasures of Learning	5	4	3	2	1	_____
Hall, Four Kinds of Reading	5	4	3	2	1	_____
Barber, Four Types of President	5	4	3	2	1	_____
Morris, Territorial Behaviour	5	4	3	2	1	_____
Twain, Two Ways of Seeing a River	5	4	3	2	1	_____
Catton, Grant and Lee: A Study in Contrasts	5	4	3	2	1	_____
Campa, Anglo vs. Chicano: Why?	5	4	3	2	1	_____
Roiphe, Confessions of a Female Chauvinist Sow	5	4	3	2	1	_____
Toffler, The 800th Lifetime	5	4	3	2	1	_____
King, The World House	5	4	3	2	1	_____
Rettie, But a Watch in the Night	5	4	3	2	1	_____
Wolfe, O Rotten Gotham	5	4	3	2	1	_____
Thomas, Natural Man	5	4	3	2	1	_____
Pirsig, Mechanics' Logic	5	4	3	2	1	_____
Petrunkevitch, The Spider and The Wasp	5	4	3	2	1	_____
Mitford, To Dispel Fears of Live Burial	5	4	3	2	1	_____

	Liked best				Liked least	Didn't read
Bok, To Lie or Not to Lie	5	4	3	2	1	______
Sheehy, $70,000 a Year, Tax Free	5	4	3	2	1	______
Halsey, What's Wrong with 'Me, Me, Me'?	5	4	3	2	1	______
Barzun, The Professions Under Seige	5	4	3	2	1	______
Selzer, All Right, What Is a Laugh, Anyway?	5	4	3	2	1	______
Lawrence, Four-Letter Words Can Hurt You	5	4	3	2	1	______
Lawrence, Pornography	5	4	3	2	1	______
Brown, The Language of Soul	5	4	3	2	1	______
Curtin, Aging in the Land of the Young	5	4	3	2	1	______
Simpson, The War Room at Bellevue	5	4	3	2	1	______
Greene, Hef's	5	4	3	2	1	______
Gansberg, 38 Who Saw Murder Didn't Call the Police	5	4	3	2	1	______
Orwell, A Hanging	5	4	3	2	1	______
Angelou, Momma's Private Victory	5	4	3	2	1	______
Cousins, How to Make People Smaller Than They Are	5	4	3	2	1	______
Jefferson, The Declaration of Independence	5	4	3	2	1	______
Mead, UFOs: Visitors from Outer Space?	5	4	3	2	1	______
Plato, Socrates "Defends" Himself	5	4	3	2	1	______
Swift, A Modest Proposal	5	4	3	2	1	______
Thoreau, From "Civil Disobedience"	5	4	3	2	1	______
Orwell, Politics and the English Language	5	4	3	2	1	______
White, Letters on the "Xerox—Esquire—Salisbury Axis"	5	4	3	2	1	______
A Guide to Terms	5	4	3	2	1	______

1. Are there any authors not included whom you would like to see represented? ______________________________
2. Were the biographical sketches and introductions useful? ________ How might they be improved? ______________
3. Will you keep this book for your library? ______________
4. Please add any comments or suggestions. ______________

____

____

5. May we quote you in our promotional efforts for this book? ________ yes ________ no

date ________ signature ______________________

mailing address ______________________________